EDWARD HEATH

A Personal and Political Biography

EDWARD HEATH

A Personal and Political Biography

George Hutchinson

Longman

LONGMAN GROUP LIMITED
LONDON

Associated companies, branches and
representatives throughout the world

Appendix III, 'Realism in British Foreign Policy' by
Edward Heath, is reproduced by kind permission of
Foreign Affairs.

First published 1970

ISBN 0 582 10371-1 cased
10372X paper

Set in Monotype Baskerville, 12 pt., 2 pt. leaded
Printed in Scotland by T. & A. Constable Ltd., Edinburgh

To Pamela

Contents

		PAGE
Foreword		ix
1	A Kentish Childhood	1
2	The Wider World	16
3	Going to War	37
4	Civil Servant	45
5	Prospective Candidate	53
6	Political Progress	66
7	On to Suez—as Chief Whip	81
8	'Into Europe'	90
9	Exit from Brussels	106
10	Time of Turmoil	119
11	Leader by Election	133
12	The Family Circle	147
13	Method and Manner	165
14	Communications	185
Appendix I 'Realism in British Foreign Policy' by Edward Heath		200
Appendix II The Berkeley Memorandum		217
Appendix III Procedure for the Selection of the Leader of the Conservative and Unionist Party		222
Index		225

Illustrations

facing page

Edward Heath at two, when the family were living in Crayford.
(*Mr W. G. Heath*) 22

Aged four, with his mother. (*Mr W. G. Heath*) 22

At fifteen, with his brother John and their mother. (*Mr W. G. Heath*) 22

Organ Scholar. (*Mr W. G. Heath*) 23

During a visit to Republican Spain in 1938 as a member of a student delegation. (*Bexley Conservative Association*) 23

Heath assails the Chamberlain Government in an Oxford Union debate and is caricatured in the *Isis*, 23 November 1938. (*Isis*) 38

With Leo Amery at a Union dinner in 1939, when Heath was President. (*Bexley Conservative Association*) 38

As a gunner officer, he was at first engaged in the anti-aircraft defence of Merseyside. (*Lafayette*) 39

Lieutenant-Colonel Heath with Captain D. J. McMintie and Lieutenant T. Shelton in 1945. (*Mr W. G. Heath*) 39

With his agent, Reginald Pye, during his first general election campaign at Bexley in 1950. (*Bexley Conservative Association*) 118

'A sad moment for European unity,' Heath called it: 29 January 1963, and the E.E.C. reject Britain's application to join. (*Associated Press*) 118

A summer morning in the garden at Broadstairs. (*Central Press Photos*) 119

Conducting his annual Christmas carol concert at Broadstairs five months after becoming Tory leader in 1965. (*Central Press Photos*) 119

Arriving at Church House, Westminster, for his formal adoption as Leader of the Conservative Party, 2 August 1965. (*Keystone*) 134

With Edward du Cann and David Howell at Villefranche, August 1965. (*Weekend Telegraph*) 134

Mr Herbert Wilson writes to Heath's father. (*Mr Herbert Wilson*) 135

Foreword

In the course of my research for this book I have received much kindness from many people, and I am grateful to them all. It is not an 'official' biography, however, and I alone must be held responsible for the outcome. While Edward Heath has co-operated with me, in a friendly and informal way, by adding to my knowledge—and I hope my understanding—of his life and career, I would not expect him to accept every view that I (or others) have expressed. I appreciate and respect his fair and reasonable attitude to what I set out to do.

I particularly wish to thank his father and his stepmother, Mr and Mrs W. G. Heath, who have made me so welcome in their home; and—on the political side—his three predecessors in the leadership of the Conservative Party: Lord Avon, Mr Macmillan and Sir Alec Douglas-Home. Others to whom I am indebted are Mr John Heath, Mr James Bird, Mr Cecil Curzon, Mr Ronald Whittell, Lord Goodman, Lord Fulton, Lord Morris of Grasmere, Mr Walt Rostow, Canon Frederick Temple, Mr Roy Jenkins, M.P., Mr Hugh Fraser, M.P., Mr Philip Kaiser, Mrs Anthony Barber, Colonel G. V. N. Chadd, Mr James Hyde, Mr Peter Masefield, Mr Edward Dines, Mr John Trevisick, Sir Giles Guthrie, Mr Ion Garnett-Orme, Lord Hailes, Lord St Helens, Lord Egremont, Mr Victor Feather, Sir Eric Roll, Mr F. A. Bishop, Sir Herbert Andrew, Mr Peter

Ramsbotham, Mr Humphry Berkeley, Mr William White-law, M.P., Lord and Lady Aldington, Mr Edward Denman, Mrs Thelma Cazalet-Keir, Mr Robert Allan, Mr and Mrs Madron Seligman, and Mr R. A. Pye.

I thank the Prime Minister's father, Mr J. Herbert Wilson, for allowing me to reproduce a letter to Mr W. G. Heath, and Sir Michael Fraser, Mr John MacGregor and Mr Douglas Hurd for their patient and helpful response to innumerable inquiries. Several valued friends—Mr Norman Collins, Mr Patrick Cosgrave and Mr J. W. M. Thompson —were good enough to read parts of the book in proof: I am grateful to them for their comments and suggestions. And I owe thanks to Cecilia Goodlad and Diana Kirk for their fortitude in producing the typescript.

London, April 1970   GEORGE HUTCHINSON

Chapter One

A Kentish Childhood

Edward Heath's rise to the leadership of the Tory party in the summer of 1965 was one of the most remarkable events of postwar politics in this country, if only because it would have seemed, even a few years earlier, such an unlikely achievement. At forty-nine, he was younger than any one of his predecessors since the office was created in 1868; more than that, he was of very modest social origin. He attained the leadership of what is pre-eminently the party of established influence and wealth without the advantage of either; and his adoption marked something much more than a milestone in the life of one individual: it was a turning point in Conservative history, with far-reaching possibilities, some of which are becoming apparent.

Even so, it would clearly be premature to attempt a thorough-going biography of Edward Heath at this point in his career. It is altogether too soon for that. What I have written is no more than an interim account, I hope accurate and detached, but tentative in some of its judgments. I have known him since he first became an M.P. and I wish him well. This is the standpoint from which I have approached the thirteenth leader of his party since Disraeli—and the first to be elected,

I

rather than to 'emerge' from what Iain Macleod has called the magic circle.

Edward Heath, born at Broadstairs in Kent on 9 July 1916, belongs to a family who originated at the other end of southern England. Until the early years of the last century they were in Devon, where John Heath (born 1739) was a tailor at Blackawton, and Richard Heath (born 1763) was a fisherman at Cockington. Another Richard, of the next generation, who was a boatman in the coastguard service, was the first of the Heaths to leave Devon—for Ramsgate, on the Thanet coast of Kent. They have been established in the neighbourhood ever since, and now think of themselves as a Kentish rather than a West Country family. Just as the second Richard Heath broke the link with the west of England, his son broke another link: George Heath (born 1830), a merchant seaman, was the last of many regular seafarers in the family. George's own son, Stephen Richard Heath, was a dairyman and then, when he fell on hard times, a porter. This was Edward Heath's grandfather.

When Edward Heath was born, his parents had been married three years. He was their first child. His mother, Edith Anne Pantony, and his father, William George Heath, were both twenty-eight. Mr Heath was a carpenter, working for a local builder. His life had not been easy. 'I first remember my father in the dairy business,' he recalls. 'He was a very lucky man up to that, but then he lost all his money and he went on the railway. He was a luggage porter, moving luggage between the station and the hotels. I remember there were three of them on a van.' In the late Victorian

2

years of which he was speaking, Broadstairs was much less bustling than Ramsgate and Margate nearby. It is still the staidest in the cluster of Thanet resorts and has changed least in the interval. The steep main street running down to the sea, the neat little bay with lowish white cliffs and sandy beach, the old black pier, and Bleak House looming out in awful Victorian Gothic, are all much as they were when William and Edith Heath made their first home together in what was then called Albion Road and is now St Peter's Park Road. No. 2 Holmwood Villas, a semi-detached house built of tawny brick, in the parish of St Peter's, was divided in two. The Bennetts (he was a retired quantity surveyor) had the upper floor, the Heaths the lower, their front window, a yard or so from the pavement, screened by a privet hedge. Before her marriage, the bride, slender and fair, had been a lady's maid with a family named Taylor. She had travelled with them and worked at their seaside house in Broadstairs and their London home in Hampstead. Her husband, dark-haired and bright-eyed, was a small and wiry man.

They had been married little more than a year when war was declared. By the following spring the rumble of the guns at Ypres could be heard across the Channel. Up the road from St Peter's, in his old manor house, Elmwood, Thanet's most illustrious resident, Lord Northcliffe, was preparing his famous onslaught on Kitchener, 'the nation's idol', for the shell shortage in France. Fourteen months later, on the summer Sunday night when Edward Heath was born, Ramsgate was bombed by a German airship, but Broadstairs escaped. In all the confusion of the attack, Mr Heath was anxious for his wife, but the birth was reasonably smooth and was duly recorded in the next issue of the *Broadstairs*

3

and St Peter's Mail—which also announced Vesta Tilley, great male impersonator, at the Margate Winter Gardens, and Horatio Bottomley, demagogue and swindler, in Ramsgate (he was making recruiting speeches, of course for money). Presently, in the parish church, the child was christened Edward, after an uncle, Richard, after his grandfather, and George after his father.

The war was less than half-way over. Asquith was Prime Minister at the head of a coalition government: Lloyd George, waiting—or poised—in the wings, first as Minister of Munitions, then as Secretary of State for War, was to dislodge him in December. The Unionist (or Tory) leader, Andrew Bonar Law, was Chancellor of the Exchequer. Churchill, previously First Lord of the Admiralty and now in eclipse after the Dardanelles calamity, was commanding a battalion in France. Haig was Commander-in-Chief. Nobody, neither the generals nor the politicians, knew how the war could be won. Everybody was floundering, Ministers and Service chiefs alike. Though Income Tax had been raised to 3s 6d in the pound a year earlier and to 5s in 1916, and 'the Government' was watering the beer, the country was not yet on a proper war footing. As late as Easter, leave-trains from France were stopped for five days so as not to interfere with holiday traffic.

More than two and a half million men had enlisted before voluntary recruitment ended in March; then came conscription. The last day of May saw the greatest sea battle of this awful war—the Battle of Jutland, with the British and German fleets mustering two hundred and fifty ships and twenty-five admirals between them. It was an inconclusive affair in which the British losses exceeded the German. Then, on 1 July,

4

there opened one of the grisliest of all land battles, the Battle of the Somme, with Haig deploying an army of continental size to tragically small effect. On the first day there were 57,000 British casualties, 19,000 killed. Before it was over, five months later, England had lost 420,000 men: three British soldiers for every two Germans. William George Heath was fortunate to escape what proved to be the graveyard of a good part of young England.

Next winter, Broadstairs was shelled from the sea—but the Heaths were now inland at Crayford. Not that fright had driven them away, though many did leave the district for their own safety, and were encouraged to do so. They moved because Mr Heath was assigned to war work as an erector at the Vickers aircraft factory in Crayford. 'It was just before Christmas 1916,' he remembers. 'Teddy wasn't six months old. It was a bitter cold Christmas, too. We couldn't get any coal, we couldn't get any potatoes.' His work outlasted the war by five years, and it was 1923 before they returned to Broadstairs. Meanwhile they lived at 106 Green Walk in Crayford, where John, the second child, was born in 1920, and where Teddy (as he has always been known in the family) went to what his father calls 'a little tin school, a wartime school'—his first. There, too, he had what was perhaps the first really frustrating experience of his childhood. He was three or four. The family had gone shopping one Saturday afternoon in Bexleyheath, and he spotted a beautiful model train in a window. He wanted it for Christmas. His father couldn't afford it and had to say no. But Mr Heath, not to be outdone by the toy manufacturers, made his son a model engine, three and a half feet long and all in scale, with a turntable in front. It was a favourite toy

5

for years and eventually fetched five shillings in an auction.

Back in Broadstairs, the Heaths settled again at St Peter's, sharing a house—Pendennis, in Albion Road—with the widow of Mrs Heath's brother, to whom it belonged, until, after a couple of years, they found a home of their own. James Bird, now retired, was one of the masters at St Peter's Church of England School, a free primary school. 'Although it is difficult to remember an individual boy out of the very many one encounters in over forty years' teaching', says Mr Bird, 'I have a distinct visual image of the small boy, Teddy Heath [aged seven] presenting himself for enrolment. Neatly dressed, and completely self-possessed, he handed me a printed transfer form from Crayford Infants School testifying to his highly satisfactory attainments in reading and arithmetic.' Mr Taylor, the boy's headmaster, found him 'too well-advanced for a class of his own age,' says his father, 'so it was decided to put him in different classes for different subjects'. This small school was associated with the parish church of the same name, in which Mrs Heath was mildly interested. As Mr Heath puts it, 'Teddy's mother was a churchwoman. I wouldn't say she went to church every Sunday, but she was certainly a churchwoman.' She was fond of music, which may have had something to do with it, and, though neither she nor her husband could play, they decided that Teddy should learn the piano. At eight, he received his first lessons from a local music teacher, Miss Lock, and to his parents' delight he took to the piano at once. At school he was also doing well enough for them to feel that he could win a scholarship to Chatham House, along the coast at Ramsgate. He did so in 1926, when he was ten. The

6

scholarship was worth some £12 a year. Chatham House (founded 1909) was the leading grammar school in the neighbourhood, and a good one. Only a quarter of its places were for scholarship boys. 'An integral part of the test,' Mr Bird recalls, 'was an oral examination conducted by the headmaster, Mr H. C. Norman, assisted by a primary school headmaster from another school district. After his oral, I asked Teddy how he had fared and what questions he had been asked. He told me that in answer to a question about what he wanted to be when he grew up he had said "an architect".'

The family had lately moved into the first house of their own—Helmdon, in King Edward Avenue, their home for many years afterwards. Mr Heath, still working for the same local builder, was by now the 'outside manager'. With a wage of perhaps £5 a week, the family had little or nothing to spare. They didn't go away for holidays—'We didn't have any', says Mr Heath. Instead, they remained at home and took in summer visitors. But they never thought of themselves as poor, and by the standards of the time they were not. More than a million were unemployed and the number was rising. By the end of 1930 it reached two and a half million. Three out of four families in the country had incomes of £4 a week or less; indeed the average wage for workers in the main industries was some £2 10s. On the eve of the great depression, the 'economic blizzard' as it came to be called, the Heaths had a comfortable home, and from all accounts it was a very happy one. The two boys, sharing a room together, were always close, but with four years between them each had his own particular friends and, as John Heath recalls, they 'didn't do much together'. John, too, was learning the piano and also the violin. He was a bit of a tearabout. Teddy was neat, pernickety, always just-so. Their mother doted on them both. Edith Heath was houseproud, delicate in all her arrangements, exacting. She was gentle in manner, yet firm, she was warm-hearted but determined. The family called her Trot, and she was very much in command. Everything had to be in apple-pie order: it was a shoes-off-at-the-door sort of regime. In contrast, her husband was easy-going, seldom ruffled, enjoying a game of darts in the kitchen with the boys. Ronald Whittell, a great friend of Teddy's when they were at school together, was often in the house. 'Mrs Heath gave us nice teas,' he remembers. 'She ruled them all, but it was a very happy household. She was one of the most determined women I've ever known. She used to complain about Teddy sitting up in his bedroom reading—he spent a tremendous amount of time reading—instead of spending more time in boyish pursuits. It was a decided shock to both his parents when he turned out the way he did—they hadn't expected such a brilliant child.'

The boy settled easily into his new school—and remained for nine years, which at Chatham House was then unusual if not unique. One of the senior masters was Cecil Curzon, who taught history, economics and the British Constitution. He remembers Heath's arrival at Chatham House with 'an excellent report on his ability and industrious concentration' from his previous headmaster. 'Although young Heath was well-learned for his age,' says Mr Curzon, 'he was no genius. His feet were always on the ground and he merged well with his environment. Throughout his first five years at Chatham House he was always two years in age below the average of his form. This was a remarkable fact because he held his own with boys who he knew were two years older. It is very doubtful whether any other boy in the school ever enjoyed the same experience.' Heath's report for the spring term of 1927 (his second at Chatham House) shows that in a form of thirty-one he came twelfth; the average age was thirteen, but he was still four months short of eleven. 'It was a practice in those days for each form as far as the fifth to have a weekly class list,' Mr Curzon recalls. 'Every subject had a maximum total which varied according to the number of periods per week. The form master classed the boys from honours (80 per cent) to fourth class (below 40 per cent). During these years the majority of Heath's classes were seconds with occasional firsts. Not once did he gain an honours. His position in class at the end of the terms moved about, from fifth to sixteenth. One can perhaps explain these moderate results by a lack of maturity or a certain satisfaction he found in being able to hold an average position. But whatever the explanation he moved in the autumn of 1929, at the age of thirteen and a half, into the fifth form with an average age of fifteen and three-quarters. He was in the senior half of the school and from this point onwards he went full steam.'

Heath was hard-working, but he couldn't be called a swot. Deeply involved though he was in all but one of the school's activities—sport—he had interests outside, and they centred on St Peter's Church. There he sang in the choir every Sunday; and there—having learned the piano—he was being taught to play the organ as well by the church organist, Alfred Tatham. He belonged to a young people's club attached to the church, and went to tennis parties in the vicarage garden on Saturday afternoons in the summer, sometimes accompanied by one or other or both daughters of a local G.P., Dr Raven. When Heath and Ronald Whittell were both fourteen, they attended confirmation classes with the vicar, the Rev. Kenneth Percival Smith. 'I think,' says Whittell today, 'that the vicar was the first man to have a very considerable influence on Heath. He opened our eyes to religion, to Christianity, and from that point on Teddy took his religion very seriously. I believe that it's a deep-seated sense of religion which may—rightly or wrongly—make him think he's a man of destiny.' The family had a tent on the beach, across from the old black pier, and during summer weekends Heath often went swimming. There were plenty of sailing-boats to admire in the harbour, and he longed to have one of his own. He and Whittell and another friend, Derek de Rome, whose father was their mathematics master, liked to go for bicycle rides in the lanes of Thanet. Their lives were as ordinary—or as representative—as thousands upon thousands of others. Up and down the country, innumerable boys of similar background were doing much the same things. If Heath's dog—a brown mongrel terrier given to him by Mrs Lyon at Elmwood Farm, part of the old Northcliffe establishment—had any distinction, it was in name alone: he called it Erg—for Edward Richard George.

At school in an inter-house piano competition, Heath was awarded a prize much valued at Chatham House though little known outside—the Belasco Prize. He played a prelude and fugue from Bach and selections from Mozart and Chopin. The judge was P. B. Tomblings, director of music at St Lawrence College,

Ramsgate. 'A very excellent and sound performance,' Mr Tomblings recorded. 'His playing shows sound musicianship and he is well equipped with technique.'

Meanwhile, as Mr Curzon recounts it, he was doing well in the fifth form. 'The fifth form contained only boys who were preparing for their first external examination, and the headmaster was of the firm opinion that Heath was too young and immature to take the examination. Heath, however, was very anxious to be allowed to sit, and correspondence passed between his father and the headmaster. In the end the head was persuaded to allow Heath to sit, although he said on his report before the examination that it was tempting Providence to allow him to do so. To the surprise of the head, however, and to most of the staff, Heath passed the examination comfortably and was the first of the school at the age of fourteen to gain a General Schools Certificate. He took the same examination the next year, passed with honours and was excused the London University Matriculation. He then moved into the sixth form and studied commerce and economics with a few subsidiary subjects. He quickly mastered the major subjects, gaining a clear understanding of the theories and some practical application of them. In 1932, he passed the London University Higher Schools Examination with exemption from Intermediate Commerce, and next year gained exemption in Intermediate Economics.'

At fifteen he was conducting the school orchestra, and he had a choir in the town which competed in various local festivals.

The one thing at school in which he never became very interested was sport. He was no good at games. Indeed, his only recorded achievement on the playing

fields was to act as scorer for the first eleven at cricket—
an honour indulgently reserved for boys who, however
useless as players, had distinguished themselves in other
ways. Heath was the secretary of the debating society,
he had charge of the library, and he became senior
prefect and captain of his house. 'He had developed a
personality and character which drew the boys towards
him,' says Mr Curzon. 'As a prefect he could be tough,
as many a younger boy discovered, especially if he were
guilty of breaking a school rule. As house captain he
carefully delegated his authority to others who were
good at games or athletics.'

Heath was also enlarging his knowledge of the world
and its ways in grown-up (and sometimes better-off)
company outside. As his father has told me, 'Teddy
always used to prefer people older than himself'. One
was Mr (now Sir) Alec Martin, of Christie's, the fine
art auctioneers, whom Heath would cycle over to see
at Kingsgate. Others were a London solicitor, Royalton
Kisch, and his wife, who had a house at Broadstairs.
Arnold Goodman (now Lord Goodman), then a young
solicitor in Kisch's office and later his partner, remembers Heath in that setting. 'Royalton Kisch,' he tells
me, 'was a prodigious rose grower who became President
of the National Rose Society. He grew his roses at
Broadstairs, where he had met the Heath family. From
time to time, Ted was asked to tea at the Kisch house
and that is where I first met him. He hadn't then gone
to the university. He was about seventeen or eighteen.
I remember him as an alert young man. I didn't get
an impression of an intellectual but of a keen general
intelligence. (I think he probably gained a great deal
more from the university than a lot of others did.) I
think of him then as an eager, questing person who was

looking for founts of experience, founts of sophistication, founts of knowledge. I think perhaps he was looking for these outside his own world and often from people older than himself. He was very genuine. He was not at all a young man on the make. He was a bright and unusual boy whom Kisch regarded as a sort of protégé and for whom both Kisch and his wife had a great affection. Kisch marked him out as a boy of great qualities— and Kisch was a very perceptive man, I may tell you.'

Heath's father was now in the building business on his own account, having bought his old firm when the owner died. He started trading under his own name in 1930 and remained his own master ever after. Politically, though never deeply committed, he differed from his father, the old dairyman turned porter. 'My father was a staunch Tory,' he says, 'absolutely staunch—a Tariff Reformer and all sorts of things. I was more inclined to be a Liberal in my young days.' The family took in one newspaper, the liberal *News Chronicle*. Once only, Mr Heath ventured directly, or tiptoed, into local politics. This was in the mid-'thirties, when he allowed himself to be persuaded 'by six rich gentlemen—one was a K.C., Trevor Watson,' into standing for the Broadstairs Urban District Council. 'Teddy spoke for me at the Bohemia, a concert hall in the High Street. Nobody was more pleased than I was when I lost. For one thing, I hadn't time for it.' Whatever Teddy may have said in his speech at the Bohemia (and neither he nor anyone else can remember), the boy wore no party label. Yet, in his father's judgment and recollection, his party allegiance was already determined: 'As far as I know, he has always been Conservative. It seemed to start in earnest at the time he was at Chatham House School.'

As the headmaster noted, Heath's interest in public affairs was both wide and informed. His forum was the school debating society, and he is remembered as an outstandingly good speaker, fluent and assured. As secretary, he was topical in his choice of subjects. In 1933, after the Oxford Union had passed what Churchill called the ever-shameful resolution 'that this House will in no circumstances fight for its King and Country', Chatham House debated the same motion, but with the contrary result. Heath led the opposition; he was then seventeen. When the MacDonald-Baldwin coalition was in office with Ramsay MacDonald as Prime Minister in a National Government, Chatham House had a mock election. Presenting himself as a National candidate, Heath won with a majority of 150. In this world of Mr Chips he had become quite a swell. He had done especially well in English, history and mathematics, well in Latin, less well in French. Academically, his record was good, but it was not brilliant and he certainly wasn't a flier, though he might just have looked like one when he was a few years younger and so much below the average age in successive forms. It may be true to say that his attainments were more artistic than intellectual, and practical rather than academic. Nor was he universally popular in the school, in the sense that 'everyone' liked him. 'He was anything but popular,' says Whittell. 'He never tried for popularity. He wasn't actively liked or actively disliked. He was respected and accepted, though a little bit intolerant.' To his brother John, looking back, 'he seemed to achieve what he wanted to achieve. He's always seemed to attain anything that he's set his mind on doing.' Heath displayed a rather grave attachment to the school as a community. He had become deeply involved in the institution. He busied himself in its internal arrangements almost as if he were a master. As Whittell expresses it, 'he seemed to achieve maturity of character earlier than others'. And in his last year he received the highest award that Chatham House had to offer—the Leslie and Douglas Prize (established in memory of two brothers killed in the 1914-18 war), and given, on the votes of the sixth and fifth forms put together, 'for character'. He shared it with the captain of school, J. E. Hobbs, who had a major science scholarship to Trinity College, Oxford (and is now prominent in the management of Tate and Lyle). Heath too had high hopes for the immediate future.

Chapter Two

The Wider World

Not only had he set his sights on Oxford. He had also decided that Balliol was the college for him. Balliol appealed to him, as he explained to his father and mother, because it was intellectually distinguished without being snobbish. But how to finance this ambition, with no scholarship? His parents undertook to find £130 a year, at substantial sacrifice to themselves, and the Kent Education Committee agreed to provide a loan of £90 a year. He would have £220 in all. It was little enough, but Heath was game, and in October 1935 he was off. He was one illustration of what Clement Attlee, then leader of the Opposition, called 'the most agreeable change in Oxford since my time'. The university, as Attlee was observing, 'has ceased to be the exclusive preserve of the better-fed classes. It is still true to say that Oxford has a very large number of undergraduates who are the sons of the rich, but intermingled with them are men from working class homes.'

Heath read Philosophy, Politics and Economics. At first, it looked as though music would occupy only a minor part of his university life, providing private pleasure but probably no more than that. In his very first term, however, music suddenly assumed a new importance in his affairs. In open competition he won the Balliol organ scholarship. He was recommended for it by Dr Herbert Howells, among others, and the adjudicator was Dr Ernest Walker, director of music at Balliol. It was a piece of good fortune for Heath and his family, worth £100 a year; and the scholarship had other consequences besides saving his parents an outlay which they could barely afford, for as time went on he began to think of music as a career. Heath also augmented his slender income by tutoring at Broadstairs during the university vacations.

Academically, his record at Oxford was not unlike his record at school: good but not brilliant. He thought himself fortunate in the Master of his college, A. D. Lindsay (later Lord Lindsay of Birker), and in his tutors, among them John Fulton (now Lord Fulton), who taught him politics, Charles Morris (now Lord Morris of Grasmere), who taught him philosophy, and Maurice Allen (until recently a director of the Bank of England), who taught him economics. Of Lindsay, who was a member of the Labour Party, Heath has told me: 'I knew him well. He didn't have much influence on me politically, but he did influence me in believing in democratic discussion. Some of us used to go to the Master's Lodgings once a week, and he was marvellously good at encouraging discussion.' As Lord Fulton expresses it today, 'Sandie Lindsay was very reserved, in the small change of social intercourse, but he was a lion in the things of the mind and he did penetrate to this group. Balliol was a remarkable place in the 'thirties because of Lindsay's influence. He was lecturing on the modern state, and had this enormous lecturing audience. It was a very interesting place for the young to be brought up in, and remember that Heath and his contemporaries belonged to a dispirited generation—they didn't know which way to turn, what to do. Lindsay was saying to them, "Here are the dictators, and what they have to offer isn't worth living for—a number rather than a name." He wrote books such as *The Two Moralities* to examine among other things the presupposition of the use of force. Lindsay was mixing up the college, too, with people from all sorts of backgrounds, quite a lot from the grammar schools.' As tutor, Fulton found Heath 'a well-organised chap, with no spectacular intellectual vice. I remember him reading his essays to me. They were full of detail, very conscientiously worked out, and he was very good at standing up for his thesis. We talked about a lot of interesting things. You couldn't but be aware that he was very much a political young man. In fact Charles Morris, who was the admissions tutor, remembers Heath telling him when they first met that he wanted to go into politics.' Looking back on this incident, Lord Morris says: 'I have a very clear recollection of his coming to see me before he came up, when he was seeking a place at the college, straight from school. I asked him what he wanted to do in life after leaving Oxford, and he replied that he wanted to be "a professional politician". I do not think I ever heard any other schoolboy answer a similar question in these terms.'

Morris's surprise was perhaps all the greater after Heath became the organ scholar, playing in the Balliol chapel at 8.5 every morning and often practising at night for the next day's service. His musical activities were blossoming. He trained the Balliol Choral Society and conducted it at the thousandth Balliol concert. He conducted the Oxford Orchestra—an orchestra composed, as he describes it, 'rather more of town than of

gown, the choir consisting of Balliol men with one or
two additions from Trinity next door and women from
Lady Margaret Hall and Somerville'. He was secretary
of the Music Society, in which he was gratified to find Dr
Lindsay taking 'the greatest possible interest'. He was
asked to arrange music for two dramatic societies. For the
O.U.D.S. he directed incidental music to *The Taming
of the Shrew*, but he was even more prominent in the
Balliol Players, who used to put on a Greek comedy in
English every summer. Walt Rostow remembers that
Heath composed the music for the Players' production
of Aristophanes' *The Frogs*, in 1937. As he tells me, 'I
had the privilege of performing some of his music in the
chorus, round the countryside of Southern England—
but keeping my voice low to avoid an excessive over-
lay of American accent'. Rostow, a White House
adviser successively to Presidents Kennedy and Johnson,
now a professor in the University of Texas, was then a
Rhodes Scholar at Balliol. Today he speaks of Heath 'as
one of the two or three most promising men I met at
Oxford: a rare example of purposefulness, amiability
and reserve'. Another friend, Frederick Temple, recalls
that the Players 'elected themselves like the Venetian
Doges and did this without reference to ability in acting
but purely with a view to congenial friendship'. Temple,
nephew of the late Archbishop, now a canon of Ports-
mouth Cathedral, has happy memories of those summer
tours, when they performed both to schools and to the
public. 'When each year people had chosen others who
would be congenial then we saw how much acting we
could get out of them. I remember Teddy being in
charge of a strange and rather weird Greek chorus and
getting remarkable music from them. These summer
evenings were among some of the happiest in my life

when we performed in the open in places like Corfe
Castle and then retired to the pub for bacon and eggs
and beer afterwards and then slept out under the
Castle or in the ruins of Old Sarum and such places
before we moved on the next day. We hired one lorry
from Cowley and enough people had broken-down
second-hand cars to transport the whole lot. Teddy, as
he was known to all of us at Oxford, and not Ted, was
completely part of this typical Balliol scene.' During
one of these tours, Heath took the opportunity of
playing on the organs of Bath Abbey and Salisbury
Cathedral, and he conducted the Wareham Silver
Band.

But he was prominent above all in undergraduate
politics. 'I started to be a politician at school', as he puts
it, 'and debating seemed to be a natural thing at Oxford.
As a boy I didn't really think of myself as a Tory or
anything else, but just as somebody political, interested
in politics. At Oxford I came to regard myself as a Tory.'
He was later to revolutionise the fortunes of the
University Conservative Association, which in the
leftward climate of undergraduate sentiment had been
in the doldrums. But in the Union Society he established
a larger reputation.

Four months after his arrival at Oxford, the *Cherwell*,
one of the university newspapers, had noted, though it
did not report, his maiden speech in the Union, whose
members were debating the motion 'That this House
considers that England is fast following in the footsteps
of Ancient Rome'. 'There followed two splendid maiden
speeches from Mr E. R. S. Heath (Balliol) and Mr D.
Hoyland (Balliol),' said the *Cherwell*, compounding
inaccuracy—as to Heath's third initial—with incom-
pleteness. From then on, until he went down in 1939,

the *Cherwell*, like the *Isis*, was sprinkled with references to Heath the undergraduate politician.

The *Isis* of 11 March 1936 reported a Union debate on the motion 'That this House considers that the present system of education is unsuited to a democratic state'. 'Mr Heath pointed out that equality of education meant equality of wealth and equality of wealth meant Communism, therefore he voted against the motion.' The report was signed I.D.H.—Ian Harvey, later a Conservative M.P. and junior minister, who added: 'Mr Heath has plenty of confidence. He must be careful not to appear too aggressive.' In the summer, Heath opposed a Union motion asserting that 'the British Fascists by their conduct have forfeited their right to freedom of speech'. In November he met Winston Churchill for the first time. This was before the abolition of university representation in Parliament. Churchill had gone to Oxford to encourage the University Conservative Association's allegiance to his friend Professor Lindemann (later Lord Cherwell), rather than Sir Arthur Salter or Sir Farquhar Buzzard, in the election, still three months away, for one of the two seats (the other was held by A. P. Herbert, sitting as an Independent). What was needed in the University, said Churchill (as the university newspapers reported him), was a definite Conservative viewpoint, a clear-cut set of principles, rather than a vague and smudgy amalgam of diverse opinions. Such real Conservatism could most properly be championed by Lindemann, a man with a fascinating mind and a definite contribution to make in matters of defence. 'The Prof.' introduced Heath to Churchill as a young man with the right outlook. In the event, it was Sir Arthur Salter (now Lord Salter) who won the day. In the same month, Heath was supporting a Union motion 'That this House would not approve the return to Germany of her former colonies'. His speech, said the *Cherwell* report,

> covered the whole ground with remarkable ease. He pointed out that Germany gave up her colonies to the Allied Powers, and not the League; that they could not be said to have been stolen in view of the fact that Germany took the risk of losing them when she went to war; and that, after all, she had only maintained 20,000 colonists before 1914. Very little of the world's raw materials came from colonies, and it was for psychological and military, rather than economic reasons that Germany claimed colonial rights. Mr Heath was very amusing about Gen. Goering, and concluded by outlining the objections on the grounds of strategy to any concession. This was an all-round attack, which perhaps combined rather too many different points. For instance, the argument, frequently reiterated during the evening, that Germany would not really enjoy having her colonies back is far less satisfactory than arguments of strategical necessity or abstract right. Nevertheless, Mr Heath's speech was well thought out, persuasively delivered, and certainly deserved the applause it received.

In the next term (February 1937) Heath opposed a motion 'That the public school would be an anomaly in a civilised society'. He 'denied that corporal punishment and fagging were necessary to the public schools system and denied also that the public schools product was incapable of creating or appreciating art', suggesting the New Oxford Art Society as proof of this. In May, in what the *Cherwell* called an 'able speech' (he 'has the great merit of always being well informed'), Heath supported a motion regretting the hostile attitude of the Congress Party towards the Indian Constitution.

(*Above left*) Edward Heath at two, when the family were living in Crayford. (*Above right*) Aged four, with his mother. (*Below*) At fifteen, with his brother John and their mother

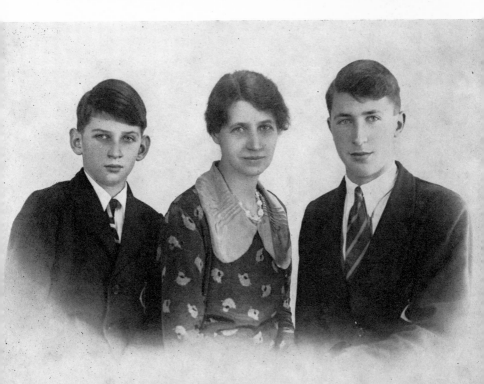

(*Above*) Organ scholar.
(*Left*) During a visit to
Republican Spain in
1938 as a member of a
student delegation

That summer, when he was just twenty-one, he visited Germany. 'I went to Germany,' he says, 'as the result of an exchange between a German family and ourselves. The German boy was the same age as myself. I think his name was Dichter. He was killed in the war. His family came from Düsseldorf. I went there first, then down with them, when they went on holiday, to Bad Homburg. After that I went on my own to Bavaria —to Munich and on to Bayrische Gmain. This was a quarter of a mile from the Austrian frontier. I stayed with a retired teacher and his wife—Dr Winckler. From there I did lots of climbing expeditions, and I learned a little German. Dr Winckler was a German liberal of the old school and he hated the Nazis and everything they were doing. We tramped around the foothills together and he would say how bad the political system was. The Wincklers suggested that I should go to the Nuremberg Rally, where I saw it all, every day for three days —the military demonstrations and Hitler himself. This was when I realised what they were really like.'

Heath returned to his home at Broadstairs rather wiser than when he set out. Back at Oxford in the autumn, he soon found himself challenging a powerfully experienced Socialist opponent, Hugh Dalton, when the Union considered Labour's so-called Immediate Programme. Heath was 'in brilliant form', according to the *Cherwell* report:

He said that Dr Dalton proved in himself that the battle of the bourgeoisie would be won on the playing field of Eton. In this motion, Labour was on the defensive. Its programme was vague, being filled with catch phrases. Who led the party? Morrison, Cole, or Cripps? What would this programme cost?—£185 millions a year increase on the social services. No wonder Dr Dalton refused to give a Socialist budget in advance. And look at the losses experienced by other countries on nationalisation of various businesses. But above all, this programme was to be condemned on its Distressed Areas policy, which would do nothing to help the situation. And with regard to foreign policy, what would the Socialists do now? Let them tell us, and be appallingly frank about it.

Heath recalls the encounter with a certain pride. 'The other speaker on my side in the debate against Dalton was the president of the Cambridge University Conservatives. We won the vote, and it was the first time the Conservatives had won in the Union on a political motion for many years—probably the first time in the 'thirties.'

The events of the following year, 1938, were of the first importance to Heath's political development. Hitler and Mussolini were tightening their grip in Europe and beyond. The Italians had conquered Abyssinia—and the British Prime Minister, Chamberlain, was ready to recognise their conquest. With Nazi Germany, the Italian Fascists were increasingly involved in Spain—five divisions of the Italian army were committed to Franco (as so-called volunteers), and in the Mediterranean a number of merchant ships had been sunk by Italian submarines masquerading as Spanish. Yet Chamberlain, as Churchill expressed it, was still 'imbued with a sense of a special and personal mission to come to friendly terms with the dictators'. Within a twelvemonth, during which he saw something of the civil war in Spain as a member of a student delegation invited by the Republican Government, Heath's mind was shaped to lasting effect.

In that year, Anthony Eden's resignation as Foreign Secretary was a turning-point for Heath. Eden found that he could no longer support, or accept, the Prime Minister's attitude to the dictators, or his manner of diplomacy. He resigned on 20 February 1938. That night, Heath was one of several undergraduates gathered in the rooms of Philip Kaiser, an American Rhodes Scholar at Balliol. They were there because Kaiser, who was a New Deal Democrat, strongly pro-Roosevelt, possessed a wireless set. 'We were all waiting for news of Eden's resignation,' Philip Kaiser recalls. 'I remember that Ted said very little that night. It affected him. Eden was important to him. When it happened—and the resignation wasn't even reported as the first item on the news—a *gravitas*, a great thoughtfulness, settled on him, more than was the case with anybody else. He thanked me and then walked out.'

Churchill, in his memoirs, has recorded his own emotions:

Late in the night a telephone message reached me as I sat in my old room at Chartwell (as I often sit now) that Eden had resigned. I must confess that my heart sank, and for a while the dark waters of despair overwhelmed me. . . . From midnight till dawn I lay in my bed consumed by emotions of sorrow and fear. There seemed one strong young figure standing up against long, dismal, drawling tides of drift and surrender, of wrong measurements and feeble impulses. My conduct of affairs would have been different from his in various ways; but he seemed to me at this moment to embody the life-hope of the British nation. . . . Now he was gone. I watched the daylight slowly creep in through the windows and saw before me in mental gaze the vision of Death.

The student delegation to Spain went out at the beginning of the long summer vacation. Heath's three companions were George Stent, a South African and a

Socialist, now dead, Richard Simons, who joined the United Nations secretariat after the war, and a Liberal, D. M. P. Tasker. 'The four of us went to Government Spain—non-Franco Spain. The Ebro River was then the front. The Government was in Barcelona. We went to Perpignan by sleeper train, then across the frontier by car to Barcelona. We went out to the front and saw the forces and the British battalion, then back to Barcelona, where we talked to members of the Government. Negrin was Prime Minister, del Vayo was Foreign Minister: they belonged to the Social Democratic Party. In Barcelona we were bombed in our hotel. People who had rushed down to the basement were killed, but we stayed upstairs and were all right—you know, the bombs went in another way. We also saw something of Catalonia. We went up to Monserrat, where we saw the pictures from the Prado, which were stored in the vaults—they were wonderful. We went along the coast and saw something of the refugee work. We were machine-gunned along the Taregona road. We tried to fly to Madrid, but we were turned back. Of course I already had fairly clear ideas about it all—Franco was backed by Hitler and Mussolini, after all, and I think everyone realised that this was the first stage of the European war. They were all using it to experiment. It was obvious that the Social Democrats had Communist support, but I was just more than ever in favour of a Government that was trying to resist the Fascists.'

Back at Oxford after the vacation, Heath became librarian of the Union, of which he had already been secretary. The *Isis* had this to say of him: 'The Librarian (Balliol) is a very good speaker indeed: reasonable, succint and lucid. Also he has shown by a particularly brilliant tenure of the secretaryship that he has real administrative ability.' Alan Wood (now dead), an Australian undergraduate who became a well-known journalist, wrote in the *Cherwell:* 'Mr E. R. G. Heath, the Union's best speaker, succeeds by the simple process of knowing more about the subject than his opponents: and, though he sometimes descends to humour, he uses it as a weapon and not as an ornament.' That year, in its account of a debate on the motion 'That this House sees little hope for the future in the present Labour and Conservative parties', the *Cherwell* reported Heath as saying that the Liberals were suffering from a sense of irresponsibility. 'Their only chance of getting back to power was a system of proportional representation, the value of which could be seen in the cases of France and Weimar Germany. In any event what Liberalism stood for—freedom of thought and trade—were the common inheritance of both the other parties and, even if this were not so, there is no room for a third one. The Conservatives stood for freedom of trade. . . . Mr Heath was not quite on his best form and had to cope with a certain amount of interruption, even so it was a competent speech.'

By now there was a growing movement for the formation of a Popular Front—a combination of Labour, Liberal and even Conservative critics of the Chamberlain administration. The Union debated its merits in June, on the motion 'That this House would welcome the replacement of the present National Government by a Popular Front Government' (carried by 154 to 113). In Heath's opinion 'a new government must have a secure basis and there was little sign that any popular front would provide that'. The *Cherwell* report continued:

he attempted to defend two clients at once: Mr Eden, who represents his own views, and Mr Chamberlain, who represents the views of the Government arraigned in the motion—and lost control of his argument for a while till he turned to what he thought the dominating European problem, the aim of Germany. Here the Government policy was unambiguous, making clear to Germany that we stood against aggression, and yet refusing to give Czechoslovakia a blank cheque. After demonstrating the failure of the idea that you need never fight provided you say you will, he ended by declaring that he thought that though this country hated war it is still ready to fight for ideals.

Hitler and Chamberlain signed the Munich Agreement in September 1938, a compact, in Chamberlain's phrase, intended to secure 'Peace with Honour'. It divided the nation. Some determined to go along with Chamberlain and uphold Munich; others—with Churchill and his parliamentary followers, such as Harold Macmillan—to condemn it. Heath was among the opponents. The following month—October—provided a spectacular opportunity to demonstrate his feelings, in the Oxford City by-election.

The Tory candidate, standing as a champion of Munich, was Quintin Hogg (later Lord Hailsham and now again Mr Hogg). His opponent was a member of the Labour Party presenting himself as a Popular Front candidate—the Master of Heath's own college, A. D. Lindsay of Balliol. Originally, as the prospective Labour candidate, Patrick Gordon Walker was to have stood against Hogg. But the Oxford City Labour Party, contriving what must have been one of the luckless Gordon Walker's earliest electoral misfortunes, decided to drop him in favour of Lindsay. According to Hugh Dalton, in his memoirs, Richard Crossman, then on the

Oxford City Council, played a leading part in this manœuvre, though I have heard that G. D. H. Cole had much more to do with it. The Liberals, for their part, withdrew their candidate and gave Lindsay full support. Heath at once declared his allegiance to Lindsay. He canvassed for him throughout the campaign, knocking on doors, urging the electors to vote for Lindsay—against Munich, against the Chamberlain Government. Macmillan went down to lend his weight to the Lindsay campaign, and he has lately recorded in his memoirs, *Winds of Change*, that 'among several Conservative undergraduates who gave energetic support, one was conspicuous for skill and enthusiasm. His name was Edward Heath.'

'A vote for Hogg is a vote for Hitler' was the Lindsay slogan and battlecry. Julian Amery, then an undergraduate and, like Heath, an anti-Chamberlain, pro-Churchill Tory, and Crossman both claim credit for its authorship. Lindsay lost the election to Hogg, though shortly afterwards a Popular Front candidate, Vernon Bartlett, did win Bridgwater in Somerset. The by-election of course created havoc among the Oxford Tories. 'A. D. Lindsay divided the Oxford Carlton Club', Hugh Fraser recalls. Fraser, then at Balliol with Heath, later a Conservative M.P. and Minister, was on Hogg's side. 'I was just rather anti-Lindsay—it was more that than policy with me', he says.

In the same month the Union debated the motion 'That this House disapproves of the policy of Peace without Honour'. Heath 'attacked the muddled policy of the Government, which had been largely responsible for bringing us to the verge of disaster', said the *Isis* report.

He maintained that the original Chamberlain declaration was indecisive and that the solution should have been autonomy. It was certainly not self-determination which resulted from Munich. He had no faith in a lasting peace, but foresaw further trouble—in Switzerland, Holland, and elsewhere. In fact, the Munich terms had now gone beyond those of Godesberg, which we had rejected. Had we won Hitler's goodwill? Was that self-evident after his last speech? Hitler could not be trusted: that was clear to everyone save Mr Chamberlain. He was prepared to give justice, but not sympathy, to Nazi Germany, for Nazism was essentially incompatible with Democracy. Finally, our defences were in a sorry state. This speech was competent if a little too long and, as a Conservative, Mr Heath must have astonished some of his confrères by his bitter attack.

A new Balliol friend, though several years younger and more recently arrived, was Roy Jenkins. 'My first debate in the Union was the immediate post-Munich debate,' he recalls. 'Heath's speech was highly polished and very effective. It was a very good speech, though I must say that Chris Mayhew's speech made an even greater impression on me.' Heath himself reported the debate in the *Cherwell*, modestly omitting his own speech. He gave great praise to Christopher Mayhew, an ex-president of the Union, who was then at Christ Church:

[Mayhew] showed the Union style at its best. He made a brilliant speech. Ridiculing the idea that the Opposition was responsible for the failure of the re-armament scheme, he went on to show that never again would our military position be so strong compared to that of Germany. We should have made a firm stand with the other countries which had been with us. Now they had left us, because of the weakness and demoralisation of the democracies. The ex-president then criticised in detail the Munich Agreement and the way it had worked out, and taunted the Tories with having lost their patriotism when there was a job worth doing to be done. He ended his speech with the cry that Chamberlain must go and a government formed worthy of the ideals of this country.

In November, Heath was again on the attack, assailing Chamberlain more fiercely still when the Union was asked to express 'No confidence in the National Government as at present constituted' (carried by 203 to 163). As the *Isis* reported, Heath said that

everywhere there was the greatest distrust of the Government. It was nothing more nor less than an organised hypocrisy, composed of Conservatives with nothing to conserve and Liberals with a hatred of liberty. As for Mr Chamberlain's foreign policy, it could only be described in the maxim, If at first you don't concede, fly, fly, fly, again. He quoted an American journalist's opinion that in the next crisis Mr Chamberlain would again turn all four cheeks at once.

Apart from reporting debates in the Union, Heath did hardly any university journalism, preferring to air his views in speech rather than print. But in February 1939, he went so far as to write an article in the *Isis* under the heading 'The Conservatives Learn to Teach', which seems worth reproducing in full:

The most interesting thing since the war must surely be the emergence of propaganda on its present scale as a national weapon. In this country we only lately realised its importance, and until recently we took no steps to counter that of other countries or to do anything positive on our own. In our internal politics we always distinguished between a more or less fair way of influencing opinion and the cruder implications of the word 'propaganda'. Nationally we thought the blatantly false propaganda of other countries couldn't work, and if it did we did not want to use the same methods against it, and we could not see any others.

The British Point of View

The position now is different. We have seen the extent to which internally people can be controlled by it, and internationally how one country can use it against another. Germany against Czechoslovakia, Italy against ourselves in Palestine. We also know that the B.B.C. can broadcast unbiassed and representative reports to other countries, which, to judge from Herr Hitler's speech, are having no inconsiderable effect. We are at least letting our ideas and opinions have a chance of standing up for themselves.

This would be important enough normally, but it is doubly important with our present foreign policy of 'appeasement'. This is largely based on the quite genuine belief that the people of other countries—as opposed to their rulers—do not want war. We must therefore show them that neither do we, that their own policy is leading them into it, and give them every chance of showing a desire for peace, thus restraining their rulers. All this is absolutely true, and the Prime Minister's visits to Germany and Italy have undoubtedly given the peaceful forces there an opportunity to show themselves sufficiently to disconcert the dictators. The question is whether this technique is sufficient in itself to achieve its ends. To many it must seem a weak plank on which to base a foreign policy.

Books and Letters

The growth of the methods of political education inside this country in the last three years has also been interesting. There have been the Book Clubs, the enormous sale of Penguin and Pelican books and the emergence of the News-letters. Of course the most universal are the News-letters, the only explanation of which can be that our normal press is not doing its job properly. On the whole the Left seems to have got one up on the Right with these new develop-

ments, but I have just received the first number of a Fort-
nightly News-letter for undergraduate Conservatives which
is being produced by Alan Fyfe, a former President of the
Union, and which has distinct possibilities of becoming a
good thing. University Conservatives have not been very well
catered for in the past; here is something in the right style.

What is a Conservative?

It concludes with press cuttings about the Universities
Conference at the beginning of the year, one of which said:
'The Federation has always had about as much backbone
as a plate of porridge, and its principal characteristic has
been willingness to fraternise with Socialists and Commun-
ists in pacifist demonstrations', and another: 'Opinions were
expressed that might more appropriately have come from
the Federation of University Socialists'—all of which is very
interesting because it revives the problem of what is a
Conservative. This is not very urgent, however, (*a*) because
the Party as such is not so keen on heresy hunts as another
I have heard of, and (*b*) because the Party is broad enough
and strong enough to contain diversity within that unity
which is constituted by Party loyalty.

In this, his final year at Oxford, Heath became
President of the Union and reached the summit of his
university career. 'He won the presidency,' Roy Jenkins
believes, 'on his anti-appeasement line. I almost certainly
voted for him, in fact I'm sure I did, though I can't
precisely remember doing so. But I would have done so
on political and personal grounds. I know that I voted,
and I'm sure it was for Teddy, as we used to call him
then. Of course he was quite senior to me. He was in his
third or fourth year when I was a freshman. He was
grave, courteous, perfectly agreeable, not sparkling, successful, old for his years. He was a thoroughly successful,
well-established Balliol figure.' The boy from the humble

but sheltered home and modest school had emerged a someone of consequence in the University, and Roy Jenkins adds: 'He seemed to me more self-confident then than he is now. He didn't show any feelings of insecurity, considering his background at Broadstairs, and although he was never arrogant, he was perfectly self-assured.'

Heath's anti-Fascist line also appealed to Philip Kaiser, his perceptive American friend at Balliol, who has lately been serving as Minister at the U.S. Embassy in London. 'He was very sound on Munich,' says Kaiser. 'You got the impression of a guy who was highly intelligent, well motivated, not a glad-hander but agreeable and congenial. He was serious, but with a good sense of fun when you were in a party with him. Retrospectively, perhaps, looking back, there was a little bit of a quality which comes out more prominently in the person presented today—essentially self-protective, a certain obliqueness about him which came through in a rather charming way in those days. Now that characteristic is, I think, part of his image problem today—it's come through rather strongly in the public man. Ideologically, he is just about where you would have expected him to be—liberal Tory, pragmatic, progressive.'

Heath was in his element as President. Just as he had revitalised the University Conservative Association by giving his mind to its organisation as well as its philosophy, he introduced practical reforms in the Union administration. Not content with arranging debates, and importuning the eminent with invitations to speak, he brought about a number of domestic changes. For example the turnover in the dining-room was at once increased when the Union adopted his businesslike proposal to let members have credit of up to £5 a term.

In this final year, Heath was also elected President of the Junior Common Room at Balliol (to be succeeded by Denis Healey, who was in turn succeeded by Roy Jenkins). To an older onlooker, his tutor John Fulton, this seemed 'almost more worthwhile than Union office'. As Lord Fulton puts it, 'He had to handle a lot of clever and individualistic chaps on issues much more varied than the purely intellectual ones which were the substance of University debates. His handling of this J. C. R. job was very important.'

As his time at the University drew to an end, he was entitled to think of himself as an Oxford success. Roy Jenkins has suggested that he was old for his years, and in a recent broadcast another Oxford contemporary, the writer Philip Toynbee, has said that he was 'a gentle, amiable, kindly, competent man, but not one with a very striking personality . . . an efficient man, but not outstanding, in no way brilliant'. Yet to Jean Asquith (now Mrs Anthony Barber) he seemed dynamically interesting: 'I was a first year when Ted was a third—I went up in 1938. I always remember standing with a friend of mine on the Broad opposite Balliol and seeing him go by in flannel bags and my friend saying: "That's Teddy Heath. He's going to be Prime Minister one day." You see, by the time I went to Oxford he was being pointed out as a person of consequence, and not only by political people. He had a certain mystique or aura. In our eyes he was absolutely splendid, and nobody questioned why.' To others he seemed a shade earnest, worthy rather than stimulating. 'He struck one as very competent, but there was no great ebullience of youth' is how Hugh Fraser puts it—adding engagingly that while at Oxford he himself spent just as much time at Cambridge because it is nearer Newmarket. 'There was nothing madcap about him, like some other characters, friends of mine—Philip Toynbee, for example. He was an extremely nice, agreeable, friendly person. He was a bright person, but not, I would say, academically brilliant.'

His examiners in the School of P.P.E. made a similar judgment: they awarded him not a first but a second-class degree. It was above the average but it was not outstanding. 'He was probably disappointed by his schools results,' says Lord Fulton, 'but then he had done a lot of other things. There was a solid virtue and steadiness about him, industry applied to the right points, sensible and self-controlled use of his time. All his non-academic work had to be done at the expense of something.' As another of his old tutors, Lord Morris, puts it, 'He was not academically brilliant by Balliol standards, but he knew what he wanted to get out of Oxford'.

As the term closed, war was very near. The *Isis*, in what proved to be its last issue before the outbreak, reported the Union as urging the Polish Government 'to resist any attempt to incorporate Danzig within the German Reich'. Underneath this report was an article about Margot Fonteyn and Pamela May by Richard Hillary. The subject seems charmingly appropriate to the gay, brave, sensitive man who was so soon to write *The Last Enemy*, his final act of authorship.

Chapter Three

Going to War

As the doom-laden summer wore on, Heath was nevertheless determined, with his great Balliol friend, Madron Seligman, to make another visit to the Continent. 'It was our last long vac,' he says. 'We knew it was likely to be the last free holiday we'd have, either because there would be a war which one wouldn't survive or else one would have a job and that would be the end of long vacs. We thought we would go to the most interesting place. Madron Seligman wanted to go to Spain and I was quite happy about that. We didn't go, however, because though he got a visa I couldn't. So we thought we'd go to Danzig, as the next most interesting place. We set off, and we went across from Dover, took a train from Brussels up to Hanover, and then went on to Berlin. In Berlin we had quite a few introductions, one to Anthony Mann of the *Daily Telegraph*, who was there, and I also had a few German introductions.'

As they moved around, however, they found 'a definite hostility and tension in the air'. The Germans were 'just hostile', though Heath is sure that this had nothing to do with the fact that Madron Seligman is Jewish. 'For a start, nobody knew. You couldn't tell from looking at him, and anyhow everyone assumed that the Jews had all been liquidated. Besides, he spoke beautiful German (and still does)—the family has a German background, way back.'

From Berlin, 'we went to Danzig—by train, you know, very much third class with hard wooden seats, rucksacks on our backs. All the youth hostels, where we meant to stay, were occupied by troops, so we put up at a sort of *pension* place. Then we went to Gdynia, in Poland, and on by rail to Warsaw. We had various other introductions there, one to Donald Hankey, who was Third Secretary at the Embassy. And we met a splendid man called Savery. He was remarkable in two ways—apparently he knew more about Poland than anyone else (he was in the consulate), and also he had the very best collection of Dresden porcelain. This was unfortunately irretrievably damaged during the war.

'From Warsaw we hitch-hiked to the German frontier, got across the border by train, and then went on hitch-hiking. Dr Winckler was staying with relations —I think it might have been his sister—just outside Breslau. He had come up from Bavaria for the summer holidays, and we had lunch together. He came with us to Leipzig and we climbed up to the top of a hill, and there we parted. We went east. We knew very well we'd never meet again. It was the date of the Ribbentrop Pact with Russia. I remember we heard a paper boy shouting it at Leipzig station. We realised that this might make it bad for us and we thought we ought to get out. The German troops were mobilising and they were moving west. In the middle of the night we got a train out of Leipzig and went down to Frankfurt. We stayed the night opposite the station and next morning got down to Kehl. This was the German side of the

'The policy of the Government is that of turning all four cheeks.'

(*Left*) Heath assails the Chamberlain Government in an Oxford Union debate and is caricatured in the *Isis*, 23 November 1938. (*Below*) With Leo Amery at a Union dinner in 1939, when Heath was President

(*Right*) As a gunner officer, he was at first engaged in the anti-aircraft defence of Merseyside. (*Below*) Lieutenant-Colonel Heath with Captain D. J. McMintie and Lieutenant T. Shelton in 1945

frontier and we crossed over the bridge into Strasburg and felt better. French troops were now mobilising. We hitch-hiked up to Paris, and it was all blacked out. We spent the night there, and next morning I managed to get a train down to the Channel coast. It was chock-a-block and so was the boat across to Dover, where my father met me. This was September, two days before war was declared. Madron didn't come back with me. As we had worked out the tour, we were both supposed to be going on from Paris to the Seligmans' holiday cottage at St Jacut de la Mer in Brittany, and he still went on to join his family there while I got back to England.'

Heath's parents had been anxious for his safety, and his father was waiting for him at Dover with the new family car—their first, a Hillman Minx.

Heath volunteered for the Army a few days after the outbreak of war. The Oxford Recruiting Board recommended him for the gunners. Months earlier, however, it had been arranged that he should undertake a debating tour in the United States, and he was advised to carry on, as he would not be called up before the following January.

'Every two years,' Heath recalls, 'a team went out from Oxford and Cambridge. This year for some reason, only Oxford had been invited. The Union committee decided that I, who had been President in the Hilary term, and Hugh Fraser, who had followed me, should go. But Hugh Fraser, because his family had been in a Territorial regiment, the Lovat Scouts, was in camp at the time and they were all told to remain, and I think they went straight from camp into formation somewhere. So Peter Street came, instead of Hugh Fraser. We went off in about the third week in October and the debating tour went on until Christmas.'

Heath and Street spoke in twenty-six universities, from Maine across to Chicago and from New Orleans to Florida: 'Before we left', he recalls, 'we were specially briefed by the Ministry of Information— no, it was the Foreign Office, I think, by a man called Frank Darwin. Our instructions were that as the U.S. were neutral we weren't publicly to discuss the war. Of course all the arguments we had privately were about this. How it worked was that a selection of motions was sent over ahead of the tour, and the universities chose from them. But Pittsburgh didn't want any of our motions. They wanted "Should America enter the war on the side of the Allies?" This was very difficult, and I thought we should probably pack up and go home. Our instructions were that if we had any problems we were to ring the British Embassy in Washington. So I spoke to Lord Lothian, who was then the Ambassador. He said that it wasn't necessary to be so drastic. What we should do, he said, was to accept the debate, and one of us should speak on either side. That would prevent any trouble, he said. What we did was to change sides every night from then on. One night I would speak for the motion while Peter Street opposed it, and next night we'd do it the other way round.' Heath still smiles at Lord Lothian's simple wisdom.

They were away till the following January. For the next seven months, Heath kicked his heels until, in August 1940, he was eventually called up in the Royal Artillery. He was sent to a training establishment on the Sussex Downs near Storrington. There he was recommended for a commission, and went on to an O.C.T.U. at Shrivenham in Wiltshire. After that, as number 179215 Second-Lieutenant Heath, Royal Artillery, he was ready for service. He was posted to Lancashire, where the 107th Heavy Anti-Aircraft Regiment were engaged in the defence of Merseyside, then under constant and often ferocious attack. His commanding officer was a Territorial Major, George Chadd, an open, frank and kindly man. Colonel Chadd (as he became) was rather taken with his new recruit, and has happily insisted ever since that in Heath he instantly recognised a future Prime Minister (in this he is supported by a fellow-officer, Anthony Race, now a City solicitor, who confirms Chadd's 'amazing prognostication'). At first, Heath was a troop commander, then adjutant to the regiment. Colonel Chadd remembers 'his industry and devotion to duty and attention to detail'. 'I've never seen him put a foot wrong,' he says. 'He was always meticulously correct in his conduct and behaviour. The men liked him. He was never impatient with dullards or arrogant to people not so bright as himself. He drank a glass of beer in the mess and he read a lot, he was always reading in bed, but he didn't go out much except with his band.' This was the battery band, a five-piece affair with 'When you're smiling, when you're smiling, the whole world smiles with you' as their signature tune. Lacking proper transport of their own, they sometimes went about in quite irregular fashion. Colonel Chadd recalls a Sunday afternoon when the band were on their way to Chester. For want of anything else, one of the R.A.M.C. doctors, Captain Williams, had produced an ambulance to take them there, and on the journey it was held up at a bridge. Just then a neighbouring and rather grand commanding officer pulled up behind in his staff car, and was dumbfounded to hear the beat of dance music from the back of the regimental ambulance. 'Typically,' says Chadd, 'Heath had got the band rehearsing to avoid wasting time.' The outraged C.O. was eventually pacified.

In the autumn of 1941, Heath had to undergo a further course of instruction. He was sent to the School of Anti-Aircraft Defence at Manorbier, near Tenby in Pembrokeshire, where Captain R. M. Fraser was his instructor. As Fraser, now Sir Michael, and deputy chairman of the Conservative Party, remembers, 'There were twenty officers on the course, of whom six failed. The records show that I picked out four from the rest as the best—Captain Reeve, Lieutenant Anderson, Lieutenant Rouston, and Second-Lieutenant Heath. Within the four, the two who really caught my eye were Captain Reeve, who was extremely knowledgeable and fairly experienced, and Second-Lieutenant Heath, who showed most drive and incisiveness.'

The Second-Lieutenant was soon promoted and before long, as a captain, he became adjutant of the regiment. During the next couple of years he was stationed in various parts of the country. With the invasion of Europe in 1944, Heath and his brother found themselves ten miles apart on the Normandy front. As John Heath, then a craftsman in R.E.M.E., remembers, 'I was amazed one night, in all the confusion, when a man in a helmet turned up on a motor-bike, and it was Teddy, who'd found out where I was and came over to see me'. Heath was at the regimental headquarters, and his duties were largely administrative. But at the end of the following winter he was given a new—and more testing—appointment, with the rank of major.

James Hyde was the orderly room sergeant of 334 Battery of the 107th Regiment, who were resting at Nieuwpoort, near Blankenberge in Belgium, after fighting their way up from Caen—through Amiens, Arras, Antwerp and Eindhoven. They had gone on to Nijmegen and beyond, for the relief of Arnhem, and had just concluded three arduous months on the Venlo front in the Ardennes. They were exhausted. Their commanding officer, a major with whom they had served continuously since 1941, was being transferred. Heath was his replacement. 'We were all wondering what sort of person he would turn out to be,' Hyde recalls, 'and we were none too happy. Up to then he had been an administrator. He hadn't done any fighting worth speaking of. I was suspicious of him. I felt my life was going to be upset. But I think it's right to say that within a fortnight or three weeks he exercised such a persuading influence that one found—much as one had loved one's previous C.O., who'd undergone all the privations—that Heath was first-class. So far as administration was concerned, he was perfect. The other reason why he was first-class—and this was to my surprise—was that he rapidly understood men and their reactions. He made no changes that were apparent on the surface, but underneath the surface, he'd made them. Within a month or two it was Heath's battery. The men liked him because they thought he was a fair man.'

The battery took part in the crossing of the Rhine. 'Heath took us across, and he was very efficient,' says Hyde. 'He led us right up to Hanover. He didn't know tiredness. I've done operation orders with him all night. He was a tough skipper. If he said the battery was going to do it this way, that was it. If he said something, that was it.'

Heath had what might fairly be called a conventionally distinguished war record. He was mentioned in despatches, awarded the M.B.E., and by the end of 1945 he was a lieutenant-colonel. While he cannot be said to have enjoyed the war, he liked the Army, so much so that he remained in it, as a Territorial, for a good many years afterwards, becoming Lieutenant-Colonel commanding the 2nd Regiment of the Honourable Artillery Company. And for three years he was Master Gunner within the Tower of London, a considerable honour.

Chapter Four

Civil Servant

Heath was approaching thirty when he was demobilised in 1946 and, like thousands of others, had to decide what to do. In his last year at Oxford, he had thought of becoming a professional musician—'I saw myself as a conductor'—and sought the advice of Sir Hugh Allen, Professor of Music in the University, who gave him both encouragement and warning. 'If you want to go in for music,' Sir Hugh had said, 'you could be a pianist, or you could be an organist, but really you ought to become a conductor. But there's no point in trying to become a conductor unless you're prepared to go right to the very top, otherwise you're going to have quite a lot of chores in life and you won't really enjoy it.' He had also considered the Bar and had a scholarship to Gray's Inn, where he ate his dinners in order to qualify. Law and music still attracted him, but the pull of politics was greater. His political ambitions had grown and clarified during the war; his mind, gaining a sharper focus and direction, turned more and more to public affairs and Parliament.

One night towards the end of 1944, returning to the Continent from leave, he ran into an older friend at Liverpool Street station—Arthur Jenkins, Labour M.P., father of Roy Jenkins, and Parliamentary Private

45

Secretary to Attlee, the deputy Prime Minister. They had often met when Mr Jenkins was visiting his son at Balliol, and also in the House of Commons, where Heath, as an undergraduate, had occasionally listened to debates from the public gallery. 'My father liked him,' Roy Jenkins recalls. That night, the P.P.S. was waiting for his master, who duly turned up. Arthur Jenkins introduced Heath, then added: 'He'd do very well as a candidate for us when the election comes.' Attlee was not overwhelmed. 'Oh yes,' he said.

Once out of uniform, Heath quickly made up his mind. He would try to get into Parliament, whatever the competition—and there was plenty of it among the Conservatives after the Labour landslide of 1945. The steps of Abbey House, then the Tory headquarters, were crowded with would-be candidates, many of them former M.P.s who had been unseated in the recent rout. Thinking logically about his future, Heath made another decision: he would earn his living meanwhile in some sphere likely to add to his equipment for a political career. Recognising that it would be no bad thing to learn more about the structure of government and the machinery of public administration, he applied for a post in the Civil Service. He took the administrative examination and passed out head of the list with another Balliol man, Ashley Raeburn (later, and still, with Shell). Not for the first time in his life, he was fortunate. Appointed to the Ministry of Civil Aviation, he was assigned to the Directorate of Long-Term Planning and Projects—a division headed by an unusually engaging and clever man. This was Peter Masefield, long distinguished in aviation, himself a temporary civil servant, and today the chairman of the British Airports Authority. As Masefield's records show,

46

Heath frankly explained that his object in joining was 'to gain experience of the workings of the Civil Service machine from the inside'. 'Whether an odd quirk of the official mind decided that this objective was "not quite cricket" in a budding politician, I know not,' says Masefield. 'But Ted was immediately despatched to what was clearly a somewhat unorthodox and untypical department—my newly formed Directorate. From there, however, he was able to range broadly throughout the Ministry's tasks.'

Under Masefield as director-general were an assistant secretary, J. G. Sims, a witty Irishman, an assistant principal, Heath, and an engineer-pilot from the Fleet Air Arm, Peter Brooks. They all four worked on the second floor of Aerial House in the Strand, once the Gaiety Hotel. In Edwardian times the rooms below them were the royal suite of the hotel, with a private passage to the leading lady's dressing room in the Gaiety Theatre, traversed by Edward VII when he was calling, as he liked to do, on Lily Langtry. Masefield and Heath once followed the passage through—to the bombed site of the theatre. Heath had a little staff of his own, one man and two girls, and he came up every morning from Swanley, in Kent, where he was living with the Bligh family. Timothy Bligh, who was at Balliol with him, was one of his greatest friends. (Sir Timothy, later Principal Private Secretary to the Prime Minister, died in 1969, aged fifty, and Edward Heath gave the address at the memorial service for him in St Margaret's, Westminster.)

Heath was also busy outside the office, furthering his parliamentary ambitions. He read the newspapers—all of them—more closely than ever before, following the fortunes of the Labour Government under Attlee and studying the Tory Opposition in Parliament, and the affairs of the party, with watchful attention. He set about strengthening his political connections and forming new ones. A good many of his Oxford friends and contemporaries, some already equipped (or born) with influential support, were doing the same, among them Ian Harvey, Julian Amery, Maurice Macmillan, Hugh Fraser, Christopher Mayhew, Roy Jenkins, Ashley Bramall, Denis Healey. Harold Wilson, another contemporary (though Heath had not known him at Oxford), was already a Minister, having been elected to Parliament in 1945. Heath met Miss Marjorie Maxse (later Dame Marjorie), a vice-chairman of the Conservative Party Organisation under Lord Woolton. He told her what he was hoping for and asked her to help him. She added his name to the list of prospective candidates maintained by the Conservative Central Office. Heath also renewed his acquaintance with Michael Fraser, who had briefly instructed him in gunnery and was now establishing himself in the Conservative Research Department; and he joined the Coningsby Club, a Tory dining club of considerable reputation with a membership of Oxbridge graduates. In the latter part of 1946, and more so in the following year as ambition drove him forward, he was increasingly associated with the intellectual end of the party which the Coningsby Club exemplified. Several entries in Fraser's diary for the early summer of 1947 provide a glimpse of Heath's life at this time:

Met David Bartlett at Carlton bar 6.30 p.m. and took him to hear Templewood [at Coningsby Club dinner]. Teddy Heath came back to the flat for drinks and music afterwards.

Took Hugo Fleury to dine and hear David Eccles at Coningsby. David Dear and Teddy Heath for music and drinks afterwards.

Coningsby Annual General Meeting followed by dinner. Teddy Heath came back to the flat afterwards for a long talk.

Day by day, at the Ministry, Heath was involved in the four principal objectives of the new directorate. The first was to press forward, in collaboration with the Ministry of Supply, the industry and the airlines, the development of new British civil aircraft—especially those evolved from the Brabazon Committee. They boiled down to four main types: those which became the Ambassador, the Viscount, the Comet and the Britannia, plus—for a time—the Princess flying boat. The second objective was to examine the long-term structure of the airline operating industry. The third was to encourage the development of British aviation in all its aspects—not just the commercial airlines. Among other things, these included light aviation, the flying clubs and the building of British light aircraft. The fourth objective was to look ahead to long-term requirements for airports and air safety, and to assess the place of British aviation in the future of world business.

One of Heath's duties was to represent Masefield on the London Airport Planning Committee—'a somewhat stodgy body', Masefield calls it, which 'was overwhelmed by the day-to-day problems of getting Heathrow going, and in our view did not look far enough ahead, though this was a general problem in those days of so much postwar initiation'. Heath and Masefield, in their own discussions on the future of the airport, were agreed about the importance of three things in particular. They both saw the need to break out of the proposed central area of Heathrow to the

49

east (i.e. the London side), to convert a restricted island site into a peninsula, even at some sacrifice of runways, so that there would be more room for expansion in years to come. They also recognised the need for aircraft piers on the front of the terminal buildings, providing covered 'walkways' almost up to the doors of a plane so that passengers would not have to be taken out by bus. And they understood the importance of adequate car parking space in the central (or the hoped-for 'peninsula') area. 'Later experience', as Masefield puts it today, 'has shown that all these long-term requirements were right. Ted Heath fought hard and long for them on the committee. He put in a lot of time and work. They met every week. He used to go and fight on the committee and come back and cry on my shoulder about all the spokes put in the wheel by bumbledom. The peninsula, perhaps the most important provision of all, is still to come. It should have been done: for lack of it we aren't as good as we should be today. The piers were put on the plan—and twenty years later they were achieved. The car parks remained inadequate until 1968.'

In a note made at the time, Masefield described Heath as 'a pleasant, sound, and highly intelligent ex-President of the Oxford Union and Colonel in the H.A.C. who clearly gets on well with people, regards our more dyed-in-the-wool civil servant colleagues with amused detachment, is first-class on paper and potentially an excellent administrator. I am indeed fortunate in him because he brings a fresh and detached mind to bear on our problems. With Sims and Brooks we are able to sit down and discuss all the aspects, looking ahead to the path we should follow. Ted Heath has a direct logic which is both stimulating and helpful. And, with all, when you get to know him (which isn't easy) he is a sensitive and warm-hearted chap who has a direct approach and an endearing sense of the ridiculous—which we so often encounter. But I fear that I shall not have him here for long because, outside the office, he lives and dreams politics and, with the Civil Service machine the way it is, as soon as he is adopted for a parliamentary seat he will have to resign. In the meantime he is invaluable—not least as a clear mind, with a lively wit, with whom to hammer out policy.'

Another of Heath's committees, but one on which he was happier, was ILAC, the Informal Light Aircraft Committee, with twenty-two members—pilots, designers, manufacturers and operators of light aircraft. Its role was to prepare recommendations for the Government to revitalise the country's light aviation, with exports much in mind. Heath had a large part in drafting the ILAC Report published early in 1948, which proposed a range of British light aircraft to be set in hand with government support.

With Peter Brooks, Heath was responsible for a significant modification to the Comet. 'They did one very important thing,' says Masefield. 'They did research on runway strengths around the world. The early Comets were quite well advanced even then, and they had a single-wheel undercarriage. Ted Heath and Peter Brooks, as a result of their researches, realised that most of the runways on the route to the Far East would not be strong enough to take them with the single carriage which they had at that stage. The bogey, the multiple-wheel carriage, is a direct result of their work. They fought quite a battle to get the change. Without it, the Comets would not have been able to use the Kangaroo Route and the Springbok Route, and BOAC would not have been able to buy them.'

Heath was sorry to leave the Ministry at the end of 1947, but he had no choice. There had been a turn for the better in his other world, in his political fortunes. He had been adopted as a prospective candidate for Parliament, and as such he could not remain in the public service. As Masefield remembers, 'he was really quite bothered about it. He was suddenly pitchforked out of a job which he thoroughly enjoyed and he was very sad about it. I sent him off to see Armstrong, in Establishments, but there was no way around it and he had to leave, and leave immediately.'

Chapter Five

Prospective Candidate

What had happened was that Heath's approach to Marjory Maxse, coupled with his other political activities, had paid off in good time. Earlier in the year he had been interviewed in three constituencies, two of which returned Conservatives at the subsequent general election and have done so ever since. In March he applied to the Conservative Association at Ashford in Kent, who were looking for a candidate. Endorsed by the Central Office, he ended up on a short-list of three: the other two were Brigadier L. D. Grande and William Deedes. To the selection committee, Deedes (Harrow, M.C. in the war, and a member of the local squirearchy long settled above the Romney Marsh) appeared the most suitable, perhaps the most promising. He was chosen, eventually became a Minister, and still sits for Ashford. A month later, on 2 April, Heath presented himself to the Tories of East Fulham—which wasn't then, and did not become, a Conservative seat. There he was short-listed with Vyvyan Adams, Colonel Peter Remnant and Major Fletcher-Wood. Heath came second. Vyvyan Adams, who had been a Member of Parliament before the war and was more in the line of the upper-class Tory candidate, was adopted. Then in August, Heath tried for Sevenoaks, a pleasant and rather prosperous place in Kent. Again he was beaten. The others on the short-list were Captain J. A. L. Duncan, Thelma Cazalet Keir, and John Rodgers. Captain Duncan and Mrs Cazalet Keir were former M.P.s, victims of the Tory rout in 1945. Rodgers, now Sir John, was chosen and he is the Member for Sevenoaks to this day. Mrs Cazalet Keir, as she has recorded in her memoirs, came third and Heath fourth. Captain Duncan, later Sir James, presently returned to Parliament as Member for South Angus; Mrs Cazalet Keir, a friend of Heath's, never did.

Heath was disappointed, but in the autumn his luck changed. The Conservative Association at Bexley, another but very different Kent constituency, were casting about for a new prospective candidate to succeed Louis May, a food manufacturer living in Letchworth. The division, consisting of the village of Old Bexley, Bexleyheath and Welling, was and is largely made up of so-called white-collar workers and artisans, the great majority occupying small semi-detached houses of their own and earning their living elsewhere—in London, or in the neighbouring boroughs of Crayford, Sidcup, Woolwich and Erith. The Tory chairman, a rugged, self-reliant sort of man, was Edward Dines, who worked for Standard Telephones and Cables. Brooding over the 'ideal' candidate, he had drawn up a specification, based not only on personal preference but on some hard-headed convictions about the constituency. Dines expressed his formula for the new candidate in five points:

1 He should be a local boy made good.
2 He should be well educated.
3 He should have made a study of political science as affecting the British way of life.

54

4 He should not be somebody rich or grand but somebody from an 'ordinary family' who could be expected
to understand from personal experience the lives and
problems of ordinary people.
5 He should be young.

With other members of the selection committee, Dines
approached more than one 'local boy made good', to
ask if they would go forward for consideration. The
first was a building tycoon named Meyer, but he was
too occupied with his business. Another was Jack
Pheasey, a well-placed colleague of Dines's in Standard
Telephones, but he declined because of the company's
valuable trade with the Post Office. The local school
attendance officer put himself forward. Dines and his
committee were also contemplating a list which they
had requested from the Conservative Central Office
when somebody mentioned Heath. His name wasn't on
the list, presumably because it had been given, more
or less concurrently, to the Sevenoaks Association, but
someone had heard about him. The agent was asked
to obtain Heath's biography. Dines liked what he saw,
and on 18 October 1947, Heath appeared before the selection committee, one of a short-list of three. The other
contenders were Patricia Marlow, then Mrs. Anthony
Marlow, wife of the Tory M.P. for Hove, and daughter of
Sir Patrick Hastings; and Eric Harrison of Orpington, a
member of the parliamentary staff of *The Times*. There
might have been another; Ian Harvey was also invited
for interview, but he was unwell and could not attend.
The selection committee consisted of Dines and
another man and five women. (Three of the seven—Mr
Dines, Mrs Lilian Evans and Mrs Edith Sharp—were
present at a party in February this year to celebrate

Heath's twentieth anniversary as Member.) Mrs Marlow was interviewed first, Heath second, then Harrison. Heath was their choice, and at a subsequent meeting of the executive he received an overwhelming majority of votes (it was at least three to one overall) —and that in effect made the decision unanimous. Dines was well pleased with the day's work. In his eyes, Heath was the (almost) local boy who had made good, and he more closely resembled the Dines specification than anyone could have expected. Heath appealed to him because 'he had come from humble origins, he had gone a long way on scholarships, he had a good war record and was still soldiering on—in fact he was in camp with the H.A.C. when we sent him a telegram asking him to come for interview. To me he personified the best sort of young British ex-serviceman. He was modest. He was very enthusiastic about it all. He'd got a grasp of the political situation. He'd travelled about a bit, too.' Mrs Marlow went on to become a Socialist, joining the Labour Party in 1956. Eric Harrison was later adopted for Uxbridge, but withdrew in 1949. (He became Assistant Secretary of the Press Council and a Baptist minister.) Harvey was later adopted (and returned) for Harrow East.

With such a preponderance of women on the selection committee, it may be thought today—when local associations seem much more interested in having married candidates—that Heath's lack of a wife (or even a fiancée) at the age of thirty-one would have told against him. Apparently it had no effect at all, except possibly to help rather than hinder him. Nothing much was ever said about it; though Dines himself was even inclined to think it a 'plus'—'If Heath had been married it could have distracted him from his constituency work.'

While Bexley had been finding out about him, Heath had been finding out about Bexley. He realised that he was on to quite a good thing—a winnable Labour seat. The political outlook was promising for the local Tories. Up to 1945, Bexley was part of the Dartford division. Then, in the general election at the end of the war, it became a separate constituency and returned the former Member for Dartford, Mrs Jennie Adamson, whose husband had also been a Socialist M.P., with a majority of 11,763. A year later, because she had accepted an office of profit under the Crown, as Vice-Chairman of the Assistance Board, there was a by-election. Her successor, Ashley Bramall, a contemporary of Heath's at Oxford, retained the seat for Labour—but with a much reduced majority of 1,851 against the Conservative candidate, Lieut.-Col. J. C. Lockwood. Churchill, against all usual practice for the leader of the party, had put in an appearance during the campaign, driving around in an open car (which he had specified). The result was exceedingly cheering to Churchill and the party chairman, Lord Woolton, and was thought to have considerable national significance. At all events, it abundantly confirmed Dines's view that in Bexley the Socialists could be unseated.

This was the recent electoral history of Bexley when Heath was selected, and he felt rather happy about the prospect ahead. His parents were elated, and they both attended his adoption meeting a few weeks later, accompanied by Timothy Bligh. The president of the association, Martin Holt, was in the chair. Holt, a City banker who lived in Kensington and had a country house in Sussex, had not been much involved in the search for a candidate.

The meeting, said the *Kentish Independent* on 14 November, was the 'biggest and most enthusiastic Tory assembly Bexley has ever known', and opened with 'the lusty singing' of 'Land of Hope and Glory'. Heath spoke at some length before being formally adopted. In the main part it was, one imagines, the sort of speech that a hundred, a thousand, Tories were making just then. Heath sailed into the Government. There were signs, he said, that the electorate were tiring of the Socialists, with their 'specious promises' and 'lack of leadership and foresight'. The public, he detected, were tired of crises, of the 'dogma of nationalisation', of a Government that had 'started so many things which could not be carried out', of 'controls which multiplied like rabbits'; and industry was 'tired of its strait-jacket'. Thus far, his speech could hardly be called original, either in content or in language. Warming to the familiar attack, he went on to predict 'fewer houses, less rations, less petrol'.

But then, in a passage that seems to me to have reflected the realism which shows itself time and again in his career, he warned his all-Tory audience that 'there is still a suspicion of our party in the minds of the people, and one of our objects is to get rid of that suspicion. Not only must Conservatives know the party's record and policy, we must prove its genuineness.' Later on he returned to this point, calling on them to build up the party's political education, as well as its finances.

Heath realised (what the subsequent general election was to prove) that the Tories had not altogether lived down their recent past. As his 'first basic point in Conservative policy' he enunciated—again in a boring old phrase—'the belief in a property-owning democracy with respect for every human being'. The party believed, he said, in a minimum standard of life for everyone, and did 'not propose to tread down any particular class'. Then 'incentives': these would lead to increased production. Then industrial relations: the Tories wanted 'a genuine relationship between employer, employee and the Government'. Then—and at the time inevitable in almost any Conservative assembly—'the development of the Empire and Empire relations'.

However ordinary, it seems from all accounts to have satisfied the Bexley Tories. And Heath ended on a more individual note. A good many Socialists, including Ashley Bramall, the local Member, had been moaning about 'sabotage' of the Labour Government by civil servants. Heath defended his colleagues in Whitehall. 'There has been a lot of irresponsible criticism,' he said. 'The civil servant is a man of great integrity, and it is nonsense to talk of his sabotaging the Government. The civil servant, quite naturally, has his political opinions, but the great majority ignore their opinions in the course of their duty.' To which he added that in accordance with custom he would himself resign from the Civil Service upon his adoption that night as a parliamentary candidate.

That is just what he did. Saying good-bye to Peter Masefield and his other friends at the Ministry of Civil Aviation, he moved off from the Strand, and some six weeks later, at the beginning of January 1948, he settled into No. 7 Portugal Street, Kingsway, the offices of the *Church Times*. He was sent there on the recommendation of the Oxford University Appointments Board, to which he had applied on learning that he must leave the Ministry. Published weekly by the Palmer family (to whom it still belongs) the *Church*

Times was and is a distinguished newspaper, though editorially it was not then as broad in outlook and appeal as it is today. Under the editorship of Humphry Beevor it had become very much the organ of the Anglo-Catholic movement, in which Beevor, a scholarly and somewhat intimidating man of lofty mind, was a considerable figure. He felt in need of a news editor, though he had never had one; and, confronted by Heath, at once accepted him. It was a bizarre appointment, for which Heath had no qualifications either as a journalist or a theologian, and nobody understood quite why he was engaged. It wasn't as if Beevor had taken an instant liking to the improbable applicant: on the contrary, he never really cared for Heath. Heath nevertheless became the first news editor of the *Church Times*, at a salary of about £650 a year, some £200 more (he recalls) than he received as an assistant principal in the Civil Service.

He spent a year and nine months in journalism. John Trevisick, the present news editor, was there then. 'Heath didn't really get on with Humphry Beevor,' he says. 'Beevor was leftish, and there was a gulf between them. They didn't understand each other. Beevor took endless delight in trying to catch Heath out, and Heath would stall on abstruse questions—damned good training for him, of course. Being detailed for diary engagements by Beevor noticeably irked Heath, especially when he had other, and to him more pressing, things to do—he was nursing his constituency at the time.' Who should cover what, was usually decided by Heath. He had a staff of two reporters: Trevisick and Nicholas Bagnall, now the education correspondent of the *Sunday Telegraph*. Besides handling their copy, that is to say marking and otherwise preparing it for the printer, he looked after all the reports coming in from local correspondents up and down the country. In those days, book reviews were 'subbed' (edited) in the newsroom, and the three of them did this as well. Heath also did a certain amount of make-up on the printer's stone, arranging the columns of type in the order in which they were to appear. But he wrote very little, and nothing except reports. He never took the opportunity to write an article on some topic of the day, lay or religious, or to try his hand at a leader, or even to do a book review himself. His work, though it need not have been so, was a mixture of administration and sub-editing. He did not attempt the more interesting things that would have attracted most young journalists wanting a say in public affairs. The reason, no doubt, is that however 'political' he was, he had no natural instinct or flair for journalism. 'He was', one of his friends has told me, 'bored stiff at the *Church Times*.' Perhaps this is why his entry in *Who's Who* (contributed by himself) makes no mention of his brief excursion into church journalism.

'Heath shook with laughter like a jelly', Trevisick remembers, 'when he heard of a colleague's misfortunes—like being bitten by a dog when on a fruitless Beevor assignment, or losing oneself in a fog when on the way to a fourth-rate religious play at Walthamstow. The laugh was on him, however, when he altered the report of an annual festival of U.M.C.A. This was his biggest bloomer: he changed the initials U.M.C.A., meaning Universities' Mission to Central Africa, to Y.M.C.A. throughout the copy. You would have thought that he might have heard of the U.M.C.A., or if he wasn't sure he might have asked somebody, but he didn't. Humphry Beevor, with his fixations on religious drama and films, was a stickler in matters trivial. He would appear in the newsroom, flap his arms like a sea-gull, and issue inarticulate directives as to who should report such-and-such an engagement. On this he was quite immovable. That was when the future leader of the Opposition (he often fulfilled the role unsuccessfully in the office on these occasions) was thrown in at the deep end. I have vivid memories of Heath's being roped in to cover the Anglo-Catholic Congress of 1948—a really tough job—with his two colleagues. But he turned in a workmanlike précis of what he had heard, reflecting his ability to master the most abstruse and highly theological arguments. Later he took a hand in reporting Bishop Wand's great Mission to London.'

Heath was never close to his colleagues on the *Church Times*, leading a rather detached and self-contained life. Unlike most people in the newspaper world, he never went 'round the corner' for a drink with any of them, or joined them at lunch. But he did once take the proprietor's son, Bernard Palmer, who is now the editor, to lunch at Armoury House, headquarters of his beloved H.A.C.

Looking back on it today, twenty years later, Heath maintains that he liked his spell with the *Church Times*. No doubt he finds it more agreeable in retrospect than he seemed to do at the time. At all events, the office was a convenient and comfortable base from which to pursue his political interests. In a sense, it was ideal, all the more so because Heath had no feeling of commit-ment or vocation: consequently he never allowed his work to become all-absorbing, as is usually the way with journalists. It can't have been a particularly good bargain for the *Church Times*, but it suited Heath. Though the office had its irritations, embodied in

Humphry Beevor, there was nothing much to distract him from his real ambitions. Today his picture hangs in the editor's room, in a galaxy of *Church Times* notabilities of the past, some of them considerable theologians.

Heath's term in Portugal Street lasted till October 1949. A little while before he left, no doubt feeling that he had had enough of church journalism and that he should now acquire some experience more directly helpful to a political career, he decided to look for work in the City, preferably in a merchant bank. He knew James Coates, who was the managing director of the North Central Finance Company in Rotherham. Coates's deputy-chairman was Sir Giles Guthrie, one of the City establishment and a managing director of Brown, Shipley and Co., the merchant bankers. At Heath's request, Coates mentioned him to Guthrie. Heath wanted to go into politics, said Coates, but realised that 'he must learn more about finance and how money works'. Would Guthrie see him with a view to taking Heath on as a trainee with Brown, Shipley for a year or two? Guthrie asked Heath to call on him at Founder's Court, in the City, where Brown, Shipley have their offices. 'I liked him,' Sir Giles tells me. 'A former public servant, good war record, pleasant manner, a good brain, musical, keen to get on by his own efforts—but I said I would have to consult my fellow directors because we seldom had more than six trainees at a time, half of them from correspondent banks overseas and the other half, young men with a future in Brown, Shipley and Co., or one of the bank's customers. Ted was a bit old to become a trainee and, of course, he did not plan to make Brown, Shipley and

Co. his career. Nevertheless, on my recommendation, my fellow directors agreed to find a place for him.'

Heath had named three referees: Daniel Orme of Vernon Myles and Clark, solicitors; Martin Holt, the banker who was president of the Bexley Conservative Association; and A. D. McKechnie, of Galloway and Pearson. On 21 October 1949, the bank wrote to him:

> With reference to your call here on the 17th instant, we have communicated with the referees whose names you were so good as to suggest to us and we confirm that we are entirely willing to admit you to a course of training in this office to commence on Monday, the 31st instant. As we explained to you, our usual course for instruction of Volunteers for this purpose extends to two years, but we understand that your present view is that you would like to have a training of one year in our offices. We will be guided accordingly when moving you round the various departments of our business. It is our custom, in cases such as this, to pay a nominal salary of £200 per annum and, in addition, to provide lunch daily from Monday to Friday inclusive in our Staff Canteen, or whilst the Trainee is working at our West End Office, we have arrangements there to provide lunch tickets available at a nearby restaurant. We therefore await your attendance on Monday, the 31st instant, and would suggest that on that first morning you report at 9.45 a.m.

He joined Brown, Shipley on the appointed day. Ion Garnett-Orme, a 'hereditary' City banker (his grandmother was a Brown) and a kindly, modest man of much charm, now the chairman, was one of the directors who took an interest in the new if oldish trainee—Heath was thirty-three. 'All the partners knew him. He was obviously highly intelligent and very interesting, so we did see quite a lot of him.' Like the other trainees, all younger than himself, Heath was

64

put through various departments one by one. First he went into Credit Information. 'This takes them out and about in the City, to other banks and offices,' Garnett-Orme explains. 'It is an introduction to the City, geographically as well as in other ways—you learn how to get about quickly and how to dodge the rain by going through a building from one side to the other.' Next, Cashiers. There, as Garnett-Orme puts it, 'you learn what a cheque is, what you can do with it and what you cannot do with it. You learn about standing orders and how to handle accounts.' Then on to the Credit Department, to Securities and Investments, and finally to Foreign Exchange. Staff reports were presented to the board at the end of the year. The departmental report on Heath, after his first two months, read: 'Only came to us recently and is on Timber Desk. A very nice man who seeks knowledge and who should learn quickly.' The manager added: 'Likely to profit by his course.'

'He had this remarkably quick brain at picking things up,' Ion Garnett-Orme recalls. 'He never really specialised in any one department—he wasn't here long enough—but he acquired a good understanding of all our work. He left a most awfully good impression here. Large numbers of people here went to help him in his election campaign. People don't do that unless they like a man.'

Chapter Six

Political Progress

By the end of 1949, the parties were all in a state of readiness for a general election. Some constituencies were of course better prepared than others. At Bexley, Heath's own association were short of money: they had none at all. This was before the Maxwell Fyfe reforms had been introduced in the Conservative Party, and Members of Parliament and adopted candidates were still expected to contribute at least £100 a year to their constituency associations. Heath's first chairman, Edward Dines, tells me that he did not himself approve of the practice. 'I remember Heath coming to me one Saturday morning about the time when his subscription was due and asking if we'd mind waiting a bit. I told him to forget all about it and that it would be soon enough to think about a contribution when I asked him for one. Of course we never did.' The president, Martin Holt, came to the treasurer's rescue with £250, by way, he said, of expressing his confidence in their candidate. With this encouragement, Heath undertook to raise a further £250. He persuaded five people to give £50 apiece, whereupon Holt, impressed by his enterprise, produced another £250. With £750 in the bank they had enough for the campaign when it came in February 1950.

Besides the Brown, Shipley contingent, a good many of Heath's friends and well-wishers in the Honourable Artillery Company also turned out. With his zeal for organisation, the campaign was planned down to the last detail, every hour committed to what seemed potentially profitable. Heath's first election address, dated 2 February 1950, the day of his adoption, ran to just under 1,000 words. The Tories, he promised, would tackle certain unwelcome legacies of the war—controls on industry, food rationing—and they would increase war pensions. They would provide incentives for hard work, reduce taxes, cut Government spending, eliminate waste, maintain and improve the Health Service, assist home ownership, develop Empire trade, put a stop to further nationalisation, stand by the U.N.

As a statement of policy, his address contained nothing new, much less anything eccentric. But if it was pretty ordinary, it was also safe—like hundreds of others.

For example: 'I want to see reductions in both direct and indirect taxation because they will be an incentive to us all and encourage National Savings. We will revise Income Tax so that men who produce more through piece-rates or overtime will not be penalised so much. We hope to make things easier for everyone by starting to reduce Purchase Tax—you'd be surprised how much of your money goes in this tax! To do this, Government spending must be pruned. If we can save a tenth of our vast expenditure our whole position will be improved. It can be done. Where there's a will there's a way. Waste—we can all think of a good many examples—must be ruthlessly cut out, defence expenditure reviewed, and the cost of food subsidies reduced by wise buying of food.'

The Health Service, he acknowledged, was 'a splendid scheme'—but 'badly organised'. On housing, a favourite Tory theme, he had this to say: 'I want to see every family with a good separate home as soon as possible. Happy and healthy homes are the basis of family life. That is why we hold that everyone who wishes to own his home must be helped to do so. We think that only 5 per cent deposit in cash should be required to buy a new house from a local authority. Private property should be more and more widely distributed among our citizens; that is the real alternative to complete ownership by the state. The private builder will be given the opportunity to build more houses for those of modest means. The local authorities' responsibilities will be to provide new houses to rent and to attack the overcrowding and slum-clearance problems. Rent control must continue until there is no housing shortage at any level.'

The passage on schools is hardly more arresting. 'I find a lot of parents who are greatly concerned about their children's education,' he said. 'We shall make a determined effort to reduce the size of classes in primary schools and to provide more technical schools and colleges. Reduced building costs and simpler standards for school building will help the voluntary schools and the religious bodies to carry out their development plans.'

It is interesting, after the passage of twenty years, to look back on what (and what little) he had to say about foreign policy. It amounted to one paragraph of precisely fifty words: 'We stand by the United Nations in all its work for peace. We believe in closer association with western Europe and America, which Mr Churchill has done so much to foster. So long as peace is threatened we must maintain National Service but we believe this burden can be reduced.'

An election leaflet claimed that 'For two years he has been almost daily in Bexley, Bexleyheath or Welling'. The Conservatives are convinced, it concluded, 'that they have in Edward Heath a man who will go far in public life and be of great service to this country'. Polling was on 23 February. Heath only just won, and then after an unnerving recount, when—as some of those present remember—he was almost beside himself with anxiety, taut, tense, hardly able to speak. He was finally declared the winner with a majority of 133. There were four candidates, and happily for Heath one of them was a Communist, Charles Job, who polled 481 votes. Heath, with 25,854 votes, was undoubtedly the beneficiary of Job's intervention, which robbed Ashley Bramall, with 25,721, of just enough Labour support to unseat him. The Liberal, Miss M. E. Hart, polled 4,186.

Though the Conservatives had gained Bexley and many other seats they had not won the election. When the new Parliament assembled, Labour was still in office, but Attlee now had to govern with a majority of six. It was a melancholy day for Labour, and there were many sad hearts as the party entered its last months of office.

Heath could no longer put in anything like full time with Brown, Shipley. More often than not he went to the bank for a few hours in the morning and spent the rest of the day at the House. 'The narrow margin between the political parties in the House keeps him away a great deal,' wrote the manager in his second report on Heath, 'but he attends here whenever possible, and, I feel, is deriving much benefit from his course.' 'Very alert and keen to absorb knowledge,' said the departmental report. 'A very good man with business faculties highly developed.'

Heath was already turning those particular faculties to account in Bexley. Recognising that the new Parliament was bound to be short-lived he decided that no time should be lost in finding a suitable headquarters from which to fight the next election. He had conducted his first campaign from one room in a private house and had no intention of doing so again. With his agent, R. A. Pye, he started looking for ampler accommodation. They turned down one house because of dry rot —which has since been vexing the Bexley Labour Party, to whom it was subsequently sold. They were offered another for £1,600, but Heath advised the association to go one better and buy a more substantial property at £4,000 in the oddly-named road Crook Log. They paid a deposit of £400, which Heath raised by extracting gifts of £150 and £250 from two friends.

That summer he was best man at the wedding of his old comrade-in-arms George Chadd. Some of their friends thought that Heath too would be marrying before long. They were expecting him to become engaged to his girl friend, a young teacher. But the affair petered out.

He made his maiden speech as an M.P. in the last week of June, just four months after the election. Lord Avon has been looking back on it, and has given me his recollections of Heath's arrival in the House and manner of approach to Parliament: 'Twenty years ago the newly elected Member who studied the precedents had a wide choice of methods by which to capture the ear

70

of the House. If he were bold and confident enough he could try to emulate F. E. Smith or Duff Cooper and take the House by storm. Alternatively he could specialise in some topic, either economic or international, and hope one day to be regarded as an authority upon it; or he might study the rules and practices of the House itself and expect in time to be considered as a reliable interpreter of those mysteries. Ted Heath, as might be expected, took the quiet but persistent way. He attended the House regularly and modestly, but missed nothing. Pains and patience are needed to learn the way at Westminster. Heath had both—and a subject also, Europe. Predictably his maiden speech was made in a two-day debate on the Schuman Plan and it was a definite success.'

Heath was already a 'European', and in this speech —one of lasting importance in view of his subsequent history—he registered the convictions which have distinguished him ever since. Early in the previous month, Robert Schuman had announced the French Government's proposals to pool the resources of the French and German coal and steel industries by placing them under a common authority in an organisation open to the other countries of Europe. These proposals had political as well as economic motives and they were, of course, a prelude to the development of the European Economic Community, and the Common Market. Britain was invited to join France, West Germany, Belgium, Italy, Luxembourg and the Netherlands in the new association. But the Labour Government declined, and in the two-day debate the Prime Minister, Mr Attlee, expressed their hostility in blunt and succinct manner: 'We on this side are not prepared to accept the principle that the most vital economic forces of this country should be handed over to an authority that is utterly undemocratic and is responsible to nobody'.

The Member for Bexley differed. Turning on the Chancellor, Sir Stafford Cripps, who had also suggested that 'we should have no say in arranging the power of the high authority', Heath said:

Surely that would not be the case. He said we should be taking a risk with the whole of our economy. We on this side of the House feel that by standing aside from the discussion we may be taking a very great risk with our economy in the coming years—a very great risk indeed. He said it would also be a great risk if we went in and then withdrew. We regard it as a greater risk to stand aside altogether at this stage. The Chancellor spoke about the position of the Empire. We all realise the importance of the Empire, and we on this side certainly think it must be supported above all. But the right hon. and learned gentlemen did not tell us what the views of the Empire are. What are the views of the Empire in this matter? Have the Government had discussions with the other Governments of the Empire about this matter? Can we be told what are their views—what are the views of our Empire statesmen? As far as we can ascertain, they have not protested against this scheme.

The Chancellor spoke all the time as though this were to be a restrictionist plan. Surely the object of the plan is to be one of expansion? Surely the task to be put upon the high authority is to be the task of expansion rather than of restriction. . . .

The position which the Government takes up is that no other country wants full employment and that no other country is capable of pursuing full employment unless it has a Socialist Government. That is obviously far from the truth.

Heath had spent part of the Whitsun recess in West Germany, where he discussed the Schuman proposals.

He went on:

Now I should like to say a word about the reasons which I found the German Government had for taking part in these talks, and what is the attitude of the German Government. I found that their attitude was governed entirely by political considerations. I believe there is a genuine desire on their part to reach agreement with France and with the other countries of Western Europe.

I believe that in that desire the German Government are genuine and I believe, too, that the German Government would be prepared to make economic sacrifices in order to achieve those political results which they desire. I am convinced that when negotiations take place between the countries about the economic details, the German Government will be prepared to make sacrifices.

The German Government sees, too, a solution of the Saar problem. Above all it sees a means of abolishing the restriction of 11·1 million tons on its steel output. That is an important point indeed for the German Government, which is capable at the moment of seeing the steel production in Germany go up to 15,500,000 or 16,000,000 tons. It sees also a means of securing a vast expansion of German coal production.

If those are advantages, there are sown in those advantages the seeds of conflict with France over this economic basis. Under Marshall Aid, France has been able to expand her steel production very considerably. She would like to see German coke go to Lorraine and German steel production to remain pegged; while the Germans see in the plan an opportunity for expanding their steel production. There possibly, is a possible seed of conflict. . . . Finally there is the grave problem of future trade with Eastern Europe which many in the Ruhr want to start to develop. There are seeds of conflict in these negotiations between France and Germany, and I submit that that is a very strong reason why we should take part in these discussions—in order

73

that we may balance out the difficulties between France and Germany which are bound to arise on the economic side.

Under the German plan, Germany may very well become once again a major factor in Europe. Anyone going to Germany today is bound to be impressed by the fact that the German dynamics have returned; that Germany is once again working hard and producing hard and that therefore Germany will become a major factor in Europe.

I suggest that there are only two ways of dealing with that situation: one is to attempt to prolong control, which the Chancellor has already dismissed as being undesirable and impracticable. The only other way is to lead Germany into the one way we want her to go, and I believe that these discussions could give us a chance to do so.

I would also submit that if we can say that we have united Europe in the matter of steel and coal, we can say to the Americans, there is an outlet for the President's Fourth Point in the capital development of a great area of the world. That might very well be most important from the United States point of view.

After the First World War, we all thought it would be extremely easy to secure peace and prosperity in Europe; after the Second World War we all realised that it was going to be extremely difficult to make a plan of this kind succeed. What I think worries many of us on this side of the House is that even if the arguments put forward by the Government are correct, we do not feel that behind those arguments is really the will to succeed and to achieve what we each most want to see. It was said a long time ago in this House that magnanimity in politics is not seldom the truest wisdom. I appeal tonight to the Government to follow that dictum and to go into the Schuman Plan to develop Europe and to co-ordinate it in the way suggested.

This speech, Harold Macmillan has said in the third volume of his memoirs, 'much impressed the House'.

Heath was no less interested in domestic and social policy. He became associated with the party's 'new thinkers' in the House, the corps of youngish, progressive radicals who, like himself, had just entered Parliament. Three of them, Iain Macleod, Reginald Maudling and Enoch Powell, had served an invaluable apprenticeship under R. A. Butler in the Conservative Research Department. With Cuthbert Alport, Angus Maude and John Rodgers, Heath became a founder-member of the One Nation Group, a designation underlining their romantic attachment to Disraeli's conception of a united people. Presently they were joined by Powell and Macleod. Other members were Gilbert Longden, Robert Carr and Richard Fort. In October 1950 they published *One Nation—A Tory Approach to Social Problems*, a substantial pamphlet of nearly a hundred pages, which is to my mind among the most sensitive and humane papers ever issued by the Conservative Political Centre. Macleod and Maude were the editors, and in every page the effect is heightened by their lucidity and distinction as writers. Their theme was Disraeli's own, the 'improvement in the well-being of the people', which—as they wrote—'runs like a thread through his political life'. Housing was the first of their social priorities, education the second. Health, the care of the old, the reform of industrial relations and of local government, and the preservation of the countryside were others.

Heath's appetite for his parliamentary duties, his apparently inexhaustible interest in the proceedings of the House, and his alert yet reserved manner, were already winning, if not golden, then appreciative, opinions on high. He caught the eye of the Opposition Chief Whip, Patrick Buchan-Hepburn, a large and charming man of patrician appearance whom he might easily—though mistakenly—have associated with the old guard, not in age but in outlook. In fact, Buchan-Hepburn (now Lord Hailes) was a person of considerable independence of mind, and more radical than his background and way of life might have suggested. He had worked for Churchill in the late 'twenties, but Buchan-Hepburn could not support Churchill's line on India, and in the 'thirties their relations were not so close. Nevertheless he became Churchill's Chief Whip in 1948. As such he was a figure of the first importance to the party in Parliament. In 1950 Buchan-Hepburn was 'sorting out the Whips' office, and looking for recruits among the new members.' He 'kept hearing good reports' about Heath, he recalls, and in February 1951, when Heath had been in the House just under a year, Buchan-Hepburn invited him to become an Assistant Whip. He did so with the concurrence and approval of all the other Whips. For it is an axiom of the Tory Whips' Office that nobody joins unless all the others want him. In this it is like a club operating a blackball system for its own protection. There are good practical reasons for such a precaution. For one thing, the Whips must all have complete confidence in each other. For another there should never be any suspicion of a 'Trojan horse' in the Whips' office, planted there by the leader of the party as a private spy.

Heath made a condition, however: he wished to be free to leave the Whips' office after eighteen months if he did not like the work. Buchan-Hepburn fell in with this. While explaining that 'there is no way to learn Parliament better than a spell in the Whips' office', he understood that Heath 'wanted to speak in the House, and of course he was curtailed as a Whip'. Looking back today, Lord Hailes remembers Heath as 'quiet, reserved, very knowledgeable, cool, calm and collected. He was a very good organiser and strategist. To start with, he didn't say much: he listened a lot and missed nothing. He was good at getting people out of bed to vote. He knew his priorities. His whole mind was on politics. He was very ambitious. He was rather inhuman at the beginning. He tended to underestimate the importance of people themselves: he was perhaps more concerned with people's brains rather than their personal qualities. The Whips' office is a good place to learn about people and human contact.'

During the summer recess that year, Heath travelled in North America for Brown, Shipley. He really proposed himself for the visit—the partners hadn't asked him to go, but 'we were very happy to let him', as Ion Garnett-Orme recalls. 'He knew and met a lot of interesting people in America. He went to Brown Brothers Harriman (with whom Brown, Shipley were originally associated) and met the partners. He called in New York on the Bank of Manhattan. As he said later, "I took the opportunity of meeting as many people as possible". He spent one weekend with Tom Watson, President of IBM, who had been a great friend of President Roosevelt, and was the father-in-law of Jack Irwin, an Oxford contemporary of Heath's. He also went up to Canada. When he came back he wrote us a fifteen-page report on the political situation and the financial situation in the United States and Canada. One of the partners made a note on the report at the time—"This is intensely interesting. I hope that our general manager will read and record his comments".'

Heath returned to London in September. The Labour Government was in a condition of collapse. Attlee (who earlier in the year had been in hospital with a duodenal ulcer) had asked for a dissolution and announced 25 October as the date of the general election. 'I was in Ottawa when it was announced,' Heath recalls. 'I remember getting into a lift in the hotel, the Chateau Laurier, and finding myself followed by Herbert Morrison and Edward Shackleton, then his P.P.S. They had just had a message from Attlee that he had called the election. I flew to New York and travelled home on the Queen Mary. I remember Shinwell, who was also on board, leaning over the rail and telling me that they would lose the election by a small majority.'

At Bexley, Heath was again opposed by the former Labour Member, Ashley Bramall. This time there was no Job's comfort for him—no Communist; and no Liberal either. It was a straight fight. Operating much more comfortably than before, from the newly-acquired headquarters, Heath organised a twelve-hour working day, 10 a.m. to 10 p.m., throughout the campaign. He was optimistic. 'I thought that having won it we could consolidate,' he says. 'It was very much an owner-occupier area and I was fairly confident.' He was troubled, however, by private sorrow. His mother was critically ill in hospital. She had cancer, and the family knew that she was dying. Every night, after a long day's electioneering, Heath drove to Broadstairs to see her. He was always back before ten next morning. A fortnight before polling his mother died. It was the most shattering blow of his life. They had always been very, very close. He was passionately devoted to her, and she to him. Sometimes, in the days after her death, he seemed almost senseless with despair, but in public he kept up a resolute appearance. Only one or two intimate friends who were with him in the campaign knew what the effort cost him.

Distraught though he was, he managed not only to carry on, but to increase his majority to 1,639. The Conservatives had won the election by a hairbreadth. As Lord Avon recalls, 'The narrow victory, a majority of eighteen seats in the Chamber and a minority of half a million votes outside of it, presented the party with a formidable organisational problem. The first condition of any achievement was survival, which depended on the faithful attendance of Members of Parliament to defend the Government's slender margin. In such conditions the Whips' office loomed more importantly than ever.' In forming his administration, Churchill had appointed Buchan-Hepburn Government Chief Whip ('Winston and I didn't think the Government would last more than six months', the latter recalls) and Heath remained with him. He now became a member of the Government, albeit a junior one, a Lord Commissioner of the Treasury. He was never again to sit on the back-benches. This was the start of a long Ministerial career—and Lord Avon, for one, has no doubt that 'his political progress owed much to the discerning championship of Patrick Buchan-Hepburn'. Lord Avon also bears witness to Heath's value as a Whip. 'The next three and a half years were testing and difficult,' he says, 'but through them all Ted Heath's reputation in the Whips' office and outside of it rose steadily.'

The association with Brown, Shipley had to end, and in November the chairman of the bank wrote to Heath:

My dear Heath,

I am reminded that I have not had a chance to speak to you about the actual details of your working arrangements with us. As you well know, you have technically been 'learning banking' for a period of two years. Those two years are now up and as I told you before you left for America, we were happy to send you on this trip and in some ways I am sorry it was a little curtailed. Now you have a full-time job in Parliament and this will keep you busy, I hope, for some years.

I suggest therefore that we say that your term of service with us finishes on 31st December next and your small salary will cease also then. We sincerely hope that this termination of financial connection will not stop our seeing you and saying to you that the doors of Founders Court are always open to you. The lunch club meets on Monday and I sincerely hope that you will make use of it. Should circumstances change, not only on our side but on yours also then I hope that we can meet and talk further under the then conditions and make new arrangements.

'With kind regards,

Yours sincerely,

Anthony Clifton-Brown

Chapter Seven

On to Suez—as Chief Whip

Early on in the new Parliament, at the beginning of 1952, Heath and all the other Whips found themselves troubled and embarrassed by Churchill himself, who was now seventy-six. One after another, they were having to report to the Chief Whip a disquieting amount of criticism from the back-benches. Conservative Members were restive for various reasons, real and imagined, because it seemed that general conditions, now that the Socialist Government had gone, were not improving as quickly as they should. There was, the Whips said, a persistent murmuring against the Prime Minister: he was presiding over affairs in too authoritarian a manner for peacetime, he was high-handed, and he ought to retire. At successive Whips' meetings, Heath and the others were unanimous that something must be done. Inevitably, it fell to Buchan-Hepburn to act, however disagreeable the duty. He went to see Churchill in the Prime Minister's room at the House. For the present, he contents himself with the observation that 'thereafter Churchill became more amenable to suggestions and people settled down. The tension was relieved.'

It had all been very disturbing to Heath, who had a deep regard for Churchill, was presently to form a congenial association with him, and was from time to time invited to Chartwell. The Prime Minister, I think, 'took him up' because he had heard about the young Whip's anti-Fascist record before the war (Heath no doubt reminded him of their encounter at Oxford with Professor Lindemann), because Heath was to him a sort of idealised Tory patriot with brains who had worn the King's uniform, and not least because Heath was a dutiful listener.

Within a few months (in May 1952) Heath was promoted to deputy Government Chief Whip, sharing the office with a National Liberal, Sir Herbert Butcher. Fourteen months later, when Butcher dropped out, Heath had the office to himself. This was a curious and unsteady period: 'testing and difficult' Lord Avon calls it. The Tories were governing with a tiny majority, and always there was speculation about Churchill's personal intentions: when would he retire and make way for Eden? Heath listened to all the gossip; he heard plenty of comment; and—characteristically—he reserved what he knew for the Chief Whip.

Churchill retired in April 1955, and Eden at last came into his inheritance. He went to the country in May, and the Tories nicely enlarged their majority to fifty-nine. At Bexley, where on this occasion his Labour opponent was the journalist and film producer R. J. Minney, Heath again increased his majority—to 4,499. As Lord Avon recalls, the election had 'reduced the tense responsibilities of the Whips' office a little. Nevertheless when in the autumn of that year a number of inescapable ministerial changes gave me the occasion to bring Buchan-Hepburn into the Cabinet, I was glad that his successor was so easy to recognise. Ted Heath took over as Chief Whip by what seemed a natural process. During the whole period of our work together as Prime Minister and Chief Whip, I came increasingly to recognise his especial qualities of patience, adroitness and dependability. His instinctive reserve could sometimes conceal these, but the rougher the weather the steadier was his advice. In such conditions, confidence and friendship had an easy passage.'

A new recruit to the Whips' office was Michael Hughes-Young, the Member for Wandsworth Central and previously a regular officer in the Black Watch. He later became the deputy Government Chief Whip and is now Lord St Helens. He was struck by Heath's taste for meetings, by his love of consultation. 'We used to have these interminable Whips' meetings,' he recalls. 'They seem, in retrospect, to have taken place every blooming night, but I suppose there were really two or three a week. Ted would chew a subject over and over and over again, not saying much himself. I would guess he loathed having to make his mind up on his own. He took the most extraordinary amount of trouble over things and people—over anybody or anything. I've seen him be very tough with Ministers, just telling them flatly that they couldn't do it, it wasn't on.'

The short-lived Eden Government was soon in difficulties. Little more than four months after the opening of the new Parliament the Chancellor, R. A. Butler, found himself introducing an autumn Budget (with increases in Purchase Tax) in an attempt to improve the balance of payments. In successive Budgets, Butler had appreciably reduced the burden of Income Tax, but by Eden's first winter as Prime Minister, rising inflation was undermining public confidence in the administration. During that winter and in the spring of 1956, Eden was increasingly under fire.

Worse was to come, however, with Nasser's declaration on the night of 26 July that Egypt was seizing the Suez Canal. Heath was not a member of the Cabinet, though as Chief Whip he usually attended Cabinet meetings. Eden's war policy was neither initiated nor hammered out in Cabinet, however: it was determined by the Prime Minister in conclave with a small group of senior colleagues including Selwyn Lloyd, the Foreign Secretary, Harold Macmillan, who had succeeded Butler as Chancellor, Antony Head, the Defence Minister, Lord Home, the Commonwealth Secretary, and Lord Salisbury, Lord President of the Council. In the decisive early weeks of the Suez crisis, when Eden committed himself to the course which—right or wrong—was to wreck his health and his career, Butler was missing from these deliberations because he had been ill and he was resting. If Heath knew the Prime Minister's mind it was because Eden told him, not because he was party to the grave and critical decisions as they were made. Earlier, while Churchill was still Prime Minister, he had supported the Egyptian Treaty negotiations, which led to Britain's withdrawal from the Suez Canal Zone. He was certainly far removed from the 'Suez rebels' of those days. In the new crisis culminating in Britain's military intervention in Egypt, as an ally of Israel and France, he was equally far removed from the new Suez rebels such as Anthony Nutting and Sir Edward Boyle, who both resigned from the Government. Outwardly, and in every practical way, he was at the Prime Minister's side, drumming up support for Eden in the House, robust in his defence of Government policy, sometimes berating his own back-bench critics, on other occasions appealing to them with honeyed word and reasoned phrase. No Chief Whip could have exerted himself more than Heath did in holding together, with some semblance of unity, a parliamentary party that was in part extravagantly warlike, in part apprehensive, in much lesser part opposed to its leader. What he really felt about the Suez policy he is not disposed to discuss. But I have reason to believe that his heart was not in it. Yet as Chief Whip he thought it his duty to do everything that energy and resource could accomplish in sustaining Eden. One and all are agreed, friend and foe alike, that he discharged this duty to perfection. He was loyal to the policy; he was tireless in helping to carry through the parliamentary tactics which the policy involved; and he was successful. But I doubt if he liked it.

Suez was a nightmare for the Whips. 'He didn't tell us awfully much in the Whips' office,' Lord St Helens recalls, 'but he kept his head perfectly throughout. Where he was frightfully good was after Suez, when Anthony went off to the West Indies.' The Prime Minister, by now exhausted, had retreated for a few weeks to a house in Jamaica called Goldeneye, the property of Ian Fleming. There was a tense interregnum with Butler left in charge of the Government. 'Ted had immense influence then,' says St Helens. 'It was very difficult for Rab or Harold to do much. Neither of these two wanted to stick his chin out at that moment. Ted was the chief of staff. The party would almost certainly have fallen apart but for him. He was immensely approachable to the back-benchers, reassuring. In a different way he was very good vis-à-vis Ministers. He was the one very tangible link between the party and the Government.'

Heath foresaw the collapse of the Eden Government. He realised that it could hardly last after such dreadful damage to the Prime Minister's health. Eden resigned on 9 January 1957. 'Everyone'—except Randolph Churchill—predicted that Butler would succeed him. Not for the first time, Randolph was right: Butler was passed over, by a vote of his Cabinet colleagues, in favour of Harold Macmillan. 'The outcome was highly acceptable to a substantial majority in the House, a majority to which I myself belonged,' Heath tells me— an avowal which may surprise some of his friends, who had thought of him as a Butler supporter. He adds that he was hopeful of the new Government's survival in the awful aftermath of Suez—'It seemed to me that we had a good chance of succeeding, a perfectly good chance'. In this assessment he seems to have been more optimistic than Macmillan—who, in a letter four months later to his friend John Wyndham, said: 'The fact is that I did not really think my administration could last more than a few weeks'.

Heath served Macmillan as Chief Whip until the general election of October 1959, two years and nine months later. From the outset he was as close to him as anyone. Their dinner together at the Turf Club on the day of Macmillan's appointment is well-remembered. Heath—and Heath alone—was the new Prime Minister's chosen companion because Heath knew more about the state of the parliamentary party than anybody else. 'What were you discussing?' somebody asked as they left the Turf Club. 'Form, of course,' said Heath. Through the ups of this time—the gradual restoration of the party's electoral fortunes, culminating in the 'Tory glory' of the hundred majority in 1959—and the downs—such as the resignation of the Treasury Ministers, Thorneycroft, Powell and Birch at the end of 1957 —Heath was never far from the Premier's side. He has a good eye for human frailty. This accounted for much of his value to Macmillan. During his years in the Whips' office he had come to know every single Conservative Member. He was able to weigh them all up dispassionately. He knew their hopes, ambitions, feelings of good-will and ill-will, deficiencies, strengths and weaknesses (over women or drink or money or whatever): Heath knew them, and he knew what they were capable of.

In addition to attending meetings of the Cabinet, he saw Macmillan on his own at 10 a.m. every day from Monday to Friday, and he often looked in at No. 10 from his office at 12 Downing Street, which is connected by a passage. He was in constant touch with Macmillan's private secretaries too. Freddie Bishop was the Principal Private Secretary. Another secretary was John Wyndham, now Lord Egremont, who believes that Heath's 'candour and fearlessness' were 'his great qualities' as Chief Whip.

A Prime Minister's private secretaries are uniquely well-placed to judge not only the Prime Minister but all his colleagues as well. In Egremont's observation, Heath was 'tremendously loyal to the Prime Minister and tremendously frank with him. I think he regarded himself as a conduit for conducting information to the Prime Minister about what the party was thinking of the P.M. He was both practical and intellectual. He was totally pragmatical. He knew what he was doing all the time—no messing about.'

Macmillan took Heath into the Cabinet as Minister of Labour once the election was behind him. Heath himself had done well at the polls. Against his old antagonist Ashley Bramall, who had reappeared at Bexley, he again increased his majority; indeed he nearly doubled it—to 8,633. He was now forty-three years of age. How effective he might have become in his new and delicate appointment, how far (if at all) he might have travelled along the road of reform in industrial relations on which he is now so conspicuously planted, no one can tell, for he wasn't at the Ministry long enough to achieve much. As things turned out, he was no more than a bird of passage; he held the office for nine months.

I have since sensed that Macmillan feels in retrospect that this very short tenure was rather to Heath's subsequent advantage. He now seems inclined to think that Heath might have found the older sort of trade union leaders temperamentally uncongenial, even tiresome, had events required him to spend more time in their company. In fact, Heath's capacities were never fully tested, let alone stretched, at the Ministry of Labour, not only because his term was so curtailed but also because it was a period of relative tranquillity. During his nine months, there were no great troubles on the industrial front beyond the threat of a railway strike in February 1960, and this was averted. Heath did however impress the leaders of the T.U.C. as a Minister who properly understood his role as a conciliator, and his mediation in the railway dispute is remembered with respect.

Eight years earlier, when the Tories returned to office, the General Council of the T.U.C., mindful of their 'second-class citizen' relationship with Conservative Governments before the war, and still understandably resentful, had issued a warning statement. 'Since the Conservative administration of pre-war days,' said the General Council, 'the range of consultation between Ministers and both sides of industry has considerably

88

increased, and the machinery of joint consultation has enormously improved. We expect of this Government that they will maintain to the full this practice of consultation. On our part, we shall continue to examine every question solely in the light of its industrial and economic implications.' Sir Walter Monckton, the first Minister of Labour in the new Tory Government, was a lifelong neutral, so to speak, who lived up to the T.U.C.'s expectations very well—though whether he was an effective Minister of Labour is open to argument. His successor, Iain Macleod, was strong meat in contrast. He was a shade assertive for the T.U.C., too positive for their taste.

In Heath, the T.U.C. found a Minister who appealed to them as both 'moderate and constructive', in the words of Victor Feather, then the Assistant General Secretary. He and George Woodcock, the General Secretary, saw quite a bit of Heath during the railway dispute. 'He was ready enough to depart from the formal procedures and see people informally,' says Feather. 'He recognised that preconceived positions by the Minister are no good—the Minister's job is to be a conciliator. He played the traditional role of being neutral. I think this rather suited his temperament. In his job he never adopted any attitude of political partisanship. He was more like an administrator or civil servant, really. He understood the need for conciliation.'

That aptitude, and all his powers of diplomacy, were soon to be tested in another and more complicated field—in the long and ramified negotiations which he was destined to conduct in Europe.

Chapter Eight

'Into Europe'

Throughout Heath's nine months at the Ministry of Labour, the Cabinet—and especially Macmillan himself—had been watching the swift development of the European Economic Community. The E.E.C. and Euratom treaties had come into effect in January 1958. The first lowering of internal customs tariffs within the E.E.C. occurred a year later. In the same year, and six weeks after the general election in this country, the conventions establishing the 'rival' or 'alternative' European Free Trade Area were signed. Macmillan and his new Cabinet faced decisions of some urgency. In the spring of 1960 a searching re-examination of European policy was set in hand by the Economic Steering Committee, whose chairman was Sir Frank Lee, joint head of the Treasury. The Committee's conclusions proved to be of the first importance in settling Macmillan's mind.

He was already an established European. During the years of Tory opposition from 1945 to 1951, he had played a leading part in the European movement. He had helped to set up the Council of Europe, Churchill's brainchild. He was an enthusiastic supporter of the Schuman Plan (which Heath, in his maiden speech, had so warmly commended to a somewhat indifferent

House of Commons and a hostile Government in 1950).
Back in office in 1951, however, and immersed in his
work as Minister of Housing, Macmillan had seemed
to lose some of his earlier interest. In fact, his heart was
always in the policy of European integration.

In July 1960, because Derick Heathcoat Amory, the
Chancellor, wished to retire, Macmillan took the opportunity to reconstruct his administration. The effect was
to fit the 'Europeans' in his Cabinet—mere handful
that they were—into spheres of delicate importance to
the development of the policy which he was already
contemplating.

Christopher Soames became Minister of Agriculture
and Duncan Sandys the Secretary of State for Commonwealth Relations. These were areas in which both could
move with knowledge and confidence, and they were
areas of the utmost importance to the European policy
as it developed. They were spheres in which Macmillan
needed Ministers of such conviction about Europe that
neither was likely to be compromised or 'nobbled'—
the one by the farming lobby at home, the other by the
Commonwealth countries, or at least some of them. For
the Foreign Office he chose Lord Home, with Heath
at his side as Lord Privy Seal. Lord Home was agreeable, but Heath was at first rather cool towards the proposal. He felt that he had not been at the Ministry
of Labour long enough to make any mark worth
speaking of, and—more than that—he was uneasy
about the projected partnership with the Foreign
Secretary. He feared, though mistakenly, that as
Lord Privy Seal he would find himself under Lord
Home, a subordinate rather than an equal. No doubt
he remembered how Eden had fared before the war
when, as Lord Privy Seal with responsibility for League

of Nations affairs at Geneva, he was frequently at odds with his colleague the Foreign Secretary, first Sir John Simon, then Sir Samuel Hoare. Macmillan remembered this too, but he was mindful of the differences as well as the similarities and he saw Heath, in his own words, as 'principal coadjutor' to the Secretary of State, with prime responsibility for European policy. Heath was reassured after a little while, and in the event he formed the happiest of relationships with Lord Home.

In August, Heath left St James's Square for the Foreign Office, explaining to anxious friends that this was really what he would most like to do. Once the European policy was decided, the Government gradually assembled one of the most accomplished teams of officials ever formed in Whitehall in time of peace, first to prepare the British application for membership of the E.E.C. and thereafter to toil with Heath night and day in the seemingly interminable negotiations which ensued. Just as there had been more than one candidate for the political—the ministerial—leadership of the delegation (for both Soames and Sandys had impeccable credentials as 'Europeans' of long standing), so there was a certain rivalry later on for the official appointments. The Foreign Office, predictably enough, were pressing for one of their own members to head the team of officials. They proposed the Ambassador in Paris, Sir Pierson Dixon. The Secretary of the Cabinet, Sir Norman Brook, was inclined to agree, though his colleague Sir Frank Lee (both were Joint Permanent Secretaries to the Treasury) rather favoured Eric Roll, then a Deputy Secretary at the Ministry of Agriculture. Roll, now Sir Eric and an important banker among other things, had lately been running a working party on the E.E.C. under his Minister, Christopher Soames. Like Sir Frank (whose Economic Steering Committee had advised the Government to apply for membership), he was a whole-hearted supporter of the policy. Sir Norman Brook consulted Heath and, though neither apparently discussed it with the Prime Minister, Sir Pierson Dixon was appointed, with Roll as his deputy. Sir Pierson was universally respected as one of the ablest members of the Foreign Service in his generation. He already enjoyed high rank and status as Ambassador to France, and above all he was on very good terms with de Gaulle—respectful to that touchy man, yet frank and never obsequious. The President liked him and consequently he had some influence at the Elysée Palace. This was precisely the reason for preferring him. In retrospect, I suggest, it was an error. Sir Pierson, once he entered the Brussels negotiations, never enjoyed quite the same influence with de Gaulle. Had he not become directly involved in them he might still have been able, as Ambassador in Paris, to maintain his old relationship with the General, perhaps to Britain's considerable advantage.

When Parliament rose at the end of July 1960, the future of Britain's relations with the European Economic Community had looked uncertain. A year passed before Macmillan felt ready to lodge the formal application to join. During the late autumn of 1960 and in the spring of 1961 a succession of visits and exchanges took place between British Ministers and member-Governments of the Community, by way of preparing the ground. Macmillan himself conferred with Chancellor Adenauer, President de Gaulle and the Italian Premier, Signor Fanfani. Heath addressed the Consultative

Assembly of the Council of Europe in September. In October, he met French Ministers in Paris. In February, in a speech to the Council of Western European Union, he announced a significant change in the Government's attitude to a common or harmonised tariff on imported raw materials and manufactured goods. Reporting his multifarious soundings and consultations to the Commons in May, Heath had this to say:

We see today in Europe a powerfully developing group of nations in the European Economic Community. Its strength is shown by its size of over 170 million people compared with 50 million in the United Kingdom and rather under 90 million in E.F.T.A. as a whole. Their reserves of manpower are much greater. In ten years' time the populations under the age of forty-five in France and Germany alone will be double that of the United Kingdom. The gross national product of the Six is two and a half times that of the United Kingdom. Their rate of industrial growth is much higher. The internal trade of the Six rose by 30 per cent in 1960 compared with 16 per cent for the internal trade of the Seven.

The Six have a strong balance of payments position and large resources. Their prospects are already attracting increased investments both from the United States and from the United Kingdom. In the past, over 50 per cent of the investment in Europe from the United States came to the United Kingdom. In 1960, it was down to 41 per cent, and in 1961, over 50 per cent of the United States' investment in Europe is expected to go to the Six.

I give these facts to the House as an indication of the strength and the size of the new group which has emerged in Europe. It has established itself and, it is showing every sign of future success.

Examining the political significance of the Community, he continued:

We now see opposite to us on the mainland of Europe a large group comparable in size only to the United States and to the Soviet Union, and as its economic power increases, so will its political influence. . . . In the political sphere we see the growth of political consultation between the countries of the Six. There is regular consultation at the level of Foreign Ministers. There is frequent and regular consultation between Ministers of other kinds at other levels, and between, for example, the Governors of the State Bank and proposals are being considered for more formalised consultation at the level of heads of Government. . . . This development poses for us and the rest of Europe, considerable political problems. I am talking now not only of the next six months, or the next two or three years, but a very much longer period. We can then see the danger which faces us of a decline in political influence in the world at large and in our Commonwealth. . . . On the political side, one of the major political achievements of the Six has been to create a Franco-German *rapprochement* which is invaluable.

By late summer, Macmillan was ready to declare and commit himself, and he announced the Government's intention to apply for membership in the House of Commons on 31 July, nine days before lodging the application. The decision was debated and approved by both Houses.

The year and a half that followed was a period of incessant negotiation. There were really three lots of negotiations going on at once: Heath and his colleagues negotiating in Brussels with the representatives of the six states of the E.E.C.; Heath negotiating with individual member-Governments in their own capitals; and at home negotiations—for that is what they amounted to—within the Cabinet, within the Conservative Party, and within the electorate at large. Parliament was divided, the Labour Opposition was divided; the Tories were divided; and the public was divided.

Anything approaching a blow-by-blow account of these long and ramified transactions is beyond the scope and purpose of this book. They deserve, and no doubt they will eventually receive, a substantial volume or two of their own—perhaps written by Heath, who alone has access to the multitude of official papers now separately housed in the Foreign Office archives. Until those archives are available, no fully objective or agreed account of the negotiations can be written. As it is, even the participants are often at loggerheads on what actually happened, and why. Everyone knows how troublesome and complicated the negotiations became. It may equally be said that everyone recognised at the time Heath's astonishing command of all the intricacies, his mastery of the thousands and thousands of details that made up the whole. On these points there is never any dispute. He began, of course, with the superb advantage of believing passionately in what he was doing: he was—as he remains—a convinced European, believing that Britain's future can best be assured by the sort of association that he was called upon to negotiate.

As he said at the outset, addressing the Council of Ministers of the E.E.C. in Paris on 10 October 1961:

The British Government and the British people have been through a searching debate during the last few years on the subject of their relations with Europe. The result of the debate has been our present application. It was a decision arrived at, not on any narrow or short-term grounds, but as a result of a thorough assessment over a considerable period of the needs of our own country, of Europe and of the Free World as a whole. We recognise it as a great decision, a turning point in our history, and we take it in all seriousness. In saying that we wish to join the E.E.C., we mean that we desire to become full, whole-hearted and active members of the European Community in its widest sense and to go forwad with you in the building of a new Europe. . . . In a world where political and economic power is becoming concentrated to such a great extent, a larger European unity has become essential. Faced with the threats which we can all see, Europe must unite or perish. The United Kingdom, being part of Europe, must not stand aside.

Because nobody has yet published a study that can be called definitive, informed opinion about the negotiations is highly fragmented, with many shades. Most commentators, moreover, are not only pro-European but pro- a politically federal Europe. Biases like these make it difficult if not impossible to come to an agreed estimate of the British attempt to enter the Community: depending on what issues—or even aspects of issues—a writer considers important, his evaluation of diplomatic conduct will vary. It may, however, be said that most pro-European commentators now believe that it was a mistake for Britain to become bogged down in economic and agricultural technicalities, because the overriding objective was to enter—to get inside—the E.E.C. Some of those who consider the negotiations ill-conducted or at best mishandled, maintain that Britain was not far enough advanced in her political concept of Europe. They are inclined, in varying degrees, to extend some sympathy to Macmillan and Heath for having to contend with a lukewarm or hostile domestic opinion. The view that the Heath mission became bogged down in technicalities is probably held much more strongly by observers who have themselves failed to master the technical issues.

As to tactics, there is the criticism that all the important concessions made by the British delegation were too late. This charge is asserted all the more forcibly because of the conviction that on each of these major issues Britain should have known from the beginning that her initial position was untenable. The argument is reinforced, moreover, by the belief that General de Gaulle was probably not strong enough to impose a veto before the French elections of November 1962, when he won complete control of the National Assembly for the first time. It is worth noting that when in May 1962, at a press conference, de Gaulle made his first hostile statement—hostile both to Britain and to the concept of political Europe favoured by most 'Europeans'—M. Pflimlin and four M.R.P. Ministers resigned from his coalition cabinet. This is perhaps the strongest charge that their critics can level against Macmillan and Heath. Both have an answer to it.

In a few words, there is now a tendency to say that the negotiations were mishandled because Britain lacked a sufficiently clear idea of the future political pattern of a united Europe and because, technically and tactically, the concessions which the Heath delegation made at Brussels were too little and too late.

Heath's speech to the E.E.C. Ministers on 10 October 1961 had established that after long introspection and self-analysis Britain had concluded that her future world role lay with Europe; that what 'Europe' meant would be defined in entry negotiations (to be conducted, it was supposed, between seven separate Governments and not between one Government and a community of six); that, in negotiations about economies and technicalities, Britain would concede to the 'European' view rather than stick out for her own as a Commonwealth

and Atlantic power; and that there were terms—
Britain would not join the Six at any price, but, on the
other hand, felt reasonably sure that good terms could
be arranged. The speech represented a definite commitment, however imprecise. No doubt Heath and
Macmillan regarded its imprecisions as negotiating
points. Perhaps they were not yet thinking of Europe
as fully shaped. They had abandoned the idea of a free
trade area alternative to the E.E.C., but they regarded
the E.E.C. itself as something that would in part be
shaped by the negotiations for British entry. As a
negotiating principle this may be considered a mistake,
for, when the bargaining began, the Six were interested
in discussing how Britain could become a member of
an entity already established, while Britain was trying
to define the nature of the entity as well as become a
member of it.

Essentially, what Heath said in his speech of 10
October was that Britain had already made a major
decision—to opt for Europe—but that turning the
decision into actuality would depend on the result of
the negotiations. It is not easy to see that he could have
done anything else. What he meant was that Britain
had come to believe that she could join Europe *without
damaging* essential Commonwealth interests, not that
she would be prepared to join *at the expense*, if necessary,
of at least some essential Commonwealth interests—
which is what the E.E.C. wanted.

Of course the nature of the choice was obscured
or hidden by certain political realities. First, there
was the domestic political sentiment in favour of
the Commonwealth—and party, and even Cabinet,
opinion, far from being decided at the beginning,
evolved only during the negotiations. Second, during

99

the period of trying to construct an alternative to the
E.E.C., Britain had contracted certain obligations to
the E.F.T.A. countries—though in practice they did not
greatly affect the negotiations. The difference between
the two sides might be summarised in this way: at
best, E.F.T.A. thought, the British application would
secure their aim (the aim of the old Free Trade Area
plans) of a single European market; while the E.E.C.
thought, at best, that the British application meant
acceptance of the idea that a free trade concept was not
enough.

In fact, Heath and Macmillan did not have a free
hand: having regard to the state of British opinion,
there was the possibility that terms which the Prime
Minister and the Lord Privy Seal might have thought
acceptable would prove inadequate to the Cabinet, the
party and the country, not to speak of the Commonwealth. On the other hand, it could be argued that,
perhaps unconsciously, Macmillan at least, and possibly
Heath, used this domestic opposition and scepticism as
an excuse for not facing up to the real choice. The Six,
after all, had come together in a union because they
felt that history had shown that the system of relations
between nation states had been proved, by events since
1914, to be inadequate; and as a result of this inadequacy they had formed an attachment to an idea called
Europe. Britain on the other hand, after trial and error,
and aware of her diminished power in the world, had
formed the idea that, to preserve and increase her world
influence, she had to join this European grouping: her
attitude to the E.E.C. was essentially egotistical. She
therefore thought of the E.E.C. as something added to
her Commonwealth and Anglo-American role and not
as an alternative to either which she was bound to

accept. Expressed epigrammatically, the Continental countries formed their concept of Europe out of various forms of defeat. Britain formed her attachment to Europe out of a sense of victory (in 1945) which had brought not rewards, but loss of power and influence.

The fact that Britain thought of an outward-looking, Commonwealth-orientated Europe as, objectively, something good, does not disprove this: it is an historical characteristic of British foreign policy to equate objective good with the British interest. It is also, historically, common to think of British foreign policy as resting on three legs—Europe, the Commonwealth and the Anglo-American alliance. This suggests, of course, that the preoccupation with the Commonwealth in 1962 was not simply sentimental or altruistic: it was basic to Britain's conception of herself—and it enabled the French to exploit doubts about Britain's commitment to Europe in the same terms as the continental powers had committed themselves.

In the event, every technicality of negotiation was impregnated with politics. Every single detail about food prices or textiles, however small in itself, had significance for the future political orientation of the new Europe. This was the true political meaning of the highly technical negotiations. The direction and intention of the negotiations and the sacrifices which Britain would make could be expressed only in the economic terms in which the negotiations in fact took place.

Strategically, therefore, Macmillan and Heath were seeking a new world role for Britain, commensurate with the role that she enjoyed in the past, and they believed that the re-direction of intention and effort which finding this role involved could be formed in negotiations about economics with political and institutional implications—though fortunately these did not all have to be spelt out for the moment. Basically, this seems to have been the correct decision—and if so, the belief of most critics that it was a mistake not to opt initially for a federal or supra-national Europe, and let the economics take care of themselves, is wrong. Moreover, if de Gaulle's opposition to British entry formed and hardened during the negotiations, how much more quickly would it have emerged if Britain had been committed from the start to the kind of federal Europe that he detested and was fighting against in discussion with his partners?

While he would not have had to impose the veto until he had won the election of November 1962, it seems certain that he would have had the will to do so, even against a much greater outcry from his partners, if Britain had from the first espoused a federal concept to which he was always opposed. Any British espousal of federal forms could not in any case have taken effect before the veto. And if espousal had meant that Britain simply conceded everything in the economic field, while de Gaulle did not impose the veto, Britain would have gone into Europe so weak that she could not have been a useful ally of federalism. Even if it is suggested that, by supporting a federal cause, Britain could have secured easier economic terms from the Five, she could not have obtained them from France: and it is important to remember that, during the negotiations, France stuck to the letter of the Treaty of Rome, which the Five could hardly have violated. In its essence, the Treaty was of course pro-French— because, when it was being drafted, the French negotiators had gained favourable terms as the price of their allegiance to the E.E.C.

Fundamentally, therefore, it may be said that the Heath delegation was right to negotiate economics at Brussels. Even if Britain had presented herself as the supporter of a federalist idea of European unity, she would have gained no advantage. What weakened her position was that she was unable to play, in negotiations, the kind of role in shaping the community that the nature of her ambitions for herself and the community alike required. Accordingly, it may reasonably be claimed that the basic terms of discussion chosen by Britain—economic rather than overtly political—were right. In terms of direction, Britain wanted an outward-looking Europe, that is a Europe whose trading and economic policies favoured the Commonwealth areas of the world. This may be considered a wise and far-seeing view of the necessary development of world trade, or as a rationalisation of British self-interest, or as both. In practice, and with exceptions, since Heath had said on 10 October 1961, that Britain would accept a common customs tariff of the enlarged E.E.C., to be imposed on non-members, it meant that Britain would want a low tariff wall, to encourage world trade. The Five, though in principle they favoured freer world trade, were less concerned with the height of the tariff wall (however much it occupied them) than with obtaining equality of treatment between E.E.C. producers and a common front against outsiders: they would not build into their arrangements a general commitment to freer world trade, though they offered to negotiate the matter later with affected countries. France was even tougher: in May 1962 and in January 1963, de Gaulle made it clear that he preferred a very high tariff wall; since this was principally an agricultural consideration it favoured French producers.

Of course all this had not crystallised when Britain decided to apply for membership. No doubt it would have been ideal for Britain if negotiations for her entry and negotiations between the Six on the formulation of stage two of the transitional period of their common agricultural policy could have been one and the same. For Britain wanted to take part in shaping the community itself. She expected the concept of the community which she wished to join to be formed as she negotiated to join it. But the Six decided to formulate a common agricultural policy before opening negotiations with Britain. It was a great pity. The result was that, although exchanges took place earlier, negotiations proper could not begin until 1962.

The pressures that made the Six anxious to come to an agreement on community agricultural policy before beginning negotiations are complex. Since the existing agricultural arrangements were very agreeable to France, she wanted to extend them. The other members of the Six wanted agricultural agreement as soon as possible as a means of really unifying the community. If France was not given her way on agriculture, however, she could delay other stages in the implementation of the process of unification, timetables for which could be made dependent on fulfilment of the agricultural schedule, due for passing to stage two of the transitional period on 1 January 1962. If this stage of the agricultural policy was not implemented by that date, France would lose some advantages, but de Gaulle would have greater negative power in other areas. Secondly, both Holland and France, as producing countries, feared that, if implementation of stage two of the agricultural policy was tied up with the British negotiations, Germany and Britain, as consumer countries, might come together to change the nature of the agricultural system to favour themselves. This might lead, it was feared, to Commonwealth agricultural producers enjoying too good a permanent access to the Common Market.

Heath's speech on 10 October 1961 did not entirely remove these fears. While he had accepted the principle of a common external tariff, which in effect meant that E.E.C. producers would all be favoured over outside countries, he was not altogether clear about the number of Commonwealth countries for which he would try to gain association with the E.E.C. To the Six it seemed that his list would be too long to be realistic. On top of that, existing association arrangements were becoming due for review. The Six thought it important to avoid mixing up these reviews with discussion of Commonwealth association, and this added impetus to the idea of concluding the agricultural arrangements before the British negotiations began.

Though Heath had made it clear that he was willing to consider arrangements short of association for some Commonwealth countries, it may be that his speech of 10 October 1961 was too balanced and thorough a survey of the situation. While leaving no doubt that Britain had made an important commitment to Europe, he had not perhaps defined the commitment explicitly enough.

Another difficulty may have been that, because of Cabinet, party and Commonwealth pressures, Macmillan and Heath did not feel able to concede too much in advance. Or again—as I think myself—it may have been that neither saw much chance of the Six letting them take part in the agricultural discussions, therefore any concessions in advance would be wasted and dangerous.

Chapter Nine

Exit from Brussels

What then was the British negotiating position? From Heath's speech of 10 October 1961, it can be summarised as follows:

1. Britain accepted that the E.E.C. would proceed towards unity and she wanted to play her part in this process. She accepted that internal tariffs between the Seven would be eliminated, that there would be a common external tariff, a common agricultural and a common commercial policy. Immediately on joining she would cut her own tariffs to what had been agreed by the Six and accept the structure of the common external tariff: this was to ease relations with G.A.T.T., member-countries of which could, in certain circumstances, have demanded a re-negotiation of the external tariff if Britain entered.

2. For Commonwealth countries, Britain would seek either association, some system which would give them access to the U.K. but not to the markets of the Six, under terms to be decided, or some system which would lower or eliminate the external tariff of the Six to protect both Commonwealth countries and countries closely associated with the E.E.C, in respect of certain products, e.g. Indian and Ceylonese tea.

3. Commonwealth interests were divided not according to country, but according to product, into tropical products, manufactured goods (from the developed Commonwealth), low-cost manufactures, mainly from Asia, and temperate zone foodstuffs. A Commonwealth country might therefore expect different treatment for different products.

4. For five raw materials, Heath suggested zero tariffs; he recognised that unrestricted access for manufactures from developed countries would not be possible; in the field of low-cost manufactures, he acknowledged that probably only Hong Kong would qualify for full association. For temperate zone foodstuffs, he laid down the doctrine that he would seek 'comparable outlets' to those already enjoyed.

5. He accepted that the Common Market would extend fully to British agriculture, but hoped to give the E.E.C. system some of the characteristics of the British.

6. For E.F.T.A. countries, Heath sought membership or association. Britain hoped that these countries would be generally agreeable to a reasonable solution.

This speech may be described as a masterly exposition of the British case. It was, however, regarded as an attempt completely to protect the Commonwealth from the effects of British entry into the E.E.C. As a result of the agreement reached by the Six on agriculture in January 1962, the principle of Community preference was built into the E.E.C. system. Which meant, first, that all farmers in the E.E.C. countries would be treated equally in respect of each other, and second, that they would be treated better than outsiders. In respect of both Commonwealth and British farmers, this was irreconcilable with the Heath position.

Up to the end of January, Britain made no serious move to resolve the implicit deadlock. At ministerial meetings in November and December, however, it did become clear that association with the E.E.C. would be possible only for under-developed countries, i.e. countries like those already associated. In January, Macmillan met Adenauer and Erhard, and while emphasising that Britain was eager to make a beginning, acknowledged his fear that this would weaken her bargaining position.

At further ministerial meetings on 22 February 1962, and one month later, Heath began to appear more flexible. These meetings saw the two major points emerge: the question of temperate foodstuffs and the problem of changing the British agricultural system. Another ministerial meeting was held on 8 May, by which time officials had made a progress report outlining the different positions. Britain and the Six now agreed to impose by phases a common tariff on industrial goods from the developed Commonwealth. This had never really been a negotiable matter. In the same month Britain proposed arrangements for the Asian nations on which a compromise seemed possible. And in June, de Gaulle and Macmillan conferred together at Château de Camps. Their meeting seemed a success, but nothing very practical was discussed and it led to no softening of the French attitude at Brussels. Perhaps it was a mistake for Macmillan not to offer de Gaulle some concession in the political-military field at this point.

What happened during the summer months was that Britain retreated slowly from the positions which (according to Heath's speech of 10 October 1961) she preferred, and began to negotiate, on Commonwealth interests, in terms preferred by the E.E.C. The object of Heath's policy appeared to be to attain through the system of the Six the same outward-looking ends as were already achieved by the Commonwealth system. In return for abandoning the Commonwealth structure, he sought assurances that the E.E.C. system would itself be given an outward-looking tendency.

The Six refused Heath's pleas for 'comparable outlets' for Commonwealth trade. This was because it seemed to them that, by allowing the Commonwealth countries access equal to their existing access (to U.K. markets), either to the U.K. or to the market of the E.E.C., during a transition period at the end of which 'comparable outlets' would be secured elsewhere, they would freeze the pattern of world trade and allow the Commonwealth to escape the difficult task of seeking outlets elsewhere, e.g. for its agricultural goods in Asia. Moreover, to allow the Commonwealth to retain its existing access during a transition period would be to give Commonwealth countries preference equal to that enjoyed by Community countries during that period— which would be a violation of the principle of community preference. Likewise, it would be a violation of that principle to allow Commonwealth countries access to the E.E.C. better than that enjoyed by other third parties after the transition was over. All this was the practical negotiating consequence of the fact that the E.E.C. had agreed on agriculture before conferring with Britain. As long as Heath fought for 'comparable outlets', France was able to argue that Britain might try to use the transition period to change the basis of the E.E.C.'s system. Some of the Five shared that fear.

At length Heath agreed to give up 'comparable outlets' and discuss, instead, 'reasonable access' for Commonwealth countries and a reorganisation of world trade that would, ultimately, rectify the imbalance between supply and need in the world agricultural situation as well as the general economic imbalance between developed and underdeveloped countries. His critics argue that he should have made a much earlier concession on comparable outlets.

The Six maintained that their system, based on a levy on goods imported from outside the Community, was not inherently restrictive: whether it would in practice prove so depended on the price level adopted by the Community; and this, of course, was something much more than a matter of agriculture alone. They believed that, with a reasonable target price inside the E.E.C., the Commonwealth countries would be assured of the same revenue for a smaller quantity of exports. The Commonwealth did not like this idea, but it was fundamentally what Heath accepted. He obtained in return some guarantee that E.E.C. prices policy would favour traditional suppliers and a certain limited promise that the E.E.C. would take remedial action in the event of sudden damage to Commonwealth trade. This was the general arrangement which he had arrived at in principle when negotiations broke down. Along with it were certain commitments to a more liberal world trading policy and special, and rather good, individual arrangements for some Commonwealth countries.

This stage was reached in August 1962. Negotiations were resumed in September, and in the main they were dominated by British agriculture. Britain proposed that there should be a twelve-year transitional period during which she would maintain her guaranteed prices and deficiency payments but would proceed progressively to adjust to the system of the Six. Levies would gradually be imposed and British prices brought to Market levels. The burden for supporting the British farmer would gradually be shifted from the Treasury to the consumer. Special arrangements would be made for certain commodities. The negotiations that followed were the toughest of all. The Six insisted that the transitional period should end on 1 January 1970, and that Britain should change to the agricultural system of the Common Market on the day of entry. This would have meant, for example, that British wheat prices would at once be raised to the lowest Market price rather than remain for the moment at their current level, which was lower than the lowest Market price. Eventually, the Six agreed to let Britain postpone price rises from the day of entry to the assembly of a new Parliament (a point of much importance to the Macmillan Government) and, on 15 January, after the veto, Heath accepted 31 December 1969 as the end of the transitional period.

In essence, Britain had to give way on domestic agriculture. His critics argue that Heath should have done so much earlier: on this issue, the critical case has dramatic point, in that the formal concession came after the veto.

It is important to remember that negotiations were by no means concluded at the time of the French veto. Many difficult problems had still to be solved, especially those concerning New Zealand and E.F.T.A. It was popularly said that January would see either a breakthrough or a breakdown. What Heath's critics have argued is that between his speech of 10 October 1961, and the following spring, and into the summer, the autumn and the winter of 1962, he delayed making concessions which, as he knew, he would have to make eventually. They maintain, moreover, that he did so in a manner which suggested that Britain had not accepted certain fundamental principles of E.E.C. organisation and that this enabled France to exploit doubts about Britain's sincerity. All this, the argument goes, gave France the time and strength to consider imposing and then to impose a veto. Alternatively, the critics argue, if concessions on all these major points had been made early enough, the Five would have been so involved in Britain's entry that France would not have been allowed to get away with a veto. This seems very doubtful for several reasons:

1. If these major points had been conceded, Britain would have been in danger of going in at any price. This would not have been tolerable to Cabinet, party, national and Commonwealth opinion. Nor would it have been in Britain's interests.

2. The French, because throughout the negotiations they relied on the letter of the Treaty of Rome, were always in a position to impose tougher terms, especially after the conclusion of the agricultural agreement, when the Six valued their own unity higher than the admission of Britain. It is very doubtful if Britain could ever have split France from her partners. Even if she had, this would almost certainly have made General de Gaulle even more determined, and, given his character, it seems unlikely that he would have lacked the nerve to impose a veto, once he concluded that it was in France's interest to do so.

3. Once the basic character of the E.E.C. was established by the agricultural agreements of January 1962, Britain could hardly expect to re-shape the Community by re-shaping its principles. Everything that the Heath delegation could do to form its workings

in ways congenial to Britain depended on technical matters like agreeing on the right tariff levels, etc. This could only be done by the negotiating posture that Heath in fact adopted—opposing Britain's principles to theirs, and giving way as they adjusted the workings of their principles. Thus, the Six were right in maintaining that there was nothing inherently restrictive in their levy system on food imports. What Heath looked like securing when negotiations broke down was not only a levy system that would not be inherently restrictive but one that would in practice be liberalising. If he had conceded too much too readily Britain would have had no power, once in, to shape things. What shaping meant lay precisely in the technical nature of the negotiations.

Most of the thirty-odd members of his delegation, some now retired from the public service, would probably agree with that appreciation. They were a gifted and varied band, drawn from half the ministries in Whitehall, and they were tough: they had to be, to withstand the strange and arduous sixteen months of negotiation. Sir Pierson Dixon, carrying a double responsibility because he remained Ambassador to France, went backwards and forwards by train, doing duty in Brussels one day, in Paris the next. Others, such as Eric Roll, Freddie Bishop, Sir Evelyn Shuckburgh, Sir Roderick Barclay and Herbert Andrew, were for ever flying between London and Brussels.

Like Heath, they all stayed in the Metropole Hotel, a somewhat ornate establishment within walking distance of the delegation's office, where each had a small room. A dozen of them met there every morning to review the previous day's work and prepare for the work of that day. Very often there were differences of opinion and clashing briefs, due to contradictory pressures from many sides. Heath's patience, and his willingness—even eagerness—to listen to other people, were important assets to him in this chaotic transaction. 'He was a wonderfully good listener,' says a former member of his staff, 'and he held things together and kept them under control. He was never simply an instrument in the hands of officials: he controlled the operation. He displayed great qualities of leadership in his handling of the team and got a lot of work out of dissimilar people. Of course he worked enormously hard himself.'

The delegations of the Six, as they confronted him across the table in their long interminable wranglings (conducted in the Belgian Foreign Ministry's new quarters), were also impressed by his patience, by his good temper even under provocation, and by his pleasant but firm way of bringing them back to the issue under consideration whenever they strayed off in another direction. From time to time, Christopher Soames went over from London to support him. It has been suggested very sensibly that Heath could have reduced the burden on himself by sharing it more with both Soames and Duncan Sandys; but he preferred to carry the bulk of the load on his own shoulders.

He was of course in constant communication with Macmillan and other Ministers and was frequently in London for Cabinet meetings, to deliver progress reports to the Commons, or to explain himself to the party. Party opinion had been brought round successfully, and the European policy, nicely launched at the Brighton conference in 1961, was overwhelmingly endorsed at Llandudno a year later, shortly after the publication of the Prime Minister's celebrated pamphlet *Britain, the Commonwealth and Europe*.

It seems fairly clear, therefore, that at Brussels Britain was moving towards a community which, while not perfectly agreeable, was as agreeable as we were likely to attain. It seems clear, too, that Britain could not have defeated France by any likely combination with the Five. Anything that could have been done to prevent a French veto would surely have had to be done directly with General de Gaulle. Yet the apparent success of his meeting with de Gaulle at Château de Camps seems to have convinced Macmillan that no radical French opposition would emerge. There is reason to believe that up to Château de Camps, de Gaulle thought that Britain would probably withdraw from the negotiations of her own accord because the economic structure and orientation of the E.E.C. would be unacceptable to her. At Château de Camps he realised that he was wrong. He then began to examine the probable political, military and economic effects of British entry, concluded that they would be undesirable, and determined to impose a veto. His objections can be summarised in the view that Britain would be an American Trojan horse. This he took to be confirmed by the Nassau negotiations between Kennedy and Macmillan, though it is probable that his mind was already made up when he met Macmillan at Rambouillet in December 1962: this is no doubt why the military matters which seemed to preoccupy him after Nassau were not raised by him at Rambouillet.

De Gaulle appeared to differ from Britain and the U.S. on three points: the political orientation of the E.E.C., whether it would have a supra-national structure or not, and whether it would be economically inward or outward looking. He evidently wanted an independent and perhaps neutralist Europe. Britain was a firm believer in the Atlantic Alliance. On the other hand, it might have been possible to meet or at least bargain with de Gaulle on this point if Britain had been able to make him some substantial offer, perhaps in nuclear knowledge or hardware. Macmillan and Kennedy seemed to have some inkling of this when, after Nassau, they offered France the Polaris on the same terms as Britain: but this was surely an unfortunate proposal in that France could at that time have supplied neither warheads nor launchers. De Gaulle felt insulted by the offer. To have made any progress in this field Macmillan would have had to re-design his foreign policy (the military principles of which, incidentally, were laid down when he was Minister of Defence).

It was commonly believed that Britain, like France, was suspicious of federal or supra-national institutions. America, on the other hand, was known to favour them. During the Brussels negotiations the Six were having discussions on the future political shape of Europe among themselves. In these discussions, France put forward schemes at variance with the existing principles of supra-nationality: she wanted to concentrate power much more in the hands of governments. Germany and Italy were brought round to accepting a variant of this point of view, but the Benelux countries refused to fall into line unless Britain could be assured of entry.

The fact is that the British Government did not anticipate early enough either the emergence or the nature of French opposition. The Brussels negotiations themselves, having regard to Britain's attempt not to be swallowed up in the Community but to shape it and turn it outwards, were well conducted and remarkably successful. Looking back, with the benefit of hindsight, one can see that if in the end we were taken by surprise, and dismayed when the General revealed his true mind, it was because we had failed to understand him. Things might have turned out differently if Sir Pierson Dixon had never been embroiled in the Brussels affair, but allowed to devote himself completely to his Embassy in Paris, where he was so well-established. He would probably have been able to keep up his old relationship with de Gaulle in all its cordiality, and even if he had not been able to influence him he would surely have learned the General's mind more fully—and in good time.

The veto was of course an appalling blow to Heath personally. He felt deeply about the setback to his cause. In his final statement to the assembled conference at Brussels, on 29 January 1963, he said:

Although this is a sad moment for European unity, I should like straightaway to say one thing. We told you, at the beginning of these negotiations, that we wanted to go forward with you in the building of a new Europe. Our words were very carefully weighed. They remain true today. We have been encouraged by the upsurge of support for the fullest British participation in a united Europe which has been demonstrated in so many quarters in these recent weeks. And so I would say to my colleagues: they should have no fear. We in Britain are not going to turn our backs on the mainland of Europe or on the countries of the Community. We are a part of Europe; by geography, tradition, history, culture and civilisation. We shall continue to work with all our friends in Europe for the true unity and strength of this continent.

At his final Press conference that day, all the assembled journalists, of many nationalities, rose to their feet and clapped as he entered the ballroom at the Metropole Hotel. And at his farewell meeting with the Commonwealth representatives in Brussels the Indian Ambassador to the E.E.C. said: 'When the British left India, many people wept. When you leave Europe tonight, many people will weep. You are the only people in the world of whom these things could be said.'

Next day, Macmillan made a television broadcast. In this he maintained that the negotiations had broken down not because they were going to fail, but because they were going to succeed. The arguments advanced against Britain's membership by the French Government could have been made at the time of Britain's application. The last few weeks had revealed a deep division of purpose as to the way in which the European Community should develop—as an outward-looking partnership, inspired by a spirit of interdependence, and determined to play a world role, not least in helping underdeveloped countries, or as a narrow and highly-protectionist group, seeking a false independence without regard to the wider responsibilities and interests of the Atlantic alliance. The first conception, said Macmillan, is that of Britain and her European friends both inside and outside the Community; the second that of the French President and Government.

Today, as Heath sees it in retrospect, the negotiations achieved three things of major importance: 'They established Britain's sincerity of intention. We got the negotiations to a point where they could only be broken off by the use of the veto: the object always was that the blame should never fall on us. And we made a series of proposals which the present Labour Government has accepted.'

(*Left*) With his agent, Reginald Pye, during his first general election campaign at Bexley in 1950. (*Below*) 'A sad moment for European unity,' Heath called it: 29 January 1963, and the E.E.C. reject Britain's application to join. *Right to left:* Christopher Soames, Eric Roll, Edward Heath; in the foreground Emilio Colombo, Italian Minister of Trade and Industry

(*Above*) A summer morning in the garden at Broadstairs: Heath with (*left to right*) his brother John, his father, his sister-in-law, his stepmother. (*Below*) Conducting his annual Christmas carol concert at Broadstairs five months after becoming Tory leader in 1965

Chapter Ten

Time of Turmoil

For Heath, the year 1963 could scarcely have opened more dismally—and further disturbance lay ahead. The nervous tensions of the Brussels negotiations, the unremitting exertion of it all, the lack of proper exercise, the irregularity of his meals (frequently of the over-rich, 'official' variety) and the final wounding blow of failure had tired him. He had put on weight, and he was puffy in the face. But he is resilient, with a strong constitution, and under a more ordered regime in London he quickly regained his normal fitness. Though the European negotiations were over, Macmillan wished him to remain in the Foreign Office. There, at the side of Lord Home, he worked happily enough for the next nine months, involved in a far wider range of business than he had been able to contemplate from Brussels.

One happy experience in a trying year was the award of the Charlemagne Prize, presented to him in a ceremony at Aachen for 'the most notable achievement in the service of encouraging international understanding and co-operation in the European sphere'. Besides an illuminated scroll and a medallion, he received the sum of £446, with which he bought a Steinway grand piano.

Macmillan was naturally depressed by the failure of

his European policy, all the more so as it followed a year of trial and anxiety. Things were no longer the same around the Cabinet table: a number of familiar faces had disappeared. In the previous July, after a winter and spring of electoral discontent highlighted by the Orpington by-election disaster and due partly to the 'pay pause', he had removed seven Cabinet ministers in one swoop. Selwyn Lloyd, Chancellor of the Exchequer, Lord Kilmuir, the Lord Chancellor, John Maclay, the Secretary for Scotland, Harold Watkinson, Minister of Defence, Lord Mills, Minister without Portfolio, Dr Charles Hill, Minister of Housing and Local Government, and Sir David Eccles, Minister of Education, had all been required to resign on Friday, 13 July. It was a staggering decision, to which—apart from Timothy Bligh and others in the Prime Minister's Private Office—only Butler, Macleod, then chairman of the party, and Martin Redmayne, the Government Chief Whip, were privy in advance. Not all the surviving Ministers approved of Macmillan's action. 'I knew nothing of what he had in mind,' Heath has told me. 'After all, I was engaged in Europe. But it was ill-advised. The timing was wrong. And to do it on such a scale!' Nor were Conservative back-benchers reassured by this display of ruthlessness. If anything, it increased the unrest in the parliamentary party.

Then in the autumn of 1962, William Vassall, an Admiralty clerk in the office of the Civil Lord, Tam Galbraith, had been arrested for spying and duly convicted. Because of imputations in the newspapers against the character of Mr Galbraith, Macmillan set up a tribunal of inquiry, which—besides clearing the Civil Lord of unfounded allegations—resulted in the jailing of two journalists. The sentences were deeply resented in Fleet Street—and of course Macmillan was blamed.

Thus the Government, after all its many troubles, was at a low ebb—and not only in Fleet Street but in Parliament and in the country—when Heath returned to London early in 1963. In no time at all came a further shock. Before the winter was out, Fleet Street and Westminster were again alive with rumours involving another member of the Government—John Profumo, the Secretary of State for War. The course and conclusion of the Profumo affair are all too familiar and hardly require recounting. It was a wretched and unhappy episode for which the Government (as well as John Profumo) paid a heavy price. While there was much public sympathy for the Prime Minister, who received several thousands of kindly letters, alarm and anxiety took hold of the party in Parliament and by the summer there were repeated reports that Macmillan would soon give up. True, he had informed the 1922 Committee that he would lead the party into the next election: but this was in April, two months before the final explosion of Profumo's resignation—which, when it occurred, gave rise to further misgivings about Macmillan's capacity and his ability to remain in office.

The reservations about him were not confined to the back-benches. Some of 'the colleagues', his fellow members of the Cabinet, were also uneasy and thought that he should go. By now (or at long last) they knew more about the Profumo affair and its consequencies than anybody else. They could measure the effects, and they realised just how close to collapse the Government had come one fine summer morning. They had been on the very edge of the precipice, and some at least felt increasingly troubled and insecure.

When Parliament rose for the long summer recess, however, the general (and even the informed) impression was that Macmillan intended to stay, whatever his critics might say. During August he gave every sign of determination to carry on. For one thing, he involved himself in some of the party's preparations for the autumn—the October conference, the opening of the new session of Parliament, and all the attendant activities that mark the beginning of the political year. He was especially interested not only in the composition but also in the production of a party pamphlet called *Acceleration*, a statement of policy bearing his photograph and signature, which was to be issued just ahead of the conference. Once a week throughout August he assembled Sir Michael Fraser, head of the Research Department, Peter Goldman, Director of the Conservative Political Centre and the present writer (then in charge of party publicity) in the Cabinet room at Admiralty House to discuss it. No detail was too small for his consideration: he even revised the captions to some of the illustrations (this of course was the old publisher as well as the Prime Minister at work). But he was not well—he had not been well for several months, though very few knew it—and in fact he was contemplating his early retirement.

By September perhaps half a dozen people understood his intentions. He confided in his son, Maurice Macmillan, in his son-in-law, Julian Amery, in Timothy

Bligh, in Lord Poole, who in April had reappeared on the political scene as joint chairman of the party with Iain Macleod, and in Butler. Macleod, to all appearances and certainly in terms of political weight the senior partner in the strange condominium then reigning in the Conservative Central Office, was neither consulted nor informed. Nor—close though he had come to Macmillan in recent years—was Heath.

The provisional plan agreed in September was that Macmillan should attend the party conference at Blackpool in October, travelling (as usual) on the Friday in order to speak on the Saturday, and then, at the very end of an otherwise 'normal' speech, announce his decision to retire on 1 January 1964. By the end of the month, however, some of those in his confidence were having second thoughts, and they were urging him to say nothing of the sort at Blackpool. I believe, nevertheless, that Macmillan's own instinct was to go ahead as arranged and announce his impending retirement. But then, providentially as it were, another course was presented to him—and there was no longer any need to pursue the September plan. As the party conference was assembling at Blackpool on the night of Tuesday 8 October, the news came through that his illness had finally struck him down: the growth in his prostate gland was such that he must enter hospital at once for an immediate operation. Heath, in company with Macleod, was addressing the Tory agents. Like Macleod, he was shocked and distressed and quite taken aback. Only Poole (as I remember) seemed less surprised than others: it appeared that he knew rather more than his colleagues, had heard something earlier, and was better prepared both for what had happened and what was to follow.

What followed was of course the struggle for the Tory leadership—the last to be determined by what Macleod later called the 'magic circle'. Macmillan's first favourite was Lord Hailsham, whose succession had become practicable because of recent legislation enabling peers to renounce their peerages. But to very many members of the party, including some of the best and most influential, Butler, the deputy Prime Minister, seemed the right and natural, almost the lawful, heir. Some months previously, when ministers and others were considering the likelihood of an early change, Rab had intimated that he was no longer to be considered a candidate for the premiership because he felt that he could not reunite the party. His friends (I believe correctly) thought differently, and they persuaded him to think differently; and by the time of Macmillan's resignation he was again ready to accept nomination. So was Maudling. Macleod, too—though he rated his prospects as very slight and made little if any attempt to promote himself. Nor did the eventual successor, Lord Home. Unlike Lord Hailsham, Lord Home did nothing to further his own claims. On the contrary, he was sought out, appealed to, and in effect drafted, as reservations were expressed about the suitability of both Hailsham and Butler and as Maudling failed to make headway.

Heath was not a contender, but—like Macleod—he had support within the constituency associations. Lord Chelmer, chairman of the executive committee of the National Union, discovered this when, with Dame Margaret Shepherd, Sir John Howard, Sir Theodore Constantine and other officers, he conducted successive polls among constituency and area chairmen. It is significant that these inquiries produced (though at different stages) only six names in all: Hailsham, Home, Butler, Maudling, Macleod and Heath. Heath had the least support. All the same, he was there in the lists without having tried, as it were. Yet he was far from being among the most senior and established members of the Cabinet. On the other hand, however, he was already exceptionally well known in the constituencies. He had visited more than most of his colleagues; he was always a willing horse, ready to accept speaking engagements up and down the country. As a result, he knew many of the associations and their officers at first hand. This has long been an important aspect of Heath's strength in the party.

Heath himself supported Lord Home in the poll of Ministers conducted by the Lord Chancellor, Lord Dilhorne. No doubt there was an element of self-interest in his preference. If either of his contemporaries, Maudling or Macleod, had secured the succession, Heath could hardly have expected to rise above them in the future. If Butler had been chosen he would probably have remained leader of the party for a long time. Lord Hailsham was not to Heath's taste or temperament as leader. But he liked Lord Home; and Lord Home, moreover, seemed unlikely to present any lasting challenge to Heath's own ambitions, if only on grounds of age.

Having voted for Home, it was natural that he should accept office in his administration—unlike Macleod and Enoch Powell, who refused to serve in the Home Government. Macleod there and then also resigned his co-chairmanship of the party. Lord Aldington, who, after being deputy chairman, had become special assistant to the joint chairmen, Macleod and Poole, also decided to call it a day. So did Lord Poole—but overnight he was persuaded to change his mind, on learning that the new Prime Minister intended to appoint John Hare chairman of the party. Hare, who shortly afterwards became Lord Blakenham, was an old friend and the brother-in-law of Lord Poole's business associate, Lord Cowdray. Poole therefore decided to stay on to assist him, assuming the rank of deputy chairman.

Heath's new and somewhat resounding role was that of Secretary of State for Industry, Trade and Regional Development and President of the Board of Trade. The first was a newly-created office designed to implement a policy of coordinated regional development throughout the country instead of the piecemeal and sometimes inconsistent development of the past. Heath was pleased with his new appointment. In the European negotiations he had acquired a first-hand knowledge of trade and industry at home and abroad, both public and private, and he was well-equipped for the post.

During the previous winter, Macmillan had asked Lord Hailsham, as Lord President of the Council, to make a survey of the North-East. His report, *The North East: A Programme for Regional Development and Growth*, was published in November, a month after Home (by now Sir Alec Douglas-Home) became Prime Minister. There was another White Paper on the development of Central Scotland, and shortly afterwards one on South-East England. All these and several other studies that were put in hand—on the West Midlands, on the North-Western region and on parts of the West Country—now came before Heath. He implemented the first two— the second in conjunction with the Secretary of State for Scotland. He has since (in an article in *Crossbow* in January 1965) described his approach to his new work:

When we started on the policy of regional development as a whole, we were faced with a number of problems. First, to think out a basic philosophy for it. Secondly, to establish the organisation necessary to handle it. Thirdly, to obtain the personnel with qualifications suitable for this work. Fourthly, to seek out the statistical basis for the formulation of policy. None of these things existed fifteen months ago and our first task was to create them. Our philosophy can be described in the three purposes we set ourselves: to develop the resources of a region whilst maintaining its own characteristics; second, to secure a more even spread of the economy over the whole country in order to enable it to operate at a higher level without strain in any particular area; third, to create a way of life appropriate to each region so that those born there would prefer to work and live there rather than emigrate, and others would be prepared to go there with their families, build up their businesses, and spend their lives there.

A fundamental aim of the new concept was to focus assistance on 'growth points'—selected areas with particular advantages for industrial expansion and growth, where the effects would spread out and encourage the development of the rest of the region. Another was to move away—for ever—from the policy of alleviating or curtailing unemployment by *ad hoc* measures and instead to generate long-term growth on a scale that would set these areas up for good.

Heath travelled the country. He went everywhere, acquainting himself with local industry, local leaders, local hopes, local prospects. In London, individuals and groups representing this or that regional interest were forever on his doorstep at the smart new offices in Victoria Street which housed both departments. Temperamentally, it was the sort of responsibility that suited him to perfection, for he is nothing if not an administrator.

He is a man who thrives on facts. Not for him the abstractions of political philosophy if he can have some hard statistical information instead.

Regional overlordship apart, he was engaged in all the established and traditional functions of the Board of Trade. He prepared legislation on monopolies, mergers and restrictive practices, though this could not be enacted before the Conservatives went out of office (the Labour Government subsequently adopted a somewhat similar Bill). Under his direction the Board also devised new safeguards for the consumer, embodied in the Hire Purchase Act, and important changes in company law designed to increase the accountability of companies to investors, creditors and the public at large. Abroad, at the United Nations Trade and Development conference in Geneva, he proposed or supported a number of initiatives, among them schemes for supplementary financing to help developing countries when their export earnings dropped as a result of long-term trends, for the re-scheduling of debt burdens with reasonable periods of grace and fair rates of interest, and for developing countries to apply a minimum amount of their own national income to helping the less-developed. In the House of Commons, Heath described this conference as 'the largest and most important ever held on international economic relations'.

It was by his abolition of Resale Price Maintenance, however, that he really left his mark on the Board of Trade and on the workaday business of household shopping and the cost of living. Many members of the Cabinet were not at all keen to disturb existing retail practices in the months before a general election. Nor were the leaders of the party organisation—not Lord Blakenham, not Lord Poole, and certainly not the officers of the National Union. Like many of the party in Parliament they were, on the contrary, vehemently opposed to a measure which was bound, they believed, to alienate the small shopkeeper and his vote. I have never myself heard a Cabinet Minister so much abused by his colleagues, so badly spoken of and so widely condemned in the party, as Heath was then. Yet he remained utterly convinced of the good sense, indeed the social necessity, of his policy. Without the support of one man he might not have been able to carry it through, however: Sir Alec backed him up in the committee that counted most of all, the Cabinet.

What Heath had done, in framing and fighting for his Resale Prices Act, was to attack the practice, a hundred years old, whereby a manufacturer fixed the price at which his goods could be resold. This practice had spread rapidly between the wars, when the 'branding' of commodities became more general. Resale Price Maintenance—R.P.M.—used to be enforced by collective boycott, when a group of manufacturers withheld supplies from a retailer accused of cutting prices, or by individual (and large) manufacturers. Collective boycott—or enforcement—was usually applied by trade associations, which had become very powerful, and in 1956, under the Eden Government, their wings were severely clipped by the Restrictive Trade Practices Act. Heath realised, however, that R.P.M. was still widespread. He was sure that it was a bad thing, he determined to extinguish it, and he decided to make its abolition one of his 'causes' in public life. He won through, and his Act received the Royal Assent in July 1964.

Of course the internal wrangle over R.P.M. had everything to do with the forthcoming general election.

When Sir Alec became Prime Minister in October 1963, he had a year at the most before seeking a dissolution: he was bound to go to the country by October 1964. During the first months of his Premiership some of his colleagues in the Cabinet were in favour of going earlier, in the spring. Maudling was one of them. Blakenham and Poole, however, the mandarins of the Central Office, were against it, and they were supported by such pillars of the organisation as Sir William Urton, the General Director, and Sir Michael Fraser of the Research Department. The Blakenham-Poole view prevailed, and it was decided to wait to the last minute. The wisdom of this decision is perhaps open to doubt, though when the general election did take place in October, the Tories only just lost.

Heath secured an exceptionally prominent role in the national campaign in this election. He appeared in four out of the party's five television broadcasts. He was not exactly an 'anchor man', but—accompanied by other Ministers—he was the one constant in the four broadcasts leading up to Sir Alec's solo performance at the end of the campaign. Maudling meanwhile took the daily press conferences at Central Office—though a few other Ministers joined him on occasion, rather in the nature of guest speakers. Originally, it was to have been the other way round: Heath at the daily press conferences, Maudling in every broadcast except the last. Heath liked the original plan, but Blakenham and Poole reversed it, preferring Maudling for the press conferences, no doubt because, as Chancellor, he was better armed against any fast bowling on economic and financial policy, both his own and Labour's.

Heath's part in the preparation of the four broadcasts took up a fair amount of his time, and—like other members of the Government—he was also carrying on with his ministerial duties throughout the campaign. Because Bexley is so close to London his constituents still saw plenty of him, however, and he was often accompanied by young Winston Churchill, Randolph's son, who was attached to him as a sort of A.D.C. He had three opponents: Leslie Reeves, Labour; Peter McArthur, Liberal; and—a phenomenon of the time— John Paul, a Conservative who had founded the Anti-Common Market League. In this four-cornered contest, Heath was returned with a much reduced majority of 4,589. Paul came bottom of the poll with 1,263 votes.

An election casualty whose misfortune directly affected Heath was Butler. Not that his beloved Saffron Walden had turned him out. But Rab had been suffering from what might perhaps be termed a weariness of the spirit. It was not to be wondered at, after the final rebuff to his hopes—and indeed to his high and legitimate claims—a year previously. He had ample cause for disenchantment. Then, in the course of a train journey a week before polling, he had spoken with some candour to the journalist George Gale of the *Daily Express*. Presciently enough, he foresaw that the result was going to be very close. 'We're running neck and neck,' he said. 'I shall be very surprised if there's much in it. . . . But things might start slipping in the last few days.' Asked about Sir Alec's praise for the 'young, dynamic' Heath, he said: 'That's interesting. I think Alec's a bit bored by him—not as a Minister, of course.' To the Lords Blakenham and Poole, these remarks seemed not only indiscreet, but damaging to the party's prospects (others—more objectively—were inclined to think that they didn't make the slightest difference to the result).

The outcome of it all, within a week of the election, was Rab's retirement from the party office that he prized above all: the chairmanship of the Research Department. This he had combined since 1945 with the chairmanship of the Advisory Committee on Policy. In the dual role he had become the principal architect of the party's post-war policies—and thereby, in great part, of its long electoral success. Nevertheless he was removed. A Central Office announcement, of doubtful propriety, said merely that Sir Michael Fraser, hitherto Director of the Research Department, was now to become deputy chairman of the party with special responsibility for that department. It did not say that Rab was out: but that is what it meant. Shortly afterwards, his demotion was complete, when he was superseded by Heath as chairman of the Advisory Committee on Policy. An illustrious reign at 24 Old Queen Street was over and Heath took possession of his room, the best in the house.

Chapter Eleven

Leader by Election

Hustle was the order of the day. Sir Alec and his colleagues on the Leader's Committee—the shadow Cabinet—recognised that, with a majority of only five, the Labour Government must be expected to go to the country again before very long. They were determined, when the time came, to present the electorate with a coherent set of policies freshly worked out under the spur of opposition. Not a moment was to be lost. With Blakenham's encouragement, Sir Alec chose Heath for the policy role in the belief that he would tackle it more energetically and single-mindedly than anybody else.

Heath meanwhile resumed his association with Brown, Shipley—but on a much grander level than before. His old friends at Founder's Court invited him on to their board. With his knowledge of European industry and commerce and his experience of the Board of Trade immediately behind him, he proved to be of considerable value to the bank, especially in its overseas business, in the months after the election. This was not the only invitation that he received. Joe Hyman offered him £25,000 a year to join Viyella. Heath was understandably attracted; he declined because he already had enough on his plate.

He gave most of his time to his new responsibility for the formulation of party policy. Within a month of his appointment he set about assembling a variety of policy study groups, and before he was through he established more than thirty, covering the entire range of national affairs. The groups were made up of M.P.s, a sprinkling of peers, and outside specialists; and each one was nominally a sub-committee of the National Advisory Committee on Policy. To an extent that the party had never previously contrived, Heath drew in experts or knowledgeable outsiders from many fields. He found little difficulty in enrolling them. In the aftermath of the Tory defeat there was no lack of willing recruits.

Nineteen groups were formed in the early months of opposition. Between them they were composed of 100 M.P.s, eight peers and about 114 non-Parliamentary members. The number of 'outsiders' varied from group to group, and a few had none. The one with the most—nineteen—was the group studying agriculture (chairman: James Scott-Hopkins), and this was because it split into seven sub-groups. Next came the Future Economic Policy group (chairman: Heath himself) with fourteen outsiders. The other fields and subjects covered by policy study groups in the early months of opposition were: Education and Careers Research; Crime; Consumer Problems; Defence; Foreign Affairs; Immigration; Land; Housing; Law Reform; Leisure; National Insurance and Health; Machinery of Government; Overseas Aid; Public Service Pensions; Rating; Technology; and Trade Unions. All the research, the collation of information, the confabulation and debate produced a huge proliferation of paper. Heath read the lot. Later he increased the number of policy groups, almost doubling the scope; and in addition (as we shall

(*Above*) Arriving at Church House, Westminster, for his formal adoption as Leader of the Conservative Party, 2 August 1965. (*Below*) With Edward du Cann and David Howell at Villefranche, August 1965

'PHONE - PAR 2523

"Riebaulx"

Biscobey,

Par,

Cornwall.

8/8/65

Dear Mr Heath,

Please accept my congratulations to you on the election of your son Edward to the Leadership of his Party. I can imagine your feelings of pride on his success as I underwent the same elation on my sons election as Leader of his Party a little over 2 years ago. I am afraid that in my case there is a difference of age of nine years as I am rapidly approaching 83 but even so its a great thrill to me to see & hear my son in the House of Commons. When I do so I look back on his years as a boy, a Boy Scout etc etc and remember with joy his youthful enthusiasm. You

Mr Herbert Wilson writes to Heath's father

see) he formed several uniquely high-powered committees to advise him personally.

Lord Blakenham, who wished to retire from the party chairmanship, had meanwhile been succeeded by Edward du Cann. Blakenham's last significant act as chairman was, after most careful reflection, to commend to Sir Alec a new method of selecting future leaders of the party. The unseemly squabble begun at Blackpool and concluded in London in 1963 had offended a lot of people. More than that, some were sceptical of the evidence which had been produced in support of the final choice, Lord Home. Lord Aldington, for one, had publicly challenged the arithmetic of the Government Chief Whip, Martin Redmayne. Then, provoked by the appearance of Randolph Churchill's tendentious, pro-Macmillan book, *The Fight for the Tory Leadership*, Iain Macleod had let fly in the *Spectator* (of which, at Ian Gilmour's invitation, he had become editor after declining to join the Home administration). This was one of the most riveting political articles of the decade, and Macleod too was at loggerheads with the Chief Whip. 'The truth,' said Macleod, 'is that at all times, from the first day of his Premiership to the last, Macmillan was determined that Butler, although incomparably the best-qualified of the contenders, should not succeed him. Once this is accepted, all Macmillan's actions become at least explicable. . . . That Butler is mystifying, complex and sometimes hard to approach, I would concede. But, on the other hand, he has the priceless quality of being able to do any job better than you think he will, and of attracting to himself wide understanding support from many people outside the Tory Party. And without such an appeal no general election can be won.'

Against this background, a good many M.P.s and others believed that the party ought to consider and lay down a standard and—as they thought—more democratic procedure for choosing its leader. One was Humphry Berkeley, the M.P. for Lancaster, who had in fact been advocating a change even before Macmillan's resignation.

On 1 January 1964, Berkeley had written to Sir Alec as follows:

Dear Prime Minister,

In March of last year, before the leadership of the Party was in dispute, I said in public that I felt that the Conservative Party should adopt a more formal method of choosing a Leader. The events of the Blackpool Conference and after have, in my view, emphasised this need and would have done so, whoever had emerged as Leader of the Party.

Since then, I have had many talks with our colleagues in the House, including senior members of the Government. I have discovered a widespread view that we should not continue with the present system, which, in any event, as practised a few months ago, bore little resemblance to what has been known as the customary process.

The fact that the Chief Whip felt obliged to reveal in public a part but not all of the results of his soundings is evidence of the misgivings which are felt about the present process throughout the Party.

No doubt there are different views as to what formalised system should be adopted. Some would advocate a secret ballot of Members of Parliament voting for openly competing candidates. Others might extend the electoral college by including representatives of the candidates, the National Union and Peers in receipt of the Party Whip. All these possibilities might be explored.

Would you consider, as Leader of the Party, setting up a small Committee to consider this matter, hear opinions and make recommendations? I am sure that the whole issue could be considered more calmly at a time when there is no likelihood of it having to be implemented for some considerable period.

Nothing which I have said, of course, implies any criticism of your Leadership of the Party.

May I take this opportunity of sending you every good wish for an outstandingly successful year.

Yours,
Humphry Berkeley

Acknowledging Berkeley's letter on 14 January, Sir Alec said: 'I am not averse to the idea of a private study of the methods which might be used on some future occasion, but I do not think that it would be wise to initiate this before the election. It would inevitably become known, and would then be taken as evidence of dissatisfaction with the present leadership—although I appreciate your assurance that it does not.' In conclusion, Sir Alec invited Berkeley to get in touch with him again later in the year.

Thanking the Prime Minister on 21 January, Berkeley intimated that he and his friends were 'all happy to leave the matter in abeyance until after the election'—though his letter added that the prospective study 'should not be so private as to prevent all interested parties from giving their views quite freely'.

There the proposal rested until after the general election in October, when the Tories went into opposition. But Sir Alec had not forgotten the subject and within three weeks—on 5 November—he informed a meeting of the 1922 Committee that he proposed to hold a review of the mechanism for choosing the leader of the party. Berkeley at once resumed his correspondence with Sir Alec. Though he was not the only private member to entertain hopes of change, he was more assiduous and articulate than anyone else in formulating and promoting his proposals, and on 9 December he submitted a memorandum to Sir Alec, which I reproduce as an appendix.

Sir Alec's principal confidants in all this were Lord Blakenham and the new Chief Whip, William Whitelaw. The upshot was the promulgation, in February 1965, of what was officially designated the *Procedure for the Selection of the Leader of the Conservative and Unionist Party*. Though not to everybody's taste, the new provisions undoubtedly appealed to many if not most Conservative M.P.s, who found it gratifying to reflect that from now on their votes, and their votes alone, would determine the party leadership. The procedure was officially expressed in thirteen points, and again the text is to be found as an appendix.

However pleasing to many M.P.s, there were misgivings in the National Union, whose officers felt that once the 'customary processes' were abandoned they too should have a direct and defined role in choosing the leader. Then there were some members of the party who thought that the new procedure should allow (as Labour's does) for annual re-election of the leader while in Opposition. I have asked Sir Alec about this. He tells me that he 'hadn't discussed it much or thought a great deal about it at the time. The thought was that once the party had elected a leader that was that, and it had better stay with him.'

Having acquired, by this innovation, such an exciting influence for the future, a good many M.P.s were keen to use it. Ill-judged or otherwise, criticism of Sir Alec was increasing, both in Parliament and in the party outside. While he was never lacking in supporters, it is also true to say that his critics were becoming more numerous. With the passage of Mr Wilson's 'first hundred days' the Tories grew more and more uneasy. Their mood was no doubt due in part to nothing nobler than resentment that Labour was in office at all. As a former leader once remarked to me, 'The Tories are awfully bad losers, you know. They've no generosity.'

To Disraeli, after a Tory defeat nearly a hundred years earlier, it had seemed that 'there are few positions less inspiriting than those of a discomfited party'. And as Harold Macmillan has observed in his memoirs, 'One of the melancholy aspects of Opposition, especially to anyone who has enjoyed high office and likes responsibility and power, is the sense of futility'. Impatience also had something to do with it: many M.P.s were anxious to batter the Wilson Government day in and day out, and they considered Sir Alec 'too nice', perhaps even too detached, for the fire-eating role in which they wished their leader to be cast. As the months passed, the murmurs of 'time for a change' took on a more determined tone.

Maudling, Macleod and Heath all had their advocates and supporters, as alternatives to Sir Alec. Hogg and Soames were also spoken of. By the spring, Heath knew that his own claims were being canvassed both vigorously and systematically in the Commons. His Parliamentary admirers were becoming more active and more open. The knowledge disturbed him. He saw their attentions at this moment as a mixed blessing, gratifying in one way, chilling in another—for Heath dreaded any suggestion that he was working against Sir Alec, to whom he had become attached. He shrank from any accusation of disloyalty. He sought out his old patron, Mr Macmillan, and told him how troubled he was.

Macmillan accepted Heath's assurance that he personally had done nothing to prompt or further the movement now developing in his favour. With the warmth of real conviction—he was quite fervent about it—Macmillan expressed the view that Sir Alec should on no account resign. To Sir Alec himself, who also went to see him, Macmillan said the same thing, begging him to 'stick it out'. Looking back today, he still has no doubt that this was the right advice. 'But,' as he said to me of Sir Alec not long ago, 'he's so generous—a lovely man.'

Perhaps Sir Alec lost the determination to continue because increasing public criticism of his leadership persuaded him that he might become a liability to the party. He is certainly not short of courage: but he is too sensitive, too honourable, ever to outstay his welcome. When the present editor of *The Times*, William Rees-Mogg, wrote in the *Sunday Times* in July that he should make way for someone else, Sir Alec was already proposing to go. Though he had grown tired of all the criticism, he could have put up with it on his own account, but he judged that it would continue if he stayed, with mounting damage to the party. Over a midsummer weekend the die was cast, and a few days later, at a meeting of the 1922 Committee on 22 July, Sir Alec announced his intention.

Sir William Anstruther-Gray was in the chair and about 200 members were present. Though some had been hoping to hear just this, and others feared it, everyone was electrified when he broke the news. Many were dismayed. Words attributed to Greville Howard, the Member for St Ives, 'We've been bulldozed into this by the Press', expressed a wider bitterness, and a feeling of shame and guilt that Sir Alec should have been driven to this. Macmillan, whose powers of persuasion had on this occasion failed, was sad when he heard the news. 'Yes,' says Sir Alec, 'Harold didn't want me to go. I was under very strong pressure from him and many others to stay on. If I'd been ten years younger [he was then sixty-two] I would have stayed on. But I really didn't see why, having been Prime Minister and Foreign Secretary and Commonwealth Secretary, I should struggle through five years or more of Opposition. It was best for the party, I think, that I resigned.'

To which he adds, with the endearing candour that sets him apart, 'I wish I'd never said that thing to Kenneth Harris [the *Observer* writer] about doing my arithmetic with matchsticks. I said it laughingly over the lunch table when he was interviewing me. I did say it and he showed it to me in typescript before he published it, but I didn't think much about it and I let it go. Of course Wilson strung it round my neck for ever more.'

Peter Emery, a former Parliamentary Private Secretary to Heath, was secretary of the 1922 Committee. It fell to him and his chairman, Sir William Anstruther-Gray, to receive the nominations in the contest which Sir Alec's decision immediately set in train. At first, nobody could be sure how many there might be. Besides Heath, Maudling and Macleod, who seemed certain runners, Hogg, Soames and Peter Thorneycroft were also expected, at one moment or another, to let their names go forward. Then Macleod, to the astonishment of some of his most ardent supporters, decided not to enter the lists. He calculated that he could not beat either Heath or Maudling, and he preferred to avoid

the contest. Hogg also remained on the sidelines, as did
Soames and Thorneycroft. In the event the only other
contender was Enoch Powell—and he was a late starter.
Nominations had to be in by 11.30 a.m. on Monday
26 July, for the first ballot to open twenty-four hours
later. Over the weekend the Chief Whip, William
Whitelaw, detected a strong feeling in the Parliamentary
party that there should be only two nominations, not
more. The Heath and Maudling camps were already at
work; but then Enoch Powell let it be known that he
too would be running.

A friend of mine in the Commons has described the
Heath and Maudling campaigns to me. 'Ted's camp
left nothing to chance,' he recalls. 'Everybody was
canvassed—everybody. Nothing was left undone. It was
a beautifully organised campaign run by Peter Walker
from H.Q. in Gayfere Street. They treated it like a war,
and they were determined to win. Reggie's campaign
was charming, easy-going, rather haphazard, very nice
—like the man himself. But his side got a lot of things
wrong. They were not fully organised. They took too
much for granted, and they made mistakes of a kind
that they ought not to have made.' Enoch Powell, who
needed nobody to tell him that he couldn't win (he knew
that perfectly well), was not the object of anything that
could properly be called a campaign: he was a loner
with just a few devoted friends behind him.

William Whitelaw and his Whips did not take sides
in any outward way. Each of them exercised his right
to vote as an individual, but as Whips they were all expected to avoid any open expression of preference. Hour
by hour, they were of course sizing things up: nobody was
better placed to judge the feeling in the House. Lord
St Aldwyn, the Opposition Chief Whip in the Lords, was

also taking soundings among Conservative peers—he consulted sixty-five of them. Within the National Union, Sir Clyde Hewlett, as chairman of the Executive Committee, spoke to the area chairmen and other officers. While neither the National Union nor the peers could have a direct say in the choice of leader it was nevertheless thought desirable, if only for reasons of tact, to know their views. Though the Lords expressed a slight preference for Heath, the upshot of all these inquiries was that most people, in the House of Commons and out of it, intimated that they would be equally happy with either Heath or Maudling. This suggested a very close contest and was gratifying to both camps—to such activists for Maudling as Robert Carr, Lord Lambton and Richard Stanley, and equally to Peter Walker, Robin Chichester-Clark and Anthony Kershaw, who were foremost in promoting Heath.

The result of the ballot stood up pretty well to the Whips' calculations. The figures, announced about two o'clock in the afternoon on Tuesday 27 July, were: Heath 150 votes, Maudling 133, and Powell 15. But the ballot was inconclusive because Heath had failed to secure the necessary 15 per cent lead—he had not received 15 per cent more of the votes cast than any other candidate. According to the rules there would have to be a second ballot. Then an hour later, having heard the outcome in the City, where—rather characteristically —he was lunching, Maudling decided to withdraw. Powell did the same. Thus the evening newspapers were able to report Heath's victory that day; and it was confirmed at 11.30 next morning when the second ballot closed and there was only one nomination—for Heath. Sir William Anstruther-Gray formally declared him the victor and his election was duly rubber-stamped at the ceremonial party meeting six days later. A total of 298 votes had been cast. There were then 304 Conservative M.P.s. William Whitelaw believes, however, that there were no abstainers: the six who did not vote were either too far away to present themselves at Westminster, or they were ill.

I personally think that Macleod let Heath in, for almost to a man his followers switched to Heath when Macleod decided not to run. If Macleod had stood he would not have won—the best estimate is that he would have received 45 votes. But he would have deprived Heath of such vital support that victory would in all probability have gone to Maudling. Macleod himself voted for Heath—and so, I believe, did Sir Alec, William Whitelaw, Sir Edward Boyle, Sir Keith Joseph and Anthony Barber.

No doubt Heath also gained from the movement which had developed in his favour earlier in the year, however much it was resented by some of Sir Alec's closest friends and admirers. Sir Alec has spoken to me about this. 'You can acquit him of any responsibility for the movement that was going on,' he says. 'I am absolutely clear that Ted Heath was not a part of it. Ted was very unhappy in case people thought that he was trying to undermine me. I am quite sure he was not.'

Though a National Opinion Poll published in the *Daily Mail* on the eve of the election had shown an overwhelming public preference for Maudling, Heath had received more editorial support from the newspapers. Both before and after the result he had an outstandingly good Press. 'The Tories have made the right choice,' said a *Daily Mirror* leader, under the heading 'The Man for the Job'. 'Faced with a difficult choice the Conservatives have decided to take a risk with Mr Heath rather than to play safe with Mr Maudling,' said the *Financial Times*. 'They have chosen their leading radical . . . he is most unusual among Conservative leaders, and his election should convince even the most sceptical that in the current Conservative Party ability counts for more than wealth or an inherited position.' 'Rightly or wrongly,' said the *Daily Telegraph*, 'a Maudling victory might have been construed as leaning slightly on the side of quietude and tradition. Mr Heath's may be construed as leaning slightly towards tough managerial pushfulness. . . . Mr Wilson as Prime Minister will find himself confronted with an opponent intellectually at least his equal and in rigorous consistency far his superior.'

Many newspapers also applauded the manner of the election—in which, as Walter Terry, the political editor of the *Daily Mail*, observed, 'outside influences did not play a major part'. To the *Mirror*, it seemed that the Tories had 'behaved with dignity as well as wisdom'. But the *Guardian* was something less than starry-eyed. Sir Alec, it said, had 'yielded to pressures within the party which were far weaker than those which Mr Macmillan resisted successfully for months during the Profumo affair in 1963. Sir Alec was obliged to go not because of anything dreadful he had done but merely because his back-benchers thought he was less good than Mr Heath. The back-benchers have had their way more easily and much more quickly than would have been imaginable under the old and customary procedures. Having decided, wrongly, to ignore Mr Butler in 1963 the Conservatives have now found a way of rectifying their mistake. If, however, they should presently find that they made another mistake yesterday, it will be far easier, this time, to remedy matters.'

Within a few days the Prime Minister's father, Mr Herbert Wilson, wrote to old Mr Heath. 'Dear Mr Heath,' he said in a charming letter from his home at Par in Cornwall, 'Please accept my congratulations to you on the election of your son Edward to the leadership of his party. I can imagine your feelings of pride on his success as I underwent the same elation on my son's election as leader of his party a little over two years ago. I am afraid that in my case there is a difference of age of some years as I am rapidly approaching eighty-three but even so it is a great thrill to me to see and hear my son in the House of Commons. When I do so I look back on his years as a boy, a Boy Scout, etc., etc., and remember with joy his youthful enthusiasms. You will undoubtedly have the same feelings at times. Trusting that you will have many years of good health to enjoy your son's success, I am, Yours very sincerely, J. Herbert Wilson. P.S. I rather enjoyed the photos and paragraph in the Telegraph the other day.'

Chapter Twelve

The Family Circle

At forty-nine, Heath was the youngest leader of the party since the office was created—for Disraeli—in 1868. Whether he would have secured the prize under the 'customary processes', admittedly variable, which produced his dozen predecessors must remain a subject of speculation. He might have done, bearing in mind that the outgoing leader wished him well. Commendation by Sir Alec would have carried great weight in the 'magic circle'. On the other hand, Sir Alec might not have wanted to assert a direct personal influence on the outcome: his invincible fair-mindedness and detachment might have inclined him to defer to his colleagues rather than express, much less promote, any preference of his own.

What can be said with certainty is that Heath was Sir Alec's beneficiary in that Sir Alec did adopt a system which, when put to the test, selected Heath. Heath has cause to be thankful for the innovation. The old method might have produced the same result: but it was under the new procedure that he did actually gain the leadership—and this is the fact that counts in assessing the value to Heath of the change which Sir Alec introduced. I have heard Heath suggest, albeit in a murmured aside, that for his part he wouldn't have minded if the 'customary processes' had been left alone. From this I conclude that he would have been equally happy to submit to them: whether he would have been equally successful in the outcome is surely open to doubt.

Heath was also the direct beneficiary of one of his political opponents, the Socialist Anthony Wedgwood Benn, whose determination to rid himself of an unwelcome peerage had important consequences for the Tory Party. Wedgwood Benn, on succeeding his father as Viscount Stansgate in 1960, at once set about attacking the law disqualifying peers from sitting in the Commons, of which he was a well-known and fairly successful member, representing Bristol South East. The Committee of Privileges upheld the existing prohibition, but Wedgwood Benn nevertheless decided to contest the by-election which his succession made necessary. Predictably, he won, but because of the law the seat passed to the Tory contender, Malcolm St Clair. Wedgwood Benn (or Lord Stansgate as he really was) did not leave it at that, however. He continued to pursue a most diverting personal campaign for reform, and he succeeded. The upshot was the Peerage Act, which came into force on 31 July 1963, and enabled peers to renounce their peerages. Wedgwood Benn was duly restored to his old seat and has since prospered exceedingly as a member of the Labour Government.

But for this timely change in the law Lord Hailsham and Lord Home could not have become eligible for the Tory leadership (and the Premiership) when Macmillan resigned less than three months later. On all the evidence, the succession would then have gone to Butler, to Maudling, or perhaps even to Macleod; and in that event (as I have suggested in an earlier chapter) it seems very unlikely that Heath could have gained such ascendancy in 1965. For the Tories, the effect of accommodating the reluctant Lord Stansgate was to replace Macmillan by one of the two peers whom he personally favoured as his successor. Perhaps it was just as well for Heath that things turned out as they did in 1963.

In social origin and background he would no doubt have seemed, only a few years before he was elected, an unlikely leader for the Tories. His predecessors were usually grand or rich or both. Of course the distinction depends to some extent on one's viewpoint or datum line. To some, the contrast is not as great as it appears to others.

I remember a conversation with Mr Macmillan as we sat by the fire in his study at Birch Grove House. 'Don't be fooled by this class thing,' he said. 'It's not as if all the leaders of the Tory Party were grandees. Most of them were nothing of the sort. Peel wasn't. [Peel led the Tories as Prime Minister before the office of Leader of the Party was created.]. Salisbury was. Disraeli certainly wasn't. Balfour was. Bonar Law wasn't. Austen Chamberlain wasn't. Baldwin wasn't. Neville Chamberlain wasn't. Churchill—well, Churchill was a special case altogether, half aristocrat and half American buccaneer. I wasn't. Alec was.' To which it might be added that, if not in wealth, then in education, in personal reputation, and in public (including military) service, Heath's record was as good as that of anyone who went before him. Some of his other qualities and claims have perhaps emerged from what I have already written, and I have more to say about them.

Heath's first act on becoming leader was to go off on holiday. It was by now the beginning of August, and his friends the Seligmans had previously invited him to join them at a house which they had taken in the South of France. He had a happy fortnight, swimming, sailing and working on papers in between times. For Nancy Joan Seligman, however, it was something less than the restful family holiday which she had planned, with journalists and photographers for ever on her doorstep and party officials turning up to do business with the new leader. As always, she and her husband accommodated themselves to the pressures on their old friend—and of course the Seligman children loved all the to-do.

The papers on which Heath was working intermittently during his Mediterranean holiday included the reports and recommendations of the various policy groups which he had set up before becoming leader. These had all been delivered to him by July and had now to be translated into some statement of policy for the party conference at Brighton in October. The result was 'a pamphlet entitled *Putting Britain Right Ahead*, carrying Heath's signature and summarised in these words:

We believe that new policies and energetic action are needed in particular at five points:

1 We must open up new opportunities for merit, talent and individual enterprise, and we must change the tax system to provide new incentives.

2 We need fresh policies to create a more competitive climate in industry and commerce, to speed up the reform of management at all levels and to re-adjust our agricultural support system.

3 We need an entirely new approach to manpower problems. In the years ahead we face an increasing demand for labour. Employment prospects must be

transformed, the trade unions' responsibilities redefined and restrictive labour practices eliminated.

4 We must make our social and community services more humane, more efficient, and better geared to people's real needs.

5 We must pursue a policy which will enable Britain to become a member of an enlarged European Community. Technological advance is making nonsense of national boundaries. Britain's future lies in a larger grouping and that grouping should be the Europe of which the Common Market is already the nucleus.

This was the essence of his first declaration of policy as leader of the party. Since those heady summer days in 1965 his policies have developed—in number, in detail, in scope. In his relationships with the party and with the larger electorate he has had his ups and downs. In coming pages I will give some account of these and other aspects of his public life while describing the private person too—his personal tastes, his likes and dislikes, his ways, his arrangements, his friends. So far, I have taken his career in chronological order, but from now on I shall look at Heath in various contexts or compartments.

The strain, both physical and nervous, imposed on the leader of a great political party, in or out of office, is nowadays quite staggering; it is enough, I should suppose, to kill or cripple most of us. Heath's term as leader of the Conservative Party has been unusually arduous and exacting—partly because of the circumstances in which he was elected, partly because of its length in opposition, and partly because he has made it so. Yet he remains very fit, and this is because he has regulated a strong constitution by eating and drinking the right things and otherwise looking after his health.

In 1959, Heath had jaundice and was laid up in King Edward VII's Hospital for Officers. It was a setback that made a strong impression on him. Immediate discomfort and inconvenience aside, he saw it as an obstacle to political ambition. Lying in 'Sister Agnes's' he realised, as a friend puts it, that 'he couldn't afford to be ill' if he were to attain the heights and hold them. Not that he had ever suffered much in the way of ill-health: measles and chickenpox as a child, appendicitis during the war—a medical record too sound to be anything but dull.

Though there is nothing of the valetudinarian about him, he has adopted a personal regimen that he follows as closely as the demands of his public life will allow. For one thing, he tends to overweight, unless he controls his diet and takes systematic exercise.

Today, with his 'comfortable' yet compact figure, good and usually sun-tanned colour, clear blue eyes and strong grey hair, he looks just what he is—a man of middle years in excellent physical condition. He stands 5 ft 10½ in and he weighs, in his own words, 165 lb—or, as most Englishmen would express it, 11 stone, 11 lb. He likes to have about seven hours' sleep ('I can sleep anywhere, in the car or on a plane: I can catnap'). Every morning, for eleven minutes, he does some of the now fashionable exercises prescribed by the Royal Canadian Air Force. In winter, when he is in London, he tries to find time for a little swimming in the evening. During the summer, at his father's seaside home, he swims and walks; and of course he has become a keen yachtsman.

'I don't drink much before meals,' he says. 'I very seldom drink sherry nowadays, and I haven't drunk gin since 1941—I just dislike it. I drink whisky—malt whisky for preference. I rarely drink port and I don't drink brandy. What I most enjoy is wine—Moselle and claret, and I like champagne.' Heath never smokes. He has a good appetite. For breakfast he always has half a grapefruit, a boiled egg, and China tea with lemon. 'I like simple food', he says. 'Yes,' his stepmother agrees, 'he likes plain things. If I try to make an elaborate sauce he doesn't want it. He likes roast lamb and he likes chicken, but plainly cooked, and he likes steak and kidney pie.' He also has a taste for chocolate biscuits at tea-time and with his mid-morning coffee (which he takes without sugar, in a small cup).

Heath is always well turned out. He has a Savile Row tailor and a preference for grey suits, invariably single-breasted. His shirts and shoes are ready-made but good. Though for many years he has maintained the public man's 'complete wardrobe'—two suits of evening clothes, morning clothes, short black jacket and striped trousers, top hat, bowler, the lot—his inclination is towards informality. Indoors, if there is no reason to dress more formally, he usually goes about in light linen trousers and a beach shirt.

Heath is comfortably off. Until about six years ago he lived, if not austerely, certainly much more modestly than he does today, in a small service flat not far from the Passport Office in Petty France, and he was able to save from his Ministerial salary. 'I have had to save because I started with no capital. Everything I have has come from my saving.' His savings have been well invested; he entrusted them to good advisers. 'Being in Government for nearly thirteen years, I left it to others

153

to do. It would not have been right for me to do it myself, and anyway there wasn't the time.' While he is not rich, he has accumulated enough capital for him to feel independent, whatever happens. Besides this, and the income from it, he has his salary of £4,500 a year as Leader of Her Majesty's Opposition, plus £1,250 of his Parliamentary pay.

His London home in Albany, the unique and elegant eighteenth-century apartments (or 'sets of chambers') off Piccadilly, provides evidence of material success. He rents his set from Peterhouse, Cambridge, who own several others as well. It comprises drawing-room, dining-room, study, bedroom, bathroom and kitchen, arranged on two floors, and above there is a small flat for his housekeeper.

Heath engaged an interior decorator, Mrs Jo Pattrick, when he took the Albany apartment. His own tastes and interests are apparent, however, in the mass of military prints and old engravings of the coastal towns of Kent, in the paintings (among them a woodland scene by Winston Churchill, who made him a present of it, and a recent Piper landscape), in the Scandinavian glass and furniture of the dining-room, in the Steinway grand piano and the delicate stereophonic equipment encased along one wall of the drawing-room. The rooms are light and airy with high ceilings. Nearly all the furniture is modern—the dark grey-green sofas in the drawing-room, the black leather chairs and huge desk in the cluttered study, the oval dining table built to his own specifications. The rooms in which he spends most time—the bedroom, with double bed, purple carpet and small table at which he usually takes breakfast—and the drawing-room and the study are grouped together; the others are on the upper floor.

It is an attractive flat; all the more so because it is not oppressively neat and tidy.

He likes to add to his possessions by buying things in antique shops as he goes about the country. Not long ago he bought a set of English dessert plates in Aberdeen. The owner of the shop offered it to him 'at the Queen Mother's price—you know the Queen Mother is always buying things here'. 'I'd rather have Queen Mary's price', said Heath—and saved himself 25 guineas.

The family home at Broadstairs, where his father lives, is in considerable contrast to Albany. No. 4 Dumpton Gap Road is a pleasant detached house, built in 1950, with a garage at the side. Old Mr Heath has called it Helmdon, the name of his previous home. The upper part of the brick facade has been plastered and painted white, and Helmdon, with its leaded windows, stands behind a high hedge in a trim, well-planted garden. The lawn is immaculate, and around it, in the summer, the flower beds are bright with roses, petunias and geraniums. Not that Edward Heath does any gardening: 'He might pick a dead rose off sometimes,' says his father. From the upstairs windows you can see the Channel, two or three hundred yards away. Down through the gap in the cliffs from which the road takes its name is a good bathing beach. This is a mile or so from the centre of Broadstairs; and if you walk along the cliffs in the other direction you come to Ramsgate.

After the death of his first wife, the mother of Edward and John, Mr Heath remarried. When his second wife died he married again. Now he lives at Dumpton Gap with his third wife, Mary, who comes from Cheshire. In the sitting-room, with its chintz covers and framed photographs of Edward Heath (sometimes accompanied by members of the family), is old Mr Heath's newest toy—a colour television set, 'a present from Teddy' on his eightieth birthday in 1968. But no piano for the musician in the family: 'We haven't got one now,' says Mr Heath. 'When we came to this house we gave it away.'

Across the hall is a small dining-room (fitted carpet, modern teak table and chairs) which, as Mrs Heath puts it, 'becomes the Central Office when Teddy is here. We leave all his papers just where they are when he is out for a walk or a sail in his boat. There are papers on the table, papers on the floor, papers everywhere. We close the door, and nothing is touched.' At Helmdon, Edward Heath is without a study. His belongings are all in his bedroom, one of three in the house. It is a simple, crowded room overlooking the garden at the back: single bed, child's basket chair at the side (a relic of his own childhood), tallboy with a photograph of Churchill on horseback and wearing a square bowler, in a corner a clutter of fishing rods, beach shoes and other seaside gear, on a shelf a Japanese wireless set shaped like a globe and a bottle of Vichy water, and along one wall four rows of books.

Facially, Edward Heath is strikingly like his father, a similarity accentuated, I daresay, now that they are both grey-haired. But the father is smaller, both shorter in height and more lightly built. He is a neat, quick, alert old man, who seems twenty years younger than his age—an impression which is heightened by his informal taste in clothes (dark green open-neck shirt, say, light linen trousers). He is fond of a good cigar (boxes of Romeo y Julieta in the sitting-room) and a glass of sherry, and he rolls his own cigarettes. Mrs Heath is a kindly, responsive person, tall, slim and younger than her stepsons. Edward Heath is always in touch with them both, wherever he may be, at home or abroad. He rings up, he sends cables and cards and presents. He is at Broadstairs pretty well every other weekend, and in the long summer recess he has two or three weeks with them.

'We fit in with his arrangements,' says Mrs Heath. 'He comes and goes as he pleases and has his meals when he wants them. One Saturday morning, after a particularly worrying period, he went out and came back saying: "I've brought you a present, Mary." It was that record *Thank you very, very much*.' Heath goes for walks along the cliffs with the family dog, Maggie May, and he watches television. 'I like anything connected with current affairs,' he says, 'and a certain amount of sport. Anything which is *good* entertainment—though most of it is appalling. I dislike watching orchestras on TV, but I like individual soloists. Ballet and opera, I think, don't come off on TV.'

They are a united family, and since the war nothing has ever prevented Heath from being present at his father's birthday party. 'I was born on 11 October 1888,' says Mr Heath, 'but we always celebrated my birthday on 10 October because somehow my birth certificate got mislaid and the real date was not established till 1967.' There is usually a party for a dozen people, and nowadays, besides John Heath and his wife and other members of the family, it invariably includes Lord and Lady Aldington, who drive over from their house above the Romney Marsh.

Toby Aldington, formerly Sir Toby Low, Conservative M.P. for Blackpool North, and his wife Araminta are two of Heath's greatest friends. Like his father, 'Punch' Low, his grandfather and his great-grandfather before him, Aldington is the chairman of Grindlays Bank. He is also the chairman of the General

Electric Company (more often identified with its managing director, Arnold Weinstock) and a director of the English China Clay Company and other blue chips of British industry. He is a wiry, very active man, always darting about, busy, yet thoughtful, even studious, and radical in outlook. The Aldingtons are both inclined to be blunt; they are as much in Heath's confidence as anyone. Araminta Aldington sings, and when Heath is visiting The Knoll Farm, their house at Aldington, he often accompanies her on the piano. Sometimes, usually on a Saturday evening, he goes out to dinner with them at the Wife of Bath at Wye, a village near Canterbury, or to a restaurant at Littlebourne. Edward Denman and his wife Joy are quite likely to join them.

Edward Denman is a City insurance broker who was at school with Heath. He lives at Broadstairs, just along the road from the Heaths, and goes up to London every day on the train. This is handy for Edward Heath when he is spending a few weeks at Broadstairs: Denman acts as courier, taking papers up and down.

'Old Mr Heath and Mary have now started calling me Edward,' says Denman. 'I have been known as Teddy all my life, but it is getting too confusing now, never knowing which Teddy they are referring to when we are both in the house.' Edward Denman, six years younger than Heath, is Commodore of the Royal Temple Yacht Club, and they have often been out sailing together. Until Heath acquired a 34-ft racing cruiser, *Morning Cloud*, in 1969, he kept two boats at Broadstairs: *Blue Heather*, a glass-fibre racing dinghy, and *White Heather*, a motor boat. Having moved into the big league with *Morning Cloud*, he has now sold *Blue Heather*, which Denman used to store in his garage

every winter, till it went down to the harbour at
Easter. *White Heather* is a speedboat with a 100
m.p.h. outboard motor, 'used for fun', as Denman
puts it, but with a rescue purpose as well. When
Heath was still sailing his small yacht the motor boat
was always at hand to fetch him in if he capsized
or was in any other sort of trouble. 'It has happened
more than once,' says Denman.

From time to time, members of his political staff
have to go down to the family home at Broadstairs to
see Heath on business, but invitations are otherwise
confined to just a few personal friends. Among them is
Thelma Cazalet Keir, the former Conservative M.P.
who (as we have seen) was short-listed with Heath at
Sevenoaks in 1947. She and her husband, David Keir,
who died in 1969, were first introduced to Heath by
Patrick Buchan-Hepburn and his wife. Until recently
they had a beautiful house near Sevenoaks—Raspit,
now the home of Malcolm MacDonald. Over the years,
Heath has been a frequent visitor to Raspit, sometimes
breaking his journey there as he drove down to
Broadstairs from London or Bexley, and to the Cazalet
Keir flat in Eaton Square, with its splendid collection
of paintings—Augustus John much to the fore. Mrs
Cazalet Keir is a great favourite of old Mr Heath, as
was her husband, who was a writer and had been a
political journalist before their marriage.

Robert and Maureen Allan are two others whose
personal friendship with Heath, like that of the
Aldingtons, had its origin in the House of Commons.
Bobby Allan, a director of several companies in the
Cowdray constellation, used to be the Tory M.P. for
Paddington South. He was in the Whips' office with
Heath, then he became Parliamentary Private Secretary

to both Eden and Macmillan and later a junior Minister. He has also been a party treasurer. The Allans live in Kensington and have another house in Hampshire, where they farm. Heath feels very much at home in their company and is fond of them both.

But of all his friends, it is Madron Seligman, I suppose, who for many years has been closer to him than anyone else. The friendship begun at Balliol before the war has never lapsed. Heath has known Nancy Joan Seligman almost as long and (needless to say) he is godfather to one of their children. All the Heaths—his father, brother John and their wives as well—are devoted to the Seligmans. Heath is often to be found at Ridge Farm, their old house at Capel, near Dorking. Madron Seligman, a cultured, kindly, open-minded man, is the export director of a company making dairy equipment and other things for farmers. He and his wife are musical, and on summer evenings they sometimes join Heath at Glyndebourne, perhaps with Moura Lympany, the pianist, who is another friend.

Heath has a lot of friends and acquaintances among professional musicians. I once asked him who they all were, and he replied: 'You could say Sir Arthur Bliss, Dr Herbert Howells, Isaac Stern, Leonard Bernstein, Carlo Maria Giulini, Moura Lympany, George Malcolm (who was also a musical scholar with me at Balliol). Then there are people like Sidney Watson, the organist in the cathedral at Oxford, Thomas Armstrong, who has just retired as principal of the Royal Academy of Music, the Glyndebourne people, and David McKenna.' As chairman of the trustees of the London Symphony Orchestra, and a member of the council of the Royal College of Music, he knows everyone on those bodies, too.

Though Heath invariably pays an autumn visit to the very rich Lord Margadale (an old Parliamentary friend as Major John Morrison, chairman of the 1922 Committee) on the island of Islay, where in 1968 he caught his first salmon, he seldom stays at the 'grand' houses frequented by some of his predecessors in the Conservative Party. However well-off some of his closest friends may be, their lives and arrangements are in the mould of the established upper middle-class business or professional family. They are, as it were, the latter-day Forsytes of this world. Heath would rather have this than the sort of ducal establishment in which higher society can still try to beguile the leader of the party. I know (but not from him) of more than one occasion when he has been invited to stay at very grand houses and has politely declined, though it might have been convenient to accept, as he was obliged to spend a night or two in the neighbourhood. Instead, he preferred to go to a hotel. 'As I'm out at meetings till eleven at night on my provincial tours,' he says, 'and off again at eight in the morning, I'd be a very poor guest.'

As I see him, Heath is an unusually self-sufficient person. To an extent that is probably rare, he does not depend on others, even close friends: while he is glad to see them, they are not essential to him. He is self-contained, detached, reserved. Though sensitive, he is not spontaneous. Nor is he good at small-talk. It may be, as one or two of his most intimate friends believe, that at heart he is a romantic—but bottled in. He never really lets his hair down. He is above all a doer. Though these characteristics may tend to isolate him, they must also insulate him against at least some of the personal stresses attaching to political leadership.

When he is playing or conducting or listening, he is entirely absorbed in the music, quite removed from anything else. His musical tastes may be described as educated, broad and tolerant. The annual carol concert which he established at Broadstairs as an undergraduate and still conducts—last year's was the twenty-sixth—is one of the simpler elements. Asked about his likes and preferences, he says: 'They cover a very wide range, especially as far as listening is concerned. Playing, as far as the organ goes, is really based on Bach and on some contemporary English composers—those who've followed on from Parry. On the piano—which I play nearly every day—it's most likely to be Beethoven, Bach, Schubert, Chopin. As to listening, well, the stereo covers the whole range: there's very little which isn't there. Yes, it includes a certain amount of jazz and pop music—mostly pop.' In the pop field he likes the Beatles: 'They're good on the beat side; they have great rhythmic ingenuity, they're very skilled'.

Last year he attended the Three Choirs Festival in Worcester Cathedral (staying nearby with Peter Walker and his wife). 'On the first evening we had the great *Missa Solemnis* of Beethoven. The impact spiritually is immense.' And, as he said afterwards in a radio interview, 'It's also an intellectual satisfaction because I've been trained in music and I therefore understand the structure'. The technicalities of composition and performance always interest him.

He has a good eye for paintings, too, and seldom misses an important exhibition. He reads incessantly, but mostly for information on current affairs. Though his study is cluttered with new books, biography and memoirs, political works of all sorts (often presented to him by their authors), 'one looks,' he says, 'for the things one wants. There is not enough time to read them all through.' He seldom even looks at a novel. In the past year he has been to the theatre twice—to see *Fiddler on the Roof* and *Hair*. He has seen one film, *The Mad Woman of Chaillot*, and that was at a private showing to which he was invited by Bryan Forbes, who made it.

Now that he is so much taken up with his expensive new boat (it cost him £7,000) he will presumably have less time than ever for other pursuits. There is no doubt that in a surprisingly short time he has become a very accomplished yachtsman. Though he had been messing about in boats for some years, and doing well enough in local regattas along the Kent coast, it was all small stuff until, a bare twelve months ago, he launched himself and his new racing cruiser, *Morning Cloud*, into serious ocean sailing. When the *Financial Times* hailed his success at the end of last year in the Sydney to Hobart race, one of the four yachting classics in the world, as a 'remarkable achievement', it expressed a universal reaction. Heath returned to London in mid-January exhilarated by his victory; and one would have had to be a recluse to miss its importance to him in terms of public feeling. 'Mr Heath has given proof,' said *The People*, 'of possessing one of the qualities that voters most admire': and the opinion polls, reflecting something of that response to a winner, at last began moving in Heath's favour.

It was, as somebody said, 'a triumph of grey matter over the rules of the Royal Ocean Racing Club'. In the months beforehand, Heath and his crew had studied all the rules in detail, taking in the fine print, as it were, and then having the boat adapted to the utmost advantage. Among other things, they increased the sail area and put in a 'stringer', a set of steel rods running round the hull, which produced a gain in speed. In the 600-mile race, the first to be won by a British entrant since 1945, they kept well out to sea, unlike many of their competitors, who stayed nearer the coast—where navigation is easier, but the wind is more likely to desert you. This was the tactical decision that counted most of all. Having taken it, neither gales nor whales could stop them.

I have asked Heath what it is that most appeals to him in sailing. Is it a sense of freedom out at sea, of welcome withdrawal from everyday experience, or has it more to do with the challenge to skill? 'It's absolutely different from anything else one does,' he says. 'Because of this it's an excellent form of relaxation: it does absorb you completely in another direction. And third it's a great contest—we always race, we never cruise— in which one engages so many different faculties. There's so much judgment involved, you're dealing with elements which are constantly changing. At the same time, you've got an important human element with a crew of six. And all the time you're going out to win.'

Chapter Thirteen

Method and Manner

Elated though he was by his rise to the party leadership, Heath recognised the trials ahead of him in July 1965, and he was troubled. It would be extravagant to suggest that he was unnerved, or thrown off balance, by his new responsibilities, but it would not be too much to say that he was unsure of himself: he was edgy, suspicious, prickly. While a lot of Tories wanted him, a lot did not. Whatever his personal qualities, he lacked many of the 'natural'—that is conventional or 'expected'—advantages of a Tory leader. Now he had to establish himself and his credentials, not only with Conservatives up and down the country but with the electorate at large. He had to communicate, to develop a relationship, with a nation in good part far removed in their workaday lives from his own cosy little hometown, from the dormitory which is his constituency, and from the House of Commons.

That is one side of the ledger—or part of it. But then Heath came to the leadership of his party with his own set of advantages, some of them peculiar to himself. For one thing, he had acquired a grip on policy of every kind. For another, he knew the party structure and its workings better than any leader since the war. (These are two respects—perhaps the only two—in which he may be likened to Chamberlain.)

Since the Tory defeat in 1964, he had been carrying special responsibility for policy. He knew the Parliamentary party inside out. More than that, he knew the party in the country, its local leaders and officers, lions and lame dogs alike, because he had met so many of them. Perhaps his own background had something to do with this originally: as neither Broadstairs nor Bexley can be called mirrors of Britain, he has had to enlarge his knowledge of the country by going about a lot. This he has done more than most. He has always been ready to accept speaking engagements in the constituencies, and at summer schools, week-end conferences, and suchlike seminars.

But there is more to it than that. For the Common Market negotiations, he was obliged to acquaint himself with every industry in the country, and to study the complexities of our agricultural system. Then, as President of the Board of Trade and Secretary of State for Industry, Trade and Regional Development, he was again immersed in industrial policy. For one reason and another he has acquired an exceptional knowledge of commercial and industrial affairs—and of the people who conduct them. His network of personal connections throughout the business world is very striking. A colleague of his put it this way: 'He has developed many friendships among leaders of industry and commerce. They are nearly always what might be called the better end of management—really intelligent, hard-working, modern-minded people who feel that in Heath they have someone who understands the problems of large-scale industry in the modern world.'

'Mr Heath's function,' said Quintin Hogg in a

Sunday Express article shortly after the leadership contest, 'is to raise the status of the Opposition to that of an alternative government. For this he needs not only the formidable debating powers which he showed in the Finance Bill but the ability to project a broad picture of Conservatism acceptable to the country as a whole.' To many a Tory stalwart in the constituencies the 'alternative government' seemed already poised for office. The close verdict of 1964, then the sensational Labour defeat in the Leyton by-election, had encouraged the sort of false optimism to which party zealots are often prone. It was soon dispelled. In the general election of March 1966, the Labour Government, in the greatest landslide since 1945, increased its majority to 97 overall. Heath had been leading the Tories for eight months. Now he knew for certain that they faced a long, long stretch in Opposition. (His own majority at Bexley, against both Labour and Liberal opponents, was 2,333.)

Yet it was generally agreed, not only by his own entourage but by journalists who saw something of his campaign, that he had done well. As Ian Trethowan wrote in *The Times* much later (in 1968), looking back on Heath's record, 'In so far as it can be said of any politician who leads his party to thumping defeat, he had a "good" election. He visibly matured. His speeches got a bit better (as well they might!), he handled himself passably on television, and he was effective at his regular press conferences. He has never been a particular favourite of journalists (he can be distinctly prickly) but during this campaign they rather warmed to him, and never more so than when he conceded defeat with good grace.'

In a neatly expressed passage, Trethowan went on

to examine Heath's policy statements and subsequent events:

In probably his best speech of the campaign—at Glasgow— he gave this warning about the state of the economy: 'The threat we are facing today is the greatest that any nation can face short of war itself. Unless we take action to avert it, we are faced with the threat of national bankruptcy.' Labour instantly condemned this as alarmist. Four months later we had the crisis of July 20, to be followed in due time by devaluation. The tocsin rang truer than those who denounced it. Then against all likelihood, Mr Heath managed to get a fair amount of election mileage out of his own pet issue—Europe. We must, he said, accept the Treaty of Rome. Certainly not, said Labour—and a year later were doing just that. We must, said Mr Heath, talk with Ian Smith. No, said Labour—within months were doing just that. We must, said Heath, bring back prescription charges. Inhuman, said Labour—and the charges are now back. There was, said Mr Heath, a danger of higher unemployment. No more than seasonal, said Mr Wilson—and within months he was putting it up deliberately.

In his first and second years there is no doubt that Heath's attempts to consolidate his leadership were handicapped by one issue—Rhodesia—and by his inability to cope with Harold Wilson in the House of Commons.

On Rhodesia, the Tories had opposed U.D.I. while in office and they were committed to the six principles. Heath and the shadow Cabinet remained true to the convictions that had guided them previously, but this hardly endeared them to their own right-wing. Even Sir Alec Douglas-Home, generous as always in support of his successor, could not save Heath from criticism. Nor was Heath shining, whatever the subject, in his tussles with the Prime Minister across the floor of the House. On the contrary, Mr Wilson was for ever knocking him about. Lacking Wilson's skill (in part natural, in part acquired) in the parliamentary rough-and-tumble, Heath was trying to do too much, because he was over-anxious. The Prime Minister was meanwhile riding high after the 1966 election. Heath rose all too readily to his often deadly bait —and time after time he was punished. He has never found it easy to relax in the face of provocation.

All this was disquieting to many Tories, in and out of the House. Though I doubt if Heath was ever in danger of desertion by any of his colleagues in the shadow Cabinet, some were uneasy about him. Many of his personal friends and followers certainly thought and said, in 1966 and 1967, that he deserved more outward support than some members of the shadow Cabinet were then displaying. The chairman of the party and others in the Central Office were conscious of this criticism. And though the Greater London Council elections in April 1967 provided a tonic for the Tories, their leader continued to trail behind the party in the public opinion polls.

One aspect of Heath's attitude to political leadership was summed up by John MacGregor, the former head of his private office: 'All along, he has always said "Let's avoid committing ourselves on anything until we know all the facts, every single one"'. His arrangements are designed to satisfy this thirst for information— and to provide a workmanlike basis for well-briefed and orderly deliberation with his colleagues.

As leader of the party, Heath deploys a considerable apparatus. He has at his service the resources of the Conservative Research Department, with a staff of no less than sixty-four, which may become even larger in the approach to a general election, and of the Central Office, with 135 in London and almost as many—about 120—in its eleven area offices. The Central Office, it should be remembered, is by its constitution the political office of the party leader, not of the National Union, and he himself appoints its principal officers— the chairman, the deputy chairman, the various vice-chairmen and the treasurers. But it does of course service the entire party. Heath has a personal staff of eleven, not counting his two Parliamentary Private Secretaries.

His expenses as leader of the party (but not as M.P. for Bexley) are met by the treasurers: he is able to draw whatever he needs for party political purposes. Travel and entertaining account for most of this outlay.

The head of his private office—which has its physical centre in the heavy, panelled room assigned to the Leader of the Opposition in the House of Commons—is Douglas Hurd, who succeeded John MacGregor, incidentally an accomplished conjurer, when the latter went off to better himself in the City. Hurd is the son of Lord Hurd, a former Conservative M.P. He is a novelist among other things, and very hard-working. He resigned from the Foreign Service because he wants to go into Parliament one day. He is, so to speak, the political element in the private office as well as its head. Cyril Townsend, a young man who was previously an Army officer, is responsible for office administration and Heath's travel arrangements, which are often complicated. Steven Dolland, with three girls to help him, looks after the heavy 'public correspondence': Heath receives 250 to 300 letters a week from members of the public. Miss Iris Jollye is the engagements secretary, keeping the diary; and there are three girls doing general secretarial work. All these are a charge on the party. Heath's personal secretary, Miss Rosemary Bush, is not. She takes care of constituency as well as personal affairs and Heath pays her out of his own pocket. His Parliamentary Private Secretaries are James Prior, M.P. for Lowestoft, and Anthony Kershaw, M.P. for Stroud, who was a contemporary of Heath's at Balliol. They are of course unpaid; for both, this service entails a sacrifice of time and income.

In discussion, Heath likes to be anchored to an agenda: not for him, if he can avoid it, the discursive stuff, the unmapped *tour d'horizon* so dear to Mr Macmillan. Thus the meetings of the shadow Cabinet, reflecting his own preference, tend to be fairly brisk. They take place at five o'clock on Mondays and Wednesdays in his room at the House of Commons. At 10 a.m. on Tuesdays, he sees the Chief Whip, William Whitelaw, and the chairman of the party, Anthony Barber, in his flat; they meet by themselves, just the three of them. On Wednesday mornings, when Barber holds a meeting of the Central Office hierarchy, Heath is represented by Douglas Hurd.

Four of his senior colleagues seem to be especially close to Heath: Sir Alec and Lord Carrington, the Opposition leader in the House of Lords, and—only partly by virtue of their office—Whitelaw and Barber. Though not formally a member of the shadow Cabinet,

Whitelaw attends all its meetings, and I believe that he has more influence than anyone else. This is not simply because he is the Chief Whip, with the party in the House to manage; it is due also to his personal qualities of straightforwardness, candour and loyalty, and to an acutely realistic yet liberal turn of mind. In this large, expansive man, rather in the mould of a genial Lakeland squire (he sits for Penrith), Heath has found a sympathetic partner. The darting, wiry Anthony Barber is an old and trusted friend, and—though nobody quite answers to the description—he and Whitelaw are perhaps the nearest approximation to parliamentary cronies that one encounters in Heath's circle. His relations with most members of the shadow Cabinet tend to focus on particular spheres of work and policy.

The neat allocation of duties within the shadow Cabinet accords with Heath's inborn taste for order, system, preparation, planning. Not for him the inspired hunch, the sudden dash, the romantic free-for-all: he likes precision, and this is what he has achieved by his shadow Cabinet arrangements, which are utterly different from those when the Tories were last in opposition under Churchill.

Then, the great man presided over a shadow Cabinet with loosely-defined, or sometimes undefined, responsibilities. Mr Macmillan was a member of it, and if Heath followed his advice he would 'drop all this shadow Minister stuff. Do what Winston did. Say that all Privy Councillors sit on the front bench. Then decide at your weekly meeting who's to speak on what in the debates coming up. You don't want rigidity in opposition: you want flexibility. It's bad enough being Postmaster-General; just think of being *shadow* Postmaster-General—some poor chap's got it now! Also, you create problems for the time you come to form your government. If you don't give the department to the shadow, what then? You upset him.' 'The new fashion,' Macmillan has written in *Tides of Fortune*, 'was adopted by the Labour Party in their long years of Opposition from 1951 to 1964. . . . There are grave disadvantages in this formality.'

He has said all this to Heath more than once, but without winning him over in the smallest degree. Heath disagrees for several reasons. He would argue, for one thing, that the Opposition under Churchill was neither as successful, nor even as 'free', as some of its surviving members maintain. There were many complaints and criticisms at the time, if only because the party failed to gain a single seat from Labour in the by-elections of the period. Heath would claim, moreover, that the Churchill manner wasn't as loose and flexible as all that: Churchill himself spoke on defence and Eden on foreign affairs, while the chairmen of various Conservative committees in the House spoke from the front bench in that capacity—e.g., Oliver Stanley, and later Oliver Lyttelton, on finance, and R. S. Hudson on agriculture.

Heath is also convinced that the party in the country expects its leading members to specialise, and that organised bodies such as trade and professional associations want to be able to discuss their affairs with one person who is clearly responsible for the particular field of policy in which they are interested.

While one can understand Macmillan's predilection, his fondness, for Churchill's seignorial sort of set-up, one can also see why Heath has chosen to manage things differently. Churchill was in any case much more than a former Prime Minister: he was the great war leader, with a uniquely exalted reputation and prestige. Heath lacks the advantage, the lifelong renown, attaching to anyone who has ever presided at 10 Downing Street. But his shadow Cabinet includes someone who has, and also contains three other members—Maudling, Macleod and Hogg—previously more prominent than himself. These circumstances, as well as personal inclination, and conviction, account for his arrangements.

His methods seem to work pretty well. So far as one can tell, they suit his colleagues. His deputy, Reginald Maudling, has accepted the Heath style happily enough. If Iain Macleod, temperamentally attracted to the Churchill manner, was at first suspicious of overmuch detail, of spelling things out too fully in opposition and thereby leaving less elbow room for office, he has since been won round.

But some people feel circumscribed to the point of oppression, hemmed-in and temperamentally imprisoned, if their roles and responsibilities are too closely defined. Enoch Powell may be one. He could not content himself with defence, which he had accepted as his subject, any more than he could confine himself to transport when that was his field. In the country, he was constantly speaking about other things as well. A brilliant mind demanded greater scope, other outlets; no doubt the compulsion was always there, as part and parcel of the intellectual ferment for ever driving him along. Given prior consultation, and within reasonable limits, this was acceptable to one and all. Without such consultation, and beyond those limits, clash and collision were probably inevitable.

They occurred on 20 April 1968, when Powell

addressed the annual general meeting of the West Midlands Area Conservative Political Centre at the Midland Hotel in Birmingham. Though present at a shadow Cabinet a few days earlier, he had given his colleagues no notice, not an inkling, that he intended to speak about immigration. Then came the thunderbolt. 'As I look ahead,' he said that Saturday, 'I am filled with foreboding. Like the Roman, I seem to see "the River Tiber foaming with much blood".'

It was more than Heath could stomach (though he had to wait for the Sunday newspapers before he could read anything like a full account of the speech, as Powell had not circulated it beforehand through the Central Office). He sent for Willie Whitelaw, who motored down from Penrith on the Sunday. He also consulted Maudling, Barber and Carrington—nobody else, not even Hogg, on whose prescribed territory Powell was guilty of serious trespass.

Heath has described his feelings to me. There is no doubt that he was deeply upset. He was saddened and offended as well as angered. He felt that if the Powell speech were to be accepted as an expression of the Conservative Party's attitude to the immigrant community, then he could not continue as its leader, nor could his colleagues in the shadow Cabinet stay on. It was something much more than a matter of individual resignations—of Hogg, say, or Macleod: it was a matter of vital importance to the party's reputation. They would all have to go, for the sake of what they believed in. He foresaw a total collapse unless he acted at once. Powell's dismissal was announced at nine o'clock that Sunday night.

The breach with Powell, so far from closing, has grown wider since that unhappy day. His disagreements with the party leadership have become more pronounced and more extensive. He assails the 'East of Suez' policy, he twists their arm on the Common Market, he challenges their economic competence. And he gains the public ear, commanding by oratorical power and timing a degree of popular interest and attention that hardly anyone can match. The gulf between him and Heath now seems unbridgable, though several mutual friends had hoped earlier on that they might be able to bring about a reconciliation. In fact, there is no longer any prospect of achieving one, in opposition or in office. Private indications apart, I do not see how you can publicly accuse someone of a lack of humanity (as Heath did after another immigration speech by Powell at Scarborough in January this year) and then invite him to rejoin your inner councils. It is all a great pity.

What will become of Enoch Powell is scarcely a subject for this book, but there can hardly be any doubt that he will continue to exercise the public. What he says, what he does, is bound to affect the Tory party—and the country generally. He is a force in British life, and his influence is not going to evaporate overnight.

Some time before the Powell affair, Heath had found himself at odds with Angus Maude. This was in January 1966, when he had been leader of the party for only six months. Maude, an old friend of One Nation days, was the front-bench spokesman on colonial affairs, though not a member of the shadow Cabinet. Under the heading 'Winter of Tory Discontent', he published an article in the *Spectator*, to which he had long been an occasional contributor (Macleod, I should add, had just ceased to be editor). 'It is obvious,' he wrote, 'that the Conservative Party has completely lost effective political initiative. Its own supporters in the country are divided and deeply worried by this failure, while to the electorate at large the Opposition has become a meaningless irrelevance.'

The Rhodesia crisis, Maude thought, was an important immediate cause—a crisis which had been inflated by the Conservative split. The right wing, he said, had played straight into the hands of the Prime Minister, and 'to those Conservative supporters who sincerely believe that the Government's whole Rhodesia policy is wrong and ought to be opposed, the present situation is doubly mortifying'. Looking more deeply into what he called the anti-political malaise, he argued that it was 'largely a frustration engendered by the increasing scale and complexity of organisation, and by the individual's growing inability to influence the development of his environment'. To which he added: 'For Tories simply to talk like technocrats will get them nowhere'.

Heath was offended. Maude was asked to present himself at the Albany flat, and on 18 January he resigned. He bears no resentment. After all, Heath was still new to the leadership, he felt a certain insecurity, the Hull North by-election was on, and a general election was looming (it occurred just two months later).

Another casualty of the Heath regime, Edward du Cann, surrendered the party chairmanship for quite different reasons: they were not political. Heath inherited du Cann from Sir Alec, and it proved to be a match of incompatibles. They had worked together in government when du Cann was Minister of State at the Board of Trade under Heath. But in the new and delicate leader-chairman relationship they jarred on each other. It was good for neither of them, and after various alarms the genial du Cann pushed off on 11 September 1967, being succeeded by Anthony Barber.

Many of the policies under review by the shadow Cabinet during their heavily publicised weekend at the Selsdon Park Hotel earlier this year were the work of the study groups originally set up by Heath in 1964 and now responsible to Maudling. Though the composition has changed from time to time, nearly every one of them has had the benefit of specialist advice, freely given, from people outside.

Thus we find, in the economic policy group (of which Heath himself has remained chairman), a leading manufacturer and a prominent merchant banker. In another group—on the Arts—the five parliamentary members are outnumbered two to one by the 'outsiders', all eminent in their fields, mostly as administrators. Because some of the volunteers have not wished to be publicly identified with what they are doing, their names have so far remained secret and are omitted from the papers circulated within the party organisation.

But besides these groups, there are private armies reporting directly to Heath. One has long since broken through the security barrier, and the world now knows that Ernest Marples is grappling with the application of scientific management techniques, cost-efficiency and suchlike practices, to the machinery of government. In this he is assisted by David Howell, the M.P. for Guildford, Mark Schreiber of the Conservative Research Department, and a galaxy of outside talents wheeled in for specific purposes. Marples's Conservative Public Sector Research Unit, as it is officially styled, has engaged the services of not one but two major firms of management consultants (British and American), both of which have been doing similar work for several foreign governments. Hence the Heath proposition to enrol in Whitehall a number of businessmen of managing director calibre.

The best description and foretaste of it all was provided by Heath himself when he had the shadow Cabinet to dinner last December and reviewed the origin, objectives and progress of the new approach. As he reminded his colleagues, major changes had taken place in Whitehall, both in structure and in procedures, since the Conservatives were last in government. Many more changes were in prospect. In particular, the implementation of the Fulton recommendations was leading to an increasing emphasis in all departments on delegation of responsibility and to the development of what the Fulton Report called accountable management units. The new Civil Service Department was providing the spearhead in these developments. The Treasury's Management Accounting Unit was also working in harness with the C.S.D. on new budgetary techniques such as the so-called programme budgeting, which placed greater emphasis on the *objectives* of different government activities, and on the costs of achieving them, than on traditional accounting procedures.

The Fulton thinking, he went on, besides helping to promote administrative reform, had political importance for the Conservative Party, which was disturbed about the excessive growth and centralisation of power in the modern state. Almost all assessments of public opinion today brought out a widespread anxiety about the capacity of party politicians to control the administrative machine. In appealing to an important section of the electorate, it was desirable that the Conservatives, as the challenging party, should speak authoritatively on government machinery and bureaucratic control. There was also a widespread expectation that the Conservatives, in contrast to the Labour Party, would be able to come to grips with public spending. But to carry conviction on this point, there would have to be more than just declarations of intent, particularly since some Conservative policies—for instance improvement in urban transport, a continued presence east of Suez, and more help for those in genuine need—clearly involved increased public spending. These policy aims would have to be reconciled with the wish to exert a tighter discipline over public expenditure and the proliferation of activities which gave rise to it.

Conservative policy leaned towards greater provision of community requirements through private enterprise, voluntary effort and the price mechanism, and less through state operations. For example, he said, they wished to see a substantial revival in the private housing sector, a halt, at the very least, to the erosion of private pension schemes, a shift in the industrial research effort to the private sector. If their intentions were to be developed into effective programmes, they would have to challenge long-established official assumptions and viewpoints. Detailed proposals for re-allocating central government responsibilities on sound organisational principles would have to be prepared if they were not to be defeated by administrative difficulties at the outset.

It was this approach to the activities of government,

Heath continued, which had opened up the argument for drafting business managers of the highest calibre into Whitehall on a new and worthwhile basis—i.e., on the basis of real responsibility for the management of clearly defined programmes and the achievement of defined policy goals. The feasibility of such a scheme, besides relying on a favourable political and administrative climate generally, would also depend heavily on support from within the Civil Service. Without full Civil Service co-operation there could be little progress. But if this and other obstacles could be surmounted, the gains might be very substantial. Clearer definition and delegation of tasks implied increased political power over the administrative machine. The overall success of the next Conservative Government could depend heavily on their ability to establish this additional degree of control over the administration and to use it effectively to carry through their policies.

It looked, he said, as though they could usefully identify a number of areas, over and above those being examined by the Civil Service Department, where there was room for a far greater emphasis on separate responsibilities, separate projects, and possible hiving off into separate agencies altogether. Precisely how any new group or unit at the centre might fit in with the existing Civil Service Department, with the Cabinet Office and other support staff available to the Prime Minister, and with the Treasury, had yet to be decided. But the arguments did seem strong for a new capability, both in order to raise the quality of information brought forward to the Cabinet and to provide the basis for a much more systematic questioning and control of departmental activities by Ministers.

Heath turned to the so-called Sundridge Park

Seminar of the previous September. This had brought together eighteen very senior executives from industry, eleven Tory back-benchers, shadow Ministers, and a number of former civil servants and specialists from abroad. The aim, Heath recalled, had been threefold. First, to enlarge their mutual understanding and to look at Conservative policy goals in a more systematic way than before. Second, to attract possible recruits from business both for the management of specific tasks under a Conservative Government and for involvement in preparatory work beforehand. Thirdly, to attract possible recruits for the kind of analytical work which a new Conservative administration would require.

The seminar was successful in achieving these aims, said Heath. All the businessmen had expressed a strong wish to continue, and in the event it was decided that fourteen of the eighteen had something further to contribute to the work of the party.

All fourteen are destined for Whitehall if Heath's hopes are fulfilled, and are now being brought into closer association with party policy under the guidance of both Lord Carrington and an important industrialist. Thus were the first of the business brigade recruited to the modern Conservative Party.

No less (and perhaps more) high-powered is another group whose principal members are five former civil servants of seniority and distinction, a woman among them. They are considering the reorganisation of government departments. Like Marples, they are occupied with considerations not only of efficiency but of economy both in costs and in numbers, and they have a bias towards a 'federal' system in Whitehall which would group appropriate ministries together. Another, but smaller, army, under Sir Con O'Neill, was disbanded in 1969 after reporting to Heath on the Diplomatic Service.

To the political editor of *The Times*, David Wood, it has seemed that 'the broad axis of Tory advance towards what may be called the businessman's takeover of Whitehall can already be seen'. But Heath sees things differently. To him, the business element would be in the nature of auxiliaries rather than principals, important but never supreme. It is not a new conception, though the Tories would hope to apply it more systematically than before.

Nor is Heath after a 'presidential' sort of set-up in Downing Street, with a corps of personal advisers in every major field of policy, forming a kind of private intellectual powerhouse—though this has sometimes been suggested. 'Preparation for government' has been a great thing of his for the last two years and more, and he now knows what he would like to do.

The Government that he would conduct, given the opportunity, is one involving a streamlining of the Civil Service with a reduction in the number of departments and staffs, a smaller Cabinet (of about sixteen), and above all a system enabling Ministers to exercise 'more direct control over the strategy of longer-term policy'. In other words, Ministers would be less immersed (or submerged) in the day-to-day running of their departments, less occupied with routine, and better able to give their minds to the objectives of overall policy. That is the theory of it all.

Heath has discussed it endlessly. For example he gave a dinner party in Albany last year ('on a somewhat ample Edwardian scale', I gather) to celebrate Mr Macmillan's seventy-fifth birthday. The other guests were people who had served Macmillan at No. 10, most of them no longer in the public service. Predictably, the conversation turned to 'preparation for government'. What was wrong with the present arrangements? What could be done to improve them? Afterwards, some of his guests committed their thoughts to paper.

Chapter Fourteen

Communications

H eath has always been a great traveller. From a young age he has been anything but insular—and even his early journeys were made (as we have seen) with a serious purpose, not just for fun. All his life he has shown an unquenchable interest in other countries. During his time as a Minister, and more recently as Leader of the Opposition, he has visited many parts of the world. Latterly, he has been covering great distances every year. He has always wanted to learn more about other nations, their ways and their systems, by seeing something of them for himself; and of course he knows many of their leaders.

If his parliamentary record proves one thing more than another, it proves that he has consistently looked at his own country in terms of its place and influence in the world, rigorously measuring his hopes for Britain against the realities of power elsewhere. Much of his domestic policy can most usefully be read in this context, moreover, for it is directly related to the wider, internationalist outlook that has distinguished him for the last twenty years.

Heath readily accepted an invitation from Harvard University to deliver the Godkin Lectures—three in all —in the spring of 1967, when he presented a lengthy and elaborate survey of modern Europe. He has since contributed a substantial assessment of Britain's rôle in the world to the distinguished American review, *Foreign Affairs*. It seems appropriate to include this important expression of his views as an appendix to the present book.

As a speaker, Heath is happier—and usually more effective—with smaller rather than larger audiences. Though he is remembered as a good speaker in school and university debates, he has not developed the oratorical powers which might have been expected in someone who took to the public platform so young. He is competent rather than inspiring, informative rather than eloquent, with no natural flair for the high style to which political leaders have normally aspired when addressing mass meetings such as party conferences. On these occasions Heath is addicted, perhaps by now incurably, to the factual statement, the plain exposition, marshalling and enumerating his facts and policies like a laundry list.

It has often been said that he reveals a curious and surprising lack of feeling for language, considering his artistic gifts. Yet I once heard him speak in public with remarkably sensitive insight and delicacy of expression. This was in March 1969, when he gave the address at the memorial service in St Margaret's, Westminster, for his old friend Sir Timothy Bligh. I was so struck by it that I made a note at the time: 'It was the finest address that I have ever heard at such a service— beautifully constructed, with never a false or extravagant note, absolutely accurate and movingly eloquent'. Three other people, all different in make-up, told me that they had felt much the same about it. My neighbour in church, Peter Hoos, was one. So was Lord Egremont. So was the editor-in-chief of the *Times* newspapers, Denis Hamilton.

Later I asked Heath for his notes. He had none. He had composed the address himself and memorised it. He showed that day that he can do it: yet he seldom does. The reason, I believe, is a fear of being thought sentimental or emotional or of striving after effect. The fact that he can, but usually does not, may be evidence of the buttoned-up romantic whom some of his friends detect beneath the surface. His final television broadcast in the 1966 election was also an eloquent performance, notably loftier in tone, more philosophical and 'grander' in its language than what had gone before; but in this he had accepted the assistance of a well-known journalist.

'People say I am better with smaller audiences,' he says. 'The smaller audience is usually more even, or perhaps specialist.' Where he always excels as a speaker is in briefing, and this was never more apparent than during the period of the Common Market negotiations. His progress reports to the Commons were models of lucidity, as were his briefings to one party committee after another. They all wanted explanations of what he was about. I attended many of these meetings. He used to speak for an hour or an hour and a half without a note, demonstrating a knowledge of every detail, and a grip on the underlying philosophy, that was staggering. He knew the facts and he had a theme—and he saw that his audience never lost track of it.

But Heath has also shown that he can rise to the really testing or tricky occasion even before the largest of audiences—not by oratory in the conventional sense of the term but by exhibiting a quality of personal conviction, of sturdiness and determination, that commands respect. Not for the first time at a party conference, he proved that in Brighton last year. Established policy on three issues—crime and punishment, immigration and the Common Market—had been under fire. If only to underline his own authority he had to reassert the official position. He did so in a speech overwhelmingly acclaimed as one of outstanding strength and persuasiveness, which produced an ovation lasting six minutes and a highly complimentary press.

As always, he was rather nervous beforehand. 'Unless you have a degree of tension,' he says, 'you don't make a good speech. It is so in any artistic performance.' His speeches on these occasions are normally constructed by Michael Wolff of the Conservative Research Department. Wolff is a journalist (*Daily Express*, *Sunday Telegraph*), and he was attached to Randolph Churchill when the latter was writing his father's Life. But Heath is always inclined to fiddle about with the draft himself, adding and subtracting and making the speech his own. More often than not, he delivers luncheon and dinner speeches off the cuff, without a note (and these are probably his best). In the House of Commons he never makes a speech that he has not written out in his own hand—working nowadays from raw material and briefs supplied to him by the Research Department.

On average, he delivers about 150 speeches a year outside Parliament. Parliamentary speeches—of course excluding interventions and off-the-cuff exchanges in the course of Questions or debates—account for a further dozen or so. In 1966, his first full calendar year as leader, he made sixteen in the House. In 1967 the number dropped to eleven and has since been running at something in between.

His engagements are a very mixed bag. Selecting some at random, I see that in 1968 his audiences included the Association of American Correspondents, the Edinburgh Junior Chamber of Commerce, the Bow Group, the Ulster Unionist Council, the Finance Houses Association, the Primrose League, the Lords Taverners, the Dickens Fellowship, and the Road Haulage Association.

Of all his direct encounters with the public, Heath probably enjoys his regional tours more than anything else. Although heavily 'political' in purpose, and largely given over to meetings with local Conservative associations, they also take him to any important industrial development that may be going on in the neighbourhood and to factories of more than humdrum consequence. By way of illustrating what he does on these occasions, I reproduce his programme for a visit to the North West at the end of 1968:

Thursday 5 December

7 p.m.	Leave Euston for Manchester. Dine on train.
9.50 p.m.	Arrive Manchester for night. Stay in hotel.

Friday 6 December

8.35 a.m.	Leave Manchester by car for Hollinwood, near Oldham.
9-11 a.m.	Visit to Ferranti's at Hollinwood.
11.15-11.45 a.m.	Attend coffee morning reception in Oldham for representatives of Oldham East and West and Heywood and Royton constituencies.

12.15-1.15 p.m.	Meeting with editors of national and local newspapers and representatives of T.V. in Manchester. (Drinks and informal discussion at Manchester hotel.)
1.30-2.50 p.m.	Speak at luncheon for officers of constituency women's organisations in the North West. Castle Irwell, Manchester.
6-7.50 p.m.	Meal and rest at Adelphi Hotel, Liverpool.
8-9.15 p.m.	Address mass meeting for Liverpool and surrounding constituencies at St George's Hall.
9.15-10.15 p.m.	Attend reception for party workers from Liverpool and surrounding constituencies at Lyceum, Bold Street.
Overnight	Stay at Adelphi Hotel, Liverpool.

Saturday 7 December

9.45-11.15 a.m.	Visit to Gladstone and Seaforth docks.
12 noon-1.50 p.m.	Attend buffet luncheon in Preston for meeting with representatives from the marginal seats of Lancaster and Preston North and South.
3-5 p.m.	Attend football match: Manchester City *versus* Burnley at Manchester City Football Ground.
5.30-6.30 p.m.	Attend cocktail party in Stockport for Stockport North and

	South and Cheadle marginal constituencies.
7.15-8.45 p.m.	Dinner with the officers of the Macclesfield Conservative Association, at the Macclesfield Arms Hotel, Macclesfield.
9-10.30 p.m.	Attend opening of new Macclesfield Conservative Club, West Bank Road, Macclesfield.
	Return to London on sleeper train.

It may of course be said that these tours are not so much encounters with 'the public' as engagements with the Tory faithful. But not all the 'party faithful' are in fact faithful, or constant in their allegiance to the leadership—far from it. They have to be wooed. Heath was in the North West to woo them—and he seems to me to be rather good at winning people's sympathy and support when he meets them face to face, or when, at a public meeting, he is addressing them individually in the question and answer session that usually follows his speech.

After the St George's Hall speech in Liverpool ('Land of Hope and Glory' on the organ to begin with, everyone—1,800—rising as he joined a platform crowded with Merseyside notabilities), he took questions for forty minutes or so. There were a dozen. In what circumstances would he re-admit Powell to the shadow Cabinet? (There are now large differences between us, he said, and he doubted whether Powell would wish to be re-admitted.) Can't the party do more for trade unionists on the shop floor? (He promised to discuss this with the chairman of the party.) Would the Tories stop grants to university students who assaulted the police? (Grants, he said, are paid by local authorities, and this is their responsibility.) These Q and A sessions always go down well, and he prefers them to set speeches.

Afterwards—it was a crisp, dry night—he chose to walk with Jim Prior to the reception at the Lyceum, calling in on the way at the Liverpool Press Club, where he chatted happily with local journalists and drank half a pint of beer. At the reception in the Lyceum, which turned out to be a handsomely appointed club and not a dance hall, he moved around, to all appearances completely at ease with the local party workers, for an hour and a half.

I am told (though I have never seen it) that he can be a bit of a handful for a neighbour who bores him at the dinner table, relapsing into lengthy silences. On the other hand, I have been struck from time to time by his geniality at parties of no special significance or importance to him. He says himself that he likes parties, especially late-night ones, after a concert or the theatre. Certainly he entertains a lot nowadays, though it is often for political purposes.

Another of Heath's lines of communication with the public is through correspondence. People are for ever writing to him. He has a huge postbag. What he calls his 'public correspondence' amounts to 250 to 300 letters a week from members of the public unknown to him personally. On top of that he receives a similar number of other letters and memoranda. As one would expect, the public correspondence is on every subject under the sun, from matters of high policy to personal problems (often to do with housing and pensions). Year after year the volume reaches its peak in October and November, because of the party conferences and the opening of the new session of Parliament.

The largest group of letters in any one week normally relates to some specific issue currently in the news. Though many people wrote to him about the Russian invasion of Czechoslovakia, about Biafra, and earlier about Rhodesia, home affairs always predominate. Much of the public correspondence is about the economy and the cost of living. One subject has remained consistently to the forefront, however, since the Powell speech of April 1968: race relations and immigration. At the time, Heath received no less than 7,000 letters; and to this day, when his correspondents are angry with him, it is more often than not on this issue. Like all public men he also comes in for a certain amount of abuse (usually anonymous), but for some reason this has lately fallen off.

However imperfect a postbag may be as a guide to public opinion, it is nevertheless an indicator, and once a fortnight the private office make him a summary and analysis, which is then related to what the party is learning from other forms of research.

Then there is Bexley, where—fortified by an able agent—his personal communication with his constituents is strong. Despite the pressures of national leadership, his links with the division (population 90,000, area eight square miles) have not diminished. He is to be found there about fifty times a year: there is seldom a week when he is not at Bexley for one reason or another.

Though it is in the London borough of Bexley, the seat is only part of the borough—which accounts for two and a half parliamentary constituencies, the other being Erith and Crayford plus half of Chislehurst. Since Heath was first returned, the electorate (a high proportion retired) has shrunk a little, to between 63,000 and 64,000. This is because quite a lot of 'young marrieds' were still sharing a house with parents in the 1950s but have since moved away to homes of their own. While there are only 4,000 council houses in the division there are 27,000 in private ownership. As Heath often tells people, 'Before the war you could buy a semi-detached house in Bexley for £395 with a £5 deposit. If you didn't have the £5 the builder would lend it to you.'

His agent, Reginald Pye, a pre-war rubber planter in Sumatra, is an energetic and self-confident man of Heath's own generation. He has a firm grip on the local party organisation. Neither the president nor the chairman writes direct to Heath: all correspondence is through Pye—which is one way of avoiding crossed wires.

One has come to expect any apparatus designed for Heath's support to be rather efficient: Pye's is no exception. The sizeable freehold house in Crook Log which Heath selected for the association twenty years ago is trim, tidy, almost antiseptically clean, a condition not universally true of constituency offices. Pye and his wife live in a pleasant flat 'over the shop', where Heath usually dines with them during election campaigns (lunch out, perhaps at the King's Head, dinner in, is his normal election drill). When Pye has urgent business with Heath he rings him in Albany at breakfast time; otherwise Rosemary Bush, Heath's personal secretary, is the link. Pye tells me that he has never regretted the lack of a Member's wife to open summer fêtes and suchlike. 'He travels fastest who travels alone,' says Pye. 'I don't believe that he could do all he does if he had a wife and family to consider and occupy some of his time.'

He and Heath attach importance to the system of 'political education' which they have followed over the years. 'Immediately an issue crops up in which E. H. is very involved,' says Pye, 'all members of the association are circulated with a memorandum on the subject, or a leaflet is produced.' Pye doesn't wait for the Central Office to provide them: guided by Heath, he manufactures them himself. For Pye the publicist the great flurry of recent years was over the Powell affair, which not only generated a quickfire memorandum to his members but gave rise to something else as well. 'For several days,' he says, 'the telephone rang in this office all day with people from all over the country shouting obscenities.' In the constituency itself—which has only about eighty coloured people, many of them nurses and doctors—'three Y.C.s were recalcitrant,' says Pye. 'I talked them round and they went out canvassing that night.' Heath has encouraged his Young Conservatives by personal effort and association. Last November he was out canvassing with them on two Saturday mornings, going from house to house.

In February this year, the Bexley Tories celebrated his twentieth anniversary as Member by making a presentation to him at a party in Crook Log. By the look of things he won't be having many more celebrations there, however. If the recommendations of the Boundary Commission are implemented, his days are numbered. What has happened is that the Commission, following the formation of the Greater London

Area, have proposed three new parliamentary constituencies in the neighbourhood to fit the new London borough boundaries. The borough of Bexley (as we have seen) comprises two and a half parliamentary seats. According to the Commission, it should be divided into three:

1 Bexley (Sidcup)—made up of half the present Chislehurst division plus that part of the Bexley seat south of the A2 road, which has 12,000—mostly Tory—voters;
2 Bexley (Bexleyheath)—the remnant of Heath's present Bexley constituency; and
3 Bexley (Erith and Crayford)—with boundaries unchanged.

One effect of all this would be to average out the local electorate at just under 51,000—which incidentally is below the national average. What will actually happen is of course uncertain, for no changes will be made before the next general election. But Heath, if he stayed where he is—that is to say in what might be called Bexley (Bexleyheath)—would probably be robbed of the best part of 12,000 votes, which would then attach to Bexley (Sidcup). As Bexley (Sidcup) would presumably include about 30,000 electors in the present Chislehurst division, as well as the 12,000—mostly Tories—taken from Heath, this would be a safe Conservative seat. It would suit him nicely. But Dame Patricia Hornsby-Smith, the former M.P. for Chislehurst, currently held by Labour, has remained the Conservative candidate there—and, naturally enough, she hopes to be adopted in the new constituency, if and when created.

What is certain is that after such an upheaval

Heath could no longer feel any lasting security at Bexley—i.e., Bexley (Bexleyheath) if that is what it became. It would be transformed into a marginal seat. The prospect has disturbed him more than most people realise. There is hardly any doubt that changes will be made after the next general election—and in that event Heath would really have to move off. He has become attached to Bexley and would be sorry to leave, but if a political leader needs one thing more than anything else, it is a sound parliamentary base. In recent months, when the nomination for the Cities of London and Westminster was on offer, he was urged to secure it for himself. He declined for more than one reason. He thought that as leader of the Tory party he ought not to be so closely identified with the City. He has received other invitations from Tory associations in safe Conservative seats, but he has declined them all: he will stay with Bexley as long as he can.

Looking at Heath's life and career, what can one make of him? Certain strands and characteristics are I think clear.

There is the aspect of service—of involvement, of participation, in community affairs from a young age: at school, at university, in the Army (not forgetting the H.A.C. after the war) and then in the wider world of parliamentary politics.

There is the thread of consistent personal endeavour, sometimes up to the point of exhaustion (as in the Common Market negotiations); of serious purpose, of stubborn determination, even inflexibility. He has always been ambitious for himself; from the start, his sights were set very high.

There is inner confidence. To do what he has done

required an indestructible belief in himself. There is resourcefulness. He has risen to the top against heavy odds by a combination of effort, intelligence and idealism (a quality which may surprise those who know him only as a practical man of affairs). Allied to these characteristics is a kind of classlessness. He has never felt inhibited by his modest beginnings. He has been guided, on the contrary, by the healthy realisation that the world and its fortunes are for those who go after them.

There is action, not words (as the Tory slogan had it in 1966). He is a doer rather than a theorist, more interested in the realities of administration than the abstractions of political philosophy.

There is moral courage, consistency of purpose and personal conviction—as for instance expressed in his attitude to the dictators before the war, in his attachment to the European ideal, in his recent vote (with the leaders of the other two parties and in the face of opposition from his own) against the restoration of capital punishment.

It is not an unattractive catalogue of personal qualities. Yet he has made less impact on the public than one would have thought likely in the leader of a party repeatedly successful in the polls that ultimately count most of all—and are represented by a dozen by-election gains from Labour since 1966. To many, I suspect, his natural reserve, suggesting a lack of personal warmth, coupled with a certain peremptoriness of manner, have been off-putting. He is not a cosy man.

In the words of a parliamentary opponent, Jo Grimond (speaking last year in the television programme *This Week*), Edward Heath 'has a genuine integrity, a desire to do well for his country, and I think he likes administration. . . . He has a very good, collected mind. He gives it to subjects and is not easily distracted. He also I think is a courageous politician. . . . Further, I think he's a fair man whom people would trust, and this is rather important in a party leader.'

Appendix
I

Realism in British Foreign Policy
By Edward Heath

Looking back at the foreign policies of Britain and the
United States since 1800 it is easy to see two strands
woven closely together—the strands of idealism and
realism. In both countries Governments, Parliaments
and peoples have been happiest when these two elements
have been brought together in apparent harmony.
Take for example two quotations from nineteenth century England:

> We have no eternal allies and we have no perpetual enemies.
> Our interests are eternal and perpetual and those interests
> it is our duty to follow. . . . With every British Minister
> the interests of England ought to be the shibboleth of his
> policy.

and then again:

> I hold that the real policy of England is to be the champion
> of justice and right: pursuing that course with moderation
> and prudence, not becoming the Quixote of the world,
> but giving her moral sanction and support wherever she
> thinks justice is, and whenever she thinks that wrong has
> been done.

The point of interest in these quotations is that they
were spoken by the same man in the same speech
without any sense of contradiction. They were the

words of Palmerston in the House of Commons in 1848; but I am sure that both quotations could be matched by almost any Foreign Secretary or Secretary of State between that time and now.

Over much of this period it has in fact been possible for idealism and realism to run fairly well together. For example in Palmerston's time the interests of England, as well as its liberal conscience, dictated that England should support those liberal and national movements which created the nation states of Europe as we see them today. At the turn of the century, for a comparatively brief period, idealistic belief in Britain's mission overseas combined with a keen sense of political and commercial opportunity to create a positive imperial policy. After the Second World War a different brand of idealism combined with a realistic sense of the change in Britain's power to produce the peaceful transfer from a colonial empire to the independent association of the Commonwealth.

But at other times there has been an obvious and inevitable tension between the claims of idealism and of realism. When this tension has occurred it has been the instinct of the British to plump for realism, to a degree which until recently has tended to shock observers on the American side of the Atlantic. It is the first and not the second of the quotations set out above which has served as a text down the years for the instruction of new entrants into the British Foreign Service. If one looks in this century at the occasional clashes between British and American policy, between Wilson and Lloyd George at the Peace Conference of 1919, between Churchill and Roosevelt in the closing years of the Second World War, between Dulles and Anthony Eden over Indo-China in 1954, one sees at each point a

British preference for realism resisted by American statesmen, who preferred to look for some master-principle which they could put forward as a universal ideal.

To the British observer one of the remarkable shifts of American policy during the last decade has been precisely a movement towards a more realistic analysis of issues of foreign policy and a partial abandonment of the search for a master-principle. I do not myself find this disturbing. For the interests of Britain and the United States in the present stage of their historical development clearly require stability and prosperity not only at home, but throughout the world. This means that we are once again in a period where the interests of our two countries coincide with any reasonable definition of the common good.

But it is clearly not enough to define these interests in such general terms. The realist has to look more closely into ways and means. It is at this point that there has been in recent years a certain question-mark over British foreign policy. We have shown some reluctance to define our course, and to hold to that course steadily in the day-to-day conduct of foreign affairs. We have tended to become pre-occupied with day-to-day difficulties, and so to miss the tide of events. We have suffered from a degree of diffidence and uncertainty which has obscured our vision of reality.

An obvious example has been the British attitude towards the movement for unity in Europe. Ever since Winston Churchill made his great post-war speeches at Zurich and in The Hague far-sighted Englishmen have seen that the movement for European unity holds enormous benefits for Britain. It promises an end to those conflicts between European powers from which the European countries, including Britain, have been the chief sufferers. It promises a voice for Europe in world affairs which individual European countries cannot hope to achieve by themselves. It promises in the long run a single market in Europe to provide a foundation from which European industry and European science can grow to match the achievements of the United States and the Soviet Union. This elementary analysis is now overwhelmingly accepted as valid, in Britain as elsewhere in Western Europe. Yet the sad fact is that each British attempt to associate Britain with the movement for European unity has failed, and that each attempt has taken place in less favourable circumstances than its predecessor. When I made my first speech in the House of Commons in 1950 I urged that Britain should join the European Coal and Steel Community. At that time, and for a few years afterwards, Britain had the opportunity to join the European Communities at their birth, and so to have a decisive say in European institutions and the way in which they were run. But by the time Mr Macmillan's Government decided in 1961 to apply for membership of the European Economic Community our task was already more difficult. During the negotiations which I conducted in 1961 and 1962 we had to reckon with a Community whose institutions and policies were already partly formed without taking account of the needs and interests of Britain. During these negotiations we came a long way to finding solutions to the practical problems resulting from that situation; but we were frustrated in January 1963 by the decision of the President of France. By the time that the Labour Government was converted to the European idea and made its own attempt to join the

Community in 1967 the policies of the Community had taken even more definite shape. In particular the Community had since the earlier negotiations adopted in detail a Common Agricultural Policy which Britain would clearly have to accept as a condition of membership. The second attempt failed without negotiations having started at all because the French President refused to alter his well-known stand. It is too early to be sure how far the basic French objection to British membership of the E.E.C. has now changed. But it is certain that Britain is now less able than she was in 1961-62, or even in 1967, to assume without special arrangements the obligations of full membership. The increase in Britain's international indebtedness and the underlying weakness of her balance of payments make more formidable the heavy short-term burden which a Common Market and the Common Agricultural Policy as it now stands would inevitably impose.

The setbacks which we have suffered in Europe have also raised in some minds a doubt as to whether we are on the right path to European unity. It has been suggested that we ought to break away from the wearisome attempt to enter the Communities and to find a short-cut by means of some dramatic political initiative aimed at finding a new formula. Recipes for this formula have varied, but I believe that they all miss the basic fact about the way in which European unity can be constructed.

In my judgment the unity of Europe will in the end be achieved by European Governments forming the habit of working together. Public and parliamentary opinion works upon Governments, but in the end it is Governments, elected Ministers and their officials, who take the decisions. Confidence between Governments is the only lasting cement for the unity of Europe. The underlying analysis of M. Monnet and the other founding fathers of the Communities was that the Governments of the Six would begin by working together for the abolition of tariffs and the creation of a Common Market. Under the stimulus of the European Commission they would then move on, as confidence in the joint taking of decisions increased, to create an economic union. They would gradually extend the range of their cooperation until it passed beyond purely economic matters into foreign policy and defence. At the same time, as confidence grew, Governments would be more ready to pool their powers in strictly European institutions. I am sure that this still remains the only realistic approach to European unity, and that short-cuts can only lead to a further round of disappointments which neither Britain nor Europe can afford. Of course the process has been slower than the signatories of the Treaty of Rome had hoped. There have been delays and setbacks; in an enterprise of this magnitude these were to be expected. But the Communities and their institutions have survived and proved their worth. It is inconceivable to me that the unity of Europe could now be established on any other basis.

There may in the next year or two be another opportunity for Britain to join in this process. If this opportunity is to succeed it must be most carefully prepared, for public opinion in Britain could not tolerate a third failure. There has understandably been some falling-off of British enthusiasm in recent years. The cause of European unity has suffered from far too high a ratio of words to action. It would be a serious miscalculation to suppose that enthusiasm could be rekindled by a new round of conferences or declarations of intent; this would merely aggravate the sense of frustration. But once there was a prospect of practical and acceptable answers being found to the real problems which now bar the way, then I believe that public interest would quickly revive and the strength of the underlying argument in favour of European unity would prevail.

Britain's application to join the E.E.C. remains on the table with those of the other applicant countries. The next step so far as Britain is concerned must be for the Six to signify that they are all ready to begin negotiations on our application. Then before negotiations between Britain and the Six as a whole can begin there must be thorough bilateral discussions between Britain and each of the Six, as well as with the European Commission if they so wish. These discussions are needed to ensure before negotiations start that enough common ground exists for their success. They will naturally cover the whole field of the Treaty of Rome. Many of the results which we achieved in the negotiations of 1961-62 are still valid and will provide a foundation for eventual British membership. Other difficulties were not resolved in the earlier negotiations and still exist today, though in the case of New Zealand for example it was acceptable in principle by the Community that a solution was essential for a successful negotiation. It is not realistic to suppose that these difficulties can be brushed aside as of no importance. But given the political will to succeed these problems are not of a magnitude to frustrate a final agreement.

But preparation must in my judgment go well beyond the scope of the Treaty of Rome. We shall not succeed unless we can work out with our future partners guidelines for the other problems which confront Europe today. We shall not achieve final solutions at this preliminary stage: as I have already said I believe that these final solutions will grow out of the confidence formed by the habit of working together. But the British Government needs to show from the beginning that it favours a common approach to these further problems, and that it has ideas on what this approach should be. The further problems fall broadly under three heads: monetary co-operation, political co-operation and defence.

The monetary predicament of the western world looms larger today than it did in 1961-62 or even in 1967. It is, of course, a problem with many facets. In 1967 a principal cause for concern was the weakness of sterling and the instability of the sterling balances. The former led to devaluation; but devaluation, in its turn, gave a shock to the sterling system which aggravated the problem of the sterling balances. In effect, a European solution had then to be found for this problem. The Basle agreements contained arrangements which could well have been a part of such a European solution.

At the same time, a general uncertainty persists—a result of the continued increase in Britain's indebtedness, the continued U.S. deficit, the weakness of the franc and the accumulated surpluses in Germany—which impedes the economic policy of each of these countries and many others besides. Obviously, there could be no purely European solution to these problems, but equally it has become clear that Europe cannot proceed much further towards economic union without a more fundamental consensus on monetary matters than is contained in the Treaty of Rome or the practice of the E.E.C. to date.

Two related issues in particular dominate the present international monetary scene. The first has world-wide ramifications; the second, in practice, is more directly the concern of the European Communities.

On the wider issue, the Bretton-Woods system (not as originally envisaged, but as in practice it has developed) has for some time been showing acute signs of strain. On the one hand there is a continuing need for increased international liquidity to satisfy the reserve require-ments of various countries without precipitating the international transmission of deflation and a return to the beggar-my-neighbour policies of the inter-war years. On the other hand, this need has been met by persistent imbalance—on the part of the Americans—creating a flow of dollars to Europe. This has eased the liquidity problem at the expense of growing doubts about the value of the dollar. While these doubts have not been resolved, the pressures to which they could have given rise have largely been neutralised by German reluctance to convert dollars into gold.

The creation of liquidity in this way has had certain unplanned and unforeseen consequences. First, the gold exchange system envisaged at Bretton-Woods has effectively been put into suspense and replaced by a dollar system. Secondly, the surplus of dollar balances, instead of accumulating in official hands, has contri-buted to the development of the Eurodollar market to supply the need for a European capital market.

These developments have both good and bad features. On the positive side, the supply of liquidity necessary for the continued growth of world trade has been main-tained; the Eurodollar market now performs an invaluable role as a flexible international money market, and America has been able to continue exporting scientific know-how and managerial skill to Europe.

On the negative side, the system depends upon a continued U.S. deficit which in turn means a flow of real resources to the richest country in the world; the Eurodollar market is also a potential source of instability, lacking as it does any overt control or 'lender of the last resort'; and under the dollar system the world is forced to march in step with the United States. The U.S. effectively determines the ebb and flow of activity throughout the rest of the world.

Europe must decide whether it really does want America to eliminate its deficit or whether to accept a world dollar system. Can the European countries agree on a viable alternative to American domination of the international monetary system?

The related, but narrower, European problem is how individual members of the Common Market can adjust imbalance between themselves. It can be argued that once the Community is fully developed scope for imbalance will be strictly limited. The ties between members of the Community will then be so close that the development of inflationary or deflationary pressures in one country will immediately be transmitted to its partners before any serious balance of payments difficulties arise.

But this does not alter the fact that a real dis-equilibrium at present exists between Germany on the one hand and France on the other. The problem is that there is a conflict between measures to eliminate a dis-equilibrium—such as exchange rate changes—and other aspects of the Community, in particular the common agricultural policy. Under this policy, agricultural prices are set in terms of units of gold which reflect the present value of the dollar. Any member which changes its exchange rate would have to accept related changes in food prices and farm subsidies, which may be undesirable. Members of the Community have therefore to come to terms with this problem, either by taking a giant stride towards integration of monetary and fiscal policies or by finding some way of permitting adjustment between members which does not undermine the existing framework of the Community.

As regards political co-operation, the first step must be an effective system of harmonising foreign policy within the Council of Ministers of the E.E.C. It is a paradox that while the E.E.C. itself has failed to establish any such pattern of consultation, the Council of the Western European Union (the Six plus Britain) had quietly and undramatically achieved a form where the seven Governments regularly exchanged views on foreign policy matters. That is one reason why I was opposed to the attempt to make W.E.U. part of the means of outflanking the French veto on British entry into the E.E.C. The only practical result has been to cause France to exclude herself from meetings of the W.E.U. which she had previously attended. It is ludicrous that countries of Western Europe are now without a means of concerting their policies on matters of such vital concern to Europe as, say, the Arab-Israeli conflict in the Middle East.

In the field of defence there has already in recent years been a movement towards creating a European voice within NATO. This tendency will inevitably increase if it becomes apparent that, despite the lesson of Czechoslovakia, the U.S. is determined to reduce the size of the forces which up to now she has been ready to station in Europe.

The chief difficulty in the way of this coming together of European countries on defence has been that France has so far been excluded as a result of President de Gaulle's withdrawal from effective co-operation with NATO. The immediate aim of European countries should be to devise a way to end this unnatural separation. It is now three years since I proposed the idea of a Joint Anglo-French Nuclear Deterrent which could be held in trust for Europe. I have been glad to notice that similar suggestions have now been made by Herr Strauss and hinted at by the new French Government. My conception has been that the non-nuclear countries of Europe could join with Britain and France in a Consultative Committee which would have exactly the same relationship to the Joint Anglo-French Deterrent as the so-called McNamara Committee has to the U.S. deterrent. There would thus be no question of infringing the non-proliferation treaty, or giving non-nuclear countries an unacceptable measure of control, commonly described as a finger on the trigger. A scheme of this kind would not in any sense be anti-American; indeed because of the provisions of the various British agreements with the U.S. in this field it could not be implemented without American support. I believe that this support would be compatible with the general principles of American policy towards Europe in recent years. The U.S. under different administrations has shown remarkable far-sightedness in being willing to make concessions of its immediate interests in order to further the creation of a European unity.

Britain's role outside Europe has been the subject of lively discussion in Britain in recent years, which has run somewhat parallel to the discussion in the United States, although the circumstances and issues are widely different. There is little dispute in Britain about the part which Britain should play in the various international enterprises in which Britain is a partner. It is widely accepted in Britain that the peace-keeping and peace-making functions of the United Nations should be supported and strengthened, and that this can be done without acknowledging that every resolution passed by the General Assembly, or its Committees, enjoys some sacred infallibility. The United Nations has shown that, in the right place and under the right conditions, it can provide a useful addition to the traditional techniques of diplomacy which no country genuinely interested in international stability can afford to neglect. Similar considerations apply to the Commonwealth, an organisation which may be on the verge of a new usefulness as the prejudices of the past evaporate. During its early years the Commonwealth suffered from the suspicion of some of its members that Britain was using the organisation to perpetuate under a new name some of the privileges of empire. Latterly it has suffered from the suspicion in Britain that other Commonwealth countries were interested in the association primarily as a means of extracting help from Britain, and as an opportunity of reading Britain lectures on British policy of a kind which would be bitterly resented if addressed to any other country. This suspicion gained ground as a result of the preoccupation of the Commonwealth with the Rhodesian question. But after the last Conference of Commonwealth Prime Ministers in London, which achieved a greater success than was recognised by some at the time, it seems at least possible that suspicions are fading. New possibilities of co-operation within the Commonwealth are opening up, based primarily on the dense network of connections between Commonwealth countries in almost every field of human activity, a network which has largely survived the vagaries of politics.

Equally there is little argument in Britain about British membership of the Alliances to which she now belongs, and in particular of the importance of the connexion with the United States. Here again much of the rhetoric of the past has vanished, leaving behind a realisation that a special relationship does not mean special privileges. It means a recognition that the two countries still hold interests in common across the world to an extent which goes well beyond the normal dealings between friendly states and peoples. This relationship will continue to the extent, and only to the extent, that each country contributes effectively to the furthering of those common interests.

Much of the argument in Britain has concentrated not on Britain's part in these common enterprises, but on the individual role of Britain in helping to keep the peace in certain well-defined areas.

In our recent history there have always been those in Britain who have opposed spending what is necessary on defence to safeguard the security of the country and protect its interests overseas. Now this group has been joined by those who divide the world up into isolated compartments and argue that the British defence effort must henceforward be confined to our own islands and the Continent of Europe.

The arguments used in defence of this thesis do not in my view stand up to serious examination. We would all prefer to see a world order in which stability was achieved by some accepted system of international enforcement. But failing such a system there is no political law of harmony in operation which ensures that the sovereign states in any given area of the world will settle down automatically into a state of peaceful co-existence. There will be circumstances in the future, as in the past, when independent nations who believe themselves to be threatened will appeal to their friends elsewhere in the world for help. It would be as foolish to claim that such appeals should always be refused as to pretend that they should always be accepted.

There have been instances since the Second World War of British military power failing to achieve the purpose for which it was deployed. But there have also been instances where British power has been strikingly successful in averting a threat not only to British interests but to the stability of the area involved. The arrival of British forces in Kuwait in 1961 ruled out the possibility of an Iraqi takeover. British military action in East Africa in 1964 prevented the overthrow of three Common-wealth East African Governments by armed mutiny. The major British military effort in Eastern Malaysia from 1964 until the change of regime in Indonesia not only maintained the integrity of Malaysia, but also averted a serious threat to the stability of South-East Asia. The lesson to be drawn from both the failures and successes during this period is that a British military presence can be effective if the political context is right. This should, I am sure, be the test for our future policy.

It happens that in the Persian Gulf and in Singapore/Malaysia the political context has been right for the successful deployment of limited British forces. These forces have, politically speaking, been part of the land-scape and their presence has been welcomed by our friends in the area. British forces have not physically protected British investment and installations, but they have helped to ensure the stability without which such British interests cannot flourish.

This analysis, rather than any nostalgia for imperial grandeur, has led the British Conservative Party to the firm conclusion that if a Conservative Government is returned to power it will consult with our friends to see in the conditions then obtaining what kind of British effort is required. In South-East Asia we have put forward a scheme for a joint five-power Commonwealth force including contingents from Britain, Australia, New Zealand, Singapore and Malaysia. We have been greatly encouraged by the fact that since I first advanced this proposal in Canberra, the Governments of Australia and New Zealand have made known in cogent statements of policy the decision of these two countries to keep troops in Singapore/Malaysia after the end of 1971. It is noticeable that informed opinion in Britain is increasingly coming round to accept our analysis. It is more and more recognised that the economies promised as a result of the policy of withdrawal are false in the sense that they expose British interests and the future of our friends to unacceptable risk.

It is sometimes said that foreign affairs are of no real interest to a democratic electorate, and that politicians should concern themselves with bread and butter issues. In my experience this is a considerable over-simplification. Certainly, so far as Britain is concerned, I find that even those who have no detailed knowledge of the particular issues of foreign affairs are nevertheless anxious that their country should not retreat into the shadows. They are quick to resent any suggestion that Britain should contract out of any interest in what happens beyond her shores or the Continent of Europe.

The pattern of future British policy which I have

outlined is I believe based on a realistic assessment of British interests. But it also offers scope for idealism, in building the unity of Europe, in helping forward the prosperity and security of the Commonwealth, and in increasing Britain's share in all those international enterprises, small and great, which are gradually edging us towards a better world.

From *Foreign Affairs*, October 1969.

Appendix
II

The Berkeley Memorandum

1 In theory, different procedures for the choice of Leader have been applied depending on whether the Party is in power and its Leader is Prime Minister, or whether it is in opposition or, as in 1921, though part of the Government, its Leader was not Prime Minister.

2 Thus, in 1911 and 1921, Bonar Law and Austen Chamberlain were confirmed as Leaders of the Party in the House of Commons. (There was a Leader of the Party in the House of Lords who, in theory, had equal status.) In 1902, 1922, 1923, 1937, 1940, 1955, 1957 and 1963, Balfour, Bonar Law, Baldwin, Neville Chamberlain, Churchill, Eden, Macmillan and Home were confirmed as Leaders of the Party as a whole. All were already Prime Minister with the exception of Bonar Law, who became so within a few hours of becoming Party Leader in October 1922.

3 In 1911 and 1921, the Leader of the Party in the House of Commons was formally endorsed in his position at meetings of the Conservative Members of Parliament. However, the Electoral College, which has always endorsed the leadership, has changed several times in this century. In 1902 and 1923 it consisted, in addition to Members of Parliament, of Peers in

possession of the whip; in 1922, adopted prospective candidates were included. In 1937, 1940, 1955, 1957 and 1963, it consisted of Members of Parliament, Peers, adopted prospective candidates and members of the Executive Committee of the National Union.

4 It is not at all clear on whose authority prospective candidates or members of the National Union Executive Committee were included in the Electoral College. However, since this College has never in fact voted, more attention may have been paid to filling a hall rather than devising a synod.

5 It is doubtful whether, in future, the Conservative Party could make a distinction between the position of Leader of the Party and that of Leader of the Party in the House of Commons. Today, whether the Party is in Government or Opposition, or whether the Party Leader in the Commons is Prime Minister or not, he is in fact the Leader of the Party as a whole.

6 In the past and until 1963, despite differences in terminology as to the Leadership and differences in the composition of the Electoral College, the same procedures so far as the Party is concerned have in practice been applied. Soundings of influential people have been taken, a contest has been avoided, and when the Party has been in power, a Prime Minister has already been appointed. The Leader was then presented, amid universal acclaim, to the Electoral College, most of whom, until 1963, had not been consulted.

7 In 1963 it was recognised that there should be broader consultation than amongst Members of the Cabinet or Members of Parliament. No doubt the announcement of Mr Macmillan's resignation to the Party Conference made this inevitable. Uncertainty as

to who was entitled to be consulted, the absence of any formalised procedure, the fact that those who took soundings both decided who were to be sounded and what weighting was to be given to the opinions of those who had been sounded and—most important of all—the fact that those who took the soundings and made the weightings were the only people to scrutinise the results of this somewhat arbitrary poll, has led to a feeling that this can never happen again.

8 If we are to adopt a formal process there should be three basic principles of procedure; Members of Parliament alone should vote, they should do so by secret ballot, and the result should be published.

9 The Election should be confined to Members of Parliament, since it is on their support that the Leader is dependent in the House of Commons. There are no constitutional arguments in favour of the present so-called Electoral College, in which Members of Parliament are heavily outnumbered by Peers, prospective candidates (who have had no Parliamentary experience) and members of the Executive Committee of the National Union—a body 150 strong, some of whom, although they do admirable voluntary work, represent nobody but themselves.

10 Any attempt to make Members of Parliament a minority voice in the Election of their Parliamentary Leader would still further erode the influence of Parliament as an institution. It would be most reprehensible for the Conservative Party to condone such a development.

11 A secret ballot is necessary so that Members of Parliament can quite freely express a preference without being subjected to any pressure or guidance from any

quarter. The system of the alternative vote is desirable since this avoids the need for a second or third ballot some weeks later, as happens with the Labour Party, with the obvious dangers of delay and intrigue.

12 A published result is desirable because this is final and decisive. The day that Harold Wilson's victory over George Brown was announced, together with the voting figures, the personality squabbles in the Labour Party ceased. Had the Conservative Chief Whip been able to produce figures to support his statement that the wish of the majority of the Party had been followed in October 1963, the result could not have been queried from any quarter.

13 It should be possible for the Party to devise rules which can be equally applicable to a situation of power or one of opposition. A Conservative Prime Minister should, in my view, resign first as Party Leader, thus enabling the Party to choose his successor. The Queen would then be spared the necessity of becoming involuntarily concerned in the internal politics of the Conservative Party by having to choose between rival Conservative leaders.

14 It is sometimes supposed that the choice by a political party, when in power, of a Parliamentary Leader who would automatically become Prime Minister represents an attack on the royal prerogative. This is not the case. Nor is the fact that a party which emerges victorious from a General Election already has a Leader an attack on the royal prerogative. The Queen had no alternative but to send for Mr Wilson in 1964, and the King had no alternative but to send for Mr Churchill in 1951. The prerogative is essentially concerned with situations such as arose in wartime in

1916 and 1940 and in a national emergency in 1931. The royal prerogative could conceivably have been involved had the result of the General Election been wholly indecisive. It is not part of the royal prerogative to do for the Conservative Party what it ought to be able to do for itself.

15 Provision should also be made for the periodical re-election of a Party Leader. It would probably be convenient for the Leader of the Party to be re-elected at the beginning of each Parliament.

Appendix III

Procedure for the Selection of the Leader of the Conservative and Unionist Party

1 There shall be a ballot of the Party in the House of Commons.

2 The Chairman of the 1922 Committee will be responsible for the conduct of the ballot and will settle all matters in relation thereto.

Nominations and Preparation of the Ballot

3 Candidates will be proposed and seconded in writing. The Chairman of the 1922 Committee and a body of scrutineers designated by him will be available to receive nominations. Each candidate will indicate on the nomination paper that he is prepared to accept nomination, and no candidate will accept more than one nomination. The names of the proposer and seconder will not be published and will remain confidential to the scrutineers. Nominations will close twenty-four hours before the first and second ballots. Valid nominations will be published.

4 The scrutineers will prepare a ballot paper listing the names of the candidates and give a copy to each voter at a meeting called by the Chairman of the 1922 Committee for the purpose of balloting and consisting of all Members of the House of Commons in receipt of the Conservative and National Liberal Whips.

First Ballot

5 For the first ballot each voter will indicate one choice from the candidates listed, and hand the ballot paper to the scrutineers who will count the votes.

6 If as a result of this ballot one candidate *both* (i) receives an overall majority *and* (ii) receives 15 per cent more of the votes cast than any other candidate, he will be elected.

7 The scrutineers will announce the number of votes received by each candidate, and if no candidate satisfies these conditions a second ballot will be held.

Second Ballot

8 The second ballot will be held not less than two days and not more than four days after the first ballot, excluding Saturdays and Sundays. Nominations made for the first ballot will be void and new nominations, under the same procedure as for the first ballot, will be submitted for the original candidates if required and for any other candidate.

9 The voting procedure for the second ballot will be the same as for the first, save that paragraph 6 above shall not apply. If as a result of this second ballot one candidate receives an overall majority he will be elected.

Third Ballot

10 If no candidate receives an overall majority, the three candidates receiving the highest number of votes at the second ballot will be placed on a ballot paper for a third and final ballot.

11 For the final ballot each voter must indicate two preferences amongst the three candidates by placing

the figure '1' opposite the name of his preferred candidate and the figure '2' opposite the name of his second choice.

12 The scrutineers will proceed to add the number of first preference votes received by each candidate, eliminate the candidate with the lowest number of first preference votes and redistribute the votes of those giving him as their first preference amongst the two remaining candidates in accordance with their second preference. The result of this final count will be an overall majority for one candidate, and he will be elected.

Party Meeting

13 The candidate thus elected by the Commons Party will be presented for election as Party Leader to the Party Meeting constituted as at present.

Index

Adams, Vyvyan, 53
Adamson, Mrs Jennie, M.P., 57
Adenauer, Chancellor, 93, 108
Aldington, Lady, 157–9
Aldington, Lord, 125, 135, 157–9
Allan, Maureen, 159
Allan Robert, 159
Allen, Sir Hugh, 45
Alport, Cuthbert, M.P., 75
Amery, Julian, M.P., 29, 122
Anderson, Lieutenant, 42
Andrew, Sir Herbert, 113
Anstruther-Gray, Sir William, M.P., 140, 141, 143
Armstrong, Thomas, 160
Asquith, Jean, *see* Barber (Mrs Anthony)
Attlee, Clement, M.P., 16, 46, 47, 69, 71, 78
Avon, Lord, 24, 25, 28, 70, 79, 82, 83, 160, 173, 217, 201; Suez policy, 84–6

Bagnall, Nicholas, 60
Barber, Anthony, M.P., 144, 171, 175, 178
Barber, Mrs Anthony (Jean), 35
Barclay, Sir Roderick, 113
Beevor, Humphry, 60–3

Berkeley, Humphry, M.P., 136, 137; his Memorandum, App. II
Bernstein, Leonard, 160
Bexley, 54, 57–9, 66, 69, 70, 72, 78, 82, 87, 131, 166, 170, 193–7
Birch, Nigel, M.P., 86
Bird, James, 6, 7
Birker, Lord Lindsay of, 17–19, 28, 29
Bishop, Frederick, 113
Blakenham, Lord, 126, 128, 130, 131, 133, 135, 138
Bligh, Sir Timothy, 47, 57, 120, 122, 186
Bliss, Sir Arthur, 160
Boyle, Sir Edward, M.P., 84, 144
Bramall, Ashley, 48, 57, 59, 69, 78, 87
Broadstairs, 2, 3, 5–9, 13, 78, 155, 157–9, 162, 166
Brook, Sir Norman, 92, 93
Brooks, Peter, 47, 50, 51
Buchan-Hepburn, Patrick, *see* Hailes, Lord
Bush, Rosemary, 171, 194
Butcher, Sir Herbert, M.P., 82
Butler, R. A., M.P., 75, 83–6, 120, 123–5, 131, 132, 135, 145, 148
Buzzard, Sir Farquhar, 21

Carr, Robert, M.P., 75, 143
Carrington, Lord, 171, 175, 182
Chadd, Colonel, G. V. N., 41, 42, 70
Chamberlain, Neville, 24, 27, 28, 31, 149, 166
Chelmer, Lord, 124
Cherwell, 20–3, 27, 30
Cherwell, Lord, 21, 82
Chichester-Clark, Robin, M.P., 143
Church Times, 59–63
Churchill, Randolph, 86, 131, 135, 188
Churchill, Sir Winston, M.P., 14, 21, 25, 57, 69, 76, 79, 81, 82, 84, 90, 149, 154, 156, 173, 201, 202, 217
Churchill, Winston, 131
Clifton-Brown, Anthony, 80
Coates, James, 63
Constantine, Sir Theodore, 124
Cooper, A. Duff, 71
Cowdray, Lord, 126
Cripps, Sir Stafford, M.P., 72
Crossman, Richard, 28, 29
Curzon, Cecil, 8, 9, 11, 12

Dalton, Dr Hugh, M.P., 23, 28
Darwin, Frank, 40
Deedes, William, M.P., 53
de Gaulle, General Charles, 93, 98, 102–4, 108, 112, 115, 117
Denman, Edward, 158, 159
Denman, Joy, 158
Dilhorne, Lord, 125
Dines, Edward, 54–7, 66
Dixon, Sir Pierson, 92, 93, 113, 117
Dolland, Steven, 171
Douglas-Home, Sir Alec, M.P., 84, 91, 92, 124, 144–8, 168, 171, 177, 217; as Prime Mini-

ster, 124, 125, 129, 130, 131, 133, 135–41
du Cann, Edward, 135, 177, 178
Duncan, Captain J. A. L., 54

Eccles, Sir David, M.P., 120
Eden, Sir Anthony, *see* Avon, Lord
Egremont, Lord, 86, 87, 187
Emery, Peter, M.P., 141
Evans, Mrs Lilian, 55

Fascism, 23, 24, 26, 28, 30, 32, 34
Feather, Victor, 89
Fletcher-Wood, Major, 53
Forbes, Bryan, 163
Fort, Richard, M.P., 75
Fraser, Hugh, M.P., 29, 35, 39, 40, 48
Fraser, Sir Michael, 42, 48, 122, 130, 132
Fulton, Lord, 17, 18, 35, 36

Galbraith, Tam, M.P., 120
Gale, George, 131
Garnett-Orme, Ion, 64, 65, 77
Gilmour, Ian, M.P., 135
Giulini, Carlo Maria, 160
Goldman, Peter, 122
Goodman, Lord, 12
Gordon Walker, Patrick, M.P., 28
Grande, Brigadier L. D., 53
Grasmere, Lord Morris of, 17, 18, 36
Grimond, Jo, M.P., 199
Guthrie, Sir Giles, 63

Hailes, Lord, 76, 77, 79, 81, 82, 159
Hailsham, Lord, *see* Hogg, Quintin, M.P.
Hamilton, Denis, 187
Hankey, Donald, 38

Hare, John, *see* Blakenham, Lord
Harris, Kenneth, 141
Harrison, Eric, 55, 56
Hart, Miss M. E., 69
Harvey, Ian, 21, 48, 55, 56
Head, Antony, M.P., 84
Healey, Denis, M.P., 35, 48
Heath, Edith Anne Pantony (mother), 2, 3, 8, 16
Heath, Edward Richard George, youth, 1–15; education (Chatham House, Broadstairs), 6–15; Oxford, 16–40; Union Society, 20–39; visits to Germany, 23, 37, 38, Spain, 25; reports in *Isis*, 26, 31–3; active service in Royal Artillery, 40–4; posts in Ministry of Civil Aviation, 45–52; *Church Times*, 59–63; and Brown, Shipley, 63–5; adoption as M.P. for Bexley, 53–9; political progress, 66–89; Suez policy, 81–6; Common Market negotiations, 90–118, App. I; Macmillan retires, 119–26; Board of Trade, 126–32; formulation of party policy, 133–5; selection of leader, 139–46; the private person, 147–64; organisation of Opposition, 165–78; manner and aims of Shadow Cabinet, 175–84; the constituencies, 185–99
Heath, John (brother), 5, 7, 14, 42, 155, 157, 160
Heath, Mary (stepmother), 155–158
Heath, Stephen Richard (grandfather), 2, 13
Heath, William George (father), 2, 3, 5, 6, 7, 12, 13, 16, 39, 146, 155–60
Heathcoat Amory, Derick, M.P., 91
Herbert, A. P., 21

Hewlett, Sir Clyde, 143
Hill, Dr Charles, M.P., 120
Hitler, Adolf, 23, 24, 26, 30, 32
Hoare, Sir Samuel, 92
Hogg, Quintin, M.P., 28, 29, 124–6, 139, 141, 142, 148, 166–7, 174–6
Holt, Martin, 57, 64, 66
Home, Lord, *see* Douglas-Home, Sir Alec, M.P.
Hoos, Peter, 186
Hornsby-Smith, Dame Patricia, 196
Howard, Greville, M.P., 140
Howard, Sir John, 124
Howell, David, M.P., 178
Howells, Dr Herbert, 160
Hudson, R. S., 173
Hughes Young, Michael, *see* St Helens, Lord
Hurd, Douglas, 170, 171
Hurd, Lord, 171
Hyman, Joe, 133

Irwin, Jack, 77
Isis, 21, 26, 29, 31, 36

Jenkins, Arthur, M.P., 45, 46
Jenkins, Roy, M.P., 30, 33–5, 45, 46, 48
Job, Charles, 69
Jollye, Iris, 171
Joseph, Sir Keith, M.P., 144

Kaiser, Philip, 25, 34
Keir, David, 159
Keir, Mrs Thelma Cazalet, 54, 159
Kershaw, Anthony, M.P., 143, 171
Kilmuir, Lord, 120
Kisch, Royalton, 12, 13

Lambton, Lord, M.P., 143
Lee, Sir Frank, 90, 92, 93
Lindemann, Professor, *see*
Cherwell, Lord
Lindsay, A. D., *see* Birker, Lord
Lindsay of
Lloyd, Selwyn, M.P., 84, 120
Lockwood, Lieutenant-Colonel
J. C., 57
Longden, Gilbert, M.P., 75
Lothian, Lord, 40
Lympany, Moura, 160
Lyttelton, Oliver, M.P., 173

McArthur, Peter, 131
MacDonald, Malcolm, 159
MacGregor, John, 169, 170
McKechnie, A. D., 64
McKenna, David, 160
Maclay, John, M.P., 120
Macleod, Iain, M.P., 2, 75, 89,
120, 123–5, 135, 139, 141, 144,
148, 174, 175, 176
Macmillan, Harold, M.P., 28,
29, 75, 139, 141, 148, 160,
171–3, 183, 203, 217, 218;
Suez policy, 84, 85; as Prime
Minister, 86–123; Common
Market negotiations, 90–118;
retirement, 119–26, 135
Macmillan, Maurice, M.P., 48,
122
Malcolm, George, 160
Margadale, Lord, 161
Marlow, Mrs Anthony
(Patricia), 55, 56
Marples, Ernest, M.P., 179, 182
Masefield. Peter, 46, 47, 49–51,
59
Maude, Angus, M.P., 75, 176,
177
Maudling, Reginald, M.P., 75,
124, 130, 139, 141–5, 148, 174,
175, 178

Maxse, Dame Marjorie, 48, 53
Mayhew, Christopher, M.P., 30,
48
Mills, Lord, 120
Minney, R. J., 82
Monckton, Sir Walter, M.P., 89
Morris, Charles, *see* Grasmere,
Lord Morris of
Morrison, Herbert, M.P., 78

Northcliffe, Lord, 3
Nutting, Anthony, M.P., 84

O'Neill, Sir Con, 182
Orme, Daniel, 64

Palmer, Bernard, 62
Pattrick, Mrs Jo, 154
Paul, John, 131
Pheasey, Jack, 55
Poole, Lord, 123, 125, 128, 130,
131
Powell, Enoch, M.P., 75, 86,
125, 142, 143, 174–6, 191
Prior, James, M.P., 171, 192
Profumo John, M.P., 121
Pye, R. A., 70, 194

Race, Anthony, 41
Reeve, Captain, 42
Raeburn, Ashley, 46
Redmayne, Martin, M.P., 120,
135
Rees-Mogg, William, 140
Reeves, Leslie, 131
Remnant, Colonel Peter, 53
Rodgers, Sir John, M.P., 54, 75
Roll, Sir Eric, 92, 93, 113
Rostow, Walt, 19
Rouston, Lieutenant, 42

St Aldwyn, Lord, 142
St Clair, Malcolm, M.P., 148
St Helens, Lord, 83, 85

Salisbury, Lord, 84
Salter, Lord, 21
Sandys, Duncan, M.P., 91, 92, 114
Schreiber, Mark, 178
Schuman, Robert, 71, 73
Scott-Hopkins, James, M.P., 134
Seligman, Madron, 37, 39, 149, 160
Seligman, Nancy, 150, 160
Shackleton, Edward, M.P., 78
Sharp, Mrs Edith, 55
Shepherd, Dame Margaret, 124
Shinwell, Emanuel, M.P., 78
Shuckburgh, Sir Evelyn, 113
Simon, Sir John, 92
Sims, J. G., 47, 50
Smith, F. E., 71
Soames, Christopher, M.P., 91-3, 114, 139, 141, 142
Spectator, 135, 176
Stanley, Oliver, M.P., 173
Stanley, Richard, M.P., 143
Stern, Isaac, 160
Street, Peter, 40

Temple, Canon Frederick, 19
Terry, Walter, 145
Thorneycroft, Peter, M.P., 86, 141
Times, The, 55, 140, 167, 183

Tomblings, P. B., 10
Townsend, Cyril, 170
Toynbee, Philip, 35
Trethowan, Ian, 167-8
Trevisick, John, 60, 61

Urton, Sir William, 130

Vassall, William, 120

Walker, Peter, M.P., 142, 143, 162
Watkinson, Harold, M.P., 120
Watson, Sidney, 160
Watson, Tom, 77
Wedgwood Benn, Anthony, M.P., 148, 149
Weinstock, Arnold, 158
Whitelaw, William, M.P., 138, 142, 144, 171
Whittel, Ronald. 8, 10, 15
Wilson, Harold, M.P., 48, 139, 141, 142, 145, 168, 169
Wilson, Herbert, 146
Winckler, Dr, 23, 38
Wolff, Michael, 188
Wood, David, 183
Woodcock, George, 89
Woolton, Lord, 48, 57
Wyndham, John, *see* Egremont, Lord

THE
ONES
WE
LEAVE
BEHIND

DEANNA LYNN SLETTEN

The Ones We Leave Behind
Copyright 2020 © Deanna Lynn Sletten

ISBN-13: 978-1-941212-56-1

Cover Designer: Deborah Bradseth of Tugboat Design

Novels by Deanna Lynn Sletten

The Women of Great Heron Lake

Miss Etta

Night Music

One Wrong Turn

Finding Libbie

Maggie's Turn

Under the Apple Blossoms

Chasing Bailey

As the Snow Fell

Walking Sam

Destination Wedding

Summer of the Loon

Sara's Promise

Memories

Widow, Virgin, Whore

Kiss a Cowboy

A Kiss for Colt

Kissing Carly

Outlaw Heroes

For Cecilia "Bunny" Edling
You are not forgotten.

THE
ONES
WE
LEAVE
BEHIND

CHAPTER ONE

Diane

Diane Martin strode down the hallway of the Rosewood Senior Living Apartments, smiling and waving to the many residents she passed. The hallway walls were painted a soothing light gray with dark gray wainscoting on the bottom half. Lovely watercolor paintings depicting lake, river, and woodland scenes decorated the walls, and each door displayed a cheerful flower or autumn leaf wreath. But the calming interior did nothing to soothe Diane's frayed nerves. It was Friday afternoon, and she'd just come from the high school where she taught history and social studies. She was tired, but she still had to take her mother shopping and out to dinner as she did every Friday. It wasn't that she minded helping her mother; it was the fact that her mother could be difficult at times and Diane could never gauge when her mother's mood might change. Diane was eager for the day to end.

Walking up to room 212, Diane steeled herself before knocking twice, then slowly opening the door. "Mom? It's me," she called.

"Come in. Come in," an impatient voice called from inside the bedroom. "I'll be ready in a minute."

Diane stepped inside the space and quietly closed the door. Her mother, Joan Hartman, had a two-bedroom apartment with a small kitchen and a good-sized living and dining room. She'd moved into the senior apartment building a year ago after she'd fallen and broken her hip. Once it had healed, the seventy-year-old had finally decided she could no longer live alone in her house and had moved in here. It wasn't exactly a care facility—many of the residents still drove and cooked their own meals. But Joan did have the choice of eating all her meals in the dining room, and there were security devices in each apartment so residents could call for help if needed.

"You'll never believe what Lucy Sutton did at lunch today," Joan said, coming out of her bedroom. She was dressed in a pair of slacks, a light sweater, and flats. Her gray hair was cut short and styled nicely. "She choked on a cut-up grape."

Diane's brows rose. "Is she okay?"

"She'll live," Joan said offhandedly. "But it was quite the spectacle when Arnold jumped up and tried to do the Heimlich maneuver on her. He grabbed her around the waist and squeezed, and they both almost fell over backward." Joan laughed. "If the lunch attendant hadn't intervened, they'd both be in the hospital."

"Mom. That's not funny," Diane said, pushing her shoulder-length blond hair behind one ear. "They could have been seriously hurt."

Joan swatted her hand through the air. "They're fine. It was funny, watching them. We're all old. It's nice to have some excitement once in a while."

Diane shook her head at her mother. Joan wasn't very tall,

and she was petite in size, but she could be a tough one when she wanted to be. She'd always been a tough cookie.

The phone on the end table started ringing, and Diane headed over to answer it.

"Leave it alone," her mother ordered. "Let's go. I have a lot of shopping to do."

Diane stopped, startled by her mother's brusque tone. Diane was fifty-one years old and three inches taller than Joan, but her mother still insisted on talking to her as if she were a child.

The phone stopped ringing, so Diane ignored it. "You should bring a light jacket," she told her mother. "The fall weather is nice right now, but once the sun goes down, it'll be chilly."

Joan nodded and walked slowly toward the closet by the door to get her jacket. She moved slower now since her hip had been replaced. She had other health issues as well, with arthritic knees and hands, and her eyesight wasn't the best, even when wearing her glasses. Moving into the senior apartments had been a relief for Diane. Living in a place where Joan could get help if needed meant Diane didn't have to worry about her mother falling and needing assistance. Winters could be harsh in their town of Minnetonka, MN, with the threat of snow and ice causing a bad fall. Having her mother live in Rosewood took a lot of stress off Diane.

The phone began ringing again. Diane watched as Joan turned and glared at it but didn't move to answer it.

"This is silly," Diane said, annoyed, heading for the phone. "I'll just answer it."

"Don't!" her mother yelled.

Diane ignored her and picked up the handset. "Hello?"

"Hello? Mrs. Hartman?" a male voice asked, sounding rushed. "I'm from the Sun-Times. I wanted to ask you a couple of questions."

Diane frowned and looked at her mother. Joan was waving her hands through the air and saying, "Hang up!"

"I'm sorry," Diane said into the receiver. "What do you want?"

"I'd like to ask you a question. How do you feel about your mother being let out of prison today after sixty-five years?"

Diane's mouth dropped open. She looked again at Joan, whose shoulders had sagged in defeat. Hanging up the phone, Diane approached her mother. "My grandmother is alive?"

Joan nodded. "Yes."

The phone began ringing again as Diane's whole life felt like it was spinning out of control.

CHAPTER TWO

Diane

Late Friday night, Diane returned home to her quiet little neighborhood in Minnetonka, feeling drained. She pulled the car into the garage, which was under one side of her split-level house, and walked upstairs to the living room. Barry Neuman, her boyfriend—how she hated that word for people their age!—was sitting on the sofa with his stocking feet on the coffee table, watching the news.

"You're home later than usual," he said, smiling over at her. "Did you have a nice dinner with your mother?"

Diane dropped her purse in the recliner and fell onto the sofa beside Barry.

"That bad?" he asked, wrapping his arm around her shoulders.

"You're never going to believe what happened." Diane glanced up at the television, and her eyes grew wide. Sitting up straight, she grabbed the remote and turned up the volume.

"Today, after serving sixty-five years for the murder of her husband, Anna Bergman Craine was released from the Shakopee

Correctional Facility at the age of ninety-five," the news anchor reported. *"It's believed she is the longest-serving female prisoner in the state of Minnesota. Craine is being released into the care of a senior care facility in St. Louis Park. No comment has been made by any of her surviving family members."*

Diane watched as they flashed several prison mugshots of Anna across the screen, starting from the time of her incarceration in the mid-1950s to the present. A complete stranger stared back at her—first as a beautiful young woman who slowly aged until she was gray and wrinkled. Diane had trouble believing this woman on the screen was her grandmother. All her life, Diane had been told her grandmother was dead. But she'd been in prison instead.

Barry straightened up and looked curiously at Diane. "That's been on the radio and news all day. Do you know this woman?"

She turned and faced him. "She's my grandmother."

Barry's expression looked as shocked as Diane had felt when her mother had confirmed the news earlier.

"Does your mother know she's out?" he asked.

Diane nodded. "We received a phone call from a reporter asking questions while I was in her apartment. My mother was angry, and I was in shock. She wouldn't even talk about it at first. She said, *'She's been dead to me all these years, and she still is!'* It's unbelievable."

Barry reached for Diane and hugged her. She could smell traces of his spicy aftershave, and she snuggled in closer to his neck, feeling safe against him. Barry always knew the right thing to do in moments of stress or uncertainty. He was laid-back by nature and one of the kindest men she'd ever met. All the children at the grade school where he worked as the principal adored him, and he also worked well with the teachers. It didn't hurt that at age fifty-two, he was still quite handsome with dark wavy hair that was graying at the temples and a kind face. Compared to her ex-husband, who she'd divorced many years ago, Barry was an angel.

"So, what did you and your mother do all evening?" Barry asked, pulling back a little. "Did you discuss this?"

Diane fell back against the cushion again. She was bone tired. The emotions of the evening and the way her mother had behaved had drained her mentally. "After the bombshell announcement, my mother still insisted that I take her shopping and out to dinner. I was in a fog most of the evening. It was so unbelievable to me that she could say her mother was still alive and then pretend it was no big deal."

"Wow," Barry said softly.

"Yeah. Wow." Diane sighed loudly and curled into him again. "Finally, as we sat at the restaurant, waiting for our food, I asked her point-blank what this was all about."

Barry reached for her hand. "What did she say?"

"She was ready to talk by then. She told me tersely that her mother had killed her father when she was five years old and her brother was two. My grandmother just blew his brains out with a pistol. My mom and my uncle went to live with their dad's sister, Aunt Bernice, and my mom said she hasn't seen her mother since. Ever."

"Goodness. That's traumatic. Did Joan see her mother kill her father?" he asked.

Diane shook her head. "No. I asked her that. She said she was told to take her brother to the neighbor's apartment, and then they heard the gunshot. She doesn't remember anything after that. Or else, she doesn't want to tell me. You know my mother. She doesn't share her secrets."

"That's a pretty big secret to keep for sixty-five years," Barry said. He gently kissed Diane's cheek. "And a lot to drop on you out of nowhere."

Diane turned and looked into his warm, brown eyes. "If it hadn't been for the reporter, I never would have known about this. My mom would have taken it to her grave."

Barry whistled low. "The secrets people kept in those days. It's incredible."

Diane nodded, pushing her hair away from her face. "I just keep thinking about that woman—my grandmother—living in prison less than thirty minutes away from me all these years. And I never knew about her."

"Your mother must have really hated her," Barry said.

"Yes." She frowned. "But you don't just shoot your husband on a whim. She must have had a reason."

He nodded. "So, what are you going to do?"

Diane's brows rose. "What do you mean?"

He gave her a small smile. "I've known you for four years. That may not be a lifetime, but it's long enough to know you won't just walk away and forget about this."

She chuckled. "You know me too well. Tomorrow, I'm going online to see what I can find out about Anna Craine's case. It'll bother me for the rest of my life if I don't know the facts."

"Yep. That sounds about right," Barry said. "I'm surprised you aren't starting your research tonight."

Diane sighed. "I can't think straight anymore tonight. I just want to go to bed and snuggle up with the only sure thing in my life right now."

He smiled. "Would that be me?"

She hit him playfully, and after turning off the television, they headed to bed, together.

* * *

The next morning, Diane sat at her kitchen counter with her laptop and began searching for information on her grandmother's case. It was a beautiful September day outside, and Barry was mowing the lawn as she researched. Even though he had his own house across town, he seldom stayed there. Diane wasn't ready to make a full commitment to live together permanently, let alone get married, so their lives were separate on paper even though they spent most nights together.

Armed with only a name and a date, Diane searched for newspaper articles about Anna's murder case. Nothing came up that she could access for free. She finally gave in and paid for a subscription to a newspaper site so she could read the old copies on file. Not knowing the exact date of the murder or trial, she searched the entire year of 1955. Finally, after several wrong hits, she found an article mentioning the murder. Surprisingly, very little was written about it except for her name and that she'd shot her husband once in the head as he slept. There were two pictures with the article, one of Anna and the other of the victim, William.

Diane studied the old, grainy, black and white photos of her grandmother and grandfather. It still seemed surreal to her. Until yesterday, she'd never seen a picture of either of them. It unnerved her that she and her grandmother had similar features. They shared the same face shape and eyes, each with a dimple on their right cheek. She also saw similarities between her grandfather's face and that of her late brother, Dale. Diane understood why no one spoke about Anna, but why had her grandfather been kept a secret?

Another clipping was only a paragraph long stating Anna Bergman Craine had pleaded guilty and been sentenced to life in prison.

Diane's phone rang, startling her. She looked at the screen and smiled. Her daughter, Natalie, was calling from California.

"Hi, sweetie. How's your senior year going?" Diane asked when she answered the phone.

"Hi, Mom. It's fine. I'm already in my routine, and classes are going well."

Diane knew that was an understatement. At twenty-one, Natalie was studying both chemistry and biology at Stanford University in preparation of going to medical school. She was a bright, energetic young woman who'd earned a full academic scholarship for all four years of schooling. She worked hard, and Diane was extremely proud of her.

"What's going on in your life?" Natalie asked.

Diane laughed. That was a loaded question. "You're never going to believe what I found out yesterday. My grandmother, your great-grandmother, is alive. She was just let out of prison here in Shakopee after serving for sixty-five years."

A long pause followed her announcement as Natalie digested what she'd been told.

"Your grandmother is alive? And was in jail? That's insane!" Natalie said, sounding shocked. "Why didn't grandma ever tell you about her?"

"Because my grandmother, Anna, killed my grandfather. His name was William. Mom was just five years old at the time, and I guess she blocked it all out."

"That's incredible! What does grandma think of all this?"

Natalie asked.

"She's still blocking it all out. She told me that her mother was dead to her and still is. She hasn't seen her since that day in 1955 and still doesn't want to see her. I'm still trying to absorb all of this. I was just researching Anna's case online when you called. There isn't much there, though. She pleaded guilty, so there was never a trial."

"Wow! So she spent sixty-five years in prison? And was never let out on parole in all those years? That's so strange. I've heard of murderers getting out after six years," Natalie said.

"I know. It's weird. I'm going to keep researching and try to learn more. I may have to go to the library to find more information. The history teacher in me is coming out in full force." She laughed.

"Why don't you just go to the source? Have you thought about meeting your grandmother?"

A chill ran up Diane's spine. Meet Anna? She was a stranger to her. "I hadn't thought about it. I'm not sure my mother would be happy about that."

"Probably not, but grandma isn't generally happy about anything," Natalie said, chuckling. "This is a once-in-a-lifetime opportunity. And Anna must be up there in years. What if you miss out on meeting her? You might regret it."

"You're right," Diane said. She gazed at the photos on her screen. The more she thought about it, the more she wanted to meet Anna. "But my mother isn't going to like it."

* * *

"Why on earth would you even consider visiting that woman?" Joan nearly screamed at Diane the next day. "She murdered your grandfather—my father. She doesn't deserve to see any of her family."

Diane grimaced as she watched her mother's face turn red with anger. As a young woman, Joan had been a force of nature with her quick temper and strong opinions. Age had not mellowed her. Diane remembered many times as a child hiding in her bedroom with her younger brother Dale until her mother's anger abated. The smallest thing could set her off. And in those days, a few cocktails in the evening had only fueled her temper. The fights between their mother and father had been epic, as were the ones between Diane's mother and her second husband. Hiding was Diane and Dale's only protection. Young Dale had been kind and soft-spoken and had been unable to cope with his mother's harsh demeanor. Often, Diane had found herself between her mother and Dale, protecting him from Joan's wrath. But as she grew older, Diane grew taller than her mother and less afraid. She'd learned Joan was mostly all bark and no bite. Still, when Joan flew into a rage, it still made Diane's heart pound a little faster.

"I'd like to hear her story. All my life, I was told she was dead, and that's why you were raised by Aunt Bernice and Uncle Jim. They were wonderful people, but I feel I should take this chance to get to know Anna."

"Bernice and Jim are the only grandparents you had. It's disrespectful of you to want to meet the woman who killed Bernice's brother. I forbid it!" Joan said firmly.

Diane held her anger in check. "You can't forbid it, Mother. I'm sorry that you don't understand my need to meet Anna, but I want to. I only told you out of respect."

Joan fumed. "If you had any respect for me, you wouldn't see that woman."

"Mom," Diane said gently. "I understand this might be difficult for you. I'm sorry. I won't talk about her again if you don't want me to."

Joan crossed her arms and sat back deeper into her recliner. "Do what you want—you will anyway. That woman should have died in prison. They never should have let her out in the first place. She's a cold-blooded killer."

Diane took a deep breath and let it out slowly. Her mother might be right. Anna might be a terrible human being for all Diane knew. But she had to meet her. Diane wanted to know the truth about her relative—a truth that had been hidden from her all these years.

CHAPTER THREE

Diane

That week, Diane searched all the newspaper accounts on Anna's release to see if she could learn where she was living. The news had said a senior care facility in St. Louis Park, but there were several. Finally, she started calling every care facility on her list, stating outright that she was Anna's granddaughter and wished to speak with her. After three phone calls, she found the right facility.

"Can you prove you're related to Mrs. Craine? We've had a tremendous amount of press requesting interviews with her, and we're trying to protect her from them," a nurse told her over the phone.

Diane thought a moment. She wasn't sure how she could prove they were related. "Would you just tell her I'm Joan Craine's daughter and mention I knew Bernice and Jim Benton, her sister and brother-in-law? Since they've passed away, I'm sure a reporter wouldn't know their names."

The nurse sighed. "Okay. I'll tell her that and see what she says. You know, Mrs. Craine is a very old woman. She tires easily, and all this fuss over her being let out of prison has been hard on her. I hope you're who you say you are."

"I'm telling the truth," Diane said gently. "If she agrees to see me, would it be possible to visit her this Saturday afternoon?"

"I'll call you back if she agrees," the nurse said.

Diane waited on pins and needles for two full days, waiting for a response. She could barely concentrate on work. Thursday night, she and Barry went out to dinner.

"I've racked my brain, but I can't figure out how to prove I'm Anna's granddaughter. I guess I could try to find my mother's birth certificate and show them mine, too, but would that be enough?" she said to Barry as they ate their meal.

"Would your mother let you use her birth certificate?" he asked.

"That's another problem. Probably not. I'd have to dig for it. I've never seen it, so I wouldn't even know where she keeps it."

Barry smiled. "That would be fun—getting caught digging through your mother's private possessions. She'd love that."

Diane rolled her eyes. "Yeah. There would be a second murder in the family then." She chuckled. "I'm obsessed with meeting Anna. I don't know why. Ever since I saw her picture and noticed how much we look alike, I feel as if I know her. Is that weird?"

"Yeah. But then, I always knew you were a bit strange." Barry winked. He reached for her hand. "I'm sure you'll get to see her. Anna hasn't seen her family in sixty-five years. She'll want to meet you."

The next day between classes, Diane's phone rang. She didn't recognize the number.

"Hello?"

"Hello? Mrs. Martin?" the woman on the other end of the line asked. "I'm Emma Alverez, Mrs. Craine's caseworker. I was told you're interested in visiting her this weekend."

Diane's heart pounded. If Anna's caseworker was calling, she might have a shot at seeing her. "Yes, Ms. Alverez. I'm her granddaughter, and I've never met her. I'd like the chance to get to know her if it's possible."

"Yes. Well, Mrs. Craine was extremely excited to hear that a relative wanted to see her. I'm not sure if you're aware or not, but no one visited her the entire time she was in prison. I'm a little surprised you'd like to see her now."

Diane thought she heard judgment in Ms. Alverez's tone. "I understand. To tell you the truth, I didn't even know my grandmother was alive, let alone living only miles from me in Shakopee. My mother and my great aunt never said a word about her. But now that I know she's alive, I'd like to meet her." Diane held her breath, hoping her answer would be yes.

"Mm. I do understand that. People were embarrassed in those days to say they had a relative in prison. May I pry and ask why you want to see her?"

Diane frowned. Did she have to give a reason? "Honestly, Ms. Alverez, I don't have a good reason other than wanting to meet her. She's my grandmother. And at ninety-five years old, I doubt if I have many years left to get to know her. Wouldn't you want to meet your grandmother if our positions were reversed?"

"Yes, I would. I'm sorry to grill you like this, but I just want to make sure your intentions are good. She's a sweet, kind woman, and as you say, very old. I don't want anyone upsetting her. She's paid her debt to society and then some. But if all you want to do is meet her and form a friendly relationship with her, I'm all for that. After over six decades in prison, she needs that."

"I understand, and that is all I want. I'm not going to berate her for the past. I don't even know what happened other than what the news has reported. My mother won't speak a word about it. I just want to meet her, nothing more."

"Okay. I know she's excited to meet you, too. Can you come tomorrow around one? I plan to be there too, just at first to introduce you to her. If all goes well, then you and she can speak in private."

Diane's heart leapt with excitement. "Yes. That'll be fine. Thank you, Ms. Alverez."

"Please. Call me Emma," she said, sounding friendlier. "I'll see you tomorrow."

Diane hung up just as the students were filing into her afternoon class. She was so happy she could burst. But first, she had work to do.

She couldn't wait to call Barry and Natalie with the good news.

* * *

The next day, Diane drove the short distance from her home to the senior care facility in St. Louis Park. She'd stopped on the way to pick up a bouquet of flowers as a gift. She hadn't wanted to come empty-handed, and flowers were the only gift she could think of. She'd also brought a few pictures of her daughter Natalie as a child and an adult to show Anna if she were interested.

Anna. Is that what she should call her? Or grandmother? It was such a strange scenario that Diane hadn't a clue what to call her own relative.

Once there, she parked and walked across the parking lot which was covered in fall leaves. The day was warm and breezy, and she could smell autumn in the air. Diane had worn slacks—she hadn't wanted to insult Anna by wearing jeans, although she had no idea where that idea came from—a blue sweater, and low heels. She hadn't wanted to look like she was trying too hard, or too little. It was all so silly.

Once inside, Diane signed in at the front desk and was directed to Anna's room. She strode down the first-floor hallway and stopped at the open door of room 114. Taking a deep breath, she knocked.

"Come in," an elderly voice called from inside the room.

Diane stepped inside and was immediately aware of how small the room was. A slender woman with short, dark hair stood by a recliner that had it's back to Diane. She guessed the younger woman was Emma Alverez. Emma waved her inside, and Diane walked up next to her.

"Diane Martin?"

Diane nodded.

"It's nice to meet you. I'm Emma." She shook hands with Diane. "And this is Anna Craine." Emma smiled down at the woman seated in the recliner.

Diane looked down into the face of her grandmother for the very first time. Her heart pounded. Anna smiled up at her expectantly. Her gray hair was twisted up into a bun, and her skin was deeply wrinkled. But her watery blue eyes were kind as she gazed up at her granddaughter.

"It's so nice to meet you, Mrs. Craine," Diane said, reaching out her free hand to shake Anna's.

Anna reached out both hands and held Diane's. "It's a pleasure to meet you, dear," the elderly woman said, her voice gentle. "Please, call me Anna. Everyone does." Her words were slow and measured, reflecting her age.

Chills ran up Diane's spine as she held her grandmother's hand. Only a week ago she hadn't even known her grandmother was alive. And now, here she was, a sweet elderly woman holding her hand as if they'd known each other for a lifetime.

"Are those for me?" Anna asked, her eyes growing brighter as she gazed at the flowers. "Thank you so much. How I love having fresh flowers."

"Oh. Yes. They are," Diane said, feeling tongue-tied. What does one say to their long-lost grandmother who had been only a few miles away the entire time you were growing up? It was such a surreal experience.

"Here. I'll put them on the table," Emma said, taking the vase of flowers from Diane and placing them on the small table beside Anna's recliner. "Why don't you pull up that chair and sit, Diane?" Emma said.

Diane glanced around and saw the padded chair by the wall next to the bathroom door. That was really all the room held; a bed, recliner, and a bathroom. A television was hung up above in the corner so it could be seen from the chair and bed. On the far wall was a curtained window looking out into a courtyard where picnic benches sat and tall trees displayed rich, beautiful colors.

Diane sat and smiled at Anna, who'd been watching her.

"It's a bit awkward, isn't it?" the older woman asked. "Us meeting for the first time?"

A relieved sigh escaped Diane, much to her surprise. She hadn't even realized she'd been holding in her breath. She laughed. "Yes, it is. But I think you just helped break the ice."

Anna smiled warmly. "Tell me everything about my little

Joanie. My, but of course she isn't little, is she? She must be what? Seventy now? It's so hard for me to believe that. How is she?"

Emma interrupted. "I'll be leaving now. You two enjoy your conversation. It was nice meeting you, Diane. I'll see you in a couple of days, Anna. Call me if you need anything."

Anna thanked her and said goodbye. Diane did also. After Emma left, Diane began answering Anna's questions.

"Mom is doing fine. She had a bad fall a year ago, and now lives in a senior apartment complex, but it's very nice, and she likes it there. She gets around well, and I take her shopping once a week since she no longer wants to drive the busy roads."

"Oh, the roads. Yes. I can't believe how big and bustling this whole area has become. I've been out and around over the years, but it still surprises me how big it's grown," Anna said. "Nothing like in the days before I went inside."

"You've been out over the years?" Diane asked, interested. "How so?"

Anna's hand moved nervously up to the collar of her floral blouse and touched the gold cross pendant she wore. "Inmates who were on good behavior were occasionally allowed to go to a play or on a picnic with staff. The system was more about reward than punishment as a way of rehabilitating the women. But enough about me. Please tell me more. Is your father still alive? Do you have siblings? Do you know if my little boy, Matthew, is still alive? There's so much I'd like to know."

Diane's heart went out to this woman who hadn't heard a word about her children all these years. How painful it must have been. If Diane had ever been separated from her daughter when she was a child, it would have ripped her heart out.

"Well, my father is no longer alive. My mom, your Joan, was married twice. She divorced my father when I was young.

He'd served a year fighting in Vietnam and came back a different person. She stayed married to him for nine more years but couldn't cope with his behavior any longer. After that, she married another man, Albert Hartman, and they were together for twenty years before he passed away. Mom hasn't married since his death."

Anna slowly shook her head. "Poor Joanie. I'm sorry her first marriage was difficult. I can certainly understand. I'm glad she married again, though."

"Yes. Well, Albert wasn't a saint either. He was very controlling. They argued a lot. But overall, they did okay, I guess." Diane hadn't liked Albert from the moment she'd met him. But her mother had married him anyway. She and Dale had stayed as far away as they could when they drank and argued. It had been a tough time growing up with all the fighting.

"I'm sorry, dear. I had hoped Joanie had a good life. But she had you. Do you have any siblings?"

Diane's heart warmed as it always did when she thought of Dale. He'd been such a sweet child and had grown into a good, caring man. "Yes. A brother, Dale. He was three years younger than me. He was perfect in every way—handsome, kindhearted, and sweet. He was married for a while, but they divorced. It nearly tore him apart." Her expression turned sad. "Unfortunately, Dale died in a car accident in 2018. He worked as a city engineer, designing roadways and city streets in Minneapolis. A very smart man and well-loved by all."

Anna moved forward in her chair and touched Diane's arm. "I'm so sorry, dear. It sounds like he was a good person. And an engineer. Just like his grandfather. I'm sure Joanie was very proud of him."

Diane's brows rose. "His grandfather? Was my grandfather an engineer?"

Anna stared at her a moment, looking puzzled. "Oh. I suppose your mother doesn't remember her father worked as an engineer for many different companies. She was so young before the incident happened."

Incident. Diane thought that was an odd way of describing the murder. "My mother has never spoken about you or my grandfather. I didn't see a photo of either of you until I saw the pictures in the newspaper."

Anna's face fell, and she sat back in the chair. The recliner's thick cushions seemed to envelop her tiny body. "I suppose your mother wouldn't have spoken about me. I was told she and her brother went to live with William's sister and brother-in-law. Bernice had no love for me, not that I blamed her. But I'm surprised Joanie never talked about her father."

Diane was unsure of what to say. She didn't want to continue being the bearer of bad news. How much terrible news could a ninety-five-year-old woman take? She decided to change the subject. "I have a beautiful daughter who's attending college in California. Would you like to see a picture of her?"

The older woman's face brightened. "Yes. Please."

Diane showed her the photos she'd brought along, and Anna fawned over what a lovely girl Natalie was.

"She looks so much like you," Anna said, smiling.

"Yes. At least how I looked when I was younger." Diane caught Anna's eyes with hers. "I was surprised at how much I resembled you when I saw the photo of you at a younger age."

Anna studied her face and nodded. "Yes. I saw it the moment you walked in. That's how I knew you were my grand-daughter. We share very strong genes. I have my mother's face and my father's eyes. She was German, and he was Swedish. I can see them in you, too."

German and Swedish. Diane hadn't known her heritage before. Everything had been kept a secret. "I'd love to hear more about them sometime."

"I'd love to tell you about them," Anna said.

Diane could tell that Anna was growing tired. She was surprised to see they'd already been talking for two hours. "I should let you rest," Diane said, although she would have loved to talk with Anna all day. "Thank you so much for seeing me."

Anna smiled at her. "No, dear. Thank you for coming. This has been the joy of my life to see you and speak with you. There's so much I'd like to talk with you about. Would you come to visit me again?"

Diane reached for her grandmother's hands. "Yes. I'd love to come again. I work all week, but I can drop by next week. On Sunday, maybe. Will that be okay?"

"Yes, dear. That'll be fine. Come whenever you are able. I look forward to it."

Diane stood and placed her chair up against the wall where she'd found it. When she turned to Anna, she saw that the older woman had risen from her chair with the aid of a walker. It was difficult for Diane to believe that this tiny, frail woman had committed cold-blooded murder. There had to be more to the story.

"Well, I'll see you next Sunday at one," Diane said, resisting the urge to hug Anna. She didn't want to act too familiar when she hardly knew her. But deep inside, she felt drawn to Anna in a way she'd never felt about her Aunt Bernice or her mother.

"I'll look forward to it," Anna said, sounding out of breath. "And dear? Do you think that Joanie might come along too?"

Diane paused a moment. She didn't want to tell this sweet woman that her daughter hated her and refused to see her. "I'll see what I can do," she said gently. With one more meaningful look between the two women, Diane left.

CHAPTER FOUR

Diane

That evening as Diane and Barry ate dinner at her house, she described her visit with her newly found grandmother. "She seems so sweet and kind. She wanted to know everything about the family, and it hurt her that my mother had never spoken about her or my grandfather to me. It was hard to believe she'd killed a man without a good reason," Diane said.

"She did it years ago. People can change as they age. Maybe she was a lot meaner and tougher when she was young," Barry suggested.

Diane snorted. "Yeah, except mean people don't usually mellow with age. Look at my mother. She's been tough her whole life, and age hasn't made her nicer—it's made her meaner."

Barry looked at her thoughtfully. "Have you ever thought that maybe life made your mother tough? Now that you know the truth of her childhood, maybe it explains why she's angry and bitter."

Diane had thought of that over the past week, but she didn't believe that was the only reason. "My childhood wasn't perfect either, but I'm not bitter and mean about it. Life is what you make of it despite your experiences. I can't give my mother a free pass on that."

Barry shrugged as he took another bite of roast beef and washed it down with a sip of soda. "I get that. You've been able to maintain a relationship with your mother despite her behavior towards you. But maybe your mother hasn't been able to reconcile her feelings about what her mother did. Until she can, if ever, I doubt she'll let go of her anger."

Diane set her fork down and stared at Barry. "Are you sure you aren't a psychologist disguised as a grade-school principal?"

He chuckled. "Nope. I'm just little ole' me. But I did have to take psychology classes to get my degree."

"Hmm. I suppose I have to accept that my mother has issues for a reason. And it couldn't have been easy living with Aunt Bernice and Uncle Jim after her father's death. I mean, they definitely would have sided against Anna. It's just terrible how families tear themselves apart."

Barry reached across the table and took her hand. "But it's amazing how wonderful a family can be when they pull together."

She smiled at him, but she knew what his underlining motivation was. Barry had proposed to her twice in the past four years. Each time, she'd told him she was afraid of marrying again. He understood but still persisted. "Unfortunately, not everyone comes from a perfect, loving family like yours," she said.

"That's true." He stood to take his plate to the kitchen. He came back with a big piece of chocolate cake he'd bought at the local bakery. "I'm positive we have a few skeletons in the closet, too, but we keep ours locked away."

She laughed.

"Want a bite?" he asked, offering her a small piece of his cake.

"A bite? I want a whole piece." She accepted his bite and then went to get her own. Barry always had a way of making her feel better in any situation. Of course, the chocolate cake helped too.

* * *

The next Friday after school, Diane went to pick up her mother for their usual outing. Joan was in a terse mood when Diane showed up, but nothing was said between them about Anna. They shopped for groceries and stopped at Target for a few items and a prescription for Joan's arthritis, then they went to the Olive Garden for dinner. They had almost finished their meal when Joan finally asked, "Did you go see that woman?"

Diane knew precisely who "that woman" was. "Yes, I did. We had a nice visit."

"Humph. I can't imagine what about. I suppose she told you all sorts of lies," Joan said.

Diane took a deep, calming breath. "Mom, I wouldn't know the truth from the lies because I don't know anything about her. It's all been a secret for so long. She was curious about everyone and how they were. She asked about you."

Joan narrowed her eyes. "I hope you didn't tell her anything. She doesn't deserve to know my business."

"Anna's an old woman, Mom. She served sixty-five years in prison to pay her debt to society. She can't harm anyone. I answered her questions. She deeply regrets missing out on your life, and mine. In fact, she said she'd love to see you."

"That's never going to happen," Joan snapped. "And I hope you've satisfied your curiosity about her and won't see her again."

"I plan on visiting her again on Sunday. I'd like to get to know her better," Diane said gently.

Joan's lips drew into a thin line. "You're only doing this to spite me."

She shook her head. "No, Mom. I'm not. I just want to get to know Anna. That's all. And you're welcome to come along if you'd like to."

"Never." Joan said the words with finality. Diane knew not to mention it again.

They were both silent on the ride back to Joan's apartment and as they put away her purchases. Picking up her purse and jacket, Diane said goodbye to her mother.

"I'll see you next Friday," she said, heading for the door.

"Wait." Joan walked into her bedroom as Diane stood by the door, waiting. Finally, her mother walked out, carrying an old wooden box a bit larger than a shoebox.

"If you insist on seeing that woman again, give her this. Aunt Bernice gave this to me before she passed away. I never wanted any of these things. I want nothing from that woman."

Diane accepted the box. It looked to be handmade with a rose carved into the lid. A latch was on it, but no lock. "What's in here?"

"Her things. I'd thought about burning it all, and now I wish I had. But since I have it, you may as well give it back to her. Good riddance." Joan turned away and headed for her living room.

"I'll make sure Anna gets it," Diane said. "Goodnight, Mom." Diane doubted if her mother even heard her because she'd already sat on the sofa and switched on the television.

That night, Diane called Natalie and told her about the box.

"Ooh. The plot thickens! What's in it?" Natalie asked, sounding intrigued. Diane had already spoken to her earlier in the week about her visit with Anna, and Natalie was very interested in the older woman.

"I don't know. I haven't opened it," Diane said. "Your grandmother said it was Anna's box. I feel like I'd be invading her privacy if I looked through it."

"Aren't you even a little curious?" Natalie asked. "I am."

"Of course I'm curious. But it's not mine. I'll bring it to her tomorrow. It's up to Anna whether or not she wants to share what's inside with me."

"Wow. You have more willpower than I do," Natalie said, laughing. "But you're right. It belongs to her. Let me know if you get to see inside."

Diane agreed before saying goodnight and hanging up. The box was sitting on the bed beside her, and she ran her hand over the smooth, aged wood. She wondered who'd made the box for Anna. Had Anna's grandfather made it? Or maybe Anna's father. Diane hoped she'd find out tomorrow.

"Are you thinking of opening it?" Barry walked in the room as he slipped out of his sweatshirt, leaving on only a T-shirt.

Diane's hand flew to her chest. "You scared me. No, I'm not going to open it. I was just wondering who'd made the box for Anna. I hope she'll tell me tomorrow."

"I'm sure she will." He slipped off his jeans and walked into the master bathroom to brush his teeth.

Diane watched Barry as he readied for bed. At fifty-two, he was still in good shape. Being tall and naturally lean helped.

But he always kept busy working around the house, and they took long walks often after dinner to stay in shape. Barry was everything her first husband hadn't been. He had the patience of a saint and always treated her respectfully. And he was cute. That last thought made her smile.

"What are you grinning at?" he asked, coming back into the room and pulling back the covers.

"You." She stood and placed the box on her nightstand, then slid into bed beside him. "Have I told you lately how much I appreciate being able to bounce all this crazy family stuff off of you?"

Barry reached over and pulled her close. She snuggled into his chest, enjoying his warmth. "I know you do. We make a good team, you and me." He brushed her hair away from her forehead and dropped a kiss on her cheek.

All the tension from the evening evaporated, and Diane snuggled in even closer. She knew she was lucky to have someone like Barry in her life. A man who didn't criticize or belittle her in any way. A partner who cared about her well-being and listened to her when she spoke. She knew first-hand that not all men were like that, and it made her appreciate him even more.

So why couldn't she commit to him?

Barry leaned over and kissed her again, brushing away all her worries as she relaxed in his embrace.

* * *

Promptly at one on Sunday, Diane showed up at Anna's door carrying the wooden box under her arm.

"Come in, dear," Anna said when Diane knocked on her door. She smiled at her words. No one except Barry had ever called her 'dear,' and she thought it was sweet.

"Hello, Anna. How are you today?" Diane asked. She set the box down on a small table by the door, took off her coat, and slipped off her shoes. It was raining outside, and she didn't want to drip water all over the laminate wood floor.

Anna was once again sitting in the recliner, facing away from her. "I'm fine, dear. I've been extremely excited about seeing you. Other than Emma and the nurses, I don't get any visitors."

"What about the other women who live here? Hasn't anyone come to introduce themselves?" Diane asked, surprised. At her mother's apartment complex, the women couldn't wait to meet new residents who'd just moved in.

"I'm afraid no one is in a rush to meet the murderer next door," Anna said, sadness in her voice. "I eat my meals in here, too. Many of the residents complained that they shouldn't have to socialize with a former prisoner, so the nurses thought it was best to keep me away from the dining room."

Diane was appalled. She moved closer to Anna and saw the unhappiness on her face. "That's terrible. People can be so mean."

Anna's features softened. "I guess I can't blame them. They don't know me. But I do miss the companionship I had at the reformatory. The women I knew there were kind to me. Many called me grandma, which tickled me."

"That's sweet," Diane said, her heart warming at the inmates who thought of Anna as family. She moved the chair over and sat in front of the recliner. "Maybe as people get used to you living here, you'll make friends. It would be nice if you could eat with them in the dining room."

"Maybe," Anna said. "You just never know." She looked at

Diane hopefully. "Did you ask Joanie to come and visit? Will she?"

Diane sighed. Anna's eyes looked so excited over the prospect of seeing her daughter. "I'm afraid she didn't want to come today. But I'm working on her. Hopefully, she'll soften to the idea soon. I'm sorry."

Anna's smile fell. "It's not your fault, dear. It's mine. I hurt her deeply. I shouldn't expect much from her. Like you said, though, one never knows. Joanie may change her mind."

It hurt to see how disappointed Anna was that Joan hadn't come to see her. But Diane couldn't force her mother to come. Still, she wished she could do something that would brighten Anna's day.

"I can't remember if you told me about my Matthew," Anna said, once again hopeful. "He'd be sixty-seven, wouldn't he? Do you think he'd come to see me?"

Diane's heart dropped. She hated being the one to tell her all the bad news. "I'm sorry, but Uncle Matt passed away in 2011. He had a heart attack and passed quickly."

Tears filled Anna's blue eyes. She reached for a tissue from the table beside her and wiped her eyes. "He was only two years old when I left them. He never even knew me." She blew her nose, then asked, "Did he have a good life?"

A smile spread across Diane's face as memories of her Uncle Matt filled her thoughts. "Yes, he did. He went to college and became an architect. He designed homes around the area and did quite well. Uncle Matt married later in life, though, so they didn't have any children. But they were happy. He was a very kind man, much like my brother, Dale. In fact, he used to take Dale out fishing and camping sometimes. My stepfather didn't do things like that. So Uncle Matt was a good role model for my brother and me."

Anna's eyes brightened. "That makes me so happy. I'm glad he had a good life. What about his wife? Does she still live around here?"

Diane shook her head. "She remarried a few years later and lives in Arizona now."

"Well, I suppose that's to be expected. I'm happy she found someone else. We all need someone."

Her words touched Diane in a way she'd hadn't expected. Yes, we all need someone in our lives. Hadn't Diane just thought that very thing last night about how lucky she was to have Barry? But why did people keep those they loved at arm's length? Why did she?

Diane looked up and saw Anna staring at her curiously. "Sorry. I was just thinking about something," she said, embarrassed she'd been caught lost in her thoughts. "Oh. I almost forgot." Diane stood and retrieved the box she'd left by the door. "My mother had this box that she said belonged to you. She told me to give it to you." As she came into Anna's view, the older woman gasped.

"My keepsake box," she said, looking stunned. "I can't believe you have it."

Diane placed it gently in Anna's lap, and the older woman ran her hands lovingly over its smooth surface. "I've had this since I was twelve years old."

Twelve years old, Diane thought. It had lasted all these years. "That's amazing. I'm glad you're able to have it again."

Anna glanced up at Diane. "Did you look inside?"

She shook her head. "No. I figured it belonged to you and was none of my business."

A slow smile crossed Anna's lips. "I wouldn't have minded.

But it's sweet that you didn't." She gazed at the box again. "I wonder if everything is still inside. I'm almost afraid of the memories it contains."

Diane hadn't thought about that. What if the items inside only reminded her of the worst part of her life? She watched as Anna slowly lifted the tarnished latch from its hook. She opened the lid, and Anna peered inside. Her grandmother's expression was unreadable.

"Come closer, dear," Anna said. "You can see what's inside."

Diane moved her chair beside the recliner. As she looked inside the old box, she saw it was filled with antique photos, letters, and what looked to be three velvet jewelry boxes.

"My entire past is in this box," Anna said. "Everything I held dear and some things that reminded me of the worst parts."

A lump formed in Diane's throat as she gazed into the box. She tried to imagine what she would put in a box if all her most treasured possession had to be in one place. Pictures of Natalie, of course. And maybe jewelry Barry had given her. It would be hard to choose. But here, all Anna held dear sat in this small container lined in purple velvet that had faded over time.

"Let me move a table over so you can place the box on it," Diane offered, noticing that Anna's thin legs were shaking under its weight. The table beside the recliner was actually three tables that stacked on top of each other. Diane removed one from underneath and placed it beside Anna so she could reach it. Then Diane moved the box from Anna's lap onto the table.

"Thank you, dear," Anna said. She moved forward and gently lifted a photo that sat on top of the pile. A sweet smile spread across her lips.

"Who is that?" Diane asked, curious to learn about everything the box contained. It was a photo of a young man standing in front of a farmhouse. He was tall and thin with a head of thick, dark hair. His clothing didn't fit very well, looking like it was homemade. And he wasn't smiling. He looked tired. And sad.

"This was my older brother, Andrew." She sighed happily. "How I adored him. He was fourteen when this was taken. I was eleven. That was the last time I saw him."

"Oh, my goodness. That's terrible. What happened to him?" Diane asked, conjuring in her mind some terrible farm accident.

Anna raised her eyes to meet Diane's. "I don't know."

CHAPTER FIVE

Anna — 1936

Anna sat on the window seat in the kitchen, quietly talking to her cloth doll. It was a warm September day, and she'd just returned from walking the mile home from the schoolhouse. Her grandmother had poured her a glass of milk and given her a biscuit, and she sat there, enjoying the breeze while eating her treat.

"Don't dally, you lazy girl," Sophia Roth scolded her granddaughter in her thick, German accent. "We have much work to do."

"Yes, Grandmother," the eleven-year-old said obediently. Anna knew better than to ignore her grandmother when she spoke to her. Once, Anna hadn't answered her and was slapped across the face and called insolent. Anna had no idea what insolent meant, but she tried hard not to be accused of being insolent again.

"Lazy child," Sophia said, clucking her tongue. "Just like your mother, you are. Useless and lazy."

Anna winced as she quickly finished her snack and slid off

the window seat. It always hurt when her grandmother talked badly about her mother. She loved her mother dearly, despite not having seen her in over six years. Her mother, Lillian Roth Bergman, was a beautiful, petite woman with a lovely face that had high cheekbones and full lips. Her eyes were a warm brown, and her dark hair was thick and wavy. Anna's aunts called Lillian the most beautiful of the Roth sisters, but everyone said she was the most headstrong, too. Anna, who proudly held the middle name of Lillian, tried not to be headstrong. She found that everyone looked badly upon a woman with strength.

Brushing the crumbs from her ankle-length, muslin dress, Anna carried her beloved doll, Lily, across the room to the table and sat in a chair. She sat quietly, awaiting whatever work her grandmother expected of her. Sophia was washing green beans in the kitchen sink under the old hand pump. Their farmhouse was built in the 1890s when Anna's grandfather, Victor, had homesteaded the acreage in central Minnesota after he, Sophia, and their family had immigrated to the United States. Since then, he'd acquired another two hundred acres that had a portion of a lake on it. It was fertile land, and they'd made a decent living raising milk cows. But now, in their seventies, Victor and Sophia were slowing down. Their two sons ran the dairy, although Victor kept his hand in it.

Anna studied her grandmother as she worked beside the sink. She was a short woman, but broad in girth, and her once dark hair, now mostly gray, was pulled back in a severe bun. She always wore dark colors. Her dress today was brown with a high collar and touched the floor. Her physical appearance matched her staunch personality. Anna never understood why her grandmother was always angry. Her papa said it was because she'd had a tough life, and maybe that was true. But sometimes Anna wished her grandmother would smile at her.

Sophia placed the colander of beans into a bowl and set it on the table in front of Anna. "Snap the ends off," she ordered, setting an empty bowl on the table too.

"Yes, ma'am," Anna said dutifully. She set Lily on the table so the doll was watching her, then brushed her short, thick hair behind her ears. Anna hated the pageboy style that her grandmother always cut her hair. She thought it made her look like a boy. Anna couldn't wait until she was older and would be allowed to grow out her hair and pin it up like a lady.

The little girl began snapping the beans and placing them carefully in the bowl. In the background, she could hear her grandmother toss two more small logs into the cookstove and place a heavy pan on it.

As Anna worked, she thought about her brother, Andrew, who she had seen walking home from school today. He was older than she, and they no longer lived together at her grandparents' house. At the beginning of summer, Andrew had been farmed out to a neighbor to work for his room and keep. Anna missed her older brother dearly. He'd always been the one who could bring a smile to her face when she was sad about her mother being gone or her father far away at work. It was Andrew who'd sewn the cloth doll for her six years ago so she wouldn't feel lonely. He'd embroidered the doll's face in a sweet smile and had braided yellow yarn for her hair. Her dress was made from an old pair of plaid flannel pants Andrew had outgrown. When Anna hugged Lily, she could still smell Andrew's scent.

"You're daydreaming again," her grandmother said, snapping Anna out of her thoughts. "Lazy girl! Finish the beans. The water is almost boiling."

Anna worked faster and finished breaking the ends off the beans. Her grandmother snatched the bowl away and dumped them into the pot of boiling water.

"Go set the table for supper," her grandmother growled. "Your aunt and uncle will be joining us."

Anna reached for Lily, but her grandmother grabbed the doll away. "Leave it here! You are too old for playing with dolls. I should burn this ragged thing in the stove."

"No! Please, Grandmother. I love my doll. Please don't hurt her. Andrew made her for me," Anna pleaded. "I'll put her away and do my work. Please don't burn her." Tears slid down her cheeks as she wrapped her arms around herself. Anna was petrified that her grandmother would destroy the only thing she had to remind her of her brother.

"Stupid, stupid, girl," Sophia said, tossing the doll back on the table. "Your brother is stupid too. Boys should not be sewing dolls for girls." She shook her head and walked away.

Anna snatched her doll from the table and hugged it close. How she wished she could run away and live with her momma and papa, far, far away from this terrible farm. Her grandfather wasn't as mean; he always had a piece of candy and a warm smile for her when he returned from town. But she spent most of her time with her grandmother and endured many insults from her. As Anna set the large table in the dining room with her grandmother's best silverware, she wished her father would take her away from here forever.

* * *

Later that night, as Anna lay in her little bed in the attic bedroom, she heard a familiar voice greeting her grandparents in the parlor. Papa! Her wish had come true! Anna sprang from the bed and ran barefoot down the two flights of stairs in her nightgown. There, wearing his work suit, stood her father smiling wide at her.

"Papa!" she cried, jumping into his arms with tears of joy running down her cheeks. "Papa! I'm so happy you're here!"

Jon Bergman hugged his daughter close. "Älskling! My sweet Anna. I'm so happy to see you." His Swedish accent was still thick even after two decades of living in America.

Grandmother Sophia glared at Anna from her rocking chair, a pair of knitting needles in her hands while Grandfather Victor only smiled at the reunion between father and child. But Anna didn't care if her grandmother was upset. Her papa was here, and that was all that mattered.

"Are you staying the whole weekend?" Anna asked, still holding her father tightly.

"I will be here a couple of days, yes," he said.

She could feel her father's thin frame tighten, and he set her down carefully before pulling a handkerchief from his pocket. A deep rumble came from his chest, and he covered his mouth as he coughed. Anna's smile faded.

"Papa? Are you sick?" she asked, looking too concerned for a child of her age.

Jon coughed again, and Anna thought she saw blood fill his handkerchief. The sight of it frightened her.

"Go to bed, Anna!" Grandmother Sophia barked. "It is too much past your bedtime."

Anna looked at her father. "Must I?" she asked, wanting to stay with him.

Jon composed himself and tucked his handkerchief into his jacket pocket. "Go along to bed, little one," he said lovingly. "I will be here in the morning, and we will eat breakfast together."

Anna smiled again and nodded. "Goodnight, Papa," she said, still elated he was here. Remembering her manners, she turned to her grandparents. "Goodnight, Grandmother and Grandfather."

Her grandfather nodded, but her grandmother ignored her and continued to work on her knitting.

Long after Anna had gone back to bed, she lay there hugging Lily tightly, unable to fall asleep. She was so excited that her father was home, even for a short visit. He came as often as possible; when his job at the railroad in Minneapolis allowed him. He was able to hop a train for free and make the trip home. But it was never long enough for Anna. Her father loved her dearly, and she knew it by the kind way he treated her. She wanted so badly for her parents to take her and Andrew away to live together as a family.

Closing her eyes, she prayed to God that her wish would come true.

The next morning, as promised, her father was waiting for her at the kitchen table. Anna helped her grandmother carry plates of food to the table, and the four of them ate pancakes, sausage, eggs, and buttered toast with homemade maple syrup that her uncle made from trees on the farm. Anna sat silently as the grown-ups talked. She wanted her father to know that she was a good girl. The more perfect she was, the greater the chance there was that he would want her to go away with him.

"It couldn't be helped," Victor said to Jon about having to send Andrew off to work and live at the neighbor's farm. "We couldn't afford the boy any longer. The Depression is hurting everyone, and this dairy farm only earns enough money to support myself and my sons' families. Besides, he is old enough to make his own way in the world."

"He could have helped with work here on the farm," Jon said. It was obvious to Anna that her father was upset that her brother had been separated from the family.

"Ack! That boy never listened to no one," Sophia said. "He was always daydreaming like his sister. And messing with the horses. That was all he cared about. Peterson will teach him to work harder."

Anna knew the truth but kept silent. Andrew had been a hard worker on the farm since he was a young child, learning to milk the cows and churn butter and so much more. But her grandfather never had patience with Andrew's sweet-natured personality. When Andrew would stop working a moment to pet one of the horses or feed one a treat from his pocket, her grandfather would hit him upside the head and tell him to go back to work. One day not long ago, as she was gathering eggs at the henhouse, she saw her grandfather hit Andrew's head so hard that blood poured from his ear. After that, Andrew was unable to hear well from that ear and still couldn't as far as Anna knew. It wasn't too long after that her grandparents decided to send Andrew away.

Jon winced, and Anna suddenly became aware of how very pale and tired he looked. She'd heard him coughing during the night in his bedroom below hers. She wondered if he was ill and what it could be.

After breakfast, Jon joined Anna as she carefully gathered eggs for her grandmother and then brought them inside and washed them in the sink. She had to stand on a small stool to reach everything, and Jon pumped the water for her. As they worked together, she noticed that her father's shirt was missing a button.

"Papa. I can sew a new button on your shirt for you," she offered, eager for him to see that she would be of great help to him.

He smiled at her, but his eyes looked sad. "Älskling. You should be playing, not working so hard. I can sew on a new button later. First, let's go outside so we can talk."

Dutifully, Anna followed her father out to the front of the house, and they sat in the shade on the cement steps. Jon began to cough again and pulled out a clean handkerchief to cover his mouth.

"I can get you a glass of water, Papa," Anna said, standing up.

Jon waved for her to sit, and she did.

"Sweet pea, I have something to talk to you about," he said solemnly. "As you can see, I am a very sick man. I need to go to a hospital for many months for treatment to get well. I should be there now, but I wanted to come and see you and Andrew one last time before I leave."

Anna's heart dropped. She didn't want her father to leave and not come back. Her mother had left, and Andrew had been sent away. She couldn't bear to lose one more person.

"Please, Papa. Please don't leave me here. I want to go with you. I love you so much and miss you so much more. Please, please take me with you." Tears flowed down her cheeks as she pleaded with her father.

Jon hugged her close. "Oh, my little darling. How I wish I could take you with me. But only those who are sick can stay in this place. And we have no one to take care of you there."

"I can take care of you, Papa. I can cook and clean, and I can wash your clothes and do anything else you need me to do."

"My älskling. It is not up to me. It is a hospital for the sick, and you cannot come there. I'm so sorry. But I will get well and come back for you. I promise you, darling."

Anna cried as her father held her. She knew that not all people who went away came back. Her mother hadn't yet come home. She knew children in school whose parents were sick and had gone to be cured and never came home. She was afraid this was the last time she'd ever see her father.

At supper that evening, Anna sat silently at the table as her aunts and their husbands chatted on about things that did not interest her. Finally, her father told the group he'd be leaving on the train on Sunday to go to Walker and stay in the sanatorium there to get well. Everyone grew quiet as they stared at him. It was her Grandmother Sophia who spoke up first.

"You will take the girl with you," she said with certainty.

"I can't take her along," Jon said. "I'm sorry. There would be no place for her."

Anna held her breath. If her grandmother forced her papa to take her, then there would be no way he could say no.

"You will take her," Sophia said again. "We have done our part. We have raised both of your children and asked for nothing. But we are getting too old for this. It is time you are responsible for Anna."

Jon frowned. "I've done the best I can. I've sent money every month for the children's care. I need your help for only a little longer."

Anna's eyes darted up at this. Her father had sent money? Yet, her grandmother had complained every time Anna had outgrown a pair of shoes or needed a new dress.

"No. You take her," Sophia insisted.

Anna watched as her father looked over at Victor, but the

older man only shrugged and shook his head. Then Jon glanced at his wife's sisters sitting around the table. "Please. Will one of you take Anna in for a year or two, until I get well. I will continue to send money to help raise her."

The little girl bit her lip. She already knew their answer. None of her aunts or uncles had offered to take her before. She knew they wouldn't now.

"We can't," the older sister, Adelaide, said, speaking for everyone. "I'm sorry, Jon, but we all have our own families and responsibilities."

"How can you not help your own sister's child?" he asked, looking at them in disbelief.

Adelaide lifted her head higher and looked down her nose at Jon. "It isn't our fault that Lillian deserted her children for others to care for them. You're their father. It's up to you."

Anna stared at her aunt with wide eyes. Deserted? Her mother hadn't abandoned her. She'd gone away because she'd been sick. She just hadn't come home yet, but Anna believed that she would. Someday.

Jon stood from the table and walked out of the room.

"Papa?" Anna attempted to leave her seat, but her grandmother placed a hand on her shoulder.

"You stay and finish your meal," the old woman demanded.

The little girl looked up into her grandmother's angry brown eyes. This woman had never wanted her here and had made that very clear. She'd never loved her, or even cared about her. She owed this woman nothing, least of all respect. Shrugging off her hand, Anna jumped from her chair and ran after her father. She could hear her grandmother's tight voice yell, "Anna!"

Anna found her father outside. He was pacing in a little

circle around the front lawn as the autumn leaves fell around him.

"Papa?" she said softly, staring up at him. He was not a tall man, and he'd become very thin. But to Anna, he was the greatest man she'd ever known.

Jon took a deep breath and let out a long sigh. He turned to his daughter. "I've failed you, sweet pea," he said. "I left you to be raised by these people who have no heart. I had no idea they were so cruel." He knelt in the grass and raised his arms to her. She ran to him and hugged him tightly.

"It will be just you and me, älskling. We will find a way for us to stay together."

The little girl's heart felt full as she hugged her father. Her wish had come true. They would be a family again.

CHAPTER SIX

Anna — 1936

Anna and her father left the house the next day with her small suitcase and his larger one despite it being a church day. But before they walked to the train station, they headed to the Peterson farm to see Andrew.

Andrew was up and dressed for church by the time they arrived. Jon greeted Mr. Peterson, a tall, thin, weatherworn man, and then waved Andrew over to speak to them.

As Andrew drew closer to his family, his smile grew wider. "Papa! Anna!" The tall, wiry boy hugged his father tightly and then his sister. Pulling back, he noticed the small suitcase on the ground beside Anna. "What is this? Are you going somewhere?"

Jon motioned for them to sit on the bench on the back porch, and the three did. "Andrew, my dear son. I'm so sorry that your grandparents sent you away to work for your keep. Are you well? Do the Petersons treat you kindly?"

Andrew glanced behind him through the back door of the house. He spoke quietly. "They are fine people. But I wish I could live with you, Papa."

Jon's face winced as he looked at his son. "I'm sorry, Andrew. I wish you could come with me. I'm very sick and am leaving to go to the sanatorium in Walker to get well." As if on cue, he began coughing and quickly grabbed his handkerchief to cover his mouth. Anna saw the horror on her brother's face.

"Papa? Do you have tuberculosis?" Andrew asked.

Jon nodded. "But they can treat it," he rushed to say. "I've known people who were cured at the sanatorium. I'll go there and rest, and in a few months, I will be well again."

Anna had never seen her brother look so frightened. Not even when their mother had left and not returned. She knew very little about tuberculosis, but her father had said he'd get better and she believed him. She didn't understand why Andrew was so upset.

"And Anna?" Andrew asked, nodding at her suitcase. "Where is she going?"

"She's coming with me." Jon wiped his mouth. "Your grandparents wouldn't keep her any longer. I'm not sure what arrangements I can make for her, but anything will be better than staying with them."

"Can I go with you too?" Andrew asked, looking hopeful. "Please, Papa. I could work and pay rent somewhere and care for Anna. Please let me come too." His eyes begged her father, and Anna could see how torn her papa was.

"I'm so sorry, my son. I only have enough to pay for my stay at the hospital. And I have to find a place for Anna. You would be better staying here until I come back for you."

Andrew's eyes watered, and he turned away, but Jon placed his hand on his son's shoulder and turned him back. "Son. I promise. I will come back for you, and then we can be a family again. Please. Just wait a little longer."

Tears filled Anna's eyes as she watched her brother nod agreement. She could tell he was hurt to be left behind. She turned to hug him, and then Jon held them both as the little family said goodbye.

Mr. Peterson drove the horse wagon up near the back door and called out, "We must leave for church now, or we'll be late." Mrs. Peterson came out the back door in her Sunday best, patted Andrew gently on the shoulder, and walked to the wagon.

Obediently, Andrew stood and brushed off his pants. He hugged his father and sister once more, then went to join the Petersons in the wagon.

"Can I give you a ride to town?" Mr. Peterson asked Jon. "We can drop you at the train station."

Jon nodded and thanked him for the offer. He lifted Anna up to sit on the back of the wagon, then climbed in too. The three sat together one last time as the rough wagon bumped along the country road toward town.

* * *

Later that day, Jon helped Anna down from the train at the depot in Walker. A truck was waiting to pick up the sanatorium's mail that came twice a day. Jon and Anna rode with the driver, who introduced himself as Earl, the two miles out of town and up the hill to where the buildings stood.

"So, are you both sick?" Earl asked, not unkindly.

Anna gazed up at him curiously. He was an older man with salt and pepper hair and beard, and he wore overalls and a red and white plaid shirt. He turned and grinned at her, and his dark eyes twinkled.

"I'm the one who's sick," Jon said. He looked pale and worn from his long, emotional day. Anna sat between the men on the bench seat and reached for her father's hand. He smiled down at her.

"I'm sure the doctors can help you," Earl said. "I've seen many come and go here over the years. More patients than not leave on their own two feet."

Anna was puzzled by what Earl had meant. Wouldn't everyone leave walking on their own two feet? She wanted to ask her father, but by then they'd pulled up in front of a large building. Stepping out of the truck, Jon thanked Earl for the ride.

Earl nodded, pulled their suitcases out of the pick-up's bed, and handed them to Jon and Anna. "This is where you can check in," he told Jon. "I'm sure I'll see you around." He grabbed the heavy mailbag from the back, hoisted it over his shoulder, and headed in the other direction.

Anna looked at the building in awe. It was so large—four stories high—and very long. A beautiful green lawn spread out in front of the building and down the hill they'd just come up. Several other buildings were in the compound, and there were trees everywhere with leaves that had turned various shades of red, orange, and yellow. But the sight that made Anna's eyes grow wide was the view of the lake down below them, spreading out for what seemed like miles to the little girl. It was unlike any lake she'd ever seen, much larger than the lake on her grandfather's farm.

"Papa! Look! Look at that big lake. Isn't it beautiful?" Anna exclaimed.

Jon smiled down at her, his eyes full of love for his daughter. "Yes, dear. It's beautiful. That's Leech Lake."

Anna wrinkled her nose. "Leech Lake? Are there a lot of leeches in it?"

Her father laughed. "I suppose there are, like any lake in our state. But nothing that you can't handle, little one."

"Do you think I'll be able to swim in the lake?" Anna asked, growing excited again.

"I'm sure you'll get a chance, my little fish." Anna loved to swim and used to spend any spare time she had swimming with Andrew. Of course, that was before her grandparents made him leave to work.

Jon waved for her to follow him, and they walked inside the grand building. Anna gazed up and down the hallway when they entered through the tall doors. Women wearing white dresses with aprons over them, and a white mask over their faces scurried about. The walls were white, as was the linoleum flooring that was speckled with dots of color. In front of them was a registration desk, and Anna followed her father to it.

The woman sitting there was also wearing a mask, but her kind eyes looked up at Jon. "How may I help you?" she asked.

"My doctor from Minneapolis sent me here to be cured," Jon told her. Although he worked in the city, his home address was the farm, so he was able to come to Ah-Gwah-Ching in Cass County where a portion of his treatment would be paid for.

"What is your name?" she asked, pulling out a large ledger full of names.

"Jon Bergman."

Anna watched as the woman ran her finger down the ledger. She noticed that her name tag read Mrs. Ottoman. It made her giggle. Her grandmother called her footstool the ottoman.

Mrs. Ottoman finally nodded. "Ah, yes. Here it is." She

waved over a young nurse who'd been passing by the desk. "Miss Swenson. We have a new patient. This is Jon Bergman. We need to get him settled in a bed and contact Dr. Clement." The nurse listened attentively as Mrs. Ottoman spoke. Anna thought Miss Swenson was pretty, even though half her face was covered with a white mask that tied at the back of her head. She had big blue eyes, and her auburn hair was pulled up in a bun with a white cap over it. Anna self-consciously ran her hand through her short hair, wishing she had beautiful hair like Miss Swenson. Her movement caught the attention of two pairs of eyes.

"And this young lady?" Mrs. Ottoman asked. "Is she also infected?"

Jon shook his head. "No, ma'am. This is Anna, my daughter. There was nowhere for her to go, and I had hoped there might be somewhere here that she could stay. I could pay her way."

The receptionist frowned as she studied Anna. "Has she been with you all this time? She could be infected."

"I picked her up from her grandparent's house just yesterday," Jon said. "I'm sure she is well." The strain of talking began a coughing fit for Jon, and he quickly placed a handkerchief over his mouth.

"She could stay in the children's ward for now," Miss Swenson suggested, looking to Mrs. Ottoman for approval.

At that moment, a tall man wearing a white coat, his mask hanging around his neck, approached the group. "Nurse. This gentleman should be in bed. Is he checked in, Mrs. Ottoman?"

The receptionist and nurse stood at attention. "We have a bit of a problem, Dr. Hanson," Mrs. Ottoman said. "Mr. Bergman brought his daughter, Anna, along, and she has nowhere to stay. Of course, we must first check to see if she's infected, but then, where will she go?"

Anna felt the doctor's eyes studying her. He was very tall and had wavy blond hair and kind blue eyes. She felt nervous with everyone staring at her but stood up straight and remained silent just as her grandmother would expect her to.

"Hello, Anna," Dr. Hanson said, smiling at her. "How old are you?"

Her face brightened at being included in the conversation. "I'll be twelve in October." Anna thought twelve sounded more mature than eleven.

"You don't say. Well, that's a fine age. Are you helpful to your mother at home?" the doctor asked.

"She's lived with her grandparents all these years," Jon interjected.

The doctor nodded. "Ah. I see. But I bet a big girl like you helped your grandmother around the kitchen and the house."

Anna nodded enthusiastically. "Yes. I helped her with cooking and cleaning. I also gathered the eggs from the chicken coop and even helped milk the cows sometimes."

The adults around her smiled, especially the doctor. Anna liked him. He seemed like a nice man.

Dr. Hanson turned to Jon. "After Anna has been cleared of infection, I would be willing to have her come live with my wife and me, if that is acceptable to you, sir. We have three young girls under the age of nine, and my wife has been wanting a mother's helper. We would make sure she attends school, and she could help around the house for her keep."

Jon looked at Anna before replying. "Would you like to live with the doctor and his family?"

Anna hated the thought of being separated from her father.

"Will I be able to see my papa?" she asked Dr. Hanson.

He smiled. "As soon as he's feeling better, yes. The first few weeks, our patients are on full bed rest, but after that, you may see him occasionally."

Jon kneeled before Anna. "Sweetie, this is a good situation for you. We can live near one another, and you will have other young girls around. What do you think?"

It all seemed scary to Anna, going off to live with a stranger's family. But he was a doctor, and he seemed very nice. And she wanted to be brave for her father and show him she was grown up enough to do this. Finally, she nodded. "I'll work very hard for Dr. Hanson," she promised her papa.

Jon hugged her. "You are a good girl, älskling. I know you'll behave for the doctor and his family." He stood and nodded at the doctor. "Thank you for offering my Anna a place to stay. I am indebted to you, sir."

Dr. Hanson shook his head. "No, it is I who am grateful. My wife has needed help for some time, so she will be thrilled. But first," he turned to Mrs. Ottoman, "let's have Anna tested and let her stay in an isolated room for a day or two. If she is fine, she may come and live at my house."

The receptionist nodded, and Miss Swenson led Jon away while Anna stood there, frightened and unsure of her future.

CHAPTER SEVEN

Diane

Diane sat listening to Anna as she spoke of Dr. Hanson's offer and how scared she'd been about her future. Already, Diane was shocked over everything Anna had been through up to the age of eleven. Such a traumatic childhood. It broke her heart.

The older woman stopped speaking and watched Diane with her watery blue eyes. "I'm so sorry, dear. I hadn't meant to go on and on."

"Oh, please don't be sorry," Diane said. "I enjoyed listening to your story. I'd love to hear more." She glanced at the wood-framed clock on the wall and saw it was getting late. "But I suppose I should be going. I don't want to tire you out."

Anna gave her a small smile. "I am a little tired. Would you mind getting me a small glass of water, dear? There are glasses in the cupboard by the sink."

"Of course." Diane rose and headed to the small sink near the door. She found a clean glass and poured water into it from the tap. Anna also had a tiny refrigerator under the counter and a one-cup coffee maker. She brought over the glass, and Anna took a sip.

"Thank you." With shaky hands, she set the glass on the table.

Diane moved her chair back against the wall, out of the way. Turning back to Anna, she asked, "What happened to your brother, Andrew? Did he stay at the neighbor's farm until your father came for him?"

"Maybe you'd like to come back, and we could continue the story," Anna said hopefully. "There's so much to tell, and if you'd like to hear it, I'd be happy to tell you."

"Oh, yes," Diane said. "I'd love to hear more. Could I come to see you during the week? I get off work at three-thirty and could come after that."

Anna's eyes grew bright. "Would you stay for supper? I'd love to have a guest. Maybe we could go to the dining room together. I just have to let them know you'll be here."

Diane's heart warmed at how excited Anna was to have a guest for supper. "I'd love to have supper with you. How about Wednesday afternoon?"

"That will be wonderful. I'll tell the nurse to expect you."

This time, before leaving, Diane bent down and gently hugged Anna. "Thank you for letting me get to know you," she said. "I'm enjoying this so much."

Anna clasped her hand in hers. "You have no idea how happy this makes me."

Diane waved and walked out the door, her heart joyful. She couldn't believe how much she enjoyed Anna's company and couldn't wait to hear more of her life story.

* * *

That night, Barry and Diane went out to dinner at their favorite little pub. He asked how her visit had gone with Anna.

"She started telling me about her childhood, and already my heart goes out to her. She grew up with her grandparents, who sounded like they were very strict and mean, and her father only came some weekends to visit."

"Where was her mother?" Barry asked, frowning.

Diane shrugged. "I'm not sure. Her mother had been gone for six years, but Anna thought she was still alive. Anna's brother was farmed out to a neighbor's farm to work. It's so sad."

Barry sighed and nodded. "A lot of families had to do that to survive. It was during the Depression. Times were tough."

"I know, but to push out a grandchild." Diane shook her head in disgust. "Anna's father, Jon, came home and she left with him, but her brother was left behind. Jon had tuberculosis. She ended the story with them arriving at Aw-Gwah-Ching in Walker. She was only eleven."

"Goodness." Barry's mouth dropped open. "And people today think they have it tough. I'll be interested in hearing more of her story."

"I'm going there on Wednesday after work to have dinner with her. Actually, supper." She smiled. "That's what she's used to calling it."

"That's good. I'm sure she'll enjoy the company." Barry looked at his phone a moment. "I don't think Ah-Gwah-Ching exists anymore. It seems to me I read a while back that it was torn down." He studied his screen another moment. "Yep. Here it is. It became a nursing home in the 1960s, then state offices were there awhile. It was torn down after closing in 2008. That's too bad."

Diane nodded. It was strange knowing that a place where her grandmother had lived didn't exist anymore.

"Do you know what the Ojibwa words Ah-Gwah-Ching mean in English?" Barry asked. "Out-of-doors. Cool, huh?"

She smiled. Only Barry would want to know every little detail. But she found it cute. "Thanks, trivia master," she said.

That night as she lay in bed beside Barry, her mind wandered again to Anna and her story. How awful to have been left at her grandparents' farm where she didn't feel wanted. And where was her mother? Anna had said her mother, Lillian, had been the beautiful one among the sisters, but what had happened to her? Why wasn't she there with her children?

Of course, Diane was no stranger to absent parents. Her father had left when she was nine years old. Although he'd paid child support, she never saw him again. He'd had many issues after returning home from Vietnam, and had health problems as he grew older, too. Diane had friends whose fathers had troubles after coming back from the war, too, so she hadn't really felt sorry for herself for not having her father around. But thinking about it now, she knew it had affected her. Her mother had spoken unkindly about her father often, and that left a mark. Diane attended her father's funeral along with her brother Dale in 1990 and had been surprised to learn he'd remarried and had been happy for a time. It had seemed odd, not knowing anything about her own father. But then, Diane hadn't known anything different.

Diane thought about her mother remarrying when she was eleven, and how Albert had never felt like a replacement for her father. He was just there. He and her mother drank a lot and fought even more. Now that Diane looked back at it, her experiences around men as a child hadn't been positive ones.

That had shaped her view of men and relationships. More like skewed her view of them. Which had led her into a verbally abusive relationship and marriage.

She sighed as she stared up at the ceiling. Was it any wonder she was afraid to marry Barry?

"Hey? Are you okay?" he asked sleepily, rolling over toward her.

"Too many memories," she said softly. She moved closer and curled around his body. "Thank you for not being like every man I've ever known."

"You're welcome." He kissed the top of her head.

Moments later, Diane could hear his steady breathing. He'd fallen asleep again. She smiled to herself. She was lucky. Very lucky.

* * *

On Wednesday after school, Diane pointed her car in the direction of Anna's care facility. It was a gorgeous fall day with unseasonably high temperatures in the low seventies and the sun shining brightly overhead. Walking inside, the receptionist told her that Anna was out in the courtyard, enjoying the sunshine. Diane headed to the outside area where there were smooth cement trails around green patches of grass. The many trees and shrubs had changed into a variety of fall colors from yellow to bright red. Diane smiled at residents as she passed them, and soon saw Anna, sitting in a wheelchair in the sunshine, with a blue plaid blanket over her legs.

"Hi, Anna," she said cheerfully as she approached her. The nurse sitting near the older woman smiled and waved. Anna looked up, and her eyes grew bright.

"You're here, just as promised," she said. "Thank you for coming."

"I'm happy to visit," Diane said, placing her purse and cardigan on the bench beside Anna. It was far too warm to wear it, but by evening, the chill would set in again. "Are you enjoying the warm day?"

"Oh, yes," Anna said. "This dear lady talked me into coming outside, and I'm so grateful she did." Anna's eyes twinkled.

The nurse stood. "It would have been a shame to miss this weather," she told Diane. "Soon enough, we'll all be stuck inside."

Diane agreed.

"Well," the nurse said. "If you're going to be here until dinner, then I'll go and attend to some of the other residents. Call me over if you need me." She headed off to the other side of the courtyard.

"All the nurses here are so sweet," Anna told Diane. "I'm so lucky to live here."

Diane supposed after spending years in a prison setting, Anna would be grateful for any small kindness. "I'm glad they're good to you. But it's easy to be nice to you." She glanced around. "Would you like me to push you around for a while?"

"Yes. We can go for a hike." Anna chuckled.

Diane slipped her purse and sweater in the pocket behind the seat and began pushing the wheelchair along the path. The courtyard was quite large, with flowerbeds sprinkled here and there and even a small fountain that was still gushing water. Birds perched around the fountain, and some ventured in to take a dip and then shake the droplets off. Their funny antics made Anna laugh.

"How does your gentleman friend feel about my taking you

away from him so often?" Anna asked after a time. "He must be quite annoyed with me."

"No, not at all. Barry is the most easy-going person you could ever meet. And he doesn't depend on me to cook his dinners or take care of him, thank goodness. We lead busy lives. He had a teacher's meeting tonight at his school, anyway. Did I tell you he was a grade-school principal?"

"Really? He must be very smart. And kind. It takes a special person to work with young children."

"He loves it. And the kids adore him. It's the perfect fit," Diane said proudly.

"You're lucky to have him," Anna said.

Diane smiled. She'd thought the same thing just last night.

She continued pushing the wheelchair at a slow pace. It felt so good to be outside in the fresh air.

"You know," Anna said. "This reminds me a little of when I lived at Ah-Gwah-Ching. The grounds were beautiful, and the fall colors were incredible. There were pines everywhere, too, and after a rain, their scent permeated the air. I can remember that scent like it was yesterday."

"It sounds wonderful. I'd always thought that sanatoriums were terrible places," Diane said.

"Oh, no. At least not there. The nurses were kind, and the doctors cared well for the patients. The rooms were clean and airy, and the patients became great friends with each other since they usually stayed there for a long time. It was almost like being a part of a large family."

"That's so good to hear," Diane said. She'd never thought of the hospitals like that. With so much sickness and people dying, she assumed they were sad places to live.

"Of course, that first few months in Walker was hard for

me. I didn't like being separated from my papa, but it was necessary, so I wouldn't become ill too. At eleven years old, though, it's difficult to understand."

CHAPTER EIGHT

Anna — 1936

Mrs. Hanson welcomed young Anna warmly when she arrived at their home near downtown Walker. Anna had been sequestered for three days at the sanatorium, tested twice, and cleared of having tuberculosis. The nurses had been cheerful and kind to her, as had Dr. Hanson. But now, as she gazed around the beautiful Tudor-style home where the doctor lived, she was nervous and excited all at once.

"I'm so happy you've come to join us, Anna," Mrs. Hanson said, smiling down at her. She was a tall, slender woman with brown hair and warm brown eyes. Anna thought her green polka-dot dress that fell below her knees looked like something a beautiful model would wear in the Sears & Roebuck Catalog. "The girls have been bursting with excitement over meeting you."

Just as she said that the three girls came into the parlor with the taller one holding the toddler's hand. They were all smartly dressed in what looked like new dresses and shoes to Anna, and she suddenly felt self-conscious about her faded, floral dress, darned stockings, and scuffed shoes.

"This is Francie, the oldest," Mrs. Hanson said, pointing to the girl holding the toddler's hand, "and Betty, and our baby, Rose. Francie is nine, Betty is six, and Rose just turned two."

Anna stared at the three girls, unsure of what to do. But then Francie let go of baby Rose's hand and rushed over to hug Anna.

"I'm so happy you're here!" she squealed. "I'll have a playmate close to my own age. We're going to be the best of friends."

"She'll be my friend too," Betty insisted, her face set in a determined expression.

Anna laughed. "I can be friends with all of you."

Betty looked pleased by Anna's words.

"I'll show you where you'll be sleeping," Francie said. "Here, I'll take your bag." Francie lifted the old leather suitcase and waved for Anna to follow.

Anna looked up at Mrs. Hanson for direction. She didn't want to do anything wrong on the very first day.

"Go along, dear," Mrs. Hanson said. "Francie will give you a tour of the house. I hope you don't mind sharing a room with her. I'm afraid this home isn't as big as the one we had in Minneapolis, but it will do."

"I'm sure it will be fine," Anna said politely. "Thank you." As she followed Francie to the staircase, she couldn't imagine why Mrs. Hanson thought this house was small. It had many more rooms than the farmhouse. Walking to the polished wood staircase with the blue paisley rug runner, Anna could see the dining room, the doorway into the kitchen, and what looked like another room around the corner, behind the staircase. Upstairs, Francie showed her to one of four bedrooms. Four! Her grandparents' farmhouse had only two rooms upstairs, and she and Andrew had shared the large room in the walk-up attic.

Betty had followed them upstairs, and the three girls entered Francie's bedroom. Anna had never seen a room so lovely. There were two twin-sized beds with gleaming brass headboards and footboards and a white nightstand in-between. Pretty pink counterpanes covered each bed. Two large windows draped in pink Pricilla curtains faced the front of the house, and sunlight streamed through them. Across the room was a small table with drawing and coloring supplies on it, and the corner held a large dollhouse with tiny furniture and dolls. Anna walked over to the dollhouse, mesmerized. She'd never had a toy so beautiful.

"You can have this bed," Francie said, setting the suitcase on the left bed. "Shall we unpack your things?"

Anna's eyes grew wide as she rushed over to stop Francie from opening her suitcase, but she wasn't quick enough. The little girl had pushed open the lid and was staring inside. Anna's belongings were pitiful compared to the things these little girls owned. Her heart dropped as she saw Francie frown at the contents.

"What's that?" Betty asked, peering inside. Francie nudged her to be quiet.

"I'll unpack it myself," Anna said, trying to regain some sense of dignity.

"Is that your doll?" Francie asked, pointing to Lily.

The faded doll lay on top of Anna's meager belongings. She lifted it up carefully. "Yes. This is Lily. My brother made her for me." She waited for the two girls to laugh at her. They had beautiful store-bought dollies sitting in a small crib near the dollhouse. What must they think of poor Lily?

"Really? You have a brother? That's nice," Francie said. "It looks like Lily has been loved a lot." The little girl smiled at Anna, making her feel warm inside. In that moment, Anna had a soft spot in her heart for the blond-haired girl whose Shirley Temple curls sprang from her head beautifully.

Betty moved closer to Anna. Her blond hair was straight, but she had the same blue eyes as her sister. "May I hold Lily while you unpack? I promise to be careful."

Anna hesitated, then decided she needed to learn to trust these girls she'd be living with. She handed Lily to Betty, and the little girl held her carefully, studying her.

"She has a pretty face," Betty said. "Did your brother embroider it?"

Anna nodded. "He surprised me with Lily for my birthday when I was five."

"That was very kind of him," Francie said. "I wish I had a brother. Is he older?"

"Yes. He's fourteen."

"Where is he now?" Betty piped up.

Anna's eyes dropped. "He's working at a farm near my grandparents' house. My papa and I hope to see him again very soon."

Francie patted Anna's back. "I'm sure you will," she said soothingly. She walked over to the closet door and opened it. "I made room to hang your dresses, and there are two drawers in the bureau for your underthings and stockings." She smiled brightly, obviously proud of what she'd done to make Anna feel welcome.

Francie brought several wooden hangers over to Anna. Once again, Anna felt inferior. She had only one other dress to hang, a sweater, one nightie, and a pair of her brother's old pants she wore when she worked outside. Her underthings were old and worn, and her stockings were shabby with many holes in them that had been darned. Anna carefully hung her dress and sweater then placed them in the closet.

"You don't have much, do you?" Betty said.

"Betty! That isn't nice." Francie turned to Anna. "I'm sure mother will buy you new dresses and other things you need."

Anna remained quiet. She doubted Mrs. Hanson would buy her anything new since she was here to work. She wasn't a member of the family.

After placing her underthings and nightie in a drawer, Anna closed her suitcase and slid it under the bed. "We should go downstairs so I can see what your mother would like me to do."

Francie looked at her curiously. "Do? You mean work? Don't be silly. I'm supposed to take you on a tour of the house, and then we can play."

Anna was sure that wasn't why they'd taken her in, but she didn't argue.

"I'll set Lily on your pillow," Betty offered. She placed the doll carefully on the bed. "I think she's pretty." Betty smiled brightly at Anna.

"Thank you. I think you're both pretty," Anna said and was rewarded with smiles from the sisters.

Francie and Betty each took one of Anna's hands and led her on a tour of the house. They took her to the walk-up attic first, where the ceiling was tall, and windows allowed bright sunlight inside. They explained that this was their father's study and their mother's sewing room. A large desk sat at one end surrounded by shelves filled with books, and a sewing machine sat at the other end.

"Although I've never seen mother sew anything," Francie confided with a giggle. Then they went to the second floor again where they showed Anna the room that Betty shared with little Rose, the guest bedroom, and then peeked into the master bedroom. Anna's eyes grew wide when she saw the grand four-poster bed and canopy in Dr. and Mrs. Hanson's bedroom.

"Sometimes we play in here and pretend that the bed is a tent," Betty said with a grin.

Anna thought it was the most beautiful room she'd ever seen. Opposite the large bed was a lovely vanity table with a mirror for Mrs. Hanson and a large bureau with eight drawers. The furniture looked expensive, nothing like the furniture in the farmhouse.

The girls took Anna back downstairs and showed her where the water closet was, and also the room behind the staircase, which was actually Mrs. Hanson's morning room. They explained that was where she sat and relaxed after breakfast, wrote letters, and sometimes knitted or did fancywork by the fire in the winter.

"And here is the kitchen," Francie said, leading Anna through a swinging door at the back of the house. A short, round woman wearing a practical flowered dress, apron, and sensible oxford shoes turned as the three girls entered.

"What have we here?" the woman asked in a thick German accent. "Are you girls multiplying?"

Francie and Betty giggled. "This is Mrs. Schmidt," Francie said to Anna. "She cooks our meals and keeps house for us. Mrs. Schmidt, this is Anna. She's come to live with us and be our friend."

Anna tried not to cower under Mrs. Schmidt's scrutinizing

brown eyes. She was older, with graying hair that was pulled back into a bun. She reminded Anna so much of her grandmother that it was hard not to shake in her shoes.

Mrs. Schmidt wiped her hands on her apron, walked over, and stuck out her hand. "Nice to meet you, Anna. I hope you enjoy living here."

Anna shook her hand, and her rapidly beating heart slowed a little. "Nice to meet you, Mrs. Schmidt."

Mrs. Schmidt nodded curtly, then returned to her work at the cutting board. After a moment, she looked up again. "Well, I suppose you girls expect to raid the cookie jar. Go ahead. One each and no more. I have a nice supper planned for Anna's arrival with chocolate cake for dessert."

Betty's eyes sparkled as she ran over to a lower cupboard and pulled out the jar with sugar cookies inside. She handed one each to Anna and Francie, then put the jar away.

"Thank you, Mrs. Schmidt," each girl said in turn, then they left the kitchen.

Later, when Anna checked in with Mrs. Hanson to see what work she'd like her to do, the kindly woman just shook her head. "You can help me later this week. Keeping the girls busy and out of trouble is all I need from you today. Play and have fun."

Anna nodded. "Yes, ma'am."

"Oh, and Anna. Tomorrow, maybe we could look through one of the catalogs and find a couple of new dresses for you. I'm sure your father was feeling too poorly to worry about such things."

Anna bit her lip as she thought this over. "Ma'am. I don't have money for anything new."

Mrs. Hanson smiled. "Don't worry about that, dear. Dr.

Hanson and I are happy to buy you a few things. You'll be doing so much to help me, it's the least I can do for you."

Anna nodded and returned to Francie's bedroom where the girls were playing, having a tea party. She felt a little better about Mrs. Hanson buying her new clothes since she'd be earning them. Still, deep down inside, her heart fluttered. New clothes. Ready-made store-bought clothes. It was all so exciting.

* * *

Anna loved living with the Hansons. Even though she had responsibilities to perform, it never felt like work. As she settled in and became comfortable, Mrs. Hanson taught her how to dress and diaper Baby Rose for when she'd look after her. Every day, she, Francie, and Betty took lessons at the local school for a few hours, then returned home. Sometimes, Anna would offer to help Mrs. Schmidt in the kitchen even though it wasn't expected of her. Other times, she'd watch the baby while Mrs. Hanson enjoyed afternoon tea with friends in the parlor or at one of their houses. Anna didn't mind babysitting little Rose. She was a chubby, sweet-tempered baby with soft blond curls and curious blue eyes. She loved playing dolls with Anna or stacking blocks and knocking them down. Francie and Betty would often join in, and they all had a wonderful time.

As September slipped into October, Anna grew troubled over not being allowed to see her father. She appreciated where she lived, and the beautiful new dresses—five in all—and two new pairs of shoes Mrs. Hanson had purchased for her. Having nice things made her feel like she was a member of the family, and that made her very happy. Still, she missed her father. Anna tried not to pester Dr. Hanson in the evening when he came home from the sanatorium, but occasionally she did ask when she would be allowed to visit her father.

"It will be a while, Anna," he told her patiently. "Your father is on complete bed rest for the next few weeks. It's necessary to rest his lungs. Once he's allowed to move around a little, I will let you see him, I promise."

Anna believed the kind doctor, but it didn't help to calm her nerves. Some nights, she cried herself to sleep in her little bed, hugging Lily tightly. A few times, Francie asked her what was wrong, but Anna told her it was nothing. "I just miss my father," she whispered one night. "But I'll be brave." But being brave all the time was difficult for an eleven-year-old girl.

One Saturday afternoon in mid-October, Dr. Hanson asked Anna to come into the parlor to talk with him. Frightened that she'd done something wrong, Anna wracked her brain, trying to think of any indiscretion she may have committed. But when they entered the parlor, he only turned and smiled at her, asking her to sit down.

"I can see you're worried. Don't be afraid, Anna. I just want to talk with you," Dr. Hanson told her as she perched on the divan. She was wearing one of her new dresses and stockings, and the oxfords Mrs. Hanson had bought for her, and she carefully smoothed out her skirt as she sat.

"I hear you've been upset about not being able to visit your father," Dr. Hanson said. "I'm sorry it's been so hard on you."

Suddenly, without warning, tears sprang to her eyes. She bit her lip, hoping to stop their flow, but she couldn't. The drops fell on her cheeks as she swiped at them with the back of her hand. "I miss him so much," she said between sobs.

Dr. Hanson moved over beside her and rubbed her back. "It's okay, dear," he said soothingly. "I understand how hard this has been for you." He handed her a clean, white handkerchief to wipe her eyes with.

"Thank you," she said, dabbing at her eyes. The handkerchief was soft and smelled slightly of the cologne the doctor wore. He was always nicely dressed in a three-piece suit, his shoes shined to perfection. Anna's father always wore a suit too, but it had never looked as nice as the many the doctor owned.

"Are you happy here, Anna?" Dr. Hanson asked. "Is there more we can do to make you feel welcomed?"

Her eyes grew wide. Would the doctor turn her out if she continued to cry? "I'm very happy here. Mrs. Hanson has been so kind, and I love the new clothes you bought for me. And I don't mind working or babysitting. Baby Rose is the sweetest girl ever, and I adore Francie and Betty."

He smiled. "I'm glad you feel that way. But it isn't really home for you, is it? That's why you miss your father."

A rush of panic gripped Anna. The only home she'd ever known before coming here was her grandparents' farm, and she hadn't been happy there. The doctor's house was so much nicer, and they were kinder than anyone had ever been to her. She twisted the handkerchief in her hands, worried. "Please don't make me leave. I promise not to cry anymore," Anna said in a rush.

Surprise fell over Dr. Hanson's face. "Oh, Anna, no. I'm not suggesting that at all. We want you to stay here. I just want to make sure you're happy."

Anna nodded. "I am. I'm very happy."

The doctor smiled again. "That's good to hear." He was silent a moment as if considering something, then he spoke. "I don't see why we couldn't pay a visit to your father for a few minutes, just to ease your mind. Why don't you get your jacket from the closet, and we'll drive up there right now?"

"Really?" Anna's heart leapt. "Thank you, Doctor." She hurried to the coat closet by the door and pulled out the blue wool coat Mrs. Hanson had bought for her. Its lining felt like satin, and it fit her perfectly. Anna had never owned a brand-new coat or one that was as nice as this one.

After telling Mrs. Hanson where they were going, Dr. Hanson led Anna outside to his Ford V8 Fordor Touring Sedan. The car was new, and the black paint gleamed in the fall sunshine. Anna stepped up into the front seat and sat as the doctor closed the door for her. The first time Anna had seen the doctor's car, she'd decided he must be very wealthy. No one in the small town where she'd lived had owned a car as fine as this one. A few of the farmers had beat-up trucks, but otherwise, most people still drove a horse and wagon. She felt like a princess when she rode in this car.

They bumped along on dirt roads the entire two miles to the sanatorium. Once there, Anna refrained from running to the building to look for her father. Instead, she walked like a proper lady beside the doctor into the main building.

Mrs. Ottoman was behind the desk when they arrived. "Dr. Hanson. What a surprise," she said, looking concerned that the doctor was there on a Saturday.

"Anna would like to visit her father," Dr. Hanson told the receptionist. "Would you please bring me a clean apron for her to wear over her clothing and a mask as well? Gloves, too."

"Of course," Mrs. Ottoman said. She left to go to the supply closet down the hall.

"Just a precaution," Dr. Hanson told Anna. "If we protect your clothing with the apron, you won't have to disinfect it. I'd hate for you to have to boil that pretty new dress."

Anna nodded. She didn't care if she had to wear a burlap potato sack, she just wanted to see her father.

The doctor also donned a jacket and mask before leading Anna down the hallway and up the stairs. They walked down another long hallway then stopped in front of a partially closed door. "Try to stay calm and not upset your father, please," he whispered to Anna.

She nodded, and he led her past two other beds in the room until they arrived at two more beds across from each other. Her father lay in the bed on the right, next to an open window that let in the crisp October air.

"You have a guest today," Dr. Hanson said to Jon.

Jon was lying on his back, his eyes shut. He opened them and turned his head, and his face lit up. "Anna? Is that you hiding behind that mask?" A big smile spread across his face.

"Papa!" she exclaimed, forgetting that she was supposed to stay quiet. She went to him with open arms, wanting to hug him, but Dr. Hanson stopped her before she touched her father.

"Remember, Anna. No touching. Here." The doctor reached for a chair next to the bed. "Sit here, dear. You can speak quietly to your father for a few minutes. I'll check on my patients and return for you."

Anna did as she was told, but her eyes filled with tears. She wanted to hug her father and feel his comforting arms around her.

"Don't cry, *älskling*," Jon said softly to his daughter. "I'm so happy you're here. Wipe your tears and tell me how you are."

Anna dried her tears with her sleeve. "I wanted so to see you, Papa. I miss you so much."

"I've missed you too," Jon said gently. "But it isn't safe for you to visit. I don't want you to become infected."

"But I had to see you. I had to make sure you were still here." Anna was fearful that her father would leave and not return just as her mother had six years before. No one would tell her where her mother was. What if that happened to her father?

"I'm still here," Jon said soothingly. "And I'll be here until I'm well. It may be a few months, or even a year or two. And the good doctor has promised me that you can stay with them as long as I'm here."

Anna nodded. She shivered from the cold air streaming in through the open window. Glancing around the room, she noticed how sparse it was. All her father had was a nightstand to store his few possessions in and a bed. She thought of all the lovely things Mrs. Hanson had bought her since she'd moved in and suddenly worried that her father didn't have everything he needed. "It's so cold in here," she said, a worried frown on her face. Hadn't her grandmother always said to stay warm when you were sick?

"It is," Jon agreed. "But I'm toasty warm under my blankets. They believe that clean, fresh air will help cure my lungs. It's one of the treatments."

"Do you like it here?" Anna asked.

"The nurses and doctors are very kind. And my roommates are also nice. Over there is Jake. And behind me is Alan. They keep me entertained."

Anna turned and looked at the man her father called Jake. He was older than her father and was balding, but he turned, smiled, and winked at her.

"I'm happy you have friends," Anna said.

Jon smiled. "Me, too. Tell me, sweet pea, how do you like living with the doctor and his family? Are they good to you?"

She nodded. "Oh, yes, Papa. The girls are kind, and we've become fast friends. And little Rose is a busy baby, but oh so sweet. I watch her sometimes when Mrs. Hanson has tea with her lady-friends. And Mrs. Hanson is very nice. She bought me new dresses and stockings and shoes. And a new coat. It's so beautiful. I wish you could see it." Anna looked down at the full-body apron she was wearing that was covering her coat. She was glad she'd kept her coat on because it was so cold in the room.

"That's wonderful to hear," Jon said. "It puts my mind at ease, knowing you are with kind people. I need you to be strong, Anna. Behave for the Hansons, do as they ask, and do well in school. It is a lot to ask, I know, but if I don't have to worry about you, I can heal faster."

"Yes, Papa," she said, although her heart felt heavy. How would she get through the next few months, or even years, without her papa? "I just miss you so much." Tears filled her eyes again.

"*Älskling*. Please. Don't cry. Once I'm feeling stronger, I will be able to see you more. You just have to be patient." He stopped a moment to catch his breath. It was evident that all this talking was wearing on him. "Sweetie. If you start feeling sad about not seeing me, you can write a letter to me and have the good doctor drop it off. And I can write to you, too. Will that help?"

The young girl wiped her tears and nodded. "Yes. I can write to you. I can tell you what I do every day, and you can tell me how you're feeling."

Jon smiled. "I will. It'll help pass the time for me, too. Lying here day after day is very boring." He gave a little laugh. "And perhaps you can write to your brother, too, and see how he is faring. That way we'll both know that he is okay."

Anna's heart skipped. With all that had happened, she'd forgotten to write to Andrew. He must be very sad to have not heard from her or their papa. "I will. I'll write to him today."

"Good, *älskling*. Good. I will be curious to know how Andrew is doing."

Anna noticed her father was growing sleepy, so she sat quietly beside him. Soon, Dr. Hanson returned, and she said goodbye to her papa.

"I know you will be a good girl, Anna. I love you so much," Jon said.

"I love you too, Papa," she whispered, holding back tears.

As she left the room with the doctor at her side, she felt a little better. She knew her father was being treated well, and she was certain he'd get better. She had to believe that; it was all she had.

CHAPTER NINE

Diane

Diane wheeled Anna into the large dining room at dinner-time as the other residents stared at them curiously. Well, some looked curious, while others looked enraged. But Diane didn't let it bother her. She maneuvered Anna's chair to an empty table in the corner.

"Do you want to sit facing them or away from them?" she asked Anna.

Anna understood perfectly. "Oh, let them see me. I don't care. Maybe, if they get used to my being in here, I'll start to feel comfortable eating here."

Diane smiled. "You're a brave lady." She rolled the chair up to the table so Anna had a view of the entire room. It was filled with more elderly women than men, all at varying stages of abilities. Some diners were in wheelchairs like Anna, some had walkers or canes, others shook and needed assistance eating. Anna looked no different than the other residents. Her slacks, blouse, and cardigan sweater were just as nice as anything the other women were wearing, and her hair was pulled back neatly. Still, they all stared at Anna as if she were a novelty. Diane glanced around the room. It was decorated in fall colors, giving off a warm, inviting feel. The tables were polished wood, and there was carpeting underneath. Windows lined the walls letting in the natural light. It was a comfortable place to enjoy meals, as long as you felt accepted.

An elderly gentleman wearing brown slacks, loafers, and a tan cardigan over a plaid shirt came through the door with the aid of his cane. He was slightly bent over and was one of the few men who still had a full head of silver hair. He stopped and looked around the room, then turned and saw Anna and Diane at the lone table. Without hesitation, he moved over to them.

"Do you mind if I join you?" he asked Anna in a gravelly voice. "I like meeting new people."

Diane saw the twinkle in his eyes. She decided he was going to teach the others a thing or two about being polite.

"Please. Do join us," Anna said. "We have plenty of room."

He chose the seat across from Anna, next to Diane. "I'm Maxwell Bordon, but you can call me Max," he said, settling into his chair.

"It's nice to meet you, Max," Anna said. "I'm Anna Craine, and this is my granddaughter, Diane."

Max nodded. "I know who you are, Anna. Everyone here does, to be blunt. I'm glad you were finally able to join us for dinner. Everyone has the right to use the dining room."

Diane noticed he'd said the last sentence louder than necessary, and it made her smile. This guy was a pistol.

An aide came over to their table to ask what they'd like to drink. She smiled when she saw Max there. "Watch out for this one," the young woman said. "He's a flirt and a scoundrel."

Max sat up straighter. "Good. My reputation is intact. I'd

like a coffee, dear lady." He winked at the young woman.

"See what I mean," she said, grinning.

Diane asked for water, and Anna requested coffee. Soon, their drinks and meals arrived. It was simple fare, but delicious. Baked chicken, mashed potatoes with gravy on the side, green beans, and a fruit cup.

"Leave room for dessert," the aide told them. "It's home-made carrot cake."

"Sounds delicious," Max said, winking at Anna.

As they ate, conversation began to fill the room as the other diners forgot about Anna and talked among themselves. After taking a few bites, Max spoke up.

"How do you like living here?" he asked Anna.

"It's very nice here," she replied. "And the nurses and staff are wonderful."

"I suppose compared to the reformatory, this is a step up, eh?" Max said.

Diane raised an eyebrow but noticed his question didn't rattle Anna.

"Actually, the reformatory isn't as bad as many believe. The staff was kind, and the food was good. But to have the freedom to spend my day as I wish does make living here so much better."

Diane was impressed at Anna's honesty. Every day that she spent with Anna made her like her even more.

"Well, I'm glad you like it here," Max said with a grin. "And if you would like a friend to eat with or watch the weekly movie with, I'm your man. I'm not here to judge you as some would." He nudged his head in the direction of the other diners.

Anna smiled. "Thank you. I wouldn't mind seeing the weekly movie. I may take you up on your offer."

Max winked again, making Diane laugh.

"But watch yourself around my grandmother," Diane told him in mock seriousness.

"I'm always a gentleman," he said proudly. Although his grin told Diane otherwise.

* * *

Later that evening, after Diane had arrived home, she changed into pajamas and curled up in bed before calling her daughter to share what she'd learned about Anna that night.

"How sad it must have been for Anna to live in a strange place while her father was so sick," Natalie said. "I can't even imagine that happening to an eleven-year-old."

"I know. I can't get the image of her as a child out of my head. She's so sweet and serene, yet she's been through so much. And I've only heard her story up to age eleven. Can you imagine what more there must be?"

"You really should be recording this, Mom. Or writing everything down afterward. It's quite a story."

"But what would I do with it?" Diane asked. She'd also thought of recording Anna's story, but for what purpose? Anna might not want her words recorded either.

"Just for our family history," Natalie said. "This story will be lost if we don't have it recorded or written down. At least think about it."

They talked some more about how Natalie was doing in school and then said goodbye. Diane felt so fortunate to have a daughter she could speak so easily with. She knew many women whose grown daughters barely talked to them. Of course, the only reason Diane still spoke to her mother was because she felt obligated to do so. It wasn't because they had a close relationship. That thought made her think of how Joan hadn't had a relationship with her mother, either. It was sad. But then, Diane still didn't know what experiences had led up to Anna killing her husband, either.

Barry came to bed soon afterward, but it took Diane a long time to fall asleep. Her thoughts kept turning back to Anna as a young girl, living and working for the doctor. Anna spoke of it as if it were a normal thing for an eleven-year-old girl to work for her keep. Diane supposed in those days, it was, which made it even sadder.

Thinking of Anna's story brought up memories of Diane's past. She was thankful she'd been able to get full custody of Natalie when she'd left her husband all those years ago. Diane couldn't imagine leaving her daughter with him. Jeffrey had been an interesting, handsome, and seemingly decent man when she'd met him, but that had only been because he'd hid his dark side from her. By the time they'd met, Jeff had already finished college and had served four years in the military. Friends had introduced them, and they'd hit it off right away. She'd been twenty-six, so by the time they'd married two years later, Diane thought she'd made a grown-up, educated decision about marrying the right man. But after a while, she realized she'd made a mistake that couldn't be fixed in any way other than divorce.

She wondered if that was how Anna had felt. Except maybe getting a divorce hadn't been a choice for Anna. Hopefully, she'd learn more as Anna's story unfolded.

* * *

After school on Friday, Diane took her mother out shopping and to dinner. Since Joan didn't ask about Anna, Diane didn't offer any information. After they'd returned to her apartment and put away her few groceries and paper products, Joan spoke up.

"So, what has she told you so far?"

Diane was surprised by her mother's interest. Even though Joan acted like she didn't care, she supposed the suspense of not knowing bothered her even more.

"I'm assuming you mean Anna," Diane said, just to annoy her.

Joan sat at her small table and crossed her arms. "Who else would I be asking about?"

Diane grinned, but not so her mother could see. "Anna has told me a little about her childhood. Did you know she grew up on her grandparents' farm in central Minnesota? And that her father had tuberculosis and went for treatment at Aw-Gwah-Ching in Walker?"

Joan wrinkled her brow. A lifetime of bad marriages and heavy drinking hadn't been kind to her mother's face. Even though Diane knew she no longer drank alcohol, it hadn't erased the damage the decades had done. Nor the damage to her memory. Diane poured two glasses of ice water and sat down at the table, opposite her mother, waiting for her response.

"I don't remember much about my mother," Joan finally said. "Except that last day. But I do remember something being said about living in Walker. With a doctor's family or something. She used to say she wanted to bring us there and show us how huge Leech Lake was. She said she swam there with some kids she took care of." Joan shook her head. "That's about all I know."

Diane sat back and took a sip of water. "Anna lived with Dr. Hanson, his wife, and their three little girls while her father was being treated at the sanatorium. She helped Mrs. Hanson with the children, and the cook in the kitchen for her keep. By the sounds of it, the family was very kind to her."

Joan nodded. "So, what happened after that?"

Diane was thrilled her mother was asking questions. She hoped that at some point, she could bring the two women together. Considering that Anna was turning ninety-five this year, there wasn't much time left to reunite mother and daughter. "That's where we ended the story this week. I'm hoping she'll tell me more on Sunday."

Joan's lips formed a thin line that Diane could only read as disapproval over her seeing Anna every week. Instead of reprimanding her for visiting the elderly lady, Joan said, "She ended up in Minneapolis somehow later in life because that's where she met my father."

Diane's ears perked up. Her mother had never spoken about her father. "What do you know about him?"

"A lot. Aunt Bernice reminisced about him quite a bit when I was younger. Then the topic became taboo. Mostly because I started asking questions about my parents when I was a teenager. I was told to never bring up the subject. So, I stopped."

"That's sad," Diane said.

"That's just how it was," Joan said with finality. "My mother disgraced the family. They didn't want to talk about her or my father because it brought up bad memories."

"It's still sad. You had a right to know about them," Diane said.

Joan shrugged.

"What do you know about your father?" Diane asked,

hoping her mother would continue talking.

Joan's face softened as she sat back in her chair. Her defenses were down for once, something Diane rarely saw. "He was born in New York state but raised in Portland, Oregon. I think it was upper New York, close to the Canadian border. But for whatever reason, they moved to Portland, where my great-grandmother had lived before marrying my great-grandfather."

"Do you remember their names?" Diane asked, hungry for any information. She'd never been told anything about her great-grandparents.

Joan squinted as if it would help her remember. "My grandmother's name was Mari. She was from Finland, but she always claimed to have been born in Portland. No one knows why. And my grandfather's name was Thomas. A common British name. His family was from England. There's some Irish and French in the family too."

"Do you know anything else?" Diane asked.

"Only that they divorced when my father was two years old and Aunt Bernice was four. Mari moved back to Portland, where she had friends from Finland, and Thomas traveled around. He lived in Buffalo, New York, up in Canada, and then in Minneapolis for a while. That's how my father ended up in Minneapolis. Around the time he was fourteen, he became troublesome for my grandmother, so she sent him to live with Thomas. I guess that wasn't a good idea. Thomas had remarried a woman from Canada and wasn't exactly the model parent. He bootlegged liquor over the Canadian border for a while and did other questionable things. He was a tough guy, according to Aunt Bernice. She said Mari was a tough cookie too. I guess in those days, you had to be."

Diane was amazed at how much her mother knew. She'd

never heard any of this before. "What else did you learn?"

Joan jolted as if being awakened from a dream. "It's all ancient history," she said, waving her hand through the air. "And it doesn't matter now." She stood and headed for her bedroom.

Diane sighed. It was just like her mother to stop abruptly when things were going well. She stood and put the glasses away in the kitchen. "Well, thanks for the information. It was interesting. I'd love to hear more if you think of anything else," she called out to her mother.

Joan came back into the room, already dressed for bed. "None of it matters. Who knows how much of it is real or fake anyway. Aunt Bernice didn't always tell the truth," she said dismissively.

Diane left after saying goodnight and headed out to her car. She wished her mother were more open about the past. What was there to hide after all these years? But it seemed that people were always hiding secrets from their past. As she drove toward home in the darkened city, she hoped Anna continued to tell her story. It was important to Diane and Natalie. Right then and there, Diane decided she would record Anna's stories. She didn't want these family stories lost. As a history teacher, she understood how important it was to remember the past. With that in mind, she turned her car toward the mall to stop at an electronics store to buy a digital recorder.

* * *

Diane arrived at Anna's place at one o'clock on Sunday afternoon. The day was cold and windy, so everyone was inside, either watching television in the recreation room, playing cards, or working on puzzles. Anna wasn't with the others as Diane had hoped. She found her alone in her room with the television on. An old movie from the 1940s was playing on TCM starring Katharine Hepburn.

"I see you have great taste in movies," Diane said, walking through the open door into the small room.

Anna smiled up at her from her recliner. The red cardigan she wore today brought color to her cheeks. "Hello, dear. Yes, I've adored Katharine Hepburn since I was a teenager in high school. All the girls did. We all wanted to be just like her; beautiful, funny, strong, and glamorous. Of course, none of us were anything like her, but it was fun to dream."

Diane pulled out the chair from beside the wall and sat, noticing the wooden box was open, and letters were strung out on the small table. "You've been reminiscing." She pointed to the letters.

Anna's eyes touched on the old letters and turned sad. "Yes. Remember how I told you I wrote to my father at the sanatorium? I wrote to Andrew as well. I've been reading through them this week. They really don't contain anything important, but they were special to me. They were my connection to the people I loved."

"I think it's sweet that you saved their letters. I wish people wrote letters today. Everything is a text or email, and it will all be lost over time."

"Yes. Times have changed. We won't know if it's for the better or not for years to come, I suppose," Anna said.

Diane set her purse down and pulled out the small digital recorder she'd purchased. "Would it be okay if I record you when we talk about the past?" she asked Anna. "I won't if it bothers you. My daughter, Natalie, is interested in your story and had hoped to hear it too." She held her breath, waiting for Anna to reply. The older woman looked confused at first, then her face softened.

"Of course you can, dear," Anna finally said. "I doubt there is much I have to say that is interesting, but I like the idea that your daughter—my great-granddaughter—is interested in anything I might have to say." She smiled.

"Oh, she's interested," Diane told her.

"Will I get a chance to meet Natalie?" Anna asked, looking hopeful.

"Hopefully, she'll be home for the holidays. I know she's eager to meet you, too."

This seemed to please Anna. Her face took on that sweet, serene look again.

Diane set the small recorder on the table. She couldn't resist running her fingers over the smooth wood of the keepsake box. "It's so lovely," she told Anna. "Was it a gift?"

Anna smiled, her eyes growing dreamy. "Yes. And from my favorite person."

CHAPTER TEN

Anna

After visiting with her father, Anna settled into her new life with the Hansons quite well. She loved sending off notes to her father and receiving his replies. Dr. Hanson was only too happy to be their messenger. Anna wrote about what she did in school, how she, Francie, and Betty spent their time together, and when she babysat for little Rose. She wrote about baking cookies with Mrs. Schmidt and helping her peel potatoes or slice carrots for dinner. Anna told her father about how much she'd grown to like the cook—even though she'd been afraid of her at first—and how Mrs. Schmidt would sometimes give her a few coins for helping her in the kitchen. *I'm saving my pennies so I can buy you something nice,* Anna wrote to her father.

Save your money to buy yourself nice things, sweet pea, Jon wrote back. *Your old papa has all he needs just hearing from his beloved älskling.*

But Anna had her mind set on how she wanted to spend her money.

She wrote a long letter to her brother at the Peterson farm

and finally received a letter back. Andrew wrote that he was happy she was living with a good family, and he hoped their papa would get well soon. *I miss you both, and I hope we will be together again very soon,* Andrew told her.

Anna hoped they would be too.

On October twenty-sixth, the Hansons surprised Anna with presents and a cake for her twelfth birthday. Anna was stunned that they'd remembered. Francie and Betty gave her a charming doll wearing a white dress that had ruffles and lace and had blond hair with long curls. Anna was mesmerized by how beautiful it was, and couldn't even fathom actually playing with it. Dr. and Mrs. Hanson gave her a new scarf and mittens that matched her blue wool coat and a pair of leather boots for when the snow arrived. And Mrs. Schmidt gave her beautiful stationery that she could write to her father and brother on. Anna couldn't remember a time when she'd received so many new and lovely gifts. That night, she placed her new doll on the bed beside her little rag doll Lily. The difference between the two dolls, just like the difference between her old and new life, was painfully obvious. Her little heart felt heavy. Just as her new doll did not belong next to Lily, Anna knew she did not belong here. She was a guest in this house, not a member of the family. But she was also grateful to be here, even if it was only for a short time.

The weeks went by quickly, and Anna worked hard to do well with her studies and help around the house. When it became too cold and snowy to go outside, Mrs. Hanson sat the girls down to learn how to do fancywork like crocheting, tatting, and knitting. Anna had learned to crochet from her grandmother, so she picked up the other techniques from Mrs. Hanson quickly. Francie was a quick learner, too, and actually enjoyed making small projects. But Betty became frustrated with the intricate work and gave up easily no matter how patient Anna was with her. Most evenings ended with the other girls running off to play while Anna sat quietly with Mrs. Hanson working on delicate lacey items like doilies and collars for dresses.

"You have a talent for this type of work," Mrs. Hanson told her one evening as they sat by the fire in the parlor. The doctor was there too, sitting on the divan and reading a book. He stood and studied Anna's crochet project, nodding his approval.

"You know, we have a craft shop at the sanatorium where patients sell the items they make to other patients. Many of the women would love these fancy collars and other items that you make. Since they spend so much time in bed, they like to dress up their pajama tops and such. If you'd like to sell a few in the shop to make a little extra money, I'd be happy to bring them there for you."

Anna's eyes lit up. "Yes. That would be wonderful!" She wasn't used to being complimented on anything she did, and she felt proud that the doctor thought her work was good enough to sell. Plus, the extra money selling items would be a great help at Christmastime.

Anna was allowed to visit her father for a few minutes on Thanksgiving, even though he was still on bed rest. She noticed again that his pajamas were getting ragged. He mentioned that they were taking him downstairs twice a week to have his lung aspirated. It was a procedure where they drew out fluid from the lung with a long needle. Jon said he had to wear a sweater over his pajamas because he didn't have a proper robe.

Anna cringed at the thought of the long needle, but she took in his idea for a robe. A few weeks before Christmas, Anna studied the J.C. Penny's catalog and marked a few pages. Then she approached Mrs. Hanson, asking if she'd be kind enough to order the items she'd tagged. Anna handed her an envelope with the money she'd saved to pay for it.

Mrs. Hanson looked over the pages. "My goodness, this is kind of you, Anna," she said. "Two pairs of pajamas, a robe, and two pairs of socks. Your father will be quite surprised."

Anna nodded enthusiastically. "He really needs them."

Mrs. Hanson smiled warmly. "You're a good daughter, Anna. To work so hard and save your money all so you can give your father these nice gifts. I hope your kindness rubs off on my daughters."

Anna felt proud to be able to buy such nice things for her father. And to be complimented by Mrs. Hanson made her feel even better. She'd marked one other item in the catalog, and Mrs. Hanson looked up at her curiously. "Levi's pants? Are these for your father, too?"

Anna shook her head. "Those are for my brother, Andrew. He's always wanted to be a cowboy, and I thought a pair of store-bought dungarees would make him happy."

"You're a sweet girl, Anna. Very thoughtful." Mrs. Hanson ordered the items, and Anna set to wrapping all the presents with paper Mrs. Hanson had offered to her. They mailed off the package to Andrew, and on Christmas Eve, Anna was allowed to visit her father for a few minutes, and Dr. Hanson helped her carry in all the gifts.

"What are all these?" Jon asked, clearly surprised.

"Merry Christmas, Papa!" Anna said happily. "These are all for you."

Jon exclaimed as he opened each of the packages, and Anna beamed with pride. "Everything is so nice, *älskling*. How on earth did you afford so many nice gifts?"

"I saved all the money Mrs. Schmidt gave me for helping her in the kitchen, and I've sold many items in the gift shop here. I even bought Andrew a pair of Levi's pants and sent them to him."

"She did it all on her own," Dr. Hanson said proudly as if Anna were his own daughter. "You should be very proud of her."

"Well, you do astonish me," Jon said. "You could have spent that money on yourself. Thank you, sweet pea, for being so unselfish. I am extremely proud of you."

Anna's heart swelled with love for her father. She was happy she could do this small thing for him.

"I don't have as many surprises for you, sweetie, but I do have something." With the doctor's help, Jon pulled out a wooden box from underneath his bed. It was about the size of a shoebox and had gold hinges and a latch. But what made it special was the rose carved out on the lid. "Merry Christmas, *älskling*."

Anna's eyes lit up as she set the box on her papa's nightstand and opened the lid. Inside, it was lined with purple velvet that felt soft to the touch. "It's beautiful, Papa. Thank you!"

"Do you remember Earl, the man who drove us up here that first day? He runs the woodshop where the patients who are feeling better can make projects. Earl made this box for me to give to you," Jon said.

"I love it. Thank you, Papa." And Anna did love the box. That night when she returned to her bedroom, she placed her most treasured keepsakes in the box. Her letters from her papa and Andrew, a picture of her mother and father when they were married, and the only jewelry she owned, a gold cross necklace. She knew she would treasure this gift for as long as she lived.

* * *

The months sped by, and the snow finally melted. Summer came, and Anna's father was allowed to sit outside in the sun and move around a little. He'd had an operation to collapse his lung so it could heal, and he seemed to be feeling better. Dr. Hanson sometimes brought Anna to work with him so she could sit with her father. They'd play checkers and enjoy the few hours alone together.

Other days Anna watched little Rose as the girls spent time outdoors. Rose was changing from a baby to a little girl and ran around everywhere, trying to keep up with her sisters. On hot days, Mrs. Hanson accompanied them to the lake, and the girls swam in the cool water. Anna loved to swim, but she also helped by watching Rose on the shore. They built sandcastles in the coarse sand, and the little girls squealed when they'd find leeches attached to their skin. Anna was always prepared with a saltshaker, and soon the leeches would curl up and fall off.

Mrs. Hanson always brought a basket lunch along, and they'd eat sandwiches by the water. These were Anna's favorite days. They were relaxed and carefree, so unlike her summers on the farm. There, she'd worked all the time either in the kitchen or outside, and her grandmother was always scolding her. Mrs. Hanson didn't scold. She'd correct her daughters lovingly if they misbehaved, but never called them names or yelled at them. Anna had great respect for her because of her easy-going nature.

A year after coming to live with the Hansons, Anna's hair had grown longer, and Mrs. Hanson taught her how to put it up as the adult women did. Anna had also grown taller and had slimmed down. She was slowly becoming a woman, and her behavior was so mature that people thought she was much older than her thirteen years.

That winter, Anna, Francie, and Betty were allowed to sit in at the weekly movies shown at the recreation center at Aw-Gwah-Ching. Dr. Hanson drove them there, and they'd sit quietly with the patients who were no longer contagious but who were still healing from tuberculosis. Anna loved watching the movies. She especially enjoyed watching Ginger Rogers dancing with Fred Astaire or the romantic comedies. The women were so beautiful in their flowing satin dresses and styled hair. Her favorites were Greta Garbo, Jean Harlow, and Katharine Hepburn. At night as she and Francie lay in their beds, the two girls would giggle and talk about the handsome male movie stars like Jimmy Stewart and Gary Cooper. Both girls dreamed about growing up and marrying handsome, courageous men like the ones in the movies.

In January of 1938, Anna's father suddenly became terribly ill. He'd been doing well and moving around as much as they would allow him, but then he came down with a fever of 105 degrees and was put on complete bed rest. When Anna heard that he was sick, she wanted to go see him immediately, but Dr. Hanson wouldn't allow it.

"I'm sorry, dear, but he's too sick right now. If his fever goes down, maybe we can let you in to see him."

Anna tried hard to be brave, but she was scared. Living around the doctor and the sanatorium, she'd heard of many cases where a patient would take a turn for the worse and then suddenly die.

"I would tell you if I thought his condition was dangerous,"

Dr. Hanson promised her. "I'll let you see him as soon as it's safe."

Her father's fever and delirium went on for two weeks as nurses tried everything to cool down his body. Each day, Dr. Hanson reported Jon's progress to Anna. But instead of making her feel better, it only worried Anna more.

Three weeks after her father's fever had started, it finally broke. The doctors had X-rayed his lungs and found that the TB infection had spread to his other lung. With one lung already collapsed, they'd have to try different treatments for the infected lung.

Dr. Hanson allowed Anna to see her father a few days after his fever broke. He'd warned her not to tire Jon as he was very weak and still recovering.

When Anna stepped up beside her father's bed, she was startled by how thin he looked under his blanket. His face was narrow and his hair thin—he looked twenty years older than when she'd last seen him. Hiding her fear, she sat, and even though she wasn't supposed to touch him, she held his hand.

"Papa?"

After a time, Jon's eyes fluttered open, and when he looked at Anna, his eyes grew wide. "Lillian?"

Anna's heart seized. Lillian was her mother. "No, Papa. It's Anna," she said softly.

He frowned, then his eyes seemed to clear. "Yes. Anna," he said. "You look so like your mother."

She took a breath. Anna had never been compared to her mother in appearance. Her mother was a beauty, and Anna had never thought of herself that way. But she thought of how she now wore her hair up, and it was the same color as her mother's. Perhaps she now resembled her a little.

"I was worried about you, Papa. But the doctor said you can rest and heal again."

Jon lay there but didn't respond. He looked so tired, it broke Anna's heart. Just as she was about to leave, Jon's eyes opened again.

"Anna?"

"Yes, Papa."

"*Älskling.* There's something you must know. If anything happens, I've made arrangements for you. I've given Dr. Hanson instructions. Be brave, sweet pea. I've done my best."

A chill ran through Anna. "But you'll get well, Papa. You and Andrew and I will be a family again very soon." Her voice cracked as she said it.

"I love you, *älskling.* Always remember that," Jon said, his voice fading.

"I love you, too, Papa," Anna whispered.

Later, when Dr. Hanson came to get her, Anna asked him to be honest with her. "Is Papa dying?"

Dr. Hanson sighed and ran his hand through his wavy blond hair. "He's very sick," he finally said. "But I have seen men in worse condition get better. We're doing our best to help your father. Please believe me, Anna."

She nodded, but her heart was ripping to pieces. That night, she wrote to Andrew telling him their papa was extremely sick, and she was praying for him. A few days later, she received a short letter back.

I'm sorry about papa. I hope he gets well soon. I miss you both very much. I've been thinking a lot about my life, and I don't know how much longer I can stay here at the Petersons. I'm fifteen now

and want to strike out on my own. I want to go
west. I dream of working with horses on a ranch
and not farming. Let me know how papa is doing.
   Love,
   Andrew

Anna was worried. Would Andrew actually go away? Papa had to get better, or else she'd lose everyone she loved.

Dr. Hanson allowed Anna to visit her father every few days, and for a while, it looked as if he might get better. He ate a little more each day, and once when she visited, he was sitting up in bed, although a nurse had helped prop him up. His breathing was labored, and he spoke in short sentences. But the nurse had smiled and said he'd eaten his lunch, which was a good sign.

"Sweet pea, there's something I need to tell you," Jon said slowly, taking a breath between each word. "I have a sister you've never met. She is older than I and lives in Minneapolis. She has agreed to take you in if something happens to me."

Anna was stunned she'd never heard of his sister before. "But you're going to get better," she insisted as if being stubborn would make it so.

Jon took another long breath. "I hope so. But if not, you must go live with May. She's a kind person and well-educated. She's not married, but she has room to take you in."

Tears filled Anna's eyes. "Why haven't I ever heard of her before?"

"She and I have had our differences, but that doesn't concern you. She is happy to give you a home. I know you'll be safe with her."

"I don't want to live with her," Anna insisted, her tears now falling. "I want to live with you and Andrew." She dropped her head in her hands and cried.

"Please, sweet pea. Don't cry. I'm telling you this so you won't be surprised in case I do not get well," Jon said, his voice growing raspier.

Anna raised her tear-stained face. Even though she'd grown more mature in looks, she was still a child at heart. "Why can't I go live with Mama if something happens?" she asked in a whisper.

Jon sighed. "I'm sorry, *älskling*. I haven't been honest with you. Your mama passed away two years ago. I couldn't bring myself to tell you that. All you have left now is my sister."

A cold chill swept through Anna. Her mother was dead. Why had no one told her that in all these years? She dropped her head once again and sobbed. Nothing was as she'd thought. And now, she feared her father would die, and she'd be all alone in the world.

She was all cried out by the time Dr. Hanson came to collect her. Her eyes were red, and her face stained with tears, but she said nothing to the doctor. In that moment, when her father told her that her mother was dead, she'd changed. Her heart tightened, and she realized that she might be all alone in the world soon. She could either cry or stand tall and be strong. *Papa would want me to be strong,* she thought. And so she was. For the next few weeks, she did as she was told, worked hard in school, and helped Mrs. Schmidt in the kitchen. She had a new resolve about her, a more mature attitude. She would save any money she earned and learn to be self-reliant. But deep down in her heart, she felt scared and alone. As if she'd always be alone.

By March, her father took a turn for the worse, and seven days after his fever spiked again, he died. Anna cried when Dr.

Hanson told her, and again at the small funeral Dr. and Mrs. Hanson held for Jon at the chapel on the sanatorium grounds. He was properly buried in the cemetery in Walker, and the doctor made sure he had a headstone so Anna could find his grave. Anna had written to her grandparents and Andrew about her father's death but had heard nothing in return. As she stood at her father's grave, she knew then that her childhood was buried along with her beloved papa. Life would never again be carefree and fun. She'd lost the only man she'd ever trusted and loved. Her heart was broken.

CHAPTER ELEVEN

Diane

Tears stung Diane's eyes as she listened to Anna's story. How heartbreaking for the poor little girl to have lost her father, and her mother, all at once. Diane couldn't imagine how difficult it had been for her.

"Did you hear from Andrew?" Diane asked once she'd regained her composure.

"I sent him several letters, and none were answered. Finally, I received a reply from Mrs. Peterson. She returned his letters in one packet and said he'd left one night, and no one knew where he'd gone. They guessed he'd jumped a train but didn't know where to. I knew, though." She smiled.

"Out west?" Diane asked.

Anna nodded. "That was my guess. It would be decades before I knew the truth."

Diane's brows rose, but before she could ask what she meant, Anna continued.

"I lived with the Hansons until the end of May. Since my aunt worked as a teacher in a high school, she had to wait until school let out to come and escort me to Minneapolis. I admit I had wished the Hansons would allow me to stay with them. They were kind people, and I knew I would be content there, but I didn't dare ask. It was too much to ask of anyone. "Auntie May arrived on the bus on the last day of May. Dr. Hanson and I greeted her at the station, and my first impression of her was she would be strict. But I was very wrong. She had high expectations of everyone around her, but she was warm and loving. The bus ride took a full day back then, so she stayed overnight at the Hansons, and we left together the next morning. I cried terribly as I said goodbye to the entire family. They'd been so kind to me, and I had many happy memories. Mrs. Schmidt packed lunch for us and even hugged me goodbye. Sadly, I never saw any of them again."

"Oh, that's too bad," Diane said. Another loss for this sweet woman. She'd lived with them for nearly two years, cared for their children, and was treated like a daughter—so much loss.

"Auntie May was very understanding. On the long ride to her apartment in Minneapolis, she told me how she'd immigrated from Sweden several years before my father. She'd learned English quite well before arriving and attended the university for her teaching certificate. She loved writing and especially loved drama, so she became an English teacher and also worked as a high school drama teacher. By the time I came to live with her, she was forty-seven years old, had worked for the school system for years, and was well-respected."

"She sounds amazing," Diane said. "So, she never married?"

Anna shook her head. "She didn't go into much detail. She told me that she'd fallen in love with a colleague, but he died in 1918 during the Great War. She never found anyone else who could compare to him."

"That's so sad," Diane said. Although, in many ways, she understood. After her bad marriage, she hadn't wanted to become involved with anyone again. Then Barry came along. Still, she was hesitant to make the relationship permanent.

They had talked so long, it was nearly dinnertime for Anna. "Are you eating in here or in the dining room?" Diane asked as she put the chair back against the wall and gathered up her purse, the recorder, and her jacket.

Anna looked thoughtful. "Well, Max keeps pestering me to eat supper with him each night in the dining room. What do you think? Should I?"

She grinned at Anna. "I think you should. Ignore the old biddies and enjoy yourself. They'll come around eventually."

The older woman laughed. The sound of her laughter warmed Diane's heart.

"Then I guess I'll take him up on it tonight. Would you mind telling one of the staff that I'll be eating in the dining room tonight?"

"I'd be happy to." Diane bent down and gave Anna a hug. She was surprised when Anna reached for her hand and held it a moment.

"Thank you for brightening up my life," Anna said warmly. "You give me something to look forward to. And telling my story to you feels right. I feel better letting it all come out after so many long years."

"I love hearing your story," Diane said. "And I love coming here to see you."

Anna beamed. "I feel so blessed."

On the way out, Diane stopped the nurse she often saw in Anna's wing of the building and told her that Anna would be eating in the dining room that night—with Max.

"I'm glad to hear that," she said to Diane. "You know, she's been so happy ever since you started coming here to visit her. I was afraid she'd have no visitors, and here you are. She's such a sweet person. She deserves a little happiness."

Diane nodded and noticed the nurse's nametag read Pauline. "I think so, too," Diane told her. "Thank you for taking such good care of Anna."

"It's my pleasure," Pauline said. "I'll go now and take her down to the dining room. I'm sure Max is already at her door, waiting for her."

Diane smiled at the idea of Max escorting Anna to supper. The image was so cute.

* * *

Diane was busy all week and was unable to visit Anna on Wednesday night as she would have liked. They had parent-teacher conferences Wednesday and Thursday nights that week, and then Friday, Diane was off work all day. She spent that day taking care of her own chores around the house like laundry and shopping for groceries. As she worked, she thought about Anna's childhood. Anna had revealed her mother had died two years before her father, but no one had told her when it happened. That seemed so strange to Diane. She wanted to ask Anna more about it and hoped it wouldn't be too painful for her to talk about it. But Diane was curious to fill in the gaps in Anna's life.

That evening, Diane headed to her mother's place to take her shopping. She hoped that her mother might share more about her childhood. Diane thought that tying together both stories from Joan and Anna might help her get to the bottom of why her mother hated Anna so much. Well, besides the obvious reason. It just seemed that if Anna was as sweet a person then as she was now, Joan would remember her mother fondly despite how it had ended. Or maybe that was just wishful thinking on Diane's part.

When Diane arrived at her mother's apartment, Joan snapped at her.

"I thought you had the day off. Why are you late?"

Diane's radar immediately went up. She'd learned from experience that when her mother was in an agitated mood, she had to walk on eggshells around her. "Sorry. Traffic was heavy for some reason tonight. Are you ready to go?"

"I've been ready for thirty minutes," Joan shot back.

Diane knew that wasn't true because she was only ten minutes late. "Well, let's get going," she said, keeping her tone light. She opened the closet where her mother kept her coats. "Which coat would you like to wear. It's a bit chilly outside."

"I can get my own coat," Joan said, pushing Diane aside.

Diane stepped back, out of her way. "Did something happen today? Aren't you feeling well?"

Joan spun on her with the agility of a woman half her age. "What's that supposed to mean?"

"You're obviously angry. What happened?"

"You were late!"

"By ten minutes," Diane said, exasperated. "Why are you making a federal case over it?"

Joan dropped her purse, stormed over to the sofa, and sat down like a petulant child.

Sighing, Diane held in her frustration and followed her. "What is this all about?"

"I don't want to go tonight," Joan said, crossing her arms.

"Why?"

"I just don't," she insisted. She set her lips into a thin line.

Diane knew that look—her mother was determined to make everyone in her path miserable, just as she had when Diane was a child. Staying calm, she asked, "Are you feeling all right?"

"I'm fine!" Joan insisted. "I just don't feel like spending time with you tonight. You obviously don't want to be here, or you wouldn't have been late. Why don't you go visit your grandmother since you seem to like her so much."

Diane sighed. "Is that what this is about? I'm here. We go out every week, Mom. Come on. Let's go do your shopping and have dinner."

Joan shook her head. "No. I'm staying in tonight. Just go."

She hated it when her mother acted like a spoiled child. And she did this quite often. When Joan was married to her second husband, Albert, she teetered between drunken rages and childish fits to get her way. Diane had hated it then, and she despised it now.

"Are you sure?" she asked calmly.

Joan sat firmly on the sofa. "Yes. Just go."

"Fine." Diane turned to leave, but anger washed over her. Turning back, she said, "Why do you do this? We had a good time last week and a nice talk. Now, you're pushing me away. Why?"

Joan pulled herself up from the sofa, her face red with anger. "Don't blame me for this! You were late. You're the one who ruined our evening, not me. Just go!"

Shaking her head, Diane turned and headed for the door. "Goodbye, Mom. I'll see you next week." She walked out the door, feeling emotionally drained.

Memories of past encounters with her mother filled Diane's thoughts on the drive home. She'd always been volatile. One minute she was the nicest person on the planet and the next she'd blow up. Diane hadn't known how to deal with her mother's roller-coaster emotions when she was a child and still had no idea how to handle it. She'd found the best way was to do as her mother wanted and walk away. But it was so frustrating.

"You're home early," Barry said when Diane entered. "Was Joan in one of her moods?"

Hearing Barry's warm, understanding voice felt like a hug after having dealt with her mother. Diane dropped her purse and coat in a chair and went to sit on the sofa next to him. Barry draped his arm around her.

"That bad, huh?" he asked, kissing the top of her head.

"That bad. I just don't get her. One week we're having a good time, the next week she's a completely different person. It's so tough to deal with."

"She's been this way your entire life. She's not going to change now," Barry said gently.

"I know. I wish our relationship could be better, but I doubt that will ever happen." Diane had been hopeful that as her mother grew older, she might mellow, and they could build a relationship. But too many years and too much water had passed under the bridge. Her mother had never been a warm, loving person, so why did Diane think her mother would change now? Again, wishful thinking.

"Do you want to go out for dinner?" Barry asked. "I haven't eaten."

She sat up and looked at Barry. "I'm exhausted. Can we just order a pizza and watch a movie?"

He smiled. "I'm game. You pick the movie, and I'll order

the pizza."

Barry always knew the right thing to do and say. And tonight, that was exactly what Diane needed—someone who understood her.

* * *

On Sunday, Diane stopped in to see Anna at one o'clock. Her grandmother was sitting in her recliner, waiting with a serene smile on her face. It was such a contrast from her own mother that Diane had trouble believing Anna and Joan were related.

"I'm so happy you're here," Anna said. "I told Max at lunch that I hoped you'd come today, and here you are."

Diane smiled. "So, you had lunch with Max?"

"Yes. I've been going to the dining room for every meal since last week. You're right—the old biddies will just have to get used to me." She giggled, which made Diane laugh. "It's nice being around other people and not hiding anymore."

"That's wonderful," Diane said. "Has anyone else spoken to you yet?"

"Well, one woman did come to our table for a moment to ask my name. When I told her, she nodded and left. Max said she has memory problems, so she may have just forgotten I was the ex-convict."

Diane's hackles raised. She didn't like that term. "Who's calling you an ex-convict?"

"Oh, don't worry, dear. It's the truth. Max teases me about being an ex-convict but in a friendly way. He doesn't mean anything by it."

Diane nodded, but it still rubbed her wrong. After serving sixty-five years in prison, Anna deserved to have it all put behind her. She'd paid her debt to society.

Discreetly, Diane pulled her recorder out of her purse and set it on the small table. "Are you up to talking about the past some more, or would you rather not?"

Anna grinned. "I've been waiting to tell you more. I even placed a picture on top of the pile in my keepsake box. Would you hand it to me, dear?"

Diane lifted the box from the table and set it closer to Anna. The older woman moved slowly, opening the lid and picking a photo.

"I thought you might be interested in my mother," Anna said.

"Wow. How'd you know I was thinking a lot about your mother?"

"I dropped the bombshell on you last week about learning she'd been deceased for over two years. We didn't discuss it further, and I thought you might have questions."

"You're a mind-reader," Diane said, grinning. "It bothered me that she'd been gone so long, and no one had told you of her death. I know your father was sick, and he'd had a lot to deal with, but still, she was your mother."

Anna nodded. "I was never angry at my father about not telling me. I suppose he thought I was too young when my mother first went away to explain why, and then it just remained a secret. But years later, I understood why my grandmother was so angry with my mother and talked badly about her." She handed Diane a black and white photo on cardboard that was from a photography studio decades ago. "This was my mother right before she married my father."

Diane stared at the woman, mesmerized. She stood near a railing with a fake garden background. Her dark hair was coiled up on her head, and she wore a long, white dress that looked like a summer frock. She was short and slender, but it was her face and expression that drew her in. Her jawline was square, and her cheekbones high, with large, dark eyes set on either side of a perfectly shaped nose. She was beautiful—her features nearly perfect except for one thing—she looked sad.

"Your mother was beautiful," Diane said.

"I think so too. In fact, everyone thought she was beautiful, and that may have been her undoing," Anna said.

Diane frowned. "Why?"

"She was the youngest and prettiest of the sisters, and they hated her for it. I guess my grandmother babied her more because she was so sweet and pretty. She must have learned that her beauty would get her anything she wanted."

"And then she married your father?" Diane asked.

"Yes. I guess, at first, my mother fell madly in love with him because he was different from all the boys she'd grown up around. He was gentle and calm, and he was quite good-looking too. But after they married, and first my brother, then I came along, all the fun left her life. My father worked down in Minneapolis for the railroad and only came home on weekends. They couldn't afford a place of their own, so she lived on the farm. I suppose to her, that wasn't the glamorous happily-ever-after she'd imagined."

"What happened?" Diane asked.

"Of course, I knew nothing of this when I was young. I guess my mother liked running around a lot, drinking and dancing at parties while my father was away, working. That left us children home with my grandparents, and my grandmother soon resented it. Then, one day, my mother just took off with another man to Minneapolis. She divorced my father and left us behind."

"That's terrible. No wonder no one told you." Diane couldn't believe a mother could do that. "How did you find this out?"

"After I moved in with Auntie May, I searched for where my mother had died and was buried. May helped me because she didn't know what had happened either. We found a record of her at the Glen Lake Sanatorium, where she'd suffered from tuberculosis. She died there in 1934 and was buried in a pauper's grave. But her death certificate had another man's last name on it. That's how we knew she'd married again."

"I'm so sorry," Diane said, feeling it was such a tragic story. "How sad that must have been for you."

"Thank you, dear," Anna said. "It was, at the time, but I forgave her. I eventually understood what it was like to be unhappy, and the lengths a person would go in order to change it. I only hope that my mother found some happiness before she died. And that it was worth leaving us."

Diane sat back and wrapped her arms around herself as if in a hug. Anna had said a lot in those few words. Anna had done the worst thing possible to leave her marriage. She had to have had a good reason. Diane's own mother had often not been there for her or her brother, either, choosing alcohol to hide behind rather than running away. Love, relationships, and family were complicated.

"I'm glad you were able to forgive your mother," Diane said. "I'm still working on it with mine."

Anna bent closer to Diane and patted her arm. "Sweetie, my Joanie has had her own demons to deal with. I'm sure that has affected you, too. I'm sorry."

She placed her hand over Anna's. "We all live through it, though, don't we?"

Anna nodded. "One way or another, we do."

CHAPTER TWELVE

Anna — 1949

Anna Bergman's black pumps clicked on the sidewalk as she hurried along, enjoying the warm spring air. It was May, and the sun was out, filtering through the new green leaves on the trees. Anna wore a dark gray suit, the skirt narrow and below her knees, and a small black hat perched on her rolled hair, staying secure in the breeze. It was after five in the afternoon, and she was heading back to the apartment she shared with Auntie May after a long day's work.

She stopped at the small neighborhood grocery store to pick up bread and crackers, then at the deli for cheese and lunchmeats. Once a month, her auntie hosted the drama group from the local playhouse, and they discussed the current play they were performing or the next one they wanted to do. Besides teaching at South High School as both an English and drama teacher, Auntie May was very active in the community theater group and directed most of their plays.

Anna smiled when she thought of how seriously her Auntie May took her drama work. Anna had performed in a few of her plays while attending South High School as well as recently with the playgroup. Her aunt was known for perfection, and each new play sold out. Anna was proud of the woman who'd taken her in eleven years before and who'd always treated her like a daughter.

With her arms full of grocery bags, Anna pushed through the door of their brownstone apartment building and started up the two flights to their floor. Halfway up, she saw a good-looking man heading down. She recognized him as the gentleman who lived one floor above them. Today, he was wearing a fine suit with highly polished shoes, a hat tipped jauntily on his head. Anna had no idea what his name was, or if he were married, but she couldn't help but be impressed by how handsome he looked.

He smiled and tipped his hat as he passed her, and Anna moved aside as best she could with all her packages. Her heel caught on the carpet, and she stumbled, dropping all her bags to catch herself on the handrail.

"Are you okay?" the gentleman asked, rushing to her aid.

She felt a warm blush creep up her neck and face. How foolish she must look to this professional-looking man, tripping over her own feet on the staircase. "I'm fine," she said, steadying herself. "Although a bit clumsy."

He smiled, showing straight, white teeth, and Anna got a closer look at his warm, brown eyes. He truly was an attractive man.

"I shouldn't have passed you on the stairs that way," he said, bending to retrieve her bags. "It was rude. I should have offered to carry your bags instead."

"Oh, no. It wasn't your fault," Anna said. She reached out her arms to take the bags, but the man shook his head.

"I'll carry them to your door," he said with a quick smile. "A gorgeous woman like you shouldn't ever have to carry her own bags."

Anna's heart leapt. No one, especially a man, had ever told her she was gorgeous. Feeling her cheeks stain red again, Anna thanked him profusely and led the way to her apartment.

"I've seen you around here before," the man said, matching her steps on the hallway carpet. "Have you lived here for a long time?"

"Over ten years," Anna said. "I live with my aunt."

"Ah, yes. The short woman with the determined look about her," he said. "She must be a professional woman, like you."

"She is. She teaches high school English and drama. And she directs plays at the local community theater."

"My goodness, that's impressive. And what about you? Where do you work?"

"I work as a secretary at a law firm. I've been there for about four years," Anna said proudly. Auntie May had insisted she attend a secondary school after high school, and she'd chosen business college. Anna enjoyed keeping the law firm organized and running smoothly. She was particularly good at it, and her employers appreciated her work.

"Well, my goodness. Beautiful and intelligent." He winked.

Anna became flustered as they stopped, and she tried to unlock the apartment door. Finally, the key went in, and the door opened. "Thank you for carrying my bags," she said, taking them from him. "It was nice meeting you."

He stood there as if to say more, then laughed and hit his palm to his head comically. "Where are my manners? I didn't introduce myself. I'm William Craine. I live on the third floor." He offered his hand to shake hers.

Anna set the bags on the table just inside the door and shook his hand. She noticed it was smooth and thought he must be a businessman and not a laborer. "I'm Anna Bergman."

His eyes twinkled. "It's nice to finally meet you, Miss Bergman."

Out of the corner of her eye, Anna saw Auntie May standing in the doorway between the kitchen and living room. "Well, Mr. Craine. Thank you again." She was about to close the door when William spoke again.

"Say, I was just heading down to the corner diner for a bite to eat. Would you like to join me? It's nothing fancy, I assure you, but it would be nice to have the company of a beautiful woman."

Anna was utterly smitten by this sharply dressed man who called her beautiful. She glanced at the bags she'd brought home, and her heart sank. She was supposed to help her aunt make snacks for tonight's get-together. But she'd much rather have dinner with William. She made her decision quicker than any she'd ever made before.

"I'd love to have dinner with you," she said. "Just give me a minute, and I'll be right out."

William nodded and waited in the hallway.

Closing the door but not hooking it, Anna picked up the packages, took a deep breath, and turned toward her aunt as she walked to the kitchen. Auntie May was studying Anna with her lips pursed. Not a good sign.

"Did you just accept that man's invitation to dinner? Do you even know him?" Auntie May asked as Anna brushed past her.

"I did," Anna said with more determination than she felt. "He was very kind to help me when I nearly fell down the stairs, and he carried my bags up here."

May's brows rose. "Fell? Are you all right?"

"Yes, yes. I'm fine. But I almost tumbled down the stairs. He was very helpful and polite."

May sighed. "And he's extremely handsome, too, I see. But what do you know about him, Anna? He might not be as gentlemanly as he appears."

"Oh, Auntie May. I've seen him around here the past few months, and he's always well-dressed. He must work because he leaves when I do and comes home about the same time. I feel as if I can trust him."

May's brow wrinkled in thought. Anna appreciated her aunt's concern, but the truth was she was twenty-four years old and still single, and Anna didn't like that. She'd hoped by now she'd have married and started a family. Despite all the schooling and the fact that Anna enjoyed her job, she still yearned to be loved by a good man and have someone to grow old with.

"Do you mind, Auntie? I know I was supposed to help you prepare for your monthly get-together, but I'd really like to go to dinner with Mr. Craine."

May's face softened. "Well, I guess it wouldn't hurt for you to have dinner. He said the diner, right? At least it's only a couple of blocks away."

Anna smiled. "Thank you for understanding."

"I was young once too, you know," May said, giving her a small smile. "But please be on your guard until you know this man better. There's just something about him that bothers me."

"I'll be careful," Anna promised as she rushed out of the kitchen and back into the living room. She checked her reflection in the mirror over the table where she'd set the groceries earlier. Snatching up her small pocketbook, she pulled out a tube of deep red lipstick and quickly smoothed it on, blotted it with a tissue, and dropped it back into her bag. Taking a deep breath, Anna walked calmly out the door.

"I'm ready," she told William, who'd been leaning against the hallway wall.

He stood up straight, smiled wide, and offered her the crook of his arm. "Then, let's be off."

* * *

Anna and William sat in a booth across from each other at the little diner. Once they'd been seated and handed menus, Anna suddenly felt shy. What on earth had possessed her to think she could go out casually with this man and have anything intelligent to say? Anna had been on a few dates through the years, but each one had ended terribly. Men either got handsy with her or never asked her out again. Anna had always been left feeling terrible about herself.

"Did your aunt give you a hard time about going out with a strange man?" William asked, glancing up from his menu with a twinkle in his eyes.

Anna's heart stopped. Had he heard their conversation? Should she come clean or lie? She chose to tell the truth. "She was a little worried, but I understand why. Sometimes she forgets that I'm not still the thirteen-year-old girl who came to live with her." She smiled and looked at him through her lashes with her head tilted down.

"So, she's a mother hen. That's not so bad. It's good to have someone looking out for you," he said, sounding as if he understood. He pulled out a pack of Camels and lit one. "Would you like one?" he offered.

"No, thank you," Anna said. She wasn't a smoker, and neither was Auntie May, but nearly everyone she knew smoked, so it didn't bother her.

The waitress came back and pulled a notepad out of her apron pocket. "So, what can I get you two?"

"I'll have half a turkey sandwich and a cup of tomato soup, please," Anna said. She knew that men didn't like women who overate, and she wanted to make a good impression on William.

"The hot roast beef sandwich, and plenty of coffee," William said. He winked at the waitress just as he'd winked at Anna earlier. The waitress was by no means young, but she smiled just the same and left.

Anna's good mood dampened. Did he flirt with everyone? But she sat quietly, waiting for him to speak first.

"Which law firm do you work at?" William asked, turning his warm gaze back on her.

"I work for Larson & Larson. They're brothers." She laughed softly. "It seems redundant to have both names on the business when they have the same name, but they're nice to work for."

William nodded and sipped his coffee. "Then you must have gone to the university."

"Business school, two years," she said.

He nodded his head. "I like a smart woman. Good for you. I studied at the university in Buffalo, New York. Mechanical Engineering."

Anna tried not to look as impressed as she felt. She'd been right—he worked with his mind, not his hands. Smiling, she asked, "What exactly does a mechanical engineer do?"

William sat up straighter and puffed out his chest. "Oh, you can do plenty with an engineering degree. But right now, I'm working at 3M, developing automotive products. It's fascinating. Before that, I worked at a company where they developed parts for aircraft. There are a multitude of jobs I can do with my degree."

"That's so exciting," Anna said, genuinely impressed. She wondered how old William was and if he'd served in the war. She couldn't really put an age on him. He'd taken off his hat, and his hair was combed back. His complexion was smooth, making her think he couldn't be much older than she was. But if he'd gone to school for four years at a university, he must be older. She didn't dare ask, though. It would be rude. She'd let him tell her the details in his own time.

Their food came, and they talked a little more about themselves. He asked if her parents had passed and if that was why she lived with her aunt. She told him a little about her story. He seemed sympathetic, and she liked that. A good-looking man with a soft heart. That was a great find.

She learned that he'd grown up with his mother and older sister in Portland, Oregon, and then lived in California. His parents divorced when he was two, and when he was fourteen, he'd moved to Buffalo, New York, to live with his father. It was his father who turned him on to engineering.

"So, your father is an engineer too?" she asked, interested in his family.

"More like a self-taught engineer," he said. "He's done a lot of things to earn a living. My father and stepmother moved back here a couple of years ago, so I did too. Now they're up in Canada, building a resort on a secluded lake. She's Canadian, so she was able to buy the land."

Anna found it interesting that he came from a broken family much as she had. She could be honest with him about her family and not feel ashamed. That connection made her more comfortable around him.

He paid for their dinner, and they walked together back to the apartment building. William lit up another cigarette as they walked. "You're not a smoker, I'm guessing."

She shook her head. "No. I lived with a doctor's family for a while when I was younger, and he was very opposed to it, so I've never even thought to smoke."

"Doctor, huh? Well, he was probably right. These things will kill you." He laughed at his own joke, and Anna laughed along.

They were almost to the building when he pointed out a car parked on the street. "Maybe you'd like to go for a ride someday after work?" he asked.

Anna looked at the maroon car with the tan soft top. A convertible. She was impressed. "Is that your car?" She knew very few people who actually owned cars. Everyone rode the bus or walked.

"Of course. I need wheels to get around, don't I?" He grinned.

"It's very nice. I'd love to go for a ride sometime."

He opened the door for her and let her climb the stairs ahead of him. Once they reached her door, her stomach suddenly twisted in knots. Would he try to kiss her? Would she let him?

"Thank you for supper," she said.

"Supper is after eight out east." He gave her a small smile and moved closer. "But I suppose that's what it was. You're very welcome."

The sound of voices could be heard from inside her apartment. Anna knew that her aunt and her theater friends would be up late. "I guess I should go inside."

He nodded. "Say, would you like to go out for a nice dinner tomorrow night. You could get all dolled up in a pretty dress, and I'll take you dining and dancing." He watched her expectantly.

Anna hesitated a moment just so she wouldn't seem too eager. "That sounds nice," she said as calmly as she could manage. Her heart was pounding, but she didn't want him to know it. "What time?"

He winked. "I'll pick you up at seven. I know a nice place a few blocks from here. We can take the car."

"Well, then. I'll see you tomorrow night," Anna said. "Goodnight."

"Goodnight, Anna," he said softly. He turned and sauntered down the hall. In that very moment, Anna was smitten.

CHAPTER THIRTEEN

Anna

Saturday morning, Anna went to Macy's and bought a beautiful dress, heels, and hat to wear out that evening with William. It was unlike her to spend her savings on frivolous things, but she couldn't help it. She wanted to look nice for him, and none of her sensible suits or dresses would have been right.

That night, she styled her hair carefully and put on a little extra make-up. Her new dress was made of turquoise-blue satin with cap sleeves, a fitted bodice, and a full skirt that fell below her knees. She wore a crinoline slip underneath to give the skirt extra fullness. She'd bought white peep-toe t-strap shoes because she knew they'd be the easiest to dance in. As she dressed, she hummed a cheery tune. She was happy. Happier than she'd been in a long time.

"My, my but don't you look lovely," Auntie May said, standing in the doorway of Anna's bedroom.

"Thank you, Auntie." Anna smiled wide. She studied her reflection in the mirror again, surprised at what she saw. Anna had come a long way from the little girl with the chubby build and Dutch-boy haircut. She'd grown up to become tall, slender, and actually pretty. When she looked in the mirror, she saw her mother's face looking back at her. A reminder, however, that beauty could be a gift and a curse, as it had cursed her mother.

Going to her closet to find her dressy coat, she glanced at her old doll, Lily, sitting against a pillow in a corner chair. Anna smiled. She still loved the old rag doll despite the fabric having turned darker and thinner with age. It reminded her of her dear brother, Andrew, who she hadn't heard from since that last letter saying he was going to leave the farm and go out west. She hoped he'd fared well and was working with horses as he'd always dreamed of. She also hoped he'd found love and had a happy family of his own.

There was a knock on the front door, and Anna draped her coat over her arm, picked up her clutch purse, and hurried out into the living room. Auntie May was just greeting William as he walked inside.

William's eyes, however, turned to Anna. "You look gorgeous." He smiled brightly, and his eyes sparkled.

Anna felt a blush creep up into her cheeks. William looked even more handsome than usual in a black suit and a crisp white dress shirt. His cuffs showed off gold cufflinks, and his tie clip sparkled in the light. Anna was sure there was a small diamond embedded in the clip.

"Thank you, William," she said, feeling shy again. "Have you met my aunt, May Bergman?"

"I was just saying hello to her before an angel walked into the room." He winked at Anna, and her heart sang.

Auntie May didn't look as impressed as Anna felt, though. "It's nice meeting you, Mr. Craine. I hope you and Anna have a lovely time out this evening."

"Please, call me William," he said to May. She nodded but remained quiet.

"Are you ready to go?" William asked Anna.

"Yes." She walked toward him, and he gestured for her walk through the door ahead of him. "Goodnight, Auntie May," Anna said as she left. She didn't bother to turn to see her aunt's expression because as they walked arm in arm toward the staircase, Anna only had eyes for William.

* * *

William drove to one of the most expensive restaurants in town. He'd made a reservation, and they had an excellent table with a good view of the band and dance floor.

"So, what do you think? Is this swanky, or what?" William asked her.

Anna gazed around, trying to take it all in. It was so grand and beautiful, like nothing she'd ever seen before. The place was lit by crystal chandeliers, and all the tables had snowy-white cloths with black linen napkins and vases of brightly colored flowers as centerpieces. The band was playing a soft tune as the patrons dined. It was the most impressive restaurant she'd ever been to.

"This place is beautiful," she said, smiling at William. He puffed up like a proud peacock then, but she didn't mind. She was sure he was proud he could take her to a place so grand.

William immediately ordered a bourbon and water, and after a moment's hesitation, Anna ordered white wine. She rarely drank, but tonight was a special occasion, and she wanted to enjoy it. As Anna looked over the menu, she was surprised there were no prices. This worried her. What if she ordered the most expensive item without knowing it? William had barely glanced at the menu and had sat back and lit a cigarette as if he weren't worried about the cost.

"Have you decided what you'd like to order?" a tall waiter dressed in black slacks, a vest, and a snowy white shirt asked.

William glanced at Anna to go first.

"Why don't you order for both of us?" she said demurely.

William sat up straighter and ordered the steak and shrimp dinner, salad, and a bottle of red wine. After the waiter left, he smiled over at Anna. "I'm celebrating tonight. I'm not only with the loveliest woman in the room, but I was also promoted yesterday at work."

"That's wonderful!" Anna said, truly happy for him. "Why didn't you tell me last night?"

"I had only just met you. I didn't want to sound like a braggart." He grinned. "I hope you don't think I am now."

"Of course not. You should be proud. I'm happy I could share this celebration with you," she said.

The band began playing, "Let Me Call You Sweetheart," and a few couples made their way to the dance floor. William stood and extended his hand to Anna. "Shall we dance?"

Smiling, she took his hand and followed him to the polished floor. As they glided across the floor, Anna was thrilled that he was an accomplished dancer. He held her at a respectful distance, but the feel of his hand on her back and his other hand holding hers made Anna tingle with delight. She adored being romanced this way, just like in the movies. Tonight, for the first time in her life, Anna felt like a princess.

They ate, drank, talked, and danced throughout the evening. It was magical. William drank the lion's share of the wine and then ordered another bourbon, but Anna didn't mind. He didn't appear drunk or sloppy in any way. And as they danced, his steps were light and perfectly in time with the music.

Anna excused herself to powder her nose and came back to the table to find William speaking with a distinguished-looking older couple.

"Ah, here she is," William said, holding out his hand to her and slipping it around her waist as she drew near. "This is Anna Bergman. Anna, I'd like you to meet Roger and Miriam Shipman. Roger is my supervisor at work."

Anna smiled and shook their hands. "It's nice to meet you both," she said. The couple looked to be in their late forties. Roger was balding and paunchy, but Mrs. Shipman was slender, and her hair was perfectly styled. She wore a large diamond wedding ring along with a cocktail ring and a diamond necklace and earring set. They looked prosperous, and Anna had the feeling that these were people William would want to impress.

"Would you care to join us?" Anna asked after a moment of silence.

"Oh, no. We don't want to intrude on your nice evening," Roger said. "I just wanted to meet William's lady-friend. Perhaps another time we can all go out together."

Anna watched William nod slightly out of the corner of her eye. She hadn't known William long, but she could tell he was trying to play it cool despite this being a good opportunity for him. Anna knew that dining with the boss was a step up the ladder.

"That would be lovely," she said, smiling brightly.

"You're a lucky man, William," Roger said. "I hope you know this woman is a keeper." He winked, then the couple turned and left.

Anna's cheeks flushed. This was really their first serious date. She hoped William wasn't put off by Roger's comment. They sat, and William smiled over at her, his eyes sparkling.

"He's right, you know. You're a keeper. The real deal."

Her heart flipped. How lucky she'd be to have a man like William in her life.

* * *

After their first date, Anna and William were inseparable. During the workweek, they ate dinner together nearly every night at the diner. On weekends, they attended parties at houses of William's friends, went out to nightclubs and high-class dining establishments, and danced many a night away. For the first time in Anna's life, she was having a ball. She was the star of her own Hollywood movie, wearing fancy dresses— which she had bought several of over the weeks—and meeting new friends. After having lived a quiet life with her aunt, and growing up in such extreme poverty, she felt as if she'd finally achieved a higher status in life. She had new friends, and most of all, she had William.

William loved showing her off to his friends, and she enjoyed being on his arm. It was incredible to her that William thought so highly of her. No one, other than her beloved father, had ever thought she was worthy of their complete attention and time. But William was different. He called her *sweetheart* and *doll* and all sorts of little endearments, even *darling*. Her father had called her *älskling*, meaning darling in Swedish. When William called her darling, her heart fluttered, and her eyes teared up. It was the ultimate endearment to her.

Anna was having such a good time with William that summer that she ignored the few times he drank too much or sometimes flashed anger at someone they were partying with. He worked hard at his job and had a lot of responsibility, so she understood his need to let loose occasionally. His anger was never directed toward her, and that was what mattered. He was always the consummate gentleman toward her. Of course, they'd kissed, quite passionately at times, but he'd never asked her to go over the line of decency. His consideration of her made her adore him even more.

On the Fourth of July, William had been invited to a party at Roger and Miriam Shipman's lake home, and he brought Anna along. It started in the late afternoon and was expected to last well into the evening to watch the fireworks over the lake. William puffed up with pride when he told Anna about the invitation. "Only the bigwigs at work are invited," he said. "So, we need to make a good impression."

Anna understood, and the day of the party she dressed in a new blue and white striped seersucker sundress with a fitted bodice and full skirt, a short, white cardigan sweater, and slip-on sandals. She'd pulled up her long, heavy hair into a loose bun, and wore the cross pendant her father had given her and simple gold earrings. She wanted William to be proud to have her on his arm that day.

"Well, look at you," William said, giving a low whistle when Anna answered the door. "You look like a sunny day, doll."

Anna blushed. "Thank you. I knew how important today was for you."

William circled around her, his hands in the pockets of his cotton trousers. When he finally faced her again, he smiled mischievously. "There's only one thing missing."

Her brows rose as she looked down at her dress, wondering what was wrong. William touched her chin with the side of his finger to lift her eyes to his. Pulling something from his blazer pocket, he handed it to her.

"What's this?" Anna asked, her eyes growing wide as she stared at the velvet jewelry box.

"Open it and see."

Anna gently lifted the lid and gasped when she saw what was inside. A delicate gold chain necklace held a pendant with a round cluster of blue gemstones and white seed pearls. A pair of matching clip-on earrings sat on the satin, too.

"They're beautiful!" Anna exclaimed. "Oh, William, you shouldn't have. But I'm so happy you did."

William smiled brightly. "I saw it and knew it was the perfect jewelry for you to wear with your sundress. Here, let me put the necklace on for you." He took the delicate chain from the box, and Anna turned so he could clip it around her neck. He kissed the nape of her neck, sending delightful chills down her spine.

"You should take off the cross necklace, so it doesn't tangle with the new one," he suggested.

"Oh, yes," Anna said. She went to the mirror by the door and took off her beloved cross necklace and her earrings. Then she clipped on the new earrings. They sparkled in the light and looked stunning. "Oh, thank you so much," she said, turning to William. "I just love them."

William winked. "Anything for you, doll."

Auntie May had been watching from her bedroom doorway and now entered the living room. "What a lovely gift, William," she said. "How thoughtful of you."

"Anna deserves beautiful things," he said.

Anna set her cross and earrings in the empty jewelry box and closed it carefully. "Are you ready to go?" she asked William.

"Ready as I'll ever be," he said.

"You two have a good time," May said as the couple headed out the door.

Anna glanced back at her aunt, but she didn't see a smile on her face. She saw concern. "I'll see you tonight, Auntie May," she said, and hurried out the door with William. She wasn't going to let her aunt's obvious dislike of William ruin her perfect summer day.

The party was a forty-minute drive away at White Bear Lake, where the Shipman's summer house was. They arrived at two, just as several other couples also did and were greeted by Roger and Miriam.

"Make yourself at home," Miriam said warmly. She was wearing a sundress with a bright floral print. "We have a bar set up or beer or soda if you prefer."

Anna thanked her as she and William strolled around, talking to the other guests. She tried hard not to gawk at their magnificent home and the lovely landscaping around the lakeshore. This wasn't a weekend cabin—it was a large, two-story house with big windows overlooking the lake, a beautiful brick patio, and an enormous green lawn that spread out to the lake.

"Amazing, isn't it?" William whispered to her. "Quite a spread." He already had a bourbon and water in hand. Anna had opted for a bottle of Coca-Cola instead.

"Yes. It's beautiful. This is their second house?" she asked.

"Yep. Roger makes a lot of money." He grinned at her. "This could be us in a few years if we play our cards right."

Anna was stunned by that bombshell. Was William

implying they'd marry someday? That they could build a life together like the Shipmans had? That would be too good to be true.

Hot and cold hor d'oeuvres were served throughout the afternoon and then they all sat down to a delicious dinner of grilled steak, baked potatoes, potato salad, other mixed salads, and plenty of raw vegetables and fruits. There were six couples in all, everyone under the age of thirty except for the Shipmans. Since the feast was being catered, servers hovered over them to pour wine and offer other beverages. William continued refilling his bourbon throughout the day until Anna grew nervous. The way he was drinking, she doubted he'd be able to drive home. But she didn't dare say anything. It wasn't her place.

After their meal, music played from the latest vinyl records on a phonograph, and couples mingled, some dancing to the mellow songs. Anna stood on the fringes, not sure what she could add to the conversations around her. All the other women were wives, and some had young children, except for Mrs. Shipman, whose children were grown. Anna was the only woman who worked for a living, and she felt as if she didn't belong with this group.

"Why aren't you talking with the other women?" William came up beside her.

She could smell the bourbon on his breath, but he looked relaxed and happy. "They're all married, some with children. I feel out of place, I guess. But I've tried to be involved whenever I can."

"Should we go for a walk?" he asked, gazing out at the lake. Anna smiled. "Yes. I'd like that."

They strolled down the path to where the water spread out, and a long, wooden dock reached out over the water. A fancy speedboat and a smaller fishing boat were tied to the dock, while a canoe sat upside-down on shore. There was a bench at the end of the dock, and they both sat down to enjoy the view.

"Isn't it amazing what a lot of money can buy?" William asked. "I'm just as smart, if not smarter, than any of these guys here today. I could have all this someday."

Anna thought that was a wonderful dream. She'd never set such lofty goals for herself. But through William's eyes, she could see herself living in a place like this, giving parties and raising children. She sighed.

"What are you thinking there, baby doll?" he asked.

"A place like this would be a dream for me. The farm I grew up on had a lake, but nothing like this one. And when I was in Walker while my father was at the sanatorium, I used to take the other girls swimming in Leech Lake. I loved it. I couldn't even imagine owning something this incredible."

William turned to her, his expression serious. "You didn't have much of a childhood, did you? I'm sorry. Mine wasn't the best either. I started working at twelve to help support my mother and sister, and then I was sent to live with my father, who isn't the greatest guy on the planet. But I've worked my way up, and I plan on going a whole lot higher."

She smiled at him. "I believe you will."

His eyes met hers. "No one has ever believed in me before." He slipped his arm around her shoulders and kissed her, right there for everyone to see. Anna didn't mind. For her, it felt like they were the only two people there.

The music, drinking, and dancing continued throughout the evening as everyone waited for the fireworks over the lake. Anna danced with Roger, with William's blessing, and she could tell the older man was quite inebriated. He slurred when he spoke and held her a bit too tight.

"You sure are a beautiful woman," Roger said. "How on earth did William get a girl like you?"

"He's a smart man," she said with a smile.

Roger snorted. "Beauty and a sense of humor. You're a doll."

Another man named Carlton cut in, and Roger staggered away. He smiled crookedly at Anna. His pupils were large, indicating he'd had too much to drink. "I had to save you from the old man," Carlton said. "He can be quite handsy, or so my wife says." Anna tried to stay as far apart from Carlton as possible as he swung her around in some crazy rendition of the Jitterbug. His hands were everywhere, too.

Finally, William saved her, but his jaw was set tight. "Don't dance with Carlton," he told her through gritted teeth. "I don't want him touching you."

"What could I do? He cut in," Anna said, surprised at his sudden anger.

William stopped dancing and pulled her to a chair at the edge of the patio. "Sit here and say no the rest of the night." He stalked off toward the bar.

Anna was stunned at the intensity of the venom in his voice. What had she done wrong? She sat there, unable to move because her body was shaking. Carlton's wife, Bonnie, brought over Anna's sweater that had been left on another chair.

"You looked chilled," Bonnie said.

"Thank you," Anna said appreciatively. She slipped it on. The sun had gone down, and it was damp near the water. But the chill she'd felt from William's rage ran deeper than the breeze.

"The men get a little silly at these parties," Bonnie said. She was a tiny woman with auburn hair cut and curled in a modern style. "I just ignore them."

Anna nodded. "Good advice."

The caterers began offering coffee and hot chocolate about a half-hour before the fireworks. Anna gratefully accepted a mug of hot chocolate and sat with Bonnie as she waited for William. They'd shut down the bar, for which Anna was grateful. She hoped William would have some coffee before their long drive back to the city.

Just before fireworks, William reappeared with a mug of coffee in one hand and a cigarette in the other. He smiled at Bonnie before addressing Anna. "Shall we go sit at the edge of the lawn and watch the fireworks?" he asked.

Anna was surprised at how cordial he sounded after how furious he'd been. "Yes. I'd like that." Bonnie had already left to go stand with Carlton. Anna and William walked to the lawn where chairs had been put out.

"I'm glad you met Bonnie," he whispered into Anna's ear. "It wouldn't hurt for you to get to know some of the wives."

Again, Anna was taken aback. What did he mean by that? Would they be socializing often with this same group of people from his work?

William dropped his cigarette butt on the grass and snuffed it out with the toe of his shoe. Then he sat beside Anna, his arm draped casually over the back of her chair. She decided to forget about earlier and moved in closer to him as the sky lit up with brilliant colors. He'd had too much to drink earlier, that was all. There was no reason to read anything else into it.

At least that was what she told herself.

CHAPTER FOURTEEN

Diane

After her last visit with Anna, all Diane thought about was how Anna hadn't seen the warning signs about William's drinking and anger issues. But then, hindsight was twenty-twenty. Diane hadn't seen the mean streak in her own husband either. Actually, she'd known he'd had it but hadn't realized how deep it ran. So, who was she to judge Anna's lapse in judgment?

That week was another short one at school because of teacher meetings, and since Diane wasn't attending the conference in St. Paul, she and Barry had the days off.

"Do you want to go on a little trip up north?" she asked Barry Tuesday evening as they ate dinner.

He grinned. "What did you have in mind?"

"I was thinking of trying to find the farm Anna grew up on and then going to Walker to see what's left of Aw-Gwah-Ching if there is anything left. I wanted to visit the cemetery where her father is buried, too."

"Your great-grandfather," Barry said softly. "I think that's a good idea. Do you know where the farm is?"

"Anna showed me on a map as best as she could remember. Who knows? Maybe I'll see a relative or two."

Barry laughed as he set his fork down on his plate. He'd surprised Diane by making lasagna that night. "Just what you need. More relatives you didn't know you had."

She swatted him playfully on the arm and laughed along. It was strange thinking she probably had a bunch of second and third cousins all over the state. Anna's mother had several sisters and two brothers. That would mean a lot of children, grandchildren, and great-grandchildren. She'd never had a big family around her. She couldn't even wrap her head around it.

Diane made arrangements for her mother's longtime friend, Gladys, to take Joan out to lunch and shopping on Friday. Gladys was a sweet lady who was still sharp as a tack and volunteered at non-profits all over town. Diane knew that she'd be more than willing to spend time with Joan.

"Don't you worry about her one bit," Gladys told her on the phone. "I'll call Joan and tell her we need to catch up. That way she'll think it was my idea."

"Thanks, Gladys. You're a lifesaver," Diane said.

"You just go on your little trip with that handsome guy of yours and have a great time," Gladys told her. "And try to talk him into making an honest woman out of you. It's about time." She laughed.

Diane grimaced but chuckled along. "He's not the problem. I am. Maybe someday."

"You aren't getting any younger, dear," Gladys said.

Diane would have been insulted if it hadn't been Gladys who'd said that. But since she adored the older woman, she took it all in stride.

The next day, she and Barry took off in his Subaru Forester, heading north. The day was cold, and the clouds looked threatening. Diane hoped it wouldn't snow this weekend. She really wanted to see her great-grandfather's grave and the other spots Anna had been to without dealing with snow.

They took Interstate 94 out of St. Cloud, and soon the road grew quieter with fewer cars. They were in the country now, passing only smaller towns. It was a three-hour drive to the small town near Anna's grandparents' farm—named Dent—and the closer they got to it, the more rural the landscape and roads became.

"We should go to the north shore sometime, for a week or weekend," Barry said as he drove the car. Soft rock music played from the 70s channel on Sirius XM Radio, and he'd been humming along with it before speaking.

"That would be fun," Diane said. She turned and studied Barry. His wavy hair was freshly cut, and he was clean-shaven—he hated the scruffy look—which suited him perfectly. He had a kind-looking face, and he rarely ever became angry. He was always open to doing something crazy on the spur of the moment—case in point, this trip—because he was a go-with-the-flow kind of guy. He was the very opposite of Diane, but she liked it.

Try to talk him into making an honest woman out of you, Gladys had said. The thought of it made Diane smile. He'd already proposed twice. If it were up to Barry, they'd be married. But Diane had told Gladys the truth—she was the problem, not Barry. There wasn't a reason on earth not to marry him except for her own private fears. The fear that he'd change after they were married. And the fear that she'd be trapped again. She couldn't let those fears go no matter how nice he was.

"Okay, navigator. We're entering Fergus Falls. Which road is next?" Barry asked, breaking into her thoughts.

They took a cutoff, then headed northeast. Diane directed him up one country road and down another. They were suddenly in an area with many small lakes as the road passed one body of water after another. Farmland spread out everywhere between the lakes, and small towns cropped up here and there. Their destination wasn't the town of Dent, but the farmland that was several miles west of it.

The sun was peeking out between the clouds as Diane told Barry to turn down another road.

"Wow. This place is in the middle of nowhere," he said with amusement. "Can you imagine how isolated it had felt in the early 1900s?"

"I can imagine. I'm sure it was Anna's entire life, except for a small schoolhouse and church. She said she used to swim in the lake on the property. It's one of her favorite memories besides spending time with her brother."

"The brother she never saw again?" Barry asked.

Diane nodded. "Yeah. That's weird, huh? Losing touch with a close family member forever." She glanced back down at the map on her phone and tucked her blond hair behind her ear. "But then, the day she left the farm, she lost touch with all of them. No one in her family wanted her. Not her aunts, uncles, or grandparents. Think of how devastating that must have felt to an eleven-year-old girl."

"Those were hard times," Barry said. "I guess people did what they had to do to survive."

"Giving away family members is a bit extreme to me," she said. "But I guess it was for the best for her because she ended up with a good education and a nice life with her Aunt May."

Diane studied the map, and then the road. "Turn left here," she said.

He did, and they were suddenly on a small road that bordered a lake. Several houses sat in a row along the lakeshore. Because winter was coming, Diane supposed they'd pulled in their docks and boats. To the left sat a farmhouse and barns, with land that had been harvested.

"Stop here," she said, suddenly realizing this might be it.

Barry slowed. "Where to?" He looked puzzled.

"Turn into that driveway," she said, pointing. "I think that's the farm."

He pulled the car into a long driveway flanked by a grove of pine trees that opened to a house, barn, and several silos. He stopped and put the car in park. "Now what?"

Diane wasn't sure. "I don't know. If these people aren't descendants of the Roths, then I guess they'll just kick us off." She opened her door and pulled on the jacket she'd discarded on the back seat during the drive. It was cold out, and the dampness from the area lakes was brisk. Barry stepped out too, and they stood together, looking around.

"All the buildings look new," Barry said. "Even the house."

She'd noticed that too, and her heart sank. Diane had hoped to see her grandmother's childhood home. But then, after all these years, that might have been expecting too much. "Look there," she said, pointing to a square spot where no grass grew a short distance from the new house. "I bet that's where the old house used to sit, and they filled the cellar in."

"Could be," Barry agreed.

The squeaking sound of a screen door made them both look up. A woman wearing boots over her jeans and a coat wrapped around her was walking toward them. She stopped a short distance away.

"Can I help you with something?" she asked, looking a bit annoyed.

Diane put a smile on her face and drew closer to her. The woman was about her height and had short blond hair. Diane estimated she was probably close to her own age. "I'm sorry to bother you," Diane said. "I think this used to be my great-great-grandfather's farm. My grandmother showed it to me on a map, and I just wanted to see how it looked."

The woman frowned. "Your grandmother is still alive?"

Diane was a bit taken aback. Did she look *that* old that it was a surprise her grandmother was alive? "Uh, yeah. But she's quite old. Ninety-five."

"I don't know much about the history of this land," the woman said. "We bought this place twenty years ago and built a new house. There was an old farmhouse over there," she pointed to the square where the grass didn't grow, "but it had fallen in, and we filled it in with gravel. There was no barn."

By now, Diane had moved close enough to the woman so she didn't have to yell. "So, your family isn't from around here?"

"No. We're actually from the cities. Minneapolis. But my husband wanted a place on a lake and some land, and this is where we ended up. We own that lakeshore across the road and fifty acres here. It's more of a hobby farm for him. He works from home for a tech business."

Diane nodded. She wasn't going to get any information from this woman. "Well, thank you. We'll be going." She turned, but the woman called her back.

"What was your great-great-grandfather's last name?" she asked.

Diane turned. "Roth. Victor Roth. His wife's name was Sophia."

The woman nodded. "Sure, I know that name. There are a lot of Roths in this area. That lake over there," she pointed to the east. "It's Roth Lake. I suppose they owned all this land at one time."

Diane's heart leapt. She looked at Barry beside her, and he stared at her, his eyes wide. "Really? That's amazing," she said.

"Yeah. I'd say if your grandmother was a Roth, you have a whole slew of relatives around here. Many of them own lake homes and other property. The farm at the end of the road is Roth property. It boarders Roth Lake."

"That's incredible," Diane said. "Thank you so much for the information."

"Sure. No problem."

Diane walked up to the woman. "I'm Diane Martin." She offered her hand. "And this is Barry Neuman. We live down in Minnetonka."

The woman shook their hands. "Ah. City folks. I miss the cities, but I do like it here, too. I'm Cathy Aimes. It's nice to meet you."

They talked a little more about the area, and after a few minutes, they thanked Cathy again and drove off. Diane had Barry pull over a few times so she could take pictures of Roth Lake, and then the other lakes as well. She'd also taken a picture of Cathy's farm earlier, with her permission. It didn't look the same, but she thought Anna might like to see it.

"Do you want to go into town and find relatives?" Barry asked.

Diane thought about that a moment. It would be interesting to meet a few, but on the other hand, Anna's relatives had tossed her aside decades ago. "No. I think we'll leave well-enough alone. Let's head to Walker."

Barry turned in the direction that Diane instructed him. "I'm sure if you ever wanted to meet any of them, you could find them on Ancestry."

She smiled over at him. "Yeah. *If* I ever want to. Maybe someday, but not yet. I'm just happy that I'm getting to know Anna and learning about her side of the family. That means more to me than meeting a bunch of relatives."

The drive took them through more back roads to the small town of Walker. Diane had made a reservation at a hotel just out of town because it was in the same direction as Aw-Gwah-Ching had been. The closer they got, the edgier she felt. In the past few weeks, she'd learned more about her family than she had in her entire life. So many secrets coming to life; secrets she hadn't even suspected existed. When she allowed herself to dwell on it, as she was right now, she felt as if her entire life had been a lie. Her mother, her aunt Bernice, and her uncle Jim had all lied to her. Her grandmother hadn't been dead. And their lies had kept her from knowing a whole side of her history. Her ancestry. Herself.

If she'd known her grandmother had killed her grandfather, would she have grown up a different person?

"We're coming to Walker. Don't blink," Barry said, laughing.

Diane refocused her attention on the small town they were driving through. It wasn't large, but there was more than she'd expected. The downtown was three blocks of businesses that catered mostly to tourists. It was cute. Charming. But a second later, Leech Lake appeared on the left in the most spectacular view, and Diane suddenly understood the attraction.

"It's beautiful," she said. "I didn't expect the lake to be so large."

Barry nodded, and, in that instant, the road turned away from the lake. Soon, they saw their hotel on the left and pulled in.

"Nice hotel for such a small town," Diane said as they grabbed their bags.

"This town is busy in the summer. Lots of summer residents and they have a rock and a country music festival around here every year. I suppose the hotel rooms come in handy," Barry said.

She looked at him, amazed. "How do you know all this?"

He shrugged. "You know me. Always doing my homework."

They checked into the hotel, then headed out again. Looking at the map, Diane found a road just a short distance out of town marked as Aw-Gwah-Ching Road. "Well, this is our best bet," she said. "It's not like they're hiding it."

They drove the short distance and pulled onto the road on the right. It curved up a tree-lined hill and out of sight. A few feet up the road, it curved off to the right. Straight ahead, however, there was a barrier blocking the road that stated, "Private Property."

Diane sighed. "Now what?"

Barry turned to her with a mischievous glint in his eyes. "Don't tell me you're going to give up that quickly. We've come too far to turn around now." He opened his door and stepped out, and Diane followed suit. "Let's just walk up the road a bit. It can't hurt."

"We could be fined for trespassing," she said.

"So, we get a fine. Come on. Let's go."

Steeling herself with a deep breath, Diane walked beside Barry as they bypassed the barrier and headed up the dirt road. "Since when are you such a rebel?" she elbowed him.

"Hey, I didn't drive all this way to see nothing." He grinned. At that moment, Diane couldn't remember when she'd loved him more.

It didn't take them long before the trees parted, and there was nothing but a large, empty field. Diane stopped and looked all around her. "It's gone. Everything. There aren't even marks on the ground where the buildings had been."

Barry nodded, looking disappointed. "I was afraid of that. I had told you before that they tore the buildings down, but you'd think there'd be something left."

Diane walked a little farther out into the open space. She felt cheated. This place once held several large buildings, a farm, outbuildings, and so much more. It had been an important part of the history of this region. All of it now gone. She thought about the many patients who'd lived here for years and who'd died here. She thought about her great-grandfather, Jon, living here nearly two years, his hopes high that he'd recover, only to fade away. And Anna. She'd walked on this ground, around these trees, maybe even played tag with Dr. Hanson's daughters, her charges, right where Diane stood. So many lives. So many ghosts. Tears filled her eyes, thinking about all of them.

Barry came over and placed his arm around her waist. "I'm sorry nothing is here, sweetie. I know how disappointing it is." He kissed her temple in his warm, tender way.

"It's sad," she said. "I feel like there should be something. A marker, a plaque. It's like it never existed."

"I know. But it did, and you have your grandmother's stories to prove it. Those are worth so much more in the end."

Diane turned to Barry, tears running down her cheeks. "You always know exactly what to say."

He smiled. "I try."

They stood there a while longer in the fading light, his arm around her and her head on his shoulder. Decades come and go, people live and die, buildings rise and fall, but stories, thank goodness, live on forever.

CHAPTER FIFTEEN

Diane

The next day, Diane and Barry checked out of their hotel and drove back through the little town of Walker toward the cemetery. Wearing winter coats to ward off the chilly air, they walked around the cemetery, searching for the spot where patients from the sanatorium were buried. Unlike many from that time, Diane knew that her great-grandfather had a headstone because of the generosity of Dr. Hanson.

The graveyard was quite large for a small town and was shaded by many old oak and pine trees. As they studied names and dates on the gravestones, Diane was shocked to see so many young people who'd died in the early to mid-1900s. She'd known that tuberculosis was prevalent during that time, and the flu could run through a town and kill whole families. But the stark reality of seeing it on the headstones was heartbreaking.

As she searched, she didn't find any type of marker stating that people from the sanatorium were buried there. This surprised her. Maybe the city had been afraid to announce where the contagious patients had been buried. Or perhaps they just didn't think it was important. Either way, she once again felt cheated that those who'd died at Aw-Gwah-Ching were left forgotten.

Finally, Diane found an old marker she could barely read. Growing excited, she realized that she'd found her great-grandfather.

"Over here," she called to Barry, who'd been searching a few feet away.

He picked his way around the graves, careful not to step on any. "The writing is really faint," he said, staring at the stone she pointed to.

"It's been over eighty years," she said. "I suppose the harsh winters have taken their toll. But from what I can read, it says Jon Peter Bergman, Born: 1897, Sweden. Died: March 28th, 1938."

"I can see it now. What's that below his name?" Barry asked.

Diane stared hard at it, and when she finally made it out, her heart clenched. It was all she could do to choke out the words. "Beloved Father."

Barry reached for her hand and squeezed it. They stood there a while in the silence of the cemetery. Leaves had already fallen from the trees and every now and then, scattered in the breeze.

A chill ran through Diane. Not a scary chill, but one that made her feel as if she'd been meant to stand here all along. Jon had waited a long time for her to find him. "I wish I'd brought flowers for his grave," she said aloud. "But I feel as if he knows we're here."

"He knows," Barry said softly. "You can feel it in the air."

She lifted her phone to take a few pictures of his gravestone. As she did, a sparrow landed on it and stared directly at her.

"See. Jon's letting you know he's here," Barry said.

Diane held back tears as she took a few more pictures, trying to capture the inscription. Finally, she stepped up closer to the headstone as the bird flew off. "Your Anna is fine. I've been visiting her. She's told me a lot about you. I just wanted you to know she's okay." The wind kicked up stronger, and the leaves rustled, then everything went still. Diane took a step back, next to Barry. She knew Jon had heard her.

* * *

On Sunday afternoon, Diane went to visit Anna. She had so much to tell her and several pictures to show her as well. When she arrived, however, Pauline approached her and told her that Anna was in the sunroom with visitors.

"Visitors? Really?" Diane couldn't think of anyone who'd come to see Anna except maybe her mother, but that was highly doubtful.

Pauline smiled. "Come on. I'll walk with you. You won't believe this story—it's incredible."

As Diane entered the sunroom, she was surprised to see two older women sitting with Anna. The smaller of the two was in a chair beside Anna's wheelchair, holding her hand. Anna's face simply glowed with happiness.

"Oh, Diane. I'm so glad you're here," Anna said when she saw her granddaughter standing in the doorway. "Come join us. I want you to meet someone very special to me."

Diane approached and smiled at the two women.

"This is my granddaughter, Diane," Anna said to the

woman still holding her hand. "I'm so very lucky she found me. Diane, this is Tonya and her sister, Angela."

Diane held out her hand to Tonya. "It's nice to meet you," she said. The woman looked up at her with a wide smile, and that was when Diane realized that Tonya had the features of one with Down Syndrome. Her face was wide and flat, her eyes almond-shaped. She had a sweet smile that melted Diane's heart. Despite Tonya's short gray hair, she radiated the energy of someone much younger. Tonya raised a small hand to shake Diane's.

"I'm happy to meet you," she said. Her words ran together quickly, but Diane understood her perfectly.

"Hi, I'm Angela," the woman next to Tonya said, rising. The two shook hands. "I'm Tonya's younger sister."

"It's so nice meeting you both," Diane said. She sat down next to Angela. "I'm curious. How do you two know Anna?"

Anna smiled. "I've known Tonya since she was four years old."

"She taught me everything!" Tonya said proudly.

Anna laughed. "Well, not everything. But enough to get you started." She looked over at Diane. "Back in the 1950s through the 60s, the Shakopee reformatory had designated a building for disabled children who were wards of the state. It was called Shaw Cottage. State workers supervised the children, but inmates could apply to work with the children too. I was allowed that honor from 1958 until Tonya left around the mid-1960s. I worked with one little girl named Glory for the first two years, and then they let me work with Tonya for five years." Her eyes sparkled. "Honestly, it was the best time of my life in prison. Working with children was so rewarding."

Diane was beyond surprised. She hadn't realized there'd

been a program like that at the prison. "That's amazing," she said. "What did you do with the children?"

"She taught me how to dress myself, tie my shoes, learn the alphabet, count numbers, and so much more," Tonya said.

Anna smiled over at Tonya. "Unfortunately, the state had designated the children who came to us as unable to learn even the simplest skills. But those of us who worked with the children showed the state that they were wrong. We were able to teach them all the same skills as any other child. They just needed more love and attention, that's all."

Diane's heart warmed at Anna's words. She knew that Anna had felt like a throw-away child once, and the thought that she'd helped other children when society had given up on them was wonderful. "That had to have felt like a great accomplishment for you," Diane said to Anna.

"Since I couldn't be with my own children, it was a joy. And look at Tonya now. A grown woman. She was just telling me that she worked at different places over the years, and now she's retired."

Tonya nodded. "A nice family took me in after I left Shaw Cottage and adopted me. They believed in kids like me. They fought to let me go to school, and I graduated from high school. I couldn't have done that without Anna."

"Things were a lot different back then," Angela said. "Children like Tonya didn't go to regular school with other children. But her adoptive parents were advocates for children's rights, and she was able to go. They were incredible people."

Diane nodded. She remembered when she was in grade school, children with Down Syndrome or who had disabilities didn't attend regular classes with the other children. They had their own room or didn't attend at all. Thank goodness so much had changed over the years.

"Were you adopted as well?" Diane asked Angela, thinking that she must have grown up in the same family as Tonya.

Angela shook her head. "No. I'm Tonya's biological sister. My parents were the ones who gave her up to the state."

Her words jolted Diane. "Oh, goodness. Did they visit her? Is that how you stayed in touch with Tonya?"

"No. Tonya and I reconnected a few years ago, in 2007. I never knew Tonya existed until then."

"Angela found me," Tonya said, smiling wide at her sister. "I love having a real sister."

"That's so sweet," Diane said.

"I'm happy I found Tonya too," Angela said. "After my mother died, I went through all her papers and had found a copy of Tonya's birth certificate and papers from the institution they left her at. Believe me, I was shocked. My parents were both good, Christian people. I couldn't believe they'd given up their child and walked away."

"It happened all the time in those days," Anna said. "I wouldn't be too hard on your parents. I'm sure some doctor told them it was for the best."

Angela nodded. "It took me a year of searching, but I finally found that Tonya had been adopted. Since her adoptive parents had passed, there wasn't a barrier for me to find her. Now Tonya lives with my husband and me, and I'm so happy to have her in our family."

"That's such a great story," Diane said. "It's wonderful that you two found each other."

"And I'm happy I found Anna, too," Tonya said. "When I read in the paper that she was out of jail, I told Angela all about her."

Angela laughed. "Yes. She was quite insistent upon seeing Anna. I had to put on my investigator's hat again and find her. I'm glad we were able to."

"I'm so happy you did find me," Anna said. "It warms my heart knowing that all turned out well with Tonya. She was like a daughter to me."

Angela turned to Diane. "Anna tells us that you found her too. She said you had no idea she was even alive until she was let out of prison. That must have been quite a shock."

"Oh, yes. It was. I'm learning so many things about my family that I never knew. It's incredible. So much was kept secret in our family for years."

"Ours too," Angela said, shaking her head. "It's all so crazy. People hid everything."

As the four visited, Diane's heart warmed at the relationship between Tonya and Anna. How wonderful it must have been for Anna to have a chance to make a difference in the young girl's life. Anna may have been in prison, but she was able to change Tonya's life for the better. It was gratifying knowing that.

Later, after Tonya and Angela left, Anna and Diane sat in her room. Diane thought the older woman looked tired— happy but worn out—and asked her if she'd rather eat her lunch in her room instead of the dining room.

"I think in here," Anna said. "I am tired. But it was so wonderful, visiting with Tonya and her sister. It does my heart good to know that she has done so well."

"It is wonderful. I had no idea there was a program like that at Shakopee."

"Yes. And I was lucky to be able to participate. I never heard what happened to the little girl, Glory, who I cared for the first two years. Her disabilities were quite severe, but she was a doll. They moved her on to another location, and I never heard about her again. But I was happy I was able to work with Tonya for five years. She was such a sweet, loving child."

Diane had wondered how Anna filled her days during her incarceration. Now, she had an opening to ask. "What other jobs did you do at the reformatory, if you don't mind me asking."

"Oh, many jobs, dear. The first year I was there, they put me on farm duty. The prison raised its own animals for meat and dairy products, and also grew fruits and vegetables. I didn't mind working outside, though. It wasn't much different from when I was a child. Then I worked in the sewing room for a couple of years. Our prison provided clothes for all the inmates around Minnesota. I didn't mind that either, except sometimes it was tiresome to be indoors all the time. Except in the winter, though. It was a good job for me, and I became friends with the other women that way."

"Then you worked with the children after that?" Diane asked.

She nodded. "I did that from around '58 to '65. Then I was recruited to work in the office. The superintendent had learned I'd gone to business college, so they asked if I'd do typing and filing and other work for them. I was happy to. I did that for years."

Pauline dropped by with Anna's lunch, and Diane stayed and visited with her a while longer. She showed Anna the photos she'd taken of her grandparents' farm, of how the Aw-Gwah-Ching property looked now, and of her father's grave. Anna stared at her father's headstone for a long time.

"It's difficult to read now," she said. "But it's nice, isn't it?"

"It is nice," Diane said. She made a mental note to check to see if the headstone could be carved again so the name and dates were visible.

"I'm glad you went to see it," Anna said. "It's nice to be remembered."

"I'm glad I went too. It made me feel closer to everyone you'd known, even though everything has changed so much."

After she'd eaten her lunch, Diane could tell Anna was tired. "I'll leave so you can rest," Diane said. "Maybe we can talk more about the past another day."

"I am tired, dear. Unfortunately, that's part of being so old." Anna smiled. "Thank you for sharing the pictures. I think of my father often. He was such a wonderful man."

"I was glad I could go visit the sites." She said goodbye and left then, driving her car through the busy streets home. Diane had learned so much about Anna's life in prison today. She hadn't expected any of it. Diane's vision of what time in prison looked like was so different from what Anna described. But it was another piece in the puzzle of Anna's life, and Diane couldn't wait to share her new information with her daughter.

CHAPTER SIXTEEN

Anna

Anna spent the summer of 1949 having a ball with William. Parties, dining out, and dancing ruled their time together. Most of William's friends loved to party, and their wives and girlfriends did too, but Anna didn't mind. For a young woman who'd lived a quiet life up until then, Anna was enjoying the carefree life William offered.

She also liked that he wasn't the type of man who pushed her for intimacies. They'd kissed, sometimes passionately, many times after an especially enjoyable evening of dancing, and once or twice he'd suggested she come up to his apartment, but Anna always had politely declined.

"Of course," he'd say. "You're too nice of a girl to do that. It's just getting very difficult for me to say goodnight."

It was getting more difficult for Anna, too. But she held firm. While she desired to feel William close to her, and her emotions were running strong, she knew she had to protect herself. Becoming an unwed mother would be the ruin of her. She couldn't give in to her desire.

As September rolled around, Anna spent so much time with William that she couldn't imagine life without him. They attended an end-of-summer celebration at Roger and Miriam's lake house one weekend, and even Miriam asked her when William was going to propose.

"It's obvious he's over the moon about you," she said. "Maybe he needs a little push."

Anna blushed a deep red. She could never be so bold as to tell William he should marry her. Although she knew women who had done that very thing.

"You know, my husband only promotes the men who are married," Miriam confided in Anna after her second martini. "Maybe if Roger mentions that to William, we could get you two together." She winked.

"Oh, please don't," Anna said hurriedly. "I want William to ask me of his own volition."

"Oh, dear," Miriam said, laughing. "Men always need a little push to get married. They'd be bachelors forever if we women didn't dangle a carrot in front of them."

The other women in the group laughed too, and most nodded their agreement. Anna prayed that nothing would be said to William. It would be too embarrassing to think he'd consider marriage just for a job promotion.

Two weeks later, William suggested a ride northwest of town to Lake Calhoun to enjoy the fall colors. It was a warm autumn day, and Anna thought a ride would be fun. They packed a picnic lunch and drove out of downtown toward the suburbs. They'd kept the top down, and she'd wrapped a color-ful silk scarf around her hair to protect it from the wind. Anna had worn a simple red print dress, and William was wearing a casual suit but had taken off his jacket and tossed it in the back seat. It felt wonderful to be out of the busy traffic and on the road.

The trees had just started to change color where they lived, and they were even more colorful several miles north. It was such a lovely day, and Anna was happy to spend some time alone with William. Most of their time together was either eating at the busy diner or going out with his friends. Today, it was just them, and she was excited about it.

After a time, they pulled into the parking lot of the public park at Lake Calhoun. The lake glittered in the sunshine, and Anna carried a blanket while William carried the basket of food she'd packed. They found a spot on the grass under a tree, overlooking the lake. Spreading out the blanket, they sat down close to each other.

"Now, that's a view, isn't it, doll?" William said, smiling over at Anna. He placed his arm around her waist. "We couldn't have picked a more romantic spot."

Anna smiled back at him. He was right—it was perfect. She unpacked the lunch and handed him a sandwich and a bottle of Coca-Cola. William pulled a small, silver flask from his back pocket and tipped a little of the liquid into the bottle.

"Just a little something to add some zing," he said with a wink.

Anna was a little disappointed he'd brought alcohol along, but he rarely overdid it, so she relaxed and enjoyed the view. Birds chirped in the trees, and gray squirrels ran this way and that, hoping to find crumbs left behind. They ate their turkey sandwiches, red grapes, and fresh potato salad that Anna had made just the night before.

"You sure know how to cook," William said. "I'll bet you make a great pot roast and even better roast beef sandwiches than that old diner does. And pie. What I'd give to have a fresh piece of homemade apple pie."

"I love baking," Anna said. "When I have the time. I'm fine with cooking, too. Auntie May and I cook meals all the time. Or, at least we used to. You should come to our place for Thanksgiving dinner. We usually invite several of the school-teachers who have no family around, and we enjoy a big meal. It's wonderful."

"It sounds wonderful," he said. "My mother wasn't much of a cook. She made mostly plain meals. It was okay, but when I moved in with my dad and his wife when I was fourteen, I found out what real home cooking tasted like. That Mattie sure can cook."

Anna was intrigued. William rarely spoke about his family. "Mattie? Is that your stepmother?"

"Yep. She's quite a woman. She was a flapper in her younger years, and my dad met her when he was running hooch over the Canadian border during prohibition. They've had some wild times together, but now they're settling down and build-ing a resort up in Canada. They figure all their rich friends from Buffalo and Minneapolis will come up there to 'rough it,' as they say. And Mattie will be the one cooking for every-one. She's good at it. And good at keeping my father in line." William laughed.

Anna had known his parents were building a lodge up in Canada, but this other information was all new to her. Running alcohol during prohibition? She'd never have imagined that. Auntie May would have a lot to say about a person who broke the law that way—and none of it good.

"What about you, Anna?" William said, turning his warm brown eyes on her. "What is it you want out of life?"

She dropped her eyes to the blanket, concentrating on the plaid pattern. "I guess I want what most women do," she said. "A good husband, children, and a nice home."

He placed the side of his finger under her chin, raising her eyes to his. "What about your work? A smart, career woman like yourself. Would you be content with just a home and a husband?"

Anna stared into the depths of his eyes. Yes. She wanted nothing more than to be a wife and a mother. She didn't want a career. She was so tired of working in a man's world and earning her keep. She wanted what all the executive wives at William's company had—a secure marriage, a home, and a future.

"I've always dreamed of having a home and family of my own. I work because I have to, not because I have any desire to build a career."

William's eyes sparkled mischievously. "Then let's get hitched."

Anna's eyes widened. "What?"

"Marry me, Anna. I adore you, and I know you love me too. Let's get married and turn this world on its ear."

The excitement in his voice made Anna's heart beat quicker. "Really?"

He pulled a small box from his jacket pocket and handed it to her. "Really. I'm serious, Anna. Marry me."

She opened the small, red velvet box and inside sat a gold band with a diamond set in the middle. Gasping, she stared at the ring, unable to believe her eyes. An engagement ring. No one she knew had one. Most women only wore a thin gold band. "I love it!" she exclaimed.

William placed his hands on her arms. "But do you love me enough to marry me?"

She smiled up at him. "Yes. Yes, I'll marry you."

He kissed her then, in a way that told her she was now his and would be his forever.

* * *

"You're what?" Auntie May stared at Anna in disbelief. "You're engaged?"

Anna nodded, showing her the ring. "With a real engagement ring," she said proudly. "He loves me, Auntie. He wants to spend the rest of his life with me. I'm so happy."

May crossed her arms and turned away a minute, something that Anna knew she did when she was thinking deeply. May turned back to Anna, keeping her voice calm. "But you hardly know this man. How can you know he's the man you want to spend the rest of your life with?"

Anna's smile faded. She was disappointed but not surprised by her aunt's reaction. That was the reason she'd decided to tell Auntie May without William in the room. She didn't want to upset William with her aunt's concerns.

"I know him well enough," Anna said soothingly. "I've been spending all my time with him. He's a good man, Auntie. He's educated, he has a stable job, and he loves me. What more could I hope for?"

May's face softened. "But you two are complete opposites. He's so...flashy. And you're more down-to-earth. He likes to drink and party with his friends all the time. I've never known you to be that way until you met him."

"I've never had a chance to be anything but the quiet woman in the corner before meeting William," Anna said. "You and I live a modest life. He's brought fun and excitement into my life. He makes me feel like I belong somewhere."

May shook her head. "How long will you be able to keep up with him, dear? How long will you want to party all night? What about when you have children? Will he calm down and become a father?"

Anna frowned. She wasn't pleased with the points her aunt was making. In truth, Anna had worried about the very same things. What if William never settled down? What if he grew tired of her when she no longer wanted to go out every night? But her desire to be married and have a family outweighed her fears. She was nearly twenty-five years old. This was her last chance for happiness and to not become an old maid like her aunt.

"I know you don't like William," Anna said. "But I'm going to marry him."

Frustration creased May's face. "Anna, please. He's not good enough for you. He drinks too much, and he calls you 'doll.' Does he think he's a gangster or something? You're just too good for him."

"No, Auntie. I'm not too good for him. I'm lucky that a man like William wants to marry me. This is my last chance to marry and build my own life. I'm going to take it." Anna turned away, trying hard to hold in the anger rising inside her.

"You don't need a man to build a life," May said, sounding desperate. "You can support yourself. You can take care of yourself. And you can wait for the right man to come along."

Anna spun around. "No. *You* don't need a man. But *I* do! I don't want to live alone, like you, for the rest of my life. William loves me, and I'm going to marry him. We're getting married at the courthouse on Wednesday. You can either support me and my decision or not. That's your choice. But I'm going to marry him." Anna stormed out of the living room and into her bedroom. She hated fighting with her beloved aunt, but she was going to stand firm on this.

May followed her into the bedroom. "You know I only want what's best for you, don't you, dear?" she asked, her voice gentle. "I've cared about your well-being since the day you came to live with me after your father died. You're like a daughter to me. And while I'm not thrilled with you marrying William, I'm also not going to stand in your way. Losing you over this would break my heart. So, I'll support your decision."

Anna turned. The tears she'd been holding back were now trickling down her cheeks. "Thank you, Auntie. I don't want to lose you. You mean so much to me. But I love him. I want this."

May walked over and hugged her close. May was several inches shorter than Anna, but Anna bent down to hug her. "I hope you'll be very, very happy," May said softly.

"I will be. I promise. This is what I want," Anna whispered back. She knew she should be the happiest woman in the world at this moment, but something felt wrong. Anna shook that feeling off and put it out of her mind.

* * *

Wednesday at three o'clock, Anna met William at the court-house downtown. They'd already bought their license and had all the necessary paperwork completed. Both of them had taken the afternoon off of work, but they did so with their employers' blessings.

Anna was nervous as they waited their turn to be married by the judge. She'd worn her dark blue suit with a white chiffon blouse underneath. William had bought her six roses for her bouquet, and he'd stuck one in the buttonhole of his jacket. Auntie May was supposed to meet them there, and the longer they waited, the more nervous Anna felt. Earlier in the week, when they'd applied for their license, the first shadow of doubt had fallen over Anna. She'd found out that William wasn't her age or older—he was two years younger.

"So, you're robbing the cradle," he'd said, his eyes sparkling as they did when he was teasing her. "What's two years? We're both adults."

Anna knew that was true, but it still made her uncomfortable. It wasn't something she wanted to broadcast to the world.

As they sat on the bench in the hallway, she suddenly realized they hadn't brought along another couple as witnesses. "Who'll sign our marriage certificate?" she asked William.

"Don't worry, doll," he said casually. "My sister and her husband will be here any minute. I invited them."

Anna was stunned. She'd known that William had an older sister but had never met her. Self-consciously, she smoothed her skirt and felt her hair to make sure it was rolled up neatly. "Why didn't you tell me she was coming?"

He shrugged. "I wanted it to be a surprise. She's the only family I have around here, and I knew we'd need witnesses. They'll be here soon, I'm sure."

Anna sat there feeling more unsure by the moment. Would William always be surprising her like this? He liked being in control and surprising her at the last minute as if she couldn't handle knowing sooner. She hadn't thought much of it before, but today it unnerved her. Meeting his sister was a big deal. Meeting her on their wedding day was overwhelming.

Auntie May arrived a few minutes later, and Anna felt a little calmer.

"I'm sorry I'm late, dear," May said, nodding over at William. "The bus was running late. I'm glad I didn't miss the ceremony."

Anna hugged her. "Thank you for coming," she said, holding her a little longer than necessary. Anna drew strength from the familiarity of her aunt's embrace.

"I brought something for you," May said, smiling. She reached into her jacket pocket and pulled out a lovely jeweled brooch shaped like a peacock. "I know how much you used to love this brooch, and I thought it might make a wonderful borrowed item for you today."

"Oh, Auntie. Thank you," Anna said. "I've always loved it. And it matches my suit."

May pinned it on her lapel and smiled up at her. "My fiancé gave this to me before he left for the war. I want you to have it."

Tears threatened to fill Anna's eyes. This was a gift from her aunt's heart, and she appreciated it so much. "I'll always cherish it," she told her.

William glanced over at the pin. "It's gorgeous, babe. Just like you." He winked at her.

A moment later, William's sister, Bernice, and her husband Jim appeared around the corner of the hallway. Her heels clicked on the linoleum floor as she strode hurriedly up to the group with a pinched face.

"There she is," William said, rising from the bench. "Anna, this is my sister Bernice and her husband, Jim Benton. Bernice, this is May Bergman, Anna's aunt."

Bernice lifted a gloved hand to shake with Anna and May. "It's nice to meet you," she said, her words clipped. Jim smiled wide and greeted both women warmly.

Bernice turned to William. "You could have given me some

warning that you were getting married. I didn't even know you were seeing anyone seriously."

"You know me, sis. I follow my heart. And I fell fast for Anna. You're going to love her. She's terrific."

Bernice quickly ran her eyes over Anna. "I'm sure I will," she said with no warmth in her tone. Bernice turned away and went to sit on the bench down the hall.

Another doubtful shadow fell over Anna. This wasn't the start of a great relationship with her soon-to-be sister-in-law. She sat once more next to William and glanced over at Bernice. The woman was tall and thin—too thin—with dark hair and a narrow face. Her tight lips had a slash of red on them that made her look even angrier. Bernice wasn't a pretty woman, and from what Anna could tell, neither was her personality. She hoped that would change as time went on.

The door beside the bench opened, and a portly woman wearing glasses called out, "Anna Bergman and William Craine?"

"That's us," William said to Anna. He took her hand and smiled at her. As she gazed up at him, she realized it didn't matter what her aunt thought or whether or not his sister liked her. Anna was about to marry William. And that was all that mattered.

With that thought in mind, the entire group walked into the judge's office.

CHAPTER SEVENTEEN

Diane

Diane sat quietly as Anna ended her story with her marriage to William. It was Wednesday evening, and Diane had come after school again to visit with Anna. In fact, this was the second time Diane had visited this week already. Monday had been Anna's ninety-fifth birthday, and Diane had come to have dinner with her and Max. She had also brought her a cake. Anna's eyes had brightened at the small birthday cake.

"You remembered," she'd said, looking truly touched.

"Of course I remembered," Diane told her. "Ninety-five is a pretty big milestone." Diane had wracked her brain for a gift for Anna and had finally decided on a framed photo of her and Natalie that had been taken the previous summer. Anna loved it, and it now sat on the nightstand next to Anna's photos of her parents and brother.

Now, Anna was looking through her wooden keepsake box. "I know it's in here somewhere. Unless Joan had decided to keep it. That would have been fine," Anna said distractedly.

"What are we looking for?" Diane asked, glancing in the box.

"The brooch. Ah, this might be it." Anna pulled out tissue paper that was wrapped tightly around a small object. She handed it to Diane. "Would you open this, dear?"

Diane carefully unwrapped the item, unwinding several layers of tissue paper. Finally, a pin, shaped like a peacock, dropped into her hands. Green and deep blue gemstones decorated the large tail feathers, and the silver body and graceful neck were sprinkled with clear stones. Three head feathers held blue and green stones. It was absolutely stunning, even after all these years.

Anna handed Diane a five-by-seven photo in black and white. "See there, on my lapel. There's the brooch. This photo was taken at my aunt's apartment after we'd married. She'd invited everyone over to celebrate with food and champagne. I thought that was sweet, considering how strongly she opposed the marriage."

Diane studied the photo. Anna and William leaned on a railing that looked like an old-fashioned fire escape. They were close together, his arm around her waist. Both were smiling sweetly. "You were certainly a good-looking couple," Diane said.

Anna nodded. "From the outside, yes. Before things began to fade, much like the jewelry William had given me."

Diane looked up at her grandmother, eyebrows raised.

Anna chuckled. "All paste and plated gold. Remember the necklace and earrings he gave me? After a while, the color of the gems clouded, and the gold turned green. The same happened with my engagement ring. It was really a zirconia, not a diamond. The band turned my finger green. Auntie had been right. William was all flash and talk, but no substance."

Diane looked down at the peacock brooch. After all these

years, it still sparkled in the light. "Your Auntie May's pin has real gemstones."

"Yes, it does. Her fiancé must have paid a pretty penny for it." She smiled. "I want you to have it, dear. It belongs to you now."

"Oh, I couldn't take your pin," Diane protested.

"Why not? I don't need it, and I suspect Joanie doesn't want it. It's yours. Or give it to your daughter. It should stay in the family." Anna began digging through the box again. "Ah, and this too," she said, pulling out a velvet ring box. Anna opened it and inside sat a very thin gold band. She handed it to Diane. "You should take this too. It's the only real piece of gold jewelry your grandfather ever gave to me."

Diane stared at it, surprised. "Isn't that your wedding band?"

"Yes, dear. It is. But I certainly don't need it any longer."

Diane felt odd taking her grandmother's jewelry, but Anna had insisted. "Thank you," she said. "I'll cherish both of these."

Anna smiled. "I'm thrilled to have someone to give them to."

Later, Diane carefully tucked the jewelry away in her purse as she left to go home. She'd seen Anna and Max off to the dining room before heading to her car. She had to admit, Max and Anna looked cute together. She was happy Anna had a friend to share meals with.

When Diane arrived home, Barry was waiting with a crockpot of pulled pork for them to make sandwiches with for dinner. She showed him the jewelry, then took photos of the pin to share with her daughter. This journey she was on with Anna was fascinating. Diane had never thought much about her ancestry before, but now she was hungry to learn it all. She couldn't wait to visit with Anna again.

* * *

Friday after school, Diane steeled herself for another confrontation with her mother. She hoped that her mother had simmered down by now, but one never knew what to expect of Joan. But when she showed up at her mother's door, she was ready as usual for their evening of shopping and dinner.

"I had the nicest visit with Gladys last week," Joan said as they ate dinner. "She called me out of the blue and took me to lunch and shopping. I miss the days when she and I used to do that all the time."

"I'm glad you got to see her," Diane said. She assumed her mother had no idea that she'd arranged for Gladys to call. "Barry and I went on a little trip north for the long weekend, so it worked out well."

Joan eyed her through her glasses. "Where did you go?"

"Oh, we just drove up north and stayed in a nice little hotel. We stopped at a casino for a while and stayed by a lake. Nothing special. It was just nice to get away and relax."

"Hmph." Joan continued eating her soup. "When is that man going to marry you? You two have been together for a long time."

Diane sighed. "He'd marry me tomorrow if I'd let him. I'm the one who's afraid to commit. After Jeffrey, I'm in no hurry to be tied to a man."

"Barry isn't anything like Jeffrey. Jeffrey was a conceited, arrogant snob who thought he was better than everyone because he had a college education. Nothing good came from him except for Natalie." Joan's expression softened. "Speaking of Natalie, how is she doing at school?"

Diane was relieved to change the subject to her daughter. Her mother could be harsh, but she had a soft spot for her granddaughter, especially since Natalie was planning on attending medical school. It gave Joan bragging rights to all her friends that her granddaughter was going to be a doctor.

All went well that night, and Diane let out a huge sigh of relief when she left her mother's place without any angry words between them. She didn't know how her mother did it. One moment she could be spitting mad, and the next she acted like all was well with the world. It was unnerving. Diane was also happy they hadn't continued the conversation about Jeffrey. She knew her mother had disliked Jeffrey from the beginning, but that hadn't meant much to Diane. Her mother hadn't exactly picked the best men to marry either, so her not liking Jeffrey was sort of a good thing. But it had turned out very wrong. The women in their family apparently didn't have good judgment when it came to choosing spouses.

Which was why Diane hadn't said yes to Barry yet. He seemed flawless, but so had Jeffrey. She feared the moment they married, Barry would turn into some crazy jerk. While this thought made her laugh out loud, she still didn't trust herself—or him—to get married.

Listening to her grandmother's story had triggered her own memories about her past, and it was hard for Diane not to analyze her marriage to Jeffrey. She didn't want to think of that time in her life, but she couldn't help it. Just like Anna, Diane hadn't seen anything wrong with Jeffrey and their relationship until after they'd married. Unlike Anna, Diane hadn't had any small doubts before marriage. Anna had experienced some things about William she'd been worried about prior to marrying him. But she'd wanted to be married so badly, that she'd pushed those fears aside. Diane, on the other hand, had seen no flaws in Jeffrey. Every time she looked back on her marriage, she wracked her brain trying to remember even a hint of what he'd become. But nothing was there. They'd been old enough to make a mature decision, and both had already started their careers. Their marriage had seemed like a perfect match. Why had it gone so wrong?

"And why did I put up with his verbal abuse for so long?" she asked aloud. She supposed she'd thought he was joking at first. Then she'd begun to believe that maybe she wasn't as smart as him, or as organized, or as competent. But after Natalie was born, the fog had cleared. Diane saw Jeffrey differently. He no longer seemed like he was smarter or more capable than she was—he was just a bully. And once he'd realized she didn't believe in him anymore, the verbal abuse grew worse. Much worse.

A psychologist would tell Diane that she had to face her past before she could move forward. Diane knew that was true. But she wasn't ready quite yet to dig too deeply into her marriage with Jeffrey, nor to move forward. She was stuck for the moment, no matter how unhealthy it was. She preferred it because it was safe. And safe was a good thing.

* * *

The first snow and November first hit on the same day that Sunday. Diane went to visit Anna despite the snow. It didn't look that threatening yet, so she felt safe driving. Once there, she found Anna in her room, dozing in her chair with a light blanket over her lap. Diane tried to be quiet, but before she could sit down, Anna's lids fluttered open.

"Oh, dear. I must have fallen asleep for a bit. Lunch was so good that I think it made me sleepy."

"Should I leave and let you rest?" Diane asked, feeling terrible that she'd awakened her. Anna looked tired, and Diane didn't want to wear her out.

"Please don't leave. I so enjoy our time together," Anna said, sitting up straighter in her chair. "What do you think of this snow? Do you think it's here to stay?"

Diane moved the chair over near Anna and sat down. "More than likely. It is November. Unless we get lucky and it melts."

"The snow is always so pretty when it first falls. It has a calming feel to it. But then it gets dirty and makes it so much harder to get around. But that first snow is magical."

"I suppose in your early years you walked through the snow a lot on your way to work or the bus stop," Diane said.

"Oh, yes. Auntie May and I didn't have the luxury of a car. We walked everywhere or took the bus. It didn't hurt us a bit, though. One of my favorite memories of my first year with Auntie was when we went to buy a tree on Christmas Eve. We bundled up and borrowed an old, red wagon from a neighbor with children. Then we walked several blocks to where they sold trees. It was snowing lightly, but it didn't feel too cold. We hauled that tree back in the wagon and decorated it while drinking hot chocolate and singing carols. It was the best Christmas I'd ever had. Simple. Sweet. Those are the best ones."

Anna's eyes shined as she spoke, and Diane could actually picture the scene in her head of the two of them walking through the streets of Minneapolis and picking out a tree. It was sweet. Memories like that were precious.

Anna reached for her keepsake box and began searching

through it. She lifted out a jewelry box and handed it to Diane. "Another memory that is bittersweet," Anna said. "One of the few pieces of jewelry William gave me early on."

Diane opened the box. Inside was a gold wristwatch. The face was small and delicate, as was the band. There was a clip that held it in place. "It's lovely. So feminine."

Anna nodded. "It is lovely. If you wind it, it will probably still work."

Diane wound the small dial and lifted it to her ear. Sure enough, the watch began to tick. "It does still work," she said excitedly.

The happiness that had shown in Anna's eyes earlier faded. "I'll never forget the day William gave that to me. It was also the first time he hit me."

CHAPTER EIGHTEEN

Anna

From the time Anna was a young girl, she'd dreamt of marrying a handsome man and living happily ever after. The day she married William, she thought her dream had come true. He was movie-star handsome, had a good job with a bright future, and loved her dearly. Or so Anna thought.

After their marriage ceremony, the small group celebrated with food and champagne at Auntie May's apartment. Bernice and Jim came for a while, and a few of May's theater and teacher friends came over too. It was a fun time, and the doubt that had been plaguing Anna disappeared. William was attentive and sweet as they drank and shared the first piece of cake that Auntie May had bought. Even Bernice's cool attitude toward Anna didn't ruin her excitement. Anna was starting a new life with the man she loved, and she wasn't going to let anything dampen that.

As the festivities dwindled, Anna hurried to pack a bag of necessities to take to William's apartment. She'd taken Thursday off as well so she could move her things into his place. Her bosses had gladly given her the time off and had also surprised her with a fifteen-cent an hour raise to entice her to continue working for them. That had been a nice boost. As far as she knew, William was more than happy for her to continue working as long as she wanted.

Auntie May came into the room as Anna packed. "Do you need any help, dear?"

"No, thank you," Anna said. "I'm just bringing a few things. I'll be here all day tomorrow, moving my things up to William's place."

May nodded. "Feel free to take anything from your room that you might need. The dresser or nightstands or lamps. Anything. I want you to feel at home there like you did here."

Tears suddenly filled Anna's eyes as her emotions bubbled to the surface. She turned and hugged May. "Thank you for everything you've done for me, Auntie. From the time I moved here as a kid to this very moment, you've been nothing but kind and loving. I hope you know how much I appreciate you."

"You're like my own daughter, dear. I was happy to take , you in and care for you. And look at what you've accomplished. You're a smart, competent woman. Please believe that no matter where life takes you."

Anna pulled back and looked into her aunt's eyes. Her message was kind but cryptic. "I'm happy, Auntie. Please be happy for me."

May smiled. "I am happy for you. I wish you nothing but the best."

William poked his head around the door frame. "Are you ready, doll?" he asked with a big grin.

"Yes. Coming." Anna hugged May once more. "I'll see you tomorrow," Anna told her and followed William out of the apartment.

William lived one floor up, so they walked up the stairs while he carried her bag. Anna had never been in his apartment before and wondered what it might look like. He'd been a bachelor for a while, but she expected that with as nicely as he dressed, he'd have newer furniture and nice things. But when William opened the door, her expectations fell. An old, droopy sofa sat in the middle of the living room with a tall shaded lamp beside it and a scratched coffee table in front. The dining room table, if it could be called that, had two chairs, and the wood was scratched, too. It was only a one-bedroom apartment. Compared to her auntie's apartment, it looked worn and, well, dumpy.

William set her suitcase down and spun her around to face him. "Alone at last," he said, smiling wide. He kissed her so passionately, it startled her. When he pulled away, his brown eyes had grown nearly black. "I've been waiting to be alone with you for a long time." He moved even closer and kissed her neck, finding the sweet spot behind her ear.

Chills of anticipation ran through Anna. She'd been nervous about their first night together, but she'd pictured it like in the movies. She'd expected to prepare for bed in a beautiful nightgown and let her hair down first. Then, William would kiss her sweetly before they went to bed. She hadn't expected that he'd be all over her the moment they walked into the apartment.

"Maybe I should change for bed first," she said, pulling away. William frowned, but then nodded.

"Sure, babe. Of course. We should get comfortable. The ladies' room is all yours."

Relieved, Anna went into the bathroom that she had to walk through the bedroom to get to. She stopped a moment to look at the bedroom furniture. There was an old brass-framed bed with a mattress that sagged in the middle. Only sheets and a blanket were on top, no comforter or bedspread. A highboy dresser stood on one wall, but it was old and banged up. As she went into the bathroom, she realized it needed a good cleaning—another thing she'd have to do tomorrow as she moved in.

Anna had purchased a beautiful filmy pale blue nightgown for her wedding night. She quickly brushed her teeth, combed out her long hair, and slipped into the gown. Her entire body vibrated with anticipation over the marriage act. She was almost twenty-five years old, and she'd never been intimate with a man. It scared her and excited her all at once. She hoped that William would be as loving and courteous in bed as he generally was out of it.

Finally, she stepped out of the bathroom, surprised to see William had already pulled down the blankets on the bed and was sitting there, waiting for her. He'd taken off his suit jacket and tie, and his shirt was half-way unbuttoned. She'd never seen him with his shirt off before and was surprised to see the dark hair on his chest around the neckline of his undershirt.

"You look gorgeous," he said, his eyes growing dark with passion. He'd made himself a drink which was already half gone. "I never realized how long your hair was. It's beautiful."

Anna felt the warmth of a blush on her face. Her hair was thick and heavy and went all the way down her back. She hadn't cut it since leaving her grandparents' farm. After years of her grandmother chopping it off so terribly, Anna had been adamant about keeping it long.

William reached his hand out to Anna. "Come sit with me."

She moved over next to him on wobbly legs and sat beside him.

"You're so beautiful, Anna. I can't believe you agreed to marry me. But I'm so happy you did." He kissed her tenderly, and she could taste the alcohol on his breath. His hands went up and through her hair, and he gently pulled her down on the bed. This was the happily-ever-after movie ending that Anna had been hoping for. She wasn't afraid. This was William, and she knew he loved her.

Suddenly, things changed. In a flash, he'd taken off his clothes and pulled her nightgown up and off her. Before she could even get beneath the covers for modesty's sake, he was on top of her. Anna held her breath and tried not to cry out. It only took seconds, and he was done.

William rolled over, took a long swig of his drink, and then pulled up the covers. Anna hurried under them too. She was too embarrassed for him to see her nude body. He bent over her, kissed her sweetly, and then rolled over. "Goodnight, doll," he said. Within seconds, he was snoring.

Anna lay motionless, too afraid to move. Tears rolled down the sides of her face, onto the pillow. She hadn't felt loved or cherished at all; she'd felt accosted. Was this how marriage was? All her ideas of romance and tender love had been crushed.

Finally, when she was sure William was sound asleep, she snuck out of bed, cleaned herself up, and put on a regular nightgown. As she climbed into bed again, careful not to touch his nude body, the tears formed once more.

Maybe it'll get better. Maybe I'm to blame for not knowing what to do, she thought. Anna finally fell asleep, lying stiff as a board at the edge of the bed.

* * *

William had to be at work the next day, so he was up early, showering. Anna got up, too, and put on a heavy robe. She checked his refrigerator for food to make breakfast with, but there was nothing there. Quickly, she ran downstairs to her aunt's kitchen, borrowed eggs and bread for toast, and hurried back up. She had two eggs over easy and toast ready by the time William was dressed.

"Good morning, doll," he said, thrilled to see she'd made him food. "How lucky am I that you thought to cook breakfast?"

She served him the food along with coffee. Luckily, he had a coffeepot and a can of coffee. Anna made a mental note of all the groceries and cookware they'd need if they wanted to eat at home.

"I figured since I had the day off of work, I would make breakfast," she said, sitting down at the table to sip her coffee.

"A guy could get used to this." He winked.

She smiled. He was his old charming self again. "I was thinking, if you don't mind, that I might bring a few of my own things up here to spruce up the place. And I'll pick up some groceries today and some cookware. We may have to eat at the diner during the week, but it would be nice to cook on the weekends."

"Yeah. Great. This place could use a woman's touch," he said, obviously not insulted by what she'd suggested. "I rented this place furnished, so that's why it's a little shabby. I know you can work your magic, though."

William kissed her lightly on the cheek and hurried out the door. After cleaning up the kitchen and dressing, Anna took stock of the apartment. There was a small closet in the bedroom, hardly big enough for all her suits and dresses. She saw William owned only two good suits for work, a black suit for dressier occasions, two pairs of shoes, and a few shirts. His clothes took up very little of the closet. She decided she'd bring down her work clothes and leave her dressier items in her closet at Auntie May's.

That day, Anna ran around trying to finish all her chores. She went quickly for groceries right away in the morning and prepared a roast and potatoes for dinner. Then she started packing up her items at her aunt's apartment. She ran into the apartment manager, and he and his son were more than happy to help her carry up some of her furniture. She brought up her dresser, nightstand, and the small tufted chair from her bedroom. She packed and unpacked her suitcase several times to bring clothing and shoes up, and then carried up her bedspread, sheets, and other items that would make the apartment feel more like home. By the time William walked through the door that evening, his apartment had been magically transformed.

"Am I in the right place?" he asked, looking around.

Anna laughed. She was wearing one of her casual dresses with an apron tied at the waist. "I just made a few changes," she said. "It's cheerier, don't you think?"

William looked around. There were doilies on the coffee table to hide the scratches as well as a tablecloth on the dining room table. In the bedroom, Anna had placed her dresser and mirror on the one empty wall, and her nightstand stood next to her side of the bed. She'd cleaned the bathroom, and borrowed rugs from Auntie May for the floor, and there was a rug in front of the sink in the kitchen, too. She'd also borrowed some old dishes of May's and hoped to get new ones for her and William soon.

"It looks amazing," he said, coming over to kiss her. "And what's that I smell?"

"Dinner. Pot roast with potatoes and carrots."

He grinned. "I'm the luckiest man alive."

She served the food as William took off his jacket and tie and rolled up his shirtsleeves. He'd also made himself a drink and looked surprised when he saw how full the refrigerator was.

"You bought groceries too? You were a busy girl today."

Anna smiled, pleased that he approved of all she'd done.

He complimented her on the dinner as they ate, and afterward, they turned on the radio and listened to music. William pulled Anna close, and they danced around the living room as if they were in a fancy ballroom. He tickled her ear with a kiss, and chills ran up her spine. This was the romantic William she knew. She hoped tonight would be more romantic than last night, and as they grew to know each other better, it would be as magical as she thought marital relations should be.

At least she hoped.

* * *

The first two months of their marriage flew by, with both of them busy working and spending time together. Anna bought a few more items for the apartment, and it was soon shaping up to look respectable. She'd purchased a navy-blue slipcover for the sofa and placed an afghan that she'd crocheted over the back. A new end table with a lamp helped to brighten up the space. She'd also brought up her small phonograph and the few records she owned. Some evenings, she and William would dance to Bing Crosby, The Glenn Miller Band, and Billie Holiday. While the romantic parts of their evenings were always delightful, Anna was still not quite used to their intimacy. But she tried as best she could to make William happy.

Anna slowly took on other duties as well. Since that first morning, when she'd cooked breakfast for William, she continued doing so, even if it meant she had to rush to get to work. He seemed to appreciate it so much that Anna thought it was the least she could do. And several times a week she'd make dinner after work. It wasn't always easy, but she did her best. She started running errands for William on her lunch break as well. She'd drop off his suit at the dry cleaners and picked it up as well. She also went to buy small things for him, like new undershirts, socks, shaving cream, or razors. She didn't mind doing these little errands for him, but it wasn't always easy to leave the office at lunchtime. And she realized that William never offered to give her money for the purchases or to buy groceries. It all came out of her earnings. But she didn't worry too much about it. She felt that since they were married, they were supposed to share their income, so she didn't complain.

One evening in mid-November, William came home with a huge grin on this face. Anna had just walked in the door minutes before and was wondering what to make for dinner. She'd been too late to pick up William's other suit at the cleaners, which had frustrated her. She'd have to make sure to press his trousers that night, so they'd looked fresh again for tomorrow. That was something he was very fastidious about.

"What's that huge grin for?" she asked when she saw his eyes twinkle mischievously.

He reached for her hand and twirled her around as if they'd been dancing. Anna laughed. She liked it when he was in a good mood.

"Put on your prettiest dress, doll. We're going out to celebrate," he said.

"Celebrate what?"

William stood up straighter, prouder. "You're looking at the new department supervisor. I've been promoted and given a big fat raise, too. Go pretty yourself up, and we'll go to the supper club for dinner and dancing."

Anna was giddy with happiness for William. She knew how hard he worked to move ahead at his company.

Since all her fancier dresses were at her aunt's place, Anna ran downstairs and knocked before walking into the apartment.

"Well, this is a surprise," May said, smiling.

"Hi, Auntie. I'm just here to get one of my dresses. William is taking me out to celebrate his promotion and raise." Anna rushed into her old bedroom and looked through the dresses hanging in the closet.

"That's wonderful," May said, following Anna inside the room. "I'm glad he's doing so well at work."

"He is, Auntie. We're both doing well. I wish I could spend more time visiting right now, but I'd better get ready." She chose a light blue dress that had a large flower print on it in darker blues. Then she pulled down a hatbox from the shelf and picked a small hat of the same color.

"Well, you two have a wonderful time," May said as Anna waved and rushed out the door.

Anna dressed quickly, and William drove them to one of the fancier supper clubs in town that had a band playing every night after eight. He ordered the most expensive thing on the menu for them both—steak and lobster tails—and a bottle of champagne along with his usual bourbon and water. After the waiter had poured the champagne, William raised his glass up toward Anna.

"To us and our successes," William said. They clinked glasses and drank.

"I'm so proud of you, dear," Anna said. "You work hard, and you're succeeding."

"And someday I'm going to run that place," William said. He laughed. "You just wait and see."

William's excitement was contagious. Anna's day had been stressful, so she was happy that it had ended well. She was careful not to drink too much since they both had to work the next day, but William didn't seem to worry about how much he drank.

After eating, when the band began playing, he rose and led her to the dance floor. Anna loved it when they danced together. He was light on his feet, and she felt special in his arms.

The celebration didn't end when they arrived home. William had consumed quite a bit of alcohol by then. He twirled her around and held her close, kissing her suggestively on the neck and collar bone. Drunk or sober, he had a huge appetite for sex, Anna had learned. And tonight was no different. They were both being silly, and soon their clothes ended up on the bedroom floor as he made love to her. For the first time since they'd married, William didn't rush. He kissed and caressed her lovingly, and she realized that this was what she'd been missing before. Afterward, they fell asleep, curled up together in a way that Anna had longed for. She felt completely loved and safe with William.

* * *

The next morning, William practically crawled out of bed when the alarm went off and headed for the bathroom. "Where's the Bromo-Seltzer?" he called out, sounding hoarse.

Anna's head was a bit fuzzy, but she woke up enough to tell him it was in the medicine cabinet. Getting out of bed, she saw his trousers and jacket on the floor and carefully hung them up. Then she went to the kitchen in her robe and slippers to make a quick breakfast before dressing for work. Even though her head ached a little from all the champagne and the late night, she smiled as she worked. William had never been as affectionate as he'd been last night. She hoped his good mood carried over for weeks to come.

Just as she flipped the eggs in the pan, William stepped into the kitchen, looking enraged.

"Look at these trousers! Look at them! They're wrinkled. Why didn't you iron them?"

Anna turned to him, startled. "I'm sorry. I hung them up," she said, but he took a step toward her and yelled in her face.

"Hung them up? What the hell is that going to do? I can't go into my first day of work as a supervisor looking like a hobo. Where's my other suit?"

Anna heard the eggs sizzling in the pan and could smell them burning. She turned to the stove to move them off the heat. "I'm sorry, honey. I couldn't get to the dry cleaners on time yesterday because I was busy at work. I'll pick up your suit today." As she turned toward him again, his hand darted out of nowhere and backhanded her across the face. Anna stumbled backward and caught herself on the counter, her hand instinctively reaching up to the red spot where he'd hit her.

"There's only one job around here that's important, and that's mine!" he bellowed. "Everything you do is second to me, you understand? You're nothing without me!" He turned on his heel and left the kitchen, and a moment later, Anna heard the apartment door slam.

Stunned, she stayed leaning against the counter a moment longer before feeling her jaw to make sure it wasn't broken. Her skin burned where he'd hit her, and her head ached from being jolted so violently. On shaky legs, she walked to the bathroom to look at her reflection in the mirror. A huge red mark showed on the side of her face. That's when the tears began to stream down her cheeks. She felt once again like the little chubby girl with the Dutch-boy haircut being berated by her grandmother at the farm. Small, defenseless, ashamed.

Knowing she had to get to work, Anna pulled herself together enough to wet a washcloth with ice-cold water and place it on her cheek. She went back to the kitchen to clean it up, tossing away the uneaten eggs, then hurried to dress for work. The mark on her face had faded a little by then, but she used some face powder to cover up the redness. She couldn't bear to have anyone know her shame. Anna left the apartment a few minutes later, ducking her head when she saw people on the stairs, still confused as to how such a beautiful evening could turn into such a horrific morning.

* * *

That evening, Anna trudged through the snow and slush on the sidewalk from the bus stop to her apartment with the dry-cleaning hanging over her arm. Somehow, she'd made it through the day, but her mind had been in turmoil the entire time. How could she stay with a man who hit her? But how could she admit she'd made a terrible mistake marrying him?

Once home, she put everything away and stared at the contents of the refrigerator for ideas for dinner. Her face still felt sore. Anna knew it had looked swollen all day, but the men she worked for were too kind to ask her about it. When Anna heard the apartment door open, she froze.

"Anna? Are you here?" William called in a kind voice.

Taking a steadying breath, she walked out to the living room, keeping her distance from him. William was carrying a dozen roses in the crook of his arm and had already set his hat down.

"Is it okay that I'm here?" he asked, not moving toward her. "After this morning, I wouldn't blame you if you kicked me out on my ass."

She studied him, puzzled by his behavior. This morning, he'd looked like a crazed beast. Tonight, he looked like a lost boy who desperately needed love. "This is your apartment. I can't kick you out," she said softly.

Encouraged, he moved closer to her and handed her the roses. "These are for you. They in no way make up for this morning, but you deserve them and dozens more for all you do for me." His face softened even more. "I'm so sorry, Anna. I don't know what got into me. Please, please forgive me. I promise I'll never do anything like that again."

Anna held the flowers, not sure what to say. Did she believe him? He'd never scared her before like he had this morning in all the months they'd dated. She searched his eyes to see if he was sincere, but he looked so sad, she couldn't tell.

"I bought you something. Something nice that you can be proud to wear. You deserve nice things, doll." He pulled a square box from his pocket and handed it to her. "Open it. And if you hate it, we'll go and buy you anything you like."

She set the flowers on the table beside her and unwrapped the box. When she lifted the lid, there sat a brand new Bulova wristwatch. It was gold with a small face and a delicate wrist band. Anna knew this wasn't a cheap watch. Bulova was one of the best.

Looking up at William, she tried to smile. "It's lovely. Thank you."

William perked up with a smile of his own. "I knew you didn't have one, and I wanted you to have the best. It's so pretty, don't you think?" he caught her eyes with his. "Just like you, baby doll." He helped her put the watch on her wrist then pulled her into a hug.

Anna still wasn't sure what to do or say. Did she believe him when he said he'd never hit her again? Should she believe him?

"How about we go to the diner tonight for dinner, so you don't have to work so hard," he offered when he pulled away.

She nodded. "That would be nice."

He smiled. "Anything for my girl." He hugged her again.

Anna knew she'd forgive him in time. Maybe even trust him again. That was how she was. She always wanted to believe the best of everyone. But she'd learn to regret that in the years to come.

CHAPTER NINETEEN

Diane

"He promised to never hit me again," Anna said softly. "Of course, it was a lie, but at the time, I believed him. I wanted desperately to believe him."

Diane shook her head as she studied the watch in her hands. "Men like that know how to manipulate women."

Anna nodded. "Yes, they do. The watch he gave me is beautiful, but I hated it. Every time I wore it, it reminded me of that terrible day, and I'd feel shame and humiliation all over again. But if I didn't wear it, he'd ask where my watch was. I've often wondered if he gave it to me to prove he loved me, or to remind me of what he was capable of."

"The ultimate control," Diane said sadly. "I'm sorry he was like that. I know what it's like to be with a man who's abusive. My husband was verbally and emotionally abusive to me. I kept coming up with excuses for why he was lashing out. He was stressed at work, he didn't feel well, and so on. It took a while for me to realize he just wasn't a good man."

Anna reached out and held Diane's hand. "I'm sorry, dear.

I guess the women in our family aren't very good at choosing men."

A small chuckle escaped Diane's lips, and Anna laughed too. "I guess we aren't. Except the guy I'm with now is a pretty good one. Too good to be true, in fact."

The older woman smiled. "Then keep him. I know there are good men out there. William never dampened my belief that there is good in almost everyone."

Diane left later that afternoon with the wristwatch in her pocket and her mind swirling over everything Anna had told her. She had a good idea now why Anna killed her husband. Although, she still didn't know to what extent the abuse had gone. Anna had been an educated woman with the ability to support herself, so leaving William would have been the smartest thing to do. But Diane knew that wasn't always the easiest thing to do, either. Hadn't she also been an educated, self-sufficient woman? Yet she'd stayed in a bad marriage for seven years. Unless you knew everything, you really couldn't judge.

What Diane did know was Anna had been raised by a tough grandmother who'd done a good job of tearing down the young girl's self-esteem. And even though it sounded like her Auntie May had tried to build up her confidence, it's easy sometimes to lose it when the first person comes along who tells you you're worthless. Diane shook her head at this as she drove. Why were people so cruel?

Diane met Barry at a local pub for dinner, and they enjoyed greasy burgers, fries, and ice-cold beer. It was comforting returning to Barry after being so engrossed in Anna's sad story. Barry knew exactly what to say and do to lift her spirits.

"Maybe you could come next Sunday to meet Anna," she said as they ate. "I'm sure she would love meeting you."

"I'd really like that," he said, looking genuinely pleased she'd asked.

Barry had just paid the check when Diane received a call from Rosewood Senior Living where her mother lived. She quickly answered.

"Diane Martin?" the woman on the other end asked. "I'm calling to let you know that your mother, Joan Hartman, had a bad fall tonight and has been rushed to Mercy Hospital."

Diane's heart pounded. "How was she when she left?"

"She was talking and complaining about going, but she had terrible swelling on the side of her head, and we know she's taking a blood thinner medication. That can be dangerous if she starts bleeding. Can you meet her there? She did seem a little confused."

"Yes, yes. Of course. We're headed there now. Thank you." Diane turned to Barry. "Mercy Hospital. We have to get there quick." She explained what the attendant at the apartments had told her. "Any kind of fall can be dangerous."

"We'll be there in a few minutes," he said gently. "We'll come back for your car later." Barry reached over and squeezed her hand. That was what she loved about him. He was always there for her one hundred percent.

They arrived at the emergency entrance, and Barry dropped Diane off and went to park. She hurried inside and explained to the receptionist behind the counter who she was there to see. The woman checked and saw that Diane was Joan's emergency contact.

"Go through those doors, and the nurse at the desk will take you to her," she told Diane.

By the time Diane entered the small room where Joan was, her mother was sitting up in the bed and drinking a cup of juice.

"I told them they were making a bigger fuss than was necessary," Joan said as if she'd been expecting Diane. "I'm fine. I just fell and hit my head."

Diane sighed. Her mother could be so difficult at times. "How are you feeling?" she asked, noting the side of her face was already bruising.

"Fine. I was a little dizzy, so they gave me some juice, but I'm fine. I'm not bleeding to death or anything. They make such a fuss just because I'm old."

"Isn't that a good thing?" Diane asked. "At least you know people care what happens to you."

Joan snorted. "They just don't want to be sued. So, are you here to take me home?"

"I need to talk to the doctor in charge first," Diane told her. "You know, with the medicine you're on, you can bleed easily. And that bruise is pretty big."

"I just want to go home." Joan crossed her arms, and a big bruise showed on one arm. "Besides. It's all your fault I fell. I was digging out a box of pictures from the shelf of my closet when I tripped down the step ladder. I knew I should have just left well-enough alone."

It didn't surprise Diane that her mother was blaming her instead of herself. Joan never did any wrong. "I'm sorry you fell, but I'm interested in the pictures you have. Maybe we can look at them later this week."

The doctor came in then and said that she'd like to keep Joan overnight to continue to check her vitals. "It's a nasty bruise, but she should be fine. We took a scan when she arrived and didn't see any internal bleeding. But you can never be too careful with patients on blood thinners."

Diane agreed, but Joan put up a fuss.

"I don't want to stay the night. I'm fine, I tell you," Joan insisted.

"Mom. Please. Stay the night. I'll bring some things for you in the morning before work and pick you up afterward. I'll feel better if you're here."

Joan sighed heavily. "Fine. But I want Gladys to pick me up. I don't want to be here a moment longer than necessary."

Diane finally left at ten o'clock after her mother had been settled in a room and was getting sleepy. Poor Barry had waited for her the entire time in the waiting room. "I'm sorry you had to wait so long. Mom didn't want to stay, and then she complained the whole time she was being moved to a room. But as far as they can tell, she'll be fine."

"I didn't mind waiting," he said, draping his arm around her shoulders as they walked out the sliding door. "I had the easy part. You had to deal with Joan." He grinned.

"Next time I'll trade you," she said, smiling back. "I'm exhausted. Let's go home."

* * *

The next morning, Diane dropped off clean clothes and toiletries at the hospital for her mother and then called Gladys to ask if she'd be able to pick Joan up.

"I'd be happy to," Gladys said. "I'm glad they kept her overnight. You just never know at our age."

"Thanks, Gladys. You're a lifesaver. I'll drop by her place after work to check on her."

A little before four, Diane showed up at her mother's apartment with a bouquet of flowers and her mother's favorite oatmeal cookies from the bakery.

"How are you feeling?" Diane asked as she put the flowers in a vase.

"Like an idiot. Old people fall down. I refuse to be old."

Diane laughed. "Mom, you're not old. But you probably shouldn't be climbing step ladders when you're alone. Next time, ask me to do it."

Joan waved her suggestion away. "It was an accident." She looked at the flowers after Diane set them on the dining room table. "Pretty. That was nice of you. Let's have a cookie."

Diane set a plate of cookies on the table and made her mother a cup of coffee from her single-cup Keurig machine. As her mother sipped the hot drink, Diane noticed how dark and ominous the bruise on her face looked.

"Should you be putting a cold pack on that bruise for the swelling?" Diane asked.

"They did in the hospital. It is what it is. I look like I was in a boxing match. The guy across the hall asked me what the other guy looked like, and I said he was toast." Joan laughed. "It'll heal. I'll just be ugly for a while."

Diane studied her mother's face, trying to see any resemblance to Anna. It was hard to tell, though. Her mother's life of heavy drinking and smoking in her early years had really damaged her skin as she grew older. Where Anna's face was full and kind looking, her mother's was narrow, with frown lines deeply embedded. If Diane hadn't known Anna was Joan's mother, she'd never have guessed by their looks.

"Can I see the box of pictures that did this to you?" Diane asked.

"Might as well. I almost killed myself getting them." Joan pointed to the box on the coffee table, so Diane retrieved it and brought it to the table. It was just an old shoebox, with a rubber band around it. She pulled off the band and opened the lid. Inside was a pile of black and white photos mixed in with faded color ones.

"We should get a couple of photo albums to put these in," Diane said.

"Yuk! That's a job for my eighties. Not now."

Diane chuckled. She lifted out a few photos and immediately recognized her mother as a young girl standing with her brother, Matthew, and her Aunt Bernice. Her heart warmed. She'd adored her Uncle Matt. He'd always been such a kind soul. "How old are you in this picture?"

Joan slid on her reading glasses and stared at it. "I suppose I was about seven. That was Easter Sunday. We weren't church people, but we always had a big dinner on Christmas and Easter. Sometimes friends of the family would come over, or we'd go to their house. Occasionally my grandfather and step-grandmother would come for Easter before they headed back up to Canada. I wasn't a big fan of theirs, so I was glad they hardly ever came."

This piqued Diane's interest. She assumed since she'd mentioned Canada, they were William's parents. "Do you have any pictures of them?"

Joan pulled the box over toward her and searched through it. She pulled out one and handed it to Diane. It was in black and white and was of an elderly couple standing outside of Bernice's house in front of an older model car. The man looked like an older version of William, except balding, and he had a hawk-like nose. He also had a mean look in his eyes. The woman was shorter and very thin with blond hair cut in a bob. Her face was narrow, but she had big, round eyes.

"Is that Thomas and Mattie?" Diane asked.

Joan looked at her with raised eyebrows. "I suppose *she* told you their names. Yes, they were my dad's parents. I think that was around 1960. Mattie was his second wife. Her real name was Matilda, but she hated it. She wasn't so bad, but he was a really mean man. I stayed as far away from him as I could when they visited. He and Bernice would get into some awful fights, but she wasn't afraid of him. She stood up to him."

Diane could believe that. Bernice had been one tough lady, although she'd always been nice to Diane. "Did you ever visit their resort up in Canada?"

"I lived there when I was really young with my mom and dad for a short while, although I really don't remember much of it. I remember being scared to death of my grandfather, and my mother trying to keep me away from him, but that's it. You'll have to ask her why we lived there. I'm not sure."

This information surprised Diane. She was sure Anna would get to that part of the story at some point. If not, she'd ask her about it.

They looked through the photos a while longer. All were from her mother's years of living with Aunt Bernice and Uncle Jim. It looked like they had a pretty good life. Bernice and Jim had been decent parents. When Diane said that, her mother nodded.

"They were good to us. I think they were unable to have children of their own, so they were thrilled to have us come live with them. And even though they weren't well-to-do, they gave us everything we needed. Aunt Bernice could be quite strict, but I knew she loved me, and that was all that mattered."

"It's good they were able to take you both in," Diane agreed.

Joan began to look tired, and she still had to go down to dinner.

Diane started putting the pictures away. "Thanks for sharing these with me. I don't think I've ever seen them before."

"Yeah, well, I've never liked looking backward," Joan said. She slid the box back toward Diane. "If you want, you can let *her* go through these. I doubt if she cares, but she can see that our lives turned out fine. Maybe even better than if she'd been our mother."

Diane winced. She really liked Anna and thought she would have been a wonderful mother. She thought about how much Tonya had loved her for all she'd done for her. But then, Joan didn't know about Tonya. "You know, Mom. I'm sure Anna would love it if you visited her. Maybe you two could put the past behind you."

Her mother's face puckered. "No. She can look at the pictures, but I don't care if I ever see her. And you can tell her I said that."

"I just thought I'd mention it," Diane said softly. "Thanks for letting me take the pictures. I'm sure she'll love seeing them." She rose and went to put on her coat. "Please be careful. If you need anything, let me know."

Joan nodded. "My face will still look terrible by Friday. Maybe I can make up a list, and you can pick up my groceries. If you don't mind."

"I'd be happy to do that. I can bring dinner here, too, if you'd like."

"That would be good. The food here is okay, but not as good as going out."

Diane left with the box tucked under her arm. She hoped her mother would be more careful. Joan was stubborn, though. Diane suspected she got that trait from her father's side.

Diane called her daughter that evening after she and Barry

had eaten to tell her all the new information she'd learned about the family.

"It's weird that after years of knowing nothing about my family, I'm suddenly getting it from both Anna and your grandmother," Diane told her. "But I love hearing about it all. It really makes me think about genetics and how it runs through families."

"So, who do I get my brains from?" Natalie asked, laughing.

"Well, your father's a chemist, so I always thought you inherited your brains from him. But it sounds like my grandfather was very smart, too. Just not very socially adept, by the sounds of it."

"Didn't grandma say William's father was mean?" Natalie asked. "Maybe William learned to be abusive from his own father. He just didn't know any better."

"I think all abusers know better or else they wouldn't apologize afterward and promise to change," Diane said. Her husband had been the same way, but he never changed.

"True," Natalie said. "You'll have to see how the story continues for Anna. William obviously provoked anger from her at some point for her to kill him. Maybe he went too far one day, and she'd had enough."

"Yeah. It'll be interesting to hear her side of the story. All the newspaper reports said she'd pleaded guilty, and she never had to make a statement. But if she'd been abused, that should have been considered."

"Probably not in those days," Natalie said. "Women weren't exactly treated as first-class citizens."

"That's the truth. Some would argue they still aren't. I'd have to agree with that, too," Diane said. She remembered when she was younger, and the only professions women were encouraged to go into were nursing, teaching, secretarial, retail, or wait-ressing. She'd never been told she could be a doctor or a lawyer or own a business of her own. Or that she could be a principal of a school or even the superintendent. Thank goodness those views have changed. She'd become a teacher because she loved history and she'd had no other recourse except teaching it. Now, Diane wished she'd continued her education to teach at the college level. She still could, she just didn't know if she had the energy to go back to school while working full-time.

Diane talked with her daughter a little longer and then ended the call. She was looking forward to visiting with Anna again on Wednesday. As she went into the bedroom to get ready for bed, she saw Barry was already in there, reading.

"Do you think I'm letting Anna and her past take over my life too much?" she asked out of the blue.

Barry looked up with his brows raised. "Where did that come from?"

She sat on the bed beside him. "I was thinking of how much time I spend with her, and then my mother. You end up being here alone quite a lot. Do you mind?"

He smiled. "No, I don't mind. What kind of guy would I be if I thought you needed to spend every waking moment with me?"

"A stalker? A controller? A jealous person?" she offered with a grin.

"I don't want to be any of those things. Besides, you've just found out that you have a grandmother who you thought was dead. Of course, you want to spend a lot of time with her. I don't have a problem with it at all." He leaned over and gave her a kiss.

"Are you sure this isn't part of your master plan? To be the nicest guy in the world so I believe that you are and finally give in and marry you, and then you turn into a real monster. No one is as nice as you," Diane teased.

"Yes. It's all a part of my plan. Is it working?"

She laughed and stood up. "Perfectly." She walked to the bathroom to get ready for bed, her heart feeling light and a smile on her lips.

* * *

Wednesday afternoon, Diane arrived at Anna's door with the box of pictures tucked under her arm. Anna was sitting in her usual spot, waiting for her.

"I just had the nicest visit from Tonya and her sister again," Anna said, her face beaming with happiness. "And now you're here. This day just keeps getting better."

"I'm glad Tonya visited again. She sure adores you. I think that's so sweet."

"It makes me happy that I did something positive in my life," Anna said. "What's in the box?"

Diane took the band off the box and placed it on Anna's lap. "My mother gave these to me to show you. They're pictures of her and Matthew growing up with Aunt Bernice and Uncle Jim."

The older woman's hand fluttered to her chest, and her eyes widened. "Really? Oh, my. I'd love to see pictures of them as children." Carefully, she pulled out a few photos from the pile and began looking at them, studying each one before going to the next. Her eyes teared up. "Look at them. Aren't they beautiful?"

Diane found a box of tissues in the bathroom and placed it

on the table next to Anna. "Yes, they are. I looked at all these pictures on Monday with mom. She'd never shown them to me before. I was surprised when she said I could bring them here to show you."

Anna looked up at her after wiping the tears that had trailed down her cheeks. "That makes me so happy. Maybe, someday soon, she'll change her mind and see me."

Diane sighed. "I'm trying to talk her into it. I think it's going to take her a little more time. But this shows she's softening."

Anna nodded and returned to looking at the photos. "Joanie was always a tough cookie. Stubborn, too. But I thought that was good. A girl needs to be tough in this world. I was never tough enough to hold my own." She shook her head.

Diane knew what she meant. She'd never been a strong person either. And her brother had been the soft-hearted one. But as she grew older, Diane had learned to stand up for herself more.

"These are so precious. I'm thankful to be able to see them," Anna said. "I know Bernice hated me, but I was always grateful she loved my children." She shook her head. "I remember when I first told William I was expecting. He was so upset. I hadn't even realized he'd never wanted children."

"Really?" Diane hadn't given much thought to how William had felt about children.

"Yes. If it had been his choice, we would never have had kids. But I wanted them. Both were so precious to me. Unfortunately, things went downhill fast after we had them."

CHAPTER TWENTY

Anna - January 1950

Anna had been sick to her stomach since before Christmas, and by mid-January, she'd lost weight and looked peaked. Food wasn't appetizing to her at all. She had to hold her breath in order to cook eggs in the morning for William, or else she'd find herself running to the bathroom to throw up.

"You've probably picked up a bug," William told her. But Anna knew differently. She was only sick in the morning and then felt well enough in the afternoon to eat lunch. Tiredness and morning sickness spelled out one thing—Anna guessed she was pregnant.

The doctor confirmed it when she went in to be tested. Anna had taken the afternoon off from work and after her appointment, she walked slowly home, wondering how William would take the news. She knew he enjoyed their life just as it was—two professionals who were free to go out every night if they chose to. Unlike many men, he was proud that his wife worked and earned money. Surprisingly, he'd never asked her how much money she earned. But he'd also never offered to give her money to buy necessities. His earnings paid the rent and for their meals out, so she'd thought it was fair she bought groceries and house items with her money. She also saved twenty percent of her earnings as her Auntie May had taught her, and only dipped into that savings for special occasions like presents at Christmas and birthdays or an occasional new dress. But what would happen when she'd no longer be able to work after the baby was born? Would losing her income change their lifestyle to the point of upsetting William?

When Anna arrived home, she started dinner—a whole chicken with walnut stuffing and cooked carrots—and tidied up the apartment. She wondered where they'd put the baby's things in their small space. Would William offer to move them into a two-bedroom apartment once the baby was born? Could they afford it? As she gazed around, she took stock of their shabby furniture and few possessions. Even though William had a good position at work, he'd never suggested buying nicer furniture or upgrading their apartment. Was he saving money so they could one day own a house? She didn't know. Anna realized that she knew very little about what William wanted for the future.

He came home at the usual time, slipped off his jacket and tie, and sat on the sofa, relaxing. Anna quickly greeted him, hung his jacket, and brought him his bourbon and water.

"Something smells good," he said. "I'm glad we're eating in tonight. I'm bushed. All I do at work is butt heads with Carlton over every little detail of my project. It just riles me. We shouldn't even be on the same project—he should be off on one of his own. You can't have two people supervising. It causes trouble."

Anna sat quietly and listened to William complain. He'd

been complaining about work a lot lately, and she knew he was frustrated with Carlton. "I'm sorry it's going so badly," she said softly.

William smiled over at her. "You're a doll, you know that? Could you get me another drink?"

Anna did, and then they sat down to the delicious meal she'd made. She wanted to tell William about the baby, but not while he was angry about work. She thought that after they'd eaten, he'd be in a better mood.

After dinner, he had his fourth drink and sat back, looking more relaxed. Anna suggested he sit on the sofa while she cleared the table, and he did just that. After cleaning up the table and setting the dishes in the sink to soak, she went into the living room. William had lit a cigarette and was lying back on the sofa. She turned the radio on to a station with soft music and sat down beside him. He smiled lazily at her, his bourbon having put him in a good mood.

"You sure know how to cook a delicious dinner," he said. "How lucky am I?"

Anna took a deep breath. "I feel lucky too. You take good care of me, and we have a good life."

William leaned his head back and took a long drag of his cigarette. "Yeah. We do have a good life. And someday, it will be even better." He smashed out his cigarette butt in the ashtray and moved closer to Anna. "How about we go relax together?" he said, leaning in to kiss her neck.

Anna stiffened involuntarily. "I have something to tell you, dear," she said softly. "Something that I hope will make you happy."

"What's that?" He wrapped his arms around her and continued kissing her up to the back of her ear.

"We're having a baby."

William stopped and pulled back. "What?"

Anna bit her lip. "You know how I've been feeling sick for the past few weeks. I went to the doctor today, and he confirmed it. I'm pregnant. We're going to be parents."

William stood suddenly and ran his hand through his hair. He began pacing the floor. "Parents? You and me?" he stopped and glared at her. "How could you let this happen? I thought you were using something."

Anna was taken aback. She'd never thought of using any type of birth control because they were married. "No, I wasn't. I'm sorry. I hadn't thought of it." Fearful of his reaction, she began to shiver. She wrapped her arms around herself to try to quell the chill.

William started pacing again. "I'm not ready to become a father. We haven't even been married that long. I never even said I wanted children." He stopped again and stared directly at Anna. "How are we going to support a child? We barely have enough to live on as it is. And you won't be working anymore after the baby is born. How could you do this?"

Tears filled her eyes and rolled down her cheeks. Anna didn't dare say a word when William was agitated like this. Even though he'd promised never to hit her again, it still sat there in the back of her mind as something that could happen.

When she didn't answer, he grew even angrier. "How do you expect me to be a father? I never wanted to have children. My own father left my mother when I was a baby. He just left us to starve, and my mother had to support us during the Depression. How could I ever be a father when I never even had one?"

She had known his parents were divorced but hadn't known

his father had left when he was so young. "I'm sorry," she said softly. "I'm sure you would make a wonderful father."

"You're sure? You say you're sure?" he yelled at her. "Stop crying. I can't stand it when you cry!"

She quickly wiped away her tears, but more came. She couldn't help it. This was going so much worse than she'd expected, and she was frightened. When William became out of control like this, she had no idea how to calm him down.

William stormed into the bedroom and came out with his jacket. "I can't look at you right now. You're acting like a simpering fool." He slammed the door on the way out of the apartment hard enough to make the framed mirror on the wall fall and hit the floor with a thud. Anna dropped her head in her hands and wept.

A few minutes later, there was a light knocking on the door. Anna had been sobbing, and the knock startled her. She didn't want anyone to see her this way. Quickly, she found a clean handkerchief and wiped her face.

"Anna? Are you in there? It's Auntie May, dear."

Hearing a familiar voice was Anna's undoing. Without thinking, she quickly skirted the mirror that had fallen and opened the door. Her aunt stood there, looking concerned.

"Oh, dear. What's wrong?" Auntie May pulled her into a hug. "I heard the door slam and then a thud on the floor. I didn't want to intrude on your privacy, but I was worried."

"Oh, Auntie. I don't know what to do. William is so mad at me." Anna began sobbing again. She felt so lost after William's outburst. What if he was through with her? What would she do?

"Now, now, dear. It can't be all that bad. Let's go inside and talk." Auntie May shut the door and led Anna to the sofa.

"What happened? Did you have a fight?"

Anna wiped away her tears again with the handkerchief. "I told him I was expecting a baby," she said, her words shaky. "I had no idea how he'd react, but he was so upset, he stormed out of here."

"A baby?" May's face lit up. "Oh, honey. That's wonderful." She hugged her niece again, but then pulled back. "Why on earth would William be angry. Didn't he realize this could happen, for Pete's sake?"

"I think he's afraid to become a father," Anna said, calming down. "He didn't have a good family life. His parents divorced when he was a baby, and I don't think he gets along with his father that well. I tried telling him he'd be a good father, but he got so angry. He just stormed out of here." She shook her head. "Auntie, what will I do if he leaves me? How will I have this baby all by myself and raise it? I'm so scared."

May patted her hand. "Dear. I'm sure it won't come to that. William will take care of you in the end." She stopped a moment and studied Anna. "Unless there's more you haven't told me about. Are you two doing okay together? Is there any reason he'd leave?"

Anna couldn't tell her aunt that William had hit her once already and that she still feared he might do it again. She felt so ashamed about it as if it were her fault he'd hit her. And she knew it would only upset her aunt. She didn't like William already. "No. He's just had a tough time at work the last few weeks, and he's stressed. I guess it wasn't a good time to tell him about the baby."

May watched her a moment but kept her thoughts to herself. "Let's go into the kitchen, and I'll make us some tea," she said. "I'm sure William will come around."

They sat at the small kitchen table and drank tea, and Anna soon felt calmer. May helped her with the dinner dishes, then told her she needed her sleep and should go to bed.

"No matter what, you and the baby are the most important things right now," May told her. "And you know if anything ever happens, you can always come back and live with me. I'll make sure you're taken care of, dear."

Anna hugged her aunt before she left. "Thank you, Auntie May. I'm glad you came up. I feel so much better."

"Get some sleep, dear. I'll see you soon."

Anna was tired, and even though William hadn't come home yet, she changed into her nightgown and crawled into bed. Despite being upset, she fell into a deep sleep.

Much later, William stumbled into the bedroom and got into bed. Anna heard him but stayed curled up on her side. He never said a word to her, and soon he began to snore. Her heart sank. She hoped tomorrow would be better.

For the next two days, William almost completely ignored Anna. She ironed his trousers each morning and made his breakfast despite feeling queasy, but he didn't acknowledge her at all. After work, she'd wait for him to come home, but he didn't until late into the night, and she could smell that he'd been drinking. This was much worse than she'd thought it would be. She didn't dare try to talk to him because she was afraid to set him off. She walked on eggshells around him, hoping he'd come around soon.

Friday night, William came home from work with a bouquet of flowers. He was sober and looked contrite. Anna had also just arrived home and had expected to spend another evening alone when he surprised her.

"These are for you, for putting up with me this week,"

William said, handing them to her.

Anna bent over and sniffed the flowers. They were a mixture of brightly-colored blooms, and they smelled wonderful. "Thank you, sweetie," she said.

He drew closer and kissed her tenderly on the lips. "I'm sorry I've been such a louse," he said. He led her to the sofa, and she set the flowers on the coffee table so he could take her hand.

"I've been thinking a lot, and I can't believe I behaved that way toward you. Of course it wasn't your fault that we're having a baby. I had a lot to do with it too." He grinned.

She sat silent, not sure where he was heading with this.

"I never thought of myself as being a father. I think I was afraid I'd be a terrible one, just like my father. But then, I realized I was acting like an ass because I was afraid. I was actually turning into my miserable father. I'm sorry, doll." He pulled her close. "It might be fun, you know, having a little one. Maybe a little girl like you, so it doesn't cause a lot of trouble."

Anna smiled back at him. She was so relieved he'd come around about the baby. "You'll be a great father, dear," she said. "I know you will. And I'll do everything I can not to put the stress of the baby on you. I know we'll be earning less money once I have to leave my job, but until then, I'll save as much as I can so you won't feel too much of the burden."

"Hey, don't worry. We'll be okay." He kissed her again, and her fears melted away. Anna knew if they worked together, they could be the happy family she'd always dreamed of. At least, she hoped.

CHAPTER TWENTY-ONE

Anna — 1950

Two months after William declared he was looking forward to becoming a father, he came home from work with a big announcement.

"We're moving to Buffalo," he said, tossing his hat on the table and heading to the kitchen to make a drink.

Anna had just walked in from a long day at work and stared at him in shock. "We're what?"

He came out with a full glass and lit up a cigarette. "I quit my job today. I couldn't stand that idiot Carlton telling me what to do any longer. And Shipman was no help at all. He just kept siding with the jerk. I don't need to kowtow to those two. I'm smarter than the both of them combined."

It was late March, and Anna was four months pregnant, although she barely showed. She was always tired, though, and this sudden news hit her hard. She sat on the sofa and stared at William, dumbfounded. How on earth does one quit a meaningful career just because he couldn't get along with a co-worker? She didn't dare say that aloud, though.

"Buffalo in New York?"

William scoffed. "Where else?"

Anna didn't mention that there was a Buffalo in Minnesota, too. It would only make him mad. "Why Buffalo?" she asked, watching him closely for any signs of aggravation. She knew when he became agitated, she had to stop talking or asking questions, otherwise he might start yelling, or worse, slap her. He had just last month when she'd asked him why Carlton bothered him so much. He'd reached out and cuffed her, then ranted on about how she was supposed to support him and not question his motives. Of course, he'd apologized profusely the next day, but the damage had been done.

"There's an aircraft company there—Bell Aircraft—and they're hiring. So, we're heading there. My father works as a machinist for them and wrote that they were looking for engineers."

"Your father?" Anna was confused. "But, I thought he was building a resort in Canada?"

William sat on one of the dining room chairs. "You can't run a resort in the winter up there," he said, his tone condescending. "He comes down to the States to work each winter and then he'll be going up there in May to open the resort. I have a bunch of relatives from his side of the family in and around Buffalo. They're all a bunch of arrogant, stupid jerks, but they're his family. That's why he goes there."

Anna tried to absorb what William was saying. She didn't want to move to Buffalo, or anywhere for that matter. She liked Minneapolis. She wanted to be near Auntie May when she had her first child. Leaving would mean starting over again. She felt like she'd done that enough in her lifetime. But William was her husband, and she didn't feel she had a choice.

"When will we be leaving?" she asked, resigned to the fact that this was going to happen. "I'll have to give notice to my employers and pack up the apartment."

"Well, then you'd better get to work because I want to leave by Friday."

"Friday?" That was only two days away. "I need to give my employers at least two weeks' notice."

"They'll manage," he said offhandedly. "You can call them tomorrow with the news while you're packing up the place. You can't bring too much, though. We're going in the car, so we're only taking our clothes and essentials."

Anna didn't argue, but her mind was in a whirl. She hated doing this to the Larson brothers. They'd always been so kind to her, and this was how she was repaying them.

"Let's run down to the diner for some food," William said, as casually as if he hadn't just dropped a bomb on Anna moments before. "I'm hungry."

Anna followed him out of the apartment feeling completely lost.

* * *

The next two days were a whirlwind of activity for Anna. She called her employer and told them the news, apologizing profusely for such short notice. They were disappointed she was leaving so quickly but said they understood and wished her well. Later that day, as Anna was packing and organizing their meager household items, a messenger came from her office with an envelope. When she opened it, she was shocked to see that not only had the lawyers written her a check for her hours worked but had added two weeks' worth of wages to it as severance pay. They thanked her for her years of work and wished her the best. She wanted to break down into tears over their generosity but held back so William wouldn't see. She decided at that moment that she wouldn't tell him about the extra money. That, plus her meager savings, would be her secret. Anna didn't know why she felt that way, but she knew that she needed a little money of her own now that she wasn't working. Not only would she need to buy necessities for the baby, but she didn't trust that William wouldn't spend her money if he got his hands on it.

She felt terrible about not trusting him, but she couldn't help it.

William and a neighbor boy moved Anna's furniture back down to May's apartment as well as anything Anna couldn't bring along. William explicitly told Anna not to tell the building super that they were leaving. He said he'd take care of it. She didn't think much about it because she was too busy deciding what to take and what to leave.

By Thursday night, all was packed and ready to go. Anna went downstairs to see Auntie May one last time before leaving because William wanted to go early the next morning.

"I'm going to miss seeing you and the baby when it comes," May said sadly. "But your place is with your husband."

Anna's heart was heavy. Auntie May had been her safety net since she was a young girl. She loved her dearly, and even though they hadn't agreed on her marriage to William, she still wanted to be near her. But Anna had chosen her path when she'd insisted on marrying William, and now she was having his child, so there was no turning back.

"I'm going to miss you too, Auntie. But William says it's

only a train ride away, and maybe I can come to visit you once the baby is born."

"Or I could visit you," May offered.

As the two women hugged goodbye, May said gently, "You'll always have a room here with me if you need it, dear. Remember that."

A few months ago, Anna would have resented such a comment, but now, she appreciated it. She nodded, and the two women parted.

"Don't worry, Anna," William said that night in bed. He'd uncharacteristically curled up next to her and held her in his arms. "This will be an adventure. You're going to like Buffalo. It's a big, busy city, and Niagara Falls is right next door, and we can go see it. I promise you, we'll be happy there."

Anna felt comforted by his closeness. He rarely showed her affection these days, but it may have had to do with his stress at work. If he liked his new position in Buffalo, maybe they would become close again.

They drove away at five the next morning before anyone in the building was awake. After four days of riding on bumpy roads and staying at fleabag hotels, they arrived in Buffalo. It was dark out when they pulled up to the brownstone apartment building near downtown, where William's father had arranged for them to live.

Anna was exhausted from their long drive and didn't pay much attention to the surrounding area. They grabbed their essential bags and headed up the stairs to the third floor. She noticed the carpet on the stairs was threadbare, and the walls needed a fresh coat of paint. William knocked on the door of one of the apartments, and after a moment, an older man who looked very much like William answered.

"Well, there you are, finally," the man said. "Get your keister in here."

Anna followed William inside. The living room was dark, with only one lamp lit by the sofa, and the furniture looked even worse than William's furniture had. A thin woman with bleached-blond hair and dark roots styled in a bob was on the sofa, smoking a cigarette.

"Anna," William said after they'd set down their bags. "This is my father, Thomas, and his wife, Mattie."

Anna lifted her hand to Thomas. "It's nice to meet you, sir," she said.

Thomas laughed. "Good God! You've got yourself a princess here." He shook Anna's hand, smiling at her with tobacco-stained teeth. "Well, it's good to finally meet you too. And I hear you've already got a bun in the oven. The Craine men work fast."

Anna was stunned by his crude words. No one she'd ever known spoke like that in mixed company.

Mattie came over and studied Anna. "Ignore the old man," she said. "He's not used to polite society. My, but you are a pretty thing. It's nice meeting you, dear."

Anna smiled at her. The woman was shorter than she was, and her face showed age lines around her mouth and eyes. But she seemed kind. "Thank you."

"Let me get you two a drink," Thomas said, turning to a side table with liquor bottles and glasses on it. He poured a bourbon straight for William.

"Sheesh. At least put some ice in it," William said when his father handed him the glass.

"Pansy," Thomas said under his breath. "There's ice in the freezer." He turned to Anna. "What about you, dear? You want one?"

"No, thank you." All she wanted to do was go to their apartment and sleep.

Mattie motioned for Anna to sit on the sofa, and she did, relieved to be off her feet.

"You look tired, dear," Mattie said.

"I am. It was a long drive."

William came back from the kitchen. "Yeah. We should head to our apartment." He glanced at his father. "I hope it's furnished."

"I told you it was, stupid," Thomas snapped. He picked up a key from the table. "Here you go. It's two doors down from here."

As William drank his bourbon, Anna took a good look at Thomas. Although he and William definitely looked like father and son, she saw that Thomas was a couple of inches shorter and not as handsome. His hair was thinning, and he combed it straight back, and his nose was hawk-like, unlike William's narrow one. But what caught her off guard was Thomas's dark eyes. There was no humor in those eyes, just anger. They made her uncomfortable.

"Come on, doll," William said, setting down his glass. "Maybe the four of us can have dinner tomorrow night," he said to his father.

"Yeah. Sure." Thomas turned to Anna, who'd already stood and lifted her suitcase. "You get some rest, dear. We have plenty of time to get to know each other."

Anna smiled and nodded, then followed William out the door and down the hallway. He jiggled the handle a little with the key in it, and it finally opened. A musty smell greeted them before they even walked in.

"Just needs some airing out," William said. He flipped the

switch, and the overhead light came on.

Anna's heart sank. The apartment was dreary, with torn and scratched furniture, threadbare carpets, and dirty walls. She dropped her bag, disappointed in the sagging gray sofa with stains, the armchair with a tear on the seat and stuffing oozing out, and the small dinette table with huge scratches across the top.

"Well, it isn't the Ritz, that's for sure," William said. "But don't worry, doll. After you work your magic on it, the place will be fine."

William's upbeat attitude stopped her from making any comments. Maybe, after she had some sleep, she'd feel more optimistic. Anna walked into the bedroom and cringed. The mattress was lumpy, and there were no sheets or blankets on it. It was stained by God knows what, and the thought of lying on it made her nauseous. When she walked into the adjoining bathroom, she stifled a scream. A huge cockroach scuttled across the floor when she turned on the overhead light bulb.

William was quicker than the bug and stomped on it. "Damn little scavengers," he said. "Don't worry, baby doll. We can get some spray in the morning."

Anna remained silent. The bathroom was tiny and dirty, and the thought of using it before she gave it a good cleaning made her stomach turn.

"I'll run down and grab the box of bed linens," William said, trying his best to be helpful. "We'll get some sleep. Tomorrow this will all look better." He leaned over and kissed Anna on the cheek. It was one of the sweetest things he'd done in a while, and it made her feel better.

"You're right. We can fix this up and make it our home," she said, encouraged by his positive attitude.

"That's my girl," he said, smiling brightly.

That night, Anna had to force herself to lay on the old mattress despite the fresh sheets that had been put on it. William had also flipped it over, which helped a little. He'd killed two more cockroaches, and it made her skin crawl, thinking of those disgusting bugs scuttling around while she slept. Anna had never lived in such a dirty, dreary place in her life. Even growing up on the farm, her grandmother had been a stickler for cleanliness, and the house was always scrubbed clean. The Hansons house in Walker had always been pristine, and Auntie May's apartment had been spotless too. Anna had never been wealthy or lived a high lifestyle, but this was so far below what she was used to that her heart ached. She missed their old place and Auntie May desperately.

"This will all be better in the morning," William said, hugging her close before he fell into a deep sleep. Anna hoped he was right.

The next morning, the place didn't look any nicer, but Anna felt better after getting some sleep. William ran out to buy cleaning supplies and roach spray and brought up the carpet sweeper Anna had packed in the car. She quickly went to work scrubbing the bathroom, and William took care of spraying for roaches.

The kitchen had looked as dumpy as the rest of the place, but Anna didn't let it get her down. She cleaned and scrubbed it as best she could and washed out all the cabinets. She wanted to put paper on the shelves before she set anything in them. She planned to buy more supplies the next day once she'd made a list of what she needed.

Anna covered the sofa with the slipcover she'd had at the other apartment, and she polished the furniture. She would try to fill in the scratches with Old English Stain later.

At lunchtime, Mattie brought over sandwiches and sodas from the diner where she worked as a prep cook each morning. "I figured you two wouldn't have any food in here yet," she said, handing the bag to Anna. "There are fresh cookies in there too."

Anna was so touched by her thoughtfulness, she hugged her. "This was so sweet of you," Anna said. "Thank you."

Mattie seemed taken aback by Anna's hug. "It's nothing. We're family. Family helps each other." She left then saying she needed a good nap because she woke up at five every morning. "We'll see you two for dinner tonight," Mattie said on her way out.

After Anna and William ate, he went with her to pick up groceries. As she stepped out of the building, Anna was surprised at how busy the street was and how crowded the neighborhood looked. Cars and busses rushed along the street, and there were businesses and bars close to their apartment building.

"I hadn't realized how busy this town was," she said to William as they walked down the sidewalk.

"It is, that's for sure. There's quite a lot of industry here, and then it also gets tourist traffic for Niagara Falls."

William knew the area well because he'd lived there before, so he showed Anna where the butcher shop and grocery store were. On the way, he pointed out the hardware store, too. There was a multitude of other little shops everywhere, as well as a laundromat just a few shops down from their building. Anna was thankful for that.

By late afternoon, Anna was so tired she thought she'd pass out. William had brought up all the boxes and suitcases, and she'd unpacked what she absolutely needed first. The place was starting to look better, although it still looked shabby. She knew she'd have to work hard to make it look even half as good as their old place.

"See, what did I tell you? It's already shaping up," William said when they both dropped onto the sofa from exhaustion.

"It is looking better," she agreed, trying to be positive. "Do you think we should paint the walls to brighten it up?"

"Let's leave it for now," he said. "They should have done that before renting it out. Maybe washing the walls would help."

Anna nodded. She was so tired she couldn't even think of cleaning one more thing.

That evening, they walked down to a small diner and ate dinner with Thomas and Mattie. Anna wasn't sure what she thought of the older couple. Mattie was likable enough, but Thomas had a foul mouth and was quick to criticize everyone and everything. The waitress was too slow, the food cold, or the coffee wasn't strong enough. He bragged about his job at Bell Aircraft and how he had a lot of pull there since he'd worked there during the war when it was even busier.

"I made thousands of parts for fighter planes that went overseas with these two hands," he said proudly, displaying his large, grease-stained hands. He was missing half of his right ring finger, but Anna didn't ask why. She didn't want to hear the gory details.

"Yeah, well, I was doing the same thing at Lockheed Aircraft in California," William said, not impressed by his dad's bragging. He turned to Anna. "I lied about my age and was hired when I was sixteen. The factory there was covered with a burlap tarp that had been painted to look like a quiet neighborhood. They even put rubber vehicles on it. From the sky, it was pretty realistic. It protected us from being bombed."

"That's interesting," Anna said, clearly impressed. She hadn't known he'd worked there during the war.

Thomas waved his hand at him as if to dismiss his words. "Braggart. Who was the one who got you started as a machinist, eh? If you hadn't been working with me for two years, you'd never have worked at your fancy Lockheed."

Anna could see that there was no love lost between these two men, which made it seem odd that Thomas had found William a job. Mattie was quiet for the most part, sitting there eating her meal. Anna thought the older woman was overdressed for a diner. She was wearing sparkly jewelry, a fancy dress, and a thick coat of make-up.

After they'd eaten, Thomas suggested stopping at a bar down the street. Anna was exhausted from her long day, but William didn't seem to notice. He was all too happy to get a nightcap.

The place was crowded and loud, with jazz music blaring from the stage in the corner. Thomas and Mattie waved to people they knew as they made their way to a small table shoved in the corner. People streamed over to them, and Thomas introduced his son and daughter-in-law to multiple people, yelling over the music to be heard. Anna overheard bits and pieces of conversation about "the good ole' days" and "running liquor for Capone during prohibition." William had told her once that his father had bootlegged alcohol over the border but hadn't mentioned it was for Al Capone. She couldn't even imagine it.

Two hours later, Anna finally begged William to take her home. "I'm so tired. Please let's go."

"Sure, doll," he said, his words slurred. "I have to get up early tomorrow anyway."

They headed out on foot, leaving Thomas and Mattie behind. The older couple was having too much fun with their friends to notice they'd left.

"How are your father and Mattie going to get up for work tomorrow after being out so late?" Anna asked William as they walked along the busy sidewalk. Cars were still buzzing by on the street, and people were milling around everywhere. Anna was surprised at how busy the streets were at this time of night.

"Ah, he can drink all night and work all day. He's always been like that. He and Mattie used to close down the speakeasies in their day." He chuckled.

"Is it true he ran liquor for Al Capone?" Anna asked in a hushed voice.

"Half his stories are either lies or exaggerated. He did run liquor over the border but for some two-bit gangster, not Capone. He just likes sounding more important than he is."

When they arrived back at the apartment, William tossed his clothes on the floor and crawled into bed. Anna was bone-tired, but she still picked up his suit and carefully hung the jacket. Then she quickly started up the iron on the drop-down ironing board and pressed his trousers. She'd learned her lesson after that one time and had never gone to bed again without making sure his trousers were wrinkle-free for the next day.

When Anna finally crawled between the sheets, she lay there a while, thinking about how their life had changed in less than a week. Buffalo wasn't like Minneapolis, but she knew she'd get used to it eventually. She had no choice.

As she lay there, she felt tiny fluttering butterflies in her stomach. Anna placed a hand on her belly. She felt the movement again, even though it was just a flutter. Anna smiled. Her baby was moving. The little life inside her was letting her know everything was going to be okay. With that sweet thought, she fell asleep.

CHAPTER TWENTY-TWO

Diane

"My mother said that her grandfather Thomas scared her," Diane said after Anna had stopped speaking. Diane had turned off her recorder and slipped it in her pocket. It was almost time for Anna to go to dinner, so she knew she'd be leaving soon.

"He could be a scary man," Anna said, staring down at her folded hands. "He had no qualms about raising his voice or hitting someone. After meeting him, I understood where William's temper came from. It wasn't an excuse, but it made sense."

"You were raised by a grandmother who insulted and hit you, but you didn't turn out that way," Diane said gently.

Anna nodded. "That's true. It just wasn't in my nature. My father and brother had been gentle souls, and I think that's what influenced me. I guess some people are just angrier than others."

"I suppose," Diane said. "It seems to me William wasn't as confident as he portrayed and that his insecurities were what prompted his anger. He was drawn to you for your calmness and the sense of security you gave him, yet those traits were also what caused him to lash out at you."

"I've had a long time to think about my life, and I came to the same conclusion. What drew him to me, he also hated me for. Because he wanted to be that way, but just couldn't."

Diane thought about her ex-husband, Jeffrey, and realized that was true of their relationship too. She'd always been self-confident but not in a showy way. Jeffrey, however, showed his confidence by tearing someone else down, because deep down inside, he didn't really believe in his abilities.

Diane waited until Max arrived and then pushed Anna down to the dining room before saying goodbye. Once Diane was home, she found Barry at her desk, working on the school budget for spring. His half-moon glasses sat low on his nose as he concentrated on the computer screen. Diane smiled at the sight of him. If ever a more peaceful man than Barry existed, she'd never met him. Barry was the ultimate in serenity.

"I'm back," she said, pulling off her coat.

Barry turned around, looking startled. "I didn't even hear you come in. I was so engrossed in this budget—it's riveting." He smiled at her, and she laughed.

"I'm sure it is. What were your thoughts about dinner?"

"Let's just order in. Your choice." He stood and stretched his long frame, then kissed her lightly. "How was your afternoon with Anna?"

"I'll tell you while we eat. Go back to work, and I'll let you know when the food arrives."

Later, they sat down to boxes of Chinese food, taking portions from each container and filling their plates.

"Have you had time to listen to some of Anna's recordings?"

Diane asked Barry. Anna had said she was fine with Diane sharing her recordings with family.

"I've listened to most of them," he said. "She sure has had a sad and interesting life."

"And she has so much more to tell, by the looks of it. It seems as if my grandfather wasn't one to settle down."

"Some people just can't," Barry said.

Diane watched Barry a moment. "Anna and I were discussing why William had a temper. It seems my great-grandfather had one too. And even my mother mentioned she'd been scared of William's father when she was a little girl. Do you think a temper is inherited or learned?"

Barry stopped chewing a moment as he thought, then swallowed down his food. "Your mother has a temper. Sometimes her foul moods don't even make sense. But you don't, and from what you've said, your brother was even more soft-hearted than you."

Diane set her fork down. "So, what are you saying? That if it's a learned behavior, then I should be angry, too?"

Barry shrugged. "I truly don't know. All I'm saying is you don't have to become an angry person just because you were raised by angry people. A lot of things can bring up anger—stress, frustration, feelings of inadequacy, failure. Mostly it seems it's all in how the person feels about themselves."

"Why aren't you ever angry?" Diane asked. "You must get frustrated at work."

"What will anger accomplish? I grew up in a very calm family. No one had anything to prove, I guess. My parents both had college degrees and were confident people. Anger solves nothing. And working with young children like I do, anger would be a detriment. A sense of humor, however, is necessary."

He winked at her.

Diane laughed. "If I didn't have a sense of humor working around teenagers, I'd go crazy."

Barry looked thoughtful for a moment. "Do you think your mother's life would have been better or worse if Anna hadn't killed her father?"

The question took Diane by surprise. "Where did that come from?"

"Well, your mother is angry and moody. Could be she inherited it, or it could be a result of losing both parents that fateful night. But, by the sound of it, William wasn't all that nice of a guy. Do you think her life would have been better if she'd grown up with an angry father?"

"Personally, no. I don't think it would have. But I think my mother believes that it would have been better. Aunt Bernice didn't help any by spewing her hatred of Anna."

"It's a complicated situation, that's for sure," Barry said. He'd finished eating and stood to rinse his plate in the sink. Diane followed him.

"I'm trying to figure out if you have a message in there somewhere," she said, handing him her plate to rinse.

He chuckled. "I wouldn't press your mother too much about seeing Anna. It might not help either of them to see each other. But as long as your mother is willing to talk, that's good. She's never had a chance to express her feelings about what happened. Maybe it would be good for her to do that."

Diane leaned back against the kitchen counter. "I hadn't thought about it that way. But you're probably right. Since she wasn't allowed to talk about her parents around Aunt Bernice, she probably never processed any of it. That's a lot of decades of holding in anger."

"That's what I was thinking," Barry said.

She eyed him. "Okay, Freud. Can you also explain why my mother had terrible taste in men? And me, too?"

He laughed. "That one I'll have to think about some more. As for you, I think your taste in men has gotten much better." He kissed her as she laughed.

* * *

On Friday, Diane left school and headed for the grocery store with her mother's list in hand. Afterward, she picked up dinner for them both at the Olive Garden, then drove to Joan's place.

"The food smells good. I'm hungry," Joan said as way of greeting when Diane came in. By the time Diane had brought in the rest of the bags, Joan had set out plates and silverware.

"We can put the groceries away later," Joan said. "Let's eat."

As Diane sat down, she noticed that the bruise on her mother's face had turned an ugly shade of yellowish-green. "How does your head feel?"

"Ugly," her mother said. "Fine. I don't have any headaches or anything."

"That's good. That was a nasty fall." The two women ate their pasta and breadsticks in silence before Diane spoke up again. "Anna appreciated seeing the photos from your childhood. I let her keep them this week to look through."

"That's good," Joan said without much enthusiasm.

"I was wondering. What made you dig out that box of pictures? I've never seen them before, and you rarely talk about your childhood."

Her mother stopped eating and stared at her. "Honestly? I wanted her to see that I had a childhood without her. To spite her, I guess. I've never talked much about my childhood because then the questions of why I lived with my aunt and uncle would have come up. My father's death wasn't something I wanted to discuss. But now, it's no secret anymore."

"The truth never goes away completely. It eventually rears its ugly head until it's let out," Diane said.

Joan studied her. "And what truths have you been hiding?"

"None. I've always been honest and upfront about my childhood and my bad marriage. I see no reason to hide the truth. It just causes grief for everyone," Diane said.

Her mother snorted. "Your childhood may not have been perfect, and I may not have been the ideal mother, but I never killed anyone." She returned to eating her dinner.

Diane chuckled. "Well, that's true enough."

They finished eating, and Diane helped her mother put away the groceries.

"I wonder," Joan said, her words trailing off.

"What?"

She turned to Diane. "I wonder how many actual truths and how many lies Anna has told you."

"Why would she lie to me?" Diane asked, frowning. "She has nothing to lose at this point."

Joan shrugged. "Why tell the truth now? She can die knowing only her side of the story was told. There's no one left to say otherwise."

"There's you," Diane said.

"I was a little girl. I don't know or remember what went on between them."

"You must remember something. You were five years old. You must have a few memories that you've hidden away."

Joan shook her head. "If I did have them, they're gone now.

That's why I've never wanted to talk about my childhood. I don't want to dredge up that part of it."

Diane left a while later, wondering what her mother actually saw as a child that she wanted so badly to stay locked away. Had she seen her father abuse Anna? Had she been abused? Sadly, Diane felt she'd never know.

But her mother's accusation that Anna could lie and no one would ever know wouldn't leave Diane's thoughts.

* * *

Sunday arrived and was another blustery day with snow falling. Diane asked Barry if he'd like to visit Anna with her, and he jumped at it.

"I can't wait to meet her," he said. "I hope she'll tell more about her story while I'm there."

"I'm sure she will," Diane said.

When they arrived, Anna was sitting in her wheelchair in the sunroom, watching the snow swirling outside.

"Oh, my," she said, smiling when she saw the two of them. "How lucky am I to have you both here? I thought you might not come with this snow outside."

"It'll take more than a little snow to keep me away," Diane said, bending down to hug Anna. "This is Barry. He's been asking to meet you. I hope you don't mind my bringing him."

"Heavens no. I'm delighted to meet you, Barry." Anna held out her hand, and they shook, and she folded her other hand over his. "My, but aren't you handsome. You two make a lovely couple."

"Thank you," Barry said, grinning. "I tell Diane that all the time." He winked at Anna.

Anna laughed. They chose to sit in one corner of the sunroom. Other residents were in there, too, visiting with family, and no one seemed to be paying any attention to the three of them.

"It was such a delight to look through Joanie's photos. I've looked at them every day since you left them. The box is in my room, ready for you to return them to her. Please tell her how thankful I am that she sent them over," Anna said, her eyes bright with happiness.

It pleased Diane that she'd thought to bring them since they gave Anna such joy. "I'll be sure to tell her."

"Do you think she's softening at all about coming to see me?" Anna asked.

It broke Diane's heart to see her looking so hopeful. "I think she's getting closer to it," she said. "The fact that she pulled down those pictures and let you see them tells me she's thinking about it."

Barry looked over at Diane with his brows raised, but she looked away quickly. She had no idea if her mother was thinking about seeing Anna, but she didn't want to squash Anna's hope.

"I hope she will, eventually. The very last time I saw her wasn't under the best of circumstances. I'd like to see her at least one more time before I leave this earth," Anna said.

"You mean when she was five years old?" Diane asked.

The older woman's face creased. "Oh, no, dear. I saw Joanie once more, twenty years later. She would have been twenty-five. She came to my parole hearing with Bernice in 1980. I sat across from them in the small room, and Joanie wouldn't even look at me. It was a sad day. Her hatred for me was palpable."

"She went to your parole hearing?" Diane couldn't believe

what she was hearing. Why hadn't her mother told her about it?

"Yes, dear. Sometime around the late seventies, a young woman fresh out of law school had heard about my case and decided to help me get out of prison. I never asked her to—as far as I knew, I was in for life. I think she was trying to make a name for herself. Anyway, she managed to get me a hearing because of the circumstances under which I shot William. Bernice came to testify against me and brought Joan along to do the same. It broke my heart, hearing Joan say I had planned the murder of her father, and I didn't deserve to ever get out. I was sure Bernice had coached her, but it didn't matter. The parole board refused my release, and after that, I never went to another parole hearing to defend myself. I just couldn't bear to think of Joan there, saying such things against me." Her eyes filled with tears. Diane grabbed a box of tissues nearby and handed them to her.

"I had no idea my mother attended one of your parole hearings," Diane said, anger welling up inside her. "How could she do that to you?"

Anna placed a hand on her arm. "She didn't realize what she was doing, dear. She was there to support Bernice, I suppose. She wouldn't even look me in the eye. It broke my heart, but I couldn't blame her. She was right about one thing—I killed her father. That was all that mattered."

Diane sat back in her chair, dumbfounded by this new information. Barry moved closer to her and wrapped his arm around her waist. Every time she thought she understood her mother, she was sideswiped by something new. So many secrets. It drove her crazy.

"I probably shouldn't have brought it up," Anna said, looking regretful. "Please don't blame your mother. Bernice had always hated me for some unknown reason, and after William's death, she had a good reason. I'm sure Joanie did it for Bernice."

Diane nodded. She didn't want to upset Anna any further by fuming over her mother's actions.

"Should we go back to my apartment and get something to drink and visit there?" Anna asked. "I'm not sure if this is a good place to talk." She glanced around where the others were sitting. Diane understood. Too many ears.

Barry pushed Anna's wheelchair while Diane went down to the dining room to get iced tea for all of them. They found another chair for Barry to sit next to Diane, and the three of them sat in a cozy circle.

"Where did I leave off last time?" Anna asked, looking up at Diane.

"You'd just moved to Buffalo."

"Aw, yes. Buffalo. Not the happiest of times for us, except for one thing. Joanie was born, and that changed my life."

CHAPTER TWENTY-THREE

Anna — 1950

William was given a position at Bell Aircraft but not the one he'd expected. They offered him a machinist job, something he had experience in but not a job he wanted to do. It didn't pay as well, and he felt it was underneath his skill level. But he had to earn money, so he went into work grudgingly.

Anna was dismayed to learn from Auntie May that William hadn't paid the last two months' rent on their apartment before leaving. The superintendent had complained to May about it. It embarrassed Anna because she'd lived there for years, and she hated to be thought of as dishonest. But she knew she couldn't say anything to William about it because it might trigger his anger. Anna wrote to May and told her to take the money out of her savings account to pay the back rent, but May told her not to. "You may need that money for yourself someday," her aunt had written back. "The owner of the apartment will be fine." Still, it was yet another dishonest move from William that bothered Anna.

Despite that, Anna settled in and did her best to make the

shabby apartment a home. Anna met the woman across the hall one warm day when she'd opened all the windows and the door to get a breeze in the apartment. Out in the hallway, children were running around and playing, and the door across the way was open, too.

"I hope they're not bothering you," a woman with a thick New York accent said as Anna watched the children play. "I'm trying to work, and I can't take them to the park to run off steam."

"I don't mind at all," Anna said. "They're just having fun." She introduced herself and learned the women's name was Edith Lewis, and her husband was Martin. Edith looked to be in her late thirties, even though gray strands were already winding through her hair. "What type of work do you do?" Anna asked.

"I sew for people. Repairs, new clothes, hems. Just about anything people need. I get a lot of alteration work from the department store downtown and the dry cleaners."

"I love to sew, but I don't own a machine," Anna said. "My aunt has a wonderful Singer machine. I grew up doing all types of tatting, crocheting, and knitting, too."

"If you ever want to make extra money, let me know. I have people wanting lace collars repaired or new ones made. I'm not one to do that delicate work myself," Edith said. "I don't have the patience."

Anna hadn't thought about doing anything to make extra money, but she liked the idea. "Thanks. I'll consider it."

Edith studied Anna a moment, making her feel uncomfortable. Anna was now over five months pregnant, and her clothing was getting tight. She knew she had to buy some maternity wear, but she didn't want to ask William for the money. He already got testy when she asked for grocery money each week, plus money for the dry cleaners and laundromat. Anna still had some money tucked away from her past paychecks, but she wanted to use that for baby items. Her savings account she'd had before meeting William was still at the bank in Minneapolis. She didn't want to touch that unless she absolutely had to.

"I hope you don't mind me saying so, but you look like you're expecting," Edith said. "And you could use something that fits."

Anna felt the heat of a blush in her cheeks. "I am expecting. I was hoping to wait as long as possible before buying any clothes. I hate to waste money."

"Hmm," Edith said. She looked from her two children to Anna again. "I'll make you a deal. If you'd take the children to the park an hour or so two times a week, I'll make you a couple of maternity dresses. I can make loose ones that you can belt after the baby is born, that way they'll get more use."

Anna loved the idea. "That would be wonderful. I'd love to take the kids to the park."

Edith waved her into the apartment to take her measurements. She let Anna go through a pile of material to pick what she liked. Anna chose a soft, blue and white print material and red fabric with tiny white flowers on it.

"I can whip these up really quick for you. And I'll make matching tie belts, too. The red one would look nice with a lace collar if you have one," Edith said.

The next day, Anna walked the two blocks over to the park with the children, Linda and Ronald. At ages five and seven, they were an easy age to watch, and Edith promised her that they behaved well. Edith had been right. The kids stayed within Anna's sight from the park bench she sat on as they played on the swings, bars, and teeter-totter. It was a busy place with many other children and mothers, and after a few days of bringing the children there, Anna met some of the other mothers.

"Your children are very well-behaved," one woman with two young boys told Anna. "And I see you have another on the way. You'll be terribly busy."

Anna laughed. "The two are my neighbor's children. I'm expecting my first."

As Anna chatted with the woman, her friend came over too, and both women gave Anna advice on where she could find the best deals on baby furniture as well as baby clothing.

"Who's your doctor?" The first woman asked.

"I don't have one yet," Anna told them, and they both looked shocked.

"Well, I'm glad we ran into you then. I know the best doctor. You'll love him." She found a pen and paper in her purse and wrote down his name and which hospital he worked at. "You should make an appointment soon for a check-up, and then he can be your designated physician," she told Anna. "Believe me, you don't want just anyone delivering your baby."

Anna thanked them for the advice, and when she brought the children back to Edith's apartment, Anna asked her about the doctor they'd suggested.

"Oh, I've heard good things about him. I didn't have my kids here, so I don't know him personally, but other women I know really like him." Edith had just finished both dresses for Anna and was just touching them up with the iron.

Anna loved the dresses. Both had large buttons going down the front and cute tie belts. She immediately tried on the blue one, and it fit perfectly.

"Thank you so much," she told Edith, giving her a hug. "I love these dresses."

"Oh, it was nothing, dear. In fact, if you keep taking the kids to the park, I thought I'd make you a couple of smock tops to wear with skirts or capri pants. I could even make a matching skirt with a stretch panel. What do you think?"

"You're too kind. I enjoy bringing the kids to the park. It's nice to be outdoors," Anna told her.

"Wait until July and August, dear. It won't be much fun then," Edith warned.

That night, Anna wore the new blue print dress when William came home from work. As she served dinner, she waited for him to notice her dress, but he just ate and complained about work.

Anna was disappointed. Over the past few months, since they'd moved there, William had practically ignored her. Almost every night after dinner, Thomas and Mattie stopped by, and he'd go off with them to the bar for a few hours. After the first two weeks, Anna had stopped going along. She was too tired in the evenings to go out, and sometimes William would be out until midnight or one. Anna spent the evenings alone, listening to the radio and knitting baby booties or adding lace or embroider to simple baby gowns she'd purchased. She was also hand-sewing a quilt for the baby made of scraps of fabric Edith had given her. Each panel had an embroidered animal on it that Anna had created.

Anna was unhappy about the influence Thomas and Mattie had over William. She wished he stayed home more. She'd come to realize that his parents were all about being showy on the outside but had no real character. Thomas liked to pretend he had money to throw around, and Mattie followed suit by wearing expensive clothing and jewelry, most of which had obviously been purchased years ago. But their apartment was basically a dump, and they both had to work hard to keep up the pretense that they were rich. William always talked big about buying a house someday and having nice things, but he spent money just as freely as Thomas did for dining out or drinking, then had none left over for essentials. It scared Anna because all she'd ever wanted was to feel secure.

But Anna knew that Mattie had a kind side as well. She worked from five to eleven each morning and would bring Anna lunch from the restaurant several days a week for free, as well as fresh bread and rolls. They'd often eat lunch together at Anna's kitchen table, and Mattie would tell her stories about what had happened at the bar with their friends the night before. Anna appreciated Mattie's generosity and did enjoy their lunches together. She was an entirely different person when she wasn't around Thomas.

"The resort will force Thomas to settle down, at least during the summers," Mattie said one day as they sipped Coca-Colas and ate sandwiches. Mattie had her hair tied back with a folded scarf and wore capris and a sleeveless, button-up shirt. The shirt emphasized how thin her arms were. "He'll be bogged down with work, as will I, but I don't mind. I cook at the restaurant, and I'll do the same at the resort. The difference is we'll be working for ourselves, and we like that."

"I often think William would like it better if he worked for himself," Anna said. "He's not very happy with the machinist job right now. I hope they offer him an engineering position soon."

Mattie laughed as she lit a cigarette and sat back. "William's doing exactly what he's trained for, so I don't know what he's complaining about."

Anna stared at Mattie, confused. "But he has an engineering degree. That's what he should be doing."

"Is that what he told you?" Mattie asked.

"Yes. From the university here in Buffalo."

Mattie laughed even harder. "Darling, that boy never even finished high school, let alone attended a university. He's got an eighth-grade education. Everything he knows has been learned on-the-job, and he's lucky he's passed himself off as more than he is."

Anna was stunned. Another lie. She felt as if she hardly knew William at all.

Mattie kindly touched Anna's arm. "I'm sorry, dear. I thought you knew. I guess I shouldn't have blown William's cover. He's a sneaky one, that man. But smart, too. I mean, you'd have to be smart to be able to work as an engineer with no training at all. He's a quick learner, and I think he has a photographic memory. Unfortunately, he lets it all go to his head."

Anna just nodded, not sure what to say. She'd thought William was a college graduate with a good future ahead of him. Now, she wasn't so sure what their future held.

In May, Thomas and Mattie left for Ontario, Canada, to open their resort. Things were pretty quiet after they'd left, but William still went out in the evenings. Anna had no idea what he was doing or who he was out with. He said it was important that he go out after work with his co-workers, but she knew that wasn't true. To keep the peace, she didn't complain and filled her time with other things.

Just as Edith had warned, July was hot and muggy. Anna took the kids to the park to try to cool off, but it was getting harder to get around now that she was eight months pregnant.

She felt like a whale, and the heat didn't help. Feeling sorry for her, Edith had made her a sleeveless dress out of blue and white striped cotton fabric. Anna wore it on her walks and even to sit on the fire escape balcony outside the kitchen's back door to cool off. A month before, she'd made an appointment with Dr. Rickman, who'd been recommended to her, and she was pleased with him. He was an older gentleman with a calm disposition. Her exam went well, and the baby's heartbeat was strong, which she was relieved to hear.

Auntie May had offered to pay for the baby's bassinette as a gift. She sent Anna a check, and Anna went out and bought a white bassinette on a rolling stand so she wouldn't have to bend over too far after the baby was born. She'd also bought linens and blankets for the baby, as well as dozens of diapers. Anna couldn't afford a diaper service, so she'd needed several, so there were enough between trips down to the laundromat.

Now that she was almost due to have the baby, Anna missed her Auntie May dearly. Even though her aunt had no experience with young children, just having her gentle presence around would have helped. She was happy that she'd met Edith and the two women at the park. It was nice having friends again.

Late one night in August, about a week before she was due, Anna heard William come stumbling into the apartment, drop his clothes on the floor, and fall into bed. She detected a sweet scent, overpowering the smell of alcohol. Anna's heart clenched. William had come home many times before with that same fragrance on his clothes, and he'd just brushed it away. He claimed that many of the women in the bar wore too much perfume, and it attached to his clothes. She knew he was lying—as he'd lied about so many other things before—but tonight, it hit her like a slap in the face.

Exhausted, she slipped out of bed to hang his jacket and trousers and put his shirt in the laundry basket. She did this each night, no matter how late he came in. Anna would iron his trousers in the morning before making breakfast in case he wore the same suit again.

As she went to place his white shirt in the basket, she saw a dark stain on it. Going to the bathroom, Anna closed the door and turned on the light. A smear of make-up stained the collar, and the shirt reeked of another woman.

Anna knew that William had a huge sexual appetite. Because he hadn't touched her since she'd become pregnant, she was realistic enough to know he wouldn't abstain entirely. Part of her was relieved that he'd found sex somewhere else, but it scared her, too. What if he left her for another woman, precisely as his father had done to his mother? Raising a child on her own would be difficult. All she'd ever wanted was a loving husband and a home to raise their children in. Anna didn't want to be a broken family like the one she'd grown up in. But William wasn't exactly giving her a good reason to stay with him, either.

Brushing away tears, Anna placed the shirt in the bottom of the laundry basket and slipped back into bed. She wouldn't confront him about his cheating. He'd only lie to her, adding another untruth to the pile she was collecting. She could only hope that once their baby was born, he'd find it in his heart to become a good father, and maybe even settle down. Anna had always lived on hope as a child, and she hid behind it now.

CHAPTER TWENTY-FOUR

Anna

One sweltering evening in August around eight o'clock, Anna's water broke after having only experienced mild contractions all afternoon. She was in the apartment alone, mopping the kitchen floor in a spurt of last-minute energy when she felt the water trickling down her leg before it gushed.

A sudden pain gripped her and brought Anna to her knees. Frightened, she headed for the bedroom and grabbed the bag she'd packed in anticipation of this moment. How she wished William would have stayed home tonight. Over the past week, she'd begged William to stay close to home, but each night he'd gone out anyway, promising he'd be gone for only a short time. Without a phone and not knowing exactly where he was, Anna walked across the hall and pounded on Edith's door. The woman took one look at Anna's panicked face and knew exactly what was happening.

"Martin! Go hail a cab for us. I have to take Anna to the hospital," Edith called out to her husband.

Another pain hit Anna, and she doubled over. Edith held

her arm to steady her. Martin squeezed past them and headed down the stairs to get a cab.

"Let's get you downstairs before you can't make it on your own. Where's that husband of yours?" Edith asked.

"He...went...out," Anna said, gasping for breath. "Proba-bly...at a...bar...down the...street."

"God have mercy," Edith said under her breath. She led Anna downstairs, stopping once as another pain enveloped her. "Your pains are so close together. We'll be lucky to get to the hospital on time."

Tears rolled down Anna's cheeks. "I have to get there."

"I know, dear. We'll get you there."

Edith helped Anna into the back of the cab and told her husband to find a neighbor to watch the kids and then go down the street and search for William. He ran off to do her bidding.

"How did you train him so well?" Anna asked between pains, giving Edith a smile that looked more like a grimace.

"I'm a lucky woman," Edith said.

Edith told the cabbie to take them to the hospital down-town, and he sped off. Anna's pains were intense and occurred every few minutes. She was so out of breath between them that the two women didn't speak.

They arrived at the hospital a few minutes later, and Edith paid the cabbie before helping Anna out. A pain gripped Anna, and she cried out, her knees buckling from the intensity of it.

"Just a few more steps to go," Edith said soothingly, letting Anna lean on her heavily. As soon as they walked in the door, Edith called out to the receptionist at the desk that she needed help. An orderly came quickly with a wheelchair, and Anna thankfully dropped into it. In the short time it took Edith to check her in, Anna had three more contractions.

"Those are coming close together," the woman behind the desk said, frowning. "Did you already call the doctor?"

Anna shook her head as another contraction seized her body.

"It's Dr. Rickman," Edith told the receptionist. "Please call him for us. And for heaven's sake, get her to a room!"

The orderly took off down the hallway with Anna before Edith could say goodbye. Anna's body shook with pain as each contraction grew stronger. She was handed off to a nurse in a snowy white uniform and helped into a hospital gown and onto a bed. Anna remembered little to nothing after that. The pains were coming so fast, the nurses rolled her into the delivery room quickly, and she was given a shot. Everything went hazy, then dark.

* * *

Anna's eyes fluttered open as a nurse stood over her with a bundle in her arms. "Mrs. Craine? Mrs. Craine? Would you like to see your daughter now?" She lowered the baby so Anna could see her face. Groggily, Anna stared at the perfect little baby with the button nose and round eyes. "She's beautiful," Anna said, but she could barely keep her eyes open and once again fell back to sleep.

The next morning Anna awoke slowly to the sun streaming in the large window beside her and the hum of activity going on outside her door. She looked around, startled at first, then remembered she'd come in to have the baby. Pushing herself up to a sitting position with considerable pain, she saw that someone had left a tray of food on the rolling table beside her bed. She lifted the lid, and the smell of eggs and toast drifted toward her. The smell made her nauseous, so she covered it again and opted to drink the orange juice and some of the cold coffee.

"Ah, you're finally awake," a young nurse with a cheery expression said as she walked into the room. "The sedation really knocked you out, didn't it?"

"Can I see my baby?" Anna asked. She vaguely remembered a nurse showing her the baby but couldn't even remember if it was a little girl or boy.

"Of course. I'll bring her in a moment. First, we need to check your vitals." She went about checking Anna's blood pressure and temperature, then left to get the baby.

Anna glanced around the room. It held two beds, but the other bed was empty. The clock on the wall said eight-fifteen. She wondered if William had ever come to the hospital or even knew she was here. She still felt a little woozy, and it seemed strange to have given birth to a baby and not remember it.

"Here she is. She's a doll," the nurse said, carrying the tiny bundle wrapped in a pink blanket. She carefully handed the baby to Anna.

Anna gazed down into her daughter's sweet little face. At that moment, she knew exactly what true love felt like. She'd never felt so much affection for anything or anyone before. It was as if her heart had opened up, and all the love she'd ever desired had rushed in.

The nurse taught Anna how to hold the baby to breastfeed, and the little girl ate hungrily. It had hurt when she'd first latched on but otherwise wasn't painful. The nurse told Anna that her milk wouldn't come in for a couple of days, but the baby could be supplemented with bottles of formula if she was hungry.

"Do you know if my husband has been here?" Anna asked.

"Oh, no. I don't know. I wasn't working last night when you came in, though. I'm sure he'll be here later today." She smiled warmly at Anna and left the room.

Anna gazed down into the watchful eyes of her little girl. She couldn't believe how alert the newborn was. "Would you like the name Joan?" she asked the infant. "Joan May Craine. It's a good name, a strong name. Joan Fontaine was the actress who played Jane Eyre in the movie, and she's beautiful like you." Ever since Anna had seen the movie as a teenager, she'd felt a strong connection with the character who'd been an orphan that nobody wanted and then grew up to be a quiet governess. Anna understood what it was like to be unwanted, and the story of Jane Eyre had touched a chord within her. Since then, she'd gone to every movie Joan Fontaine had starred in and had idolized her as a young woman.

"Yes. Joan it is," Anna said gently.

The doctor came in on his rounds that morning to check on Anna. "You sure gave us a scare yesterday," he said. "You lost a lot of blood after the delivery, and we had to give you blood, but your color looks good now."

Anna was surprised. She'd never had a problem with bleeding intensely before. "Is that something I should be worried about?" she asked the doctor.

Dr. Rickman shook his head. "I'm sure it was the result of the delivery. I'd just make sure any future doctors or surgeons are aware if you have any other procedures."

He checked her chart and then looked her over to make sure all was well. "I looked in on the baby earlier this morning before she came in here," he said. "She looks strong and healthy. Eight pounds, six ounces is a big first baby. Be aware that babies tend to lose a little weight at first, but then will gain it back again. If she has any big changes in weight, let me know."

He left then, after suggesting she stay in the hospital for a minimum of four days. He wanted to make sure there was no more bleeding before she left. Anna was pretty sure William would have other ideas. There was no chance he'd want to pay the bill for that many days. She'd stay overnight again and see how she felt.

Edith came to visit later that morning, bringing along flowers in a vase and a gift for the baby. "Congratulations! I saw the little sweetheart in the nursery. Isn't it wonderful how they now have a big window so you can see the babies?" She sighed. "I loved when my kids were babies, but I'm certainly not having any more."

Anna laughed and opened the gift. Edith had sewn two little drawstring nightgowns for the baby in yellow and green, and a cute playsuit with a smock top and ruffled diaper cover. "They're adorable!" Anna said. "Thank you so much. And the colors are perfect for a little girl."

"You're welcome, dear," Edith said. "Come to me when you need more clothes, and I'll sew them up in a jiff." She glanced around. "Did William make it here last night?"

Anna's smile faded as she placed the clothing back in the box. "I'm not sure. They sedated me pretty heavily. I only saw the baby for a minute and then slept all night. He hasn't been here yet this morning."

Edith set her mouth into a thin line. "Well, he better have been here last night. Martin found him in a bar down the street and told him. He said he'd rush to the hospital right away."

"Well, I'm sure he must have been here then," Anna said, although she wasn't sure at all.

Anna slept the rest of the afternoon, and after dinner, she fed the baby again. She was holding Joan in her arms, admiring her perfect cupid's bow mouth and chubby cheeks when William walked through the door smiling, carrying a pink teddy bear.

"There are my girls," he said, coming up beside Anna's bed and placing a sweet kiss on her cheek. "And look at her," he said softly. "Isn't she the prettiest thing you've ever seen?"

The warmth in his voice touched Anna's heart. She hadn't expected William to be so happy to see the baby after months of ignoring the pregnancy. "She is. She's perfect," Anna said.

He smiled down at Anna as he set the teddy bear on the bed. "I didn't forget you, either," he said, pulling a long, narrow box from his pocket. "Before she left, Mattie said that any man who didn't buy his wife a gift after having a baby is a cad. And she's right. I hope you like it."

Anna was stunned to see that he'd bought her a gift. "Would you like to hold the baby while I open it?" she asked.

William hesitated a moment, looking nervous, then nodded. "Sure. I'd better get used to the little thing, hadn't I?" He leaned down, and Anna placed the baby in his arms. He lifted her up like a pro and gently rocked her as he gazed down into her face. The sight of her husband holding their child so lovingly brought tears to Anna's eyes.

Anna unwrapped the box and saw that it was from the jewelry store downtown. She lifted the lid, and there, lying on black velvet, was a string of small pearls, glistening in the light. "William! They're beautiful. Thank you." She ran her fingers over the smooth, round pearls. "They're perfect, just like our baby."

He smiled. "I know how to treat my girls right," he said proudly.

Anna didn't ask him if he'd come to the hospital the night before. It didn't matter anymore. All that mattered was he was here now, and he seemed pleased with their baby girl.

William sat on the edge of the bed, still holding the baby snug in his arms. "So, what are we going to call this baby doll?" he asked.

She could smell bourbon on his breath but chose to ignore it. "I was thinking of naming her Joan. Joan May Craine. It sounds nice, doesn't it?"

William thought a moment. "Sure. Why not? Hey there, Joanie," he said, tickling the baby's cheek with his fingertip. "How do you like your name?" The baby's eyes fluttered open, and she yawned wide before settling back to sleep. William laughed. "Not exactly an enthusiastic response, but we'll take it."

Anna smiled, her heart full of love for her husband. She forgave him for lying to her about important details, and she forgot that he could sometimes be cruel. Right now, she saw only his love for his baby daughter and for her, and for now, that was all Anna needed.

* * *

Two days later, against the doctor's advice, Anna checked out of the hospital. William had taken half a day off work and drove them home. Climbing the stairs to the apartment was difficult for Anna. But once she was inside their place, she settled down on the sofa with Joan while William brought up the flowers and gifts. Edith came by to gush over the baby for a few minutes, and her children came along to see little Joan too. Anna was so happy to be home.

After settling little Joan into the bassinette, Anna checked the kitchen and was thankful to see that someone had cleaned up the mess she'd left the night she went to the hospital. The refrigerator had been stacked with groceries, and two casseroles were in there too. Anna was grateful to whoever had left them. Making dinner would have tired her out.

"Edith from across the hall brought them," William said after Anna had heated one of the casseroles and they'd sat down to eat. "She offered to fill the fridge, too, so I gave her money. She's a good neighbor."

Anna was so thankful for Edith. She'd been nothing but kind to her. It was nice having a friend like her in this town where she knew practically no one.

That first couple of weeks, William was good with the baby and stayed home in the evenings. Anna was tired all the time, but it helped when William held the baby or rocked her while Anna made dinner or took a bath. But the newness soon wore off as William became increasingly tired too, being woken up by the baby every four hours during the night.

"When will that baby sleep all night?" he asked one morning as Anna made his breakfast. It had been an especially bad night with Joan waking every two hours.

"Not for a while," she said. "I'm sorry you're not getting enough sleep. Should I sleep on the sofa a few nights with the bassinette out there so you won't hear her?"

"Don't be ridiculous," he grumbled. Anna stayed quiet. She tried not to say too much when William was in a mood.

Still, as the weeks passed, Joan became increasingly fussy in the evenings and woke up more often during the night. William began going to the bar again after dinner to escape the screaming, which left Anna alone and frustrated.

"It's more than likely she's a colicky baby," the doctor said at Joan's six-week check-up. "Her weight is good, and she seems otherwise healthy. You'll just have to wait it out."

Anna tried everything everyone suggested on how to calm a colicky baby. She gave Joan a soothing bath in the evenings, she wrapped her tightly in a blanket, she tried using a pacifier, and she even tried formula instead of breast milk to see if it would fill her up so she'd sleep, but nothing worked. So, Anna held Joan day and night, rocking her and sometimes even letting the baby fall asleep on top of her as they lay on the sofa. Anna was tired, and her nerves were frayed, but what stressed her the most was worrying about William becoming agitated by all the crying.

In early October, Anna was up walking around the living room with the baby when William came in after midnight from a night at the bar. He immediately went into a rage over the baby's crying.

"Make that brat shut up!" he screamed at Anna. "How the hell is anyone supposed to sleep around here?"

"I'm trying," Anna said meekly. She controlled her emotions when she spoke so as not to give him a reason to become angrier.

He tossed off his coat and suit jacket. "Give her to me," he demanded, grabbing Joan from Anna's arms. Anna stood stock still, scared to death of what William might do. He held the baby up to his face and yelled at her, "Shut up! Stop crying! What is wrong with you?"

Joan stopped crying for an instant and stared at him with round eyes. No one had ever yelled at the baby before, and it must have scared her because after another second, Joan let out a shrieking wail louder than any Anna had ever heard before.

"Shut up!" William yelled. He shook the baby. "Shut up!"

Terrified, Anna reached for Joan. "Stop! You'll hurt her!"

William clutched the baby against his chest with one arm and shoved Anna with the other. She flew across the living room and fell on the floor, hitting her head on the corner of the coffee table.

Their next-door neighbor pounded on the wall. "Shut up in there, you big oaf! We're trying to sleep!"

"Go to hell!" William shouted back. Through it all, Joan continued to wail.

Anna's head throbbed as she tried to stand. Dizziness washed over her, and she fell backward again. "Please, William. Please. Don't hurt Joanie," she cried, tears spilling down her cheeks.

William stopped and clutched the baby, his eyes suddenly coming into focus as if coming out of a trance. He walked over to the sofa and set the baby down carefully, then went into the bedroom. A moment later, he strode out, carrying the bassinette and setting it by the sofa. "Sleep out here tonight," he said. Then he disappeared into the bedroom again.

Still shaking from fear, Anna was able to get on her knees beside the sofa and check Joan all over. Other than crying, the baby seemed fine despite being tossed around by William. She lifted the baby into her arms and cuddled her close, cooing at her, "It's okay, sweetie. You're okay." After a while, Joan settled down. Anna's head throbbed, and she reached around to the back of her head to see if there was a bump. Instead, Anna felt something sticky. When she looked at her hand, she saw blood.

Once the baby fell asleep, Anna placed her gently in the bassinette. She padded softly to the bedroom and into the bathroom to wash the blood from the top of her head. It stung, and Anna felt a lump forming. Once it stopped bleeding, she headed back through the bedroom.

Anna quietly picked up William's jacket and coat off the floor. Staring into the darkened room, she saw him lying in bed, sound asleep. She watched William for a long time, wondering how she was going to spend the rest of her life with him. He could be so kind and yet so terrifying. How could he treat his own daughter the way he had tonight? He could have hurt her, or worse, killed her. Anna's heart hardened as she looked at him. She'd do anything she had to in order to protect her baby.

Despite her anguished feelings, Anna found his trousers and hung them up along with his jacket, then hung his coat in the closet by the door. She didn't want to give him another reason to fly off the handle.

Anna walked over to the bassinet and gazed down at her sleeping baby. "He will never hurt you again. I promise," she whispered. Then she laid down on the sofa and fell into a fitful sleep.

CHAPTER TWENTY-FIVE

Diane

Anna rummaged through her keepsake box and pulled out a smaller jewelry box. She handed it to Diane. Opening it, Diane saw the yellowed pearls that William had given her after Joan's birth.

"Real pearls will yellow over time if they aren't worn," Anna said. "Yes, he actually bought real pearls, but I later learned he'd found them in a pawn shop and put them in the box from the jewelry store."

Diane shook her head. "He was a real con man, wasn't he?"

"He knew how to make things appear better than they were," Anna said. "But deep down inside, he was a deeply disturbed man."

Diane's heart went out to her grandmother. How could these stories possibly be untrue as her mother had hinted at? Why would Anna go to all the trouble of making them up? What would it accomplish? She'd already spent sixty-five years of her life in prison for the crime. What good would it do to make up stories now?

Anna asked Barry questions about his job and why he'd chosen to work with young children. He told a few stories from his years of teaching before he became a principal. Anna laughed at the stories. Anna talked a little about teaching Tonya simple tasks, and they discussed how wonderful it was that children like Tonya were now included in school and learned to be self-sufficient in life.

Diane sat back and watched as Barry and Anna talked. It was a nice exchange. Anna was genuinely interested in Barry. Joan rarely every asked about Barry, and when they were all together for the holidays, she never even had a conversation with him. Her mother was just too self-absorbed to care about anyone else's life. She'd always been that way.

Max came to tell them it was time for dinner, so Barry wheeled Anna down to the dining room while Diane walked with Max. She liked the older gentleman. He was sharp and funny, and it seemed as if he really liked Anna.

Just as they were leaving, Anna reached for Diane and hugged her. "Barry is as nice as he is handsome," she whispered to Diane. "He's a real keeper, that one."

"I think so, too," Diane whispered back.

After leaving Anna to her dinner, Barry asked Diane if she wanted to get a bite. As they drove to their chosen restaurant, Diane asked, "Do you think Anna is telling the truth or making up stories?"

Barry looked over at her in surprise. "What makes you say that?"

"Oh, my mother put that thought in my head. She said that since there's no one left to tell the truth, Anna can say whatever she likes to make herself look good. But I just don't get the feeling she's lying."

"I don't think she is, either," Barry said. "She's pretty open about everything. That would be a lot of lies to keep straight for an older person."

"True." She grinned over at Barry. "Of course, you're going to side with Anna because she likes you so much. She said you're a keeper, you know."

He laughed. "Well, I am. But honestly, I think she's the real deal. If she's not, then Anna truly is a con artist."

"I hope not," Diane said seriously. "I really like her. I'd hate to think it was all lies."

"I guess you'll never know unless your mother's memory of those days suddenly clears up," Barry said. "She must remember something. I suppose she's blocked it all out."

Diane nodded. "I guess I can't blame her for that. But I think she remembers more than she's saying."

"Well, you can always ask her." Barry pulled the car into the restaurant's parking lot.

"Yeah, we'll see," Diane said. She had asked her mother, and each time she'd denied remembering anything. But she wasn't done asking quite yet.

* * *

Monday evening after work, Diane called her mother to ask how her head felt.

"I'll live," her mother said. "The bruise is still a doozy, but my head doesn't hurt. I'm sure I just knocked a few brains cells loose."

"I'm glad it doesn't hurt. I have your box of photos back from Anna. I'll bring them to you on Friday," Diane said.

There was silence on the other end of the line. Finally,

Joan said, "Why don't you just keep them? I don't need them anymore."

This surprised Diane. "Are you sure? You might want to look at them again sometime."

"I'm sure," Joan said. "I have no use for the past."

Diane hesitated a moment. She'd planned on telling her mother about the jewelry Anna had given her to see if she wanted it. Taking a deep breath, she charged ahead. "Mom. Anna has a few pieces of jewelry that your father gave her that she's given to me. I wondered if you'd like to have them. There's a watch, a string of pearls, and her rings."

Joan didn't even hesitate. "The jewelry that was in the wooden box I gave you? No. I don't want any of it. Or the photos she had either."

So, she had gone through the items in Anna's box, Diane thought. "Are you sure?"

"Absolutely. I don't want anything that ever belonged to her. They're yours to keep."

After hanging up, Diane walked over to her dresser where the jewelry lay. She looked at the watch, held the pearls a moment, and studied the other jewelry that had tarnished and dulled over time. The only piece that still looked shiny, aside from the peacock pin May had given Anna, was the plain gold wedding band. Diane slid the band on her little finger, amazed at how small Anna's hands must have been for it to fit her ring finger. The wedding band was the only piece of jewelry that was bought out of happiness. William must have loved Anna to propose marriage. Or had he only married her on a whim because he thought it would help him obtain a promotion at work? Diane knew that was a terrible thought, but it could be true. He seemed to be the type of person who jumped before he thought. The pearls should have been a nice remembrance gift, but he'd only bought them to prove he was a good guy. Wouldn't it have been better if he'd just been a good guy instead?

Diane thought of the gifts of jewelry she'd received in the past. Her husband hadn't really been big on buying jewelry, but he'd purchased a couple of items as an apology gift. Those were the pieces she refused to ever wear again. What was it with those type of men who thought a pretty bauble would make everything better? Barry, on the other hand, had only bought her jewelry as a celebratory gift. A pair of diamond earrings for her fiftieth birthday, and a necklace for the anniversary of the day they'd met. When she looked at the jewelry Barry had given her, it made her smile. When Anna looked at the jewelry William had given her, it recalled an unhappy memory. Diane thought that was sad.

Diane kept Anna's wedding band on. She didn't know why, but it made her feel closer to her grandmother—and that made her feel good.

Diane's week at work was busy with papers to grade and teacher meetings to attend. She couldn't visit Anna that Wednesday after school. When she called to explain, Anna told her it was fine. "I don't expect you to drop everything for me, dear," she said kindly. Her words made Diane laugh because her mother did expect her to drop everything for her sometimes.

On Friday, Diane showed up at her mother's place to take her out shopping and for dinner. It was a snowy, blustery day, but that never stopped Joan. She liked routine, and since she'd missed going out the week before, she wanted to go this time.

This week, however, Diane's mother surprised her by asking

to go to a shopping mall to buy some new clothes. Diane knew her mother hadn't bought anything new in a long time, nor ever wanted anything new, but she didn't say anything and drove her there.

They went inside a store that catered to mature women, and her mother tried on several dresses, dress pants, and sweaters. She ended up buying a bright red dress, two pairs of slacks, and three sweaters plus one sweater set. She also picked out a new black wool coat.

"Wow. That's the most clothes I've seen you buy at one time in a while," Diane said as her mother paid for her purchases. "Are you planning a trip somewhere that I don't know about?" she teased.

Her mother looked at her seriously. "I just might be. Gladys and I are talking about taking one of those river cruises in Europe. We've always wanted to do that, and we both decided it was now or never."

"Really?" Diane was stunned. "That's wonderful. I guess I never knew you wanted to do that."

"Well, I do. And I have the money to do it. I'm tired of sitting around, growing old. I want to have a little fun before I die."

"I think it's a great idea," Diane told her.

They stopped at a shoe store, and her mother bought a pair of black shoes with low heels. Diane cringed, picturing her mother tripping in them, but said nothing. Her mother had the right to wear whatever made her happy. Afterward, they went to eat dinner then picked up a few groceries before returning to Joan's apartment.

"When are you and Gladys thinking of going?" Diane asked as she helped her mother put away groceries.

"Gladys was going to check and see when there are openings. We'd like to go by next March or April. I told her to book whatever dates suit her, and I'll be fine with it."

"I'm glad you're planning a trip, but I'm surprised. What made you decide to plan one now?" Diane asked.

Joan stopped what she was doing and stared at Diane. "Truthfully? My recent fall made me rethink my life. Here I am in this little apartment with nothing to do, wasting my time. After I fell, I realized something could happen to me any day now, and what would I have accomplished? Nothing. I don't want to sit here and wait to die. I still want to have a little fun. I survived a murderous mother and two terrible marriages. The only good thing I ever did was have you and your brother. So now, I just want to go see some of the world and enjoy myself."

Diane smiled. "I think you should. What's the point of living if you can't have a little fun?"

"Speaking of which," Joan said. "Isn't it time you thought about the rest of your life? In ten years, you'll be close to retiring, and then what? Will Barry still be around, waiting for you to marry him? I just don't see what you're waiting for. Marry him. He's a thousand times better than Jeffrey ever was, and he lives to make you happy. You two can retire and travel or be snowbirds or whatever. You can enjoy your life. Don't let too many more years go by, and before you know it, he's gone."

Diane crossed her arms and stared at her mother. "What brought this on?"

Joan shook her head and went to sit down at the table. Diane followed her. "I don't know. It's all this Anna stuff. Ever since she got out of prison, all these memories and thoughts have run around inside my head, and they're driving me crazy. Look at all the years she wasted, sitting in that prison. And look at all the time I wasted with the wrong men. And you, too. We created prisons of our own, staying with men who didn't make us happy. And now, you have a chance to be with a man who genuinely wants to make you happy. It's time you let go of your fear of the past and move forward with Barry. You won't be happy until you finally make that decision."

Diane tried to digest everything her mother was saying. Her first reaction was to tell her mother that she knew nothing about her past or present, but then, as she thought about it, she realized her mother was right. She'd locked herself up in her own prison, afraid to move forward and make another bad relationship decision. It was unbelievable that her mother, the queen of terrible decisions, was the one who realized it.

"Anna brought this all to the surface?" Diane asked.

"I never wanted to think about that woman again, from the time I was a child," Joan said bitterly "But now, she's all I think about. She's reminded me of my past and all that was wrong with it. I've rethought every decision I've ever made, and that's not something I ever wanted to do. I hate it. In the end, it all comes down to the fact that none of us can change the past, and all we can do is try to make the future better. And that's what I've decided to do—make it better. And I'm going to start by taking a damn cruise."

Her last sentence made Diane laugh. "I get it. I really do. So, maybe it's a good thing Anna came back into our lives. It forced you to rethink your life and move forward."

Joan swiped the air with her hand. "I'm not giving her the credit. She doesn't deserve any of it. And I'm not talking about her anymore."

Diane sighed. With that final statement, they were back to the same old Joan.

When Diane returned home, she found Barry sitting in bed, working on his laptop.

"Hmm. Another wonderful evening with your mother, I see," he said, peering over his reading glasses.

"What makes you say that?" she asked, puzzled.

"The serious look on your face. You always come back from Joan's looking serious. You come back from Anna's with a smile on your face. I can tell which person is better for your psyche."

Diane laughed. "I could have told you that." She changed into a pair of sweatpants and a cozy sweatshirt and laid down on the bed beside him. "Do you think I've locked myself away in my own personal prison, afraid to get close to people?"

Barry turned his full attention on her, looking stunned. "Where on earth did you get that from?"

"Believe it or not, my mother. She said that since my divorce, I've kept myself locked away, afraid to trust again, just like being in prison. She thinks I'm afraid to trust not only another person but my own judgment. And honestly, I think she's right. I thought for sure I knew exactly what I was getting into when I married Jeffrey. We were both adults, both college-educated, both mature. But it still ended up being the worst decision of my life."

Barry's expression softened. "I guess I can understand that. But we all make bad decisions no matter how informed we are. When it comes to trusting other people, it's always a big leap of faith. But it's hard when you've been burned once before."

"My mother and her best friend are planning on going on a cruise in Europe," Diane said, waiting to see Barry's reaction. She was not disappointed. His eyes grew wide.

"Your mother is going to travel? I've never known her to want to do anything."

She chuckled. "I know. But that's part of her theory. She's also locked herself away, out of fear. Now, she fears death and not having enjoyed life. So, she's decided to break herself out of prison and change what she can."

"Hmm. I wonder what brought all this on?" he said, a knowing smile on his face.

"Exactly what you think has. Anna. My mom has started looking back at her life and reevaluating it. And you know what? Now that I'm learning what kind of person my grandfather was, I realize why my mother chose the men she did. They were damaged for whatever reason. My father had a hard time when he came back from Vietnam, and that isn't surprising. But after him, my mother married an alcoholic because she was one too, and the abuse continued. She was marrying men like her father, consciously or unconsciously. And what did I do? I married the same kind of man. It's a cycle that I'd like to see broken."

Barry nodded. "So, you locked away your trust, and that's why you won't marry me," he said gently. "I get it. I've always understood your fear of committing. Why do you think I keep hanging around?"

This surprised Diane. She thought she'd come up with this big breakthrough, but Barry had known all along. "Why?"

He smiled. "Because I knew that someday you'd realize why you didn't want to commit, and we could finally bury the past. In the meantime, I could still love you. Because unconditional love really is what we're all searching for."

Unconditional love, Diane thought. Like her love for her daughter, and the love she'd had for her brother. Her mother had never shown her unconditional love. Neither had her father. They'd been too wrapped up in what was happening in their own lives to ever place their children first.

Diane gazed up into Barry's warm brown eyes and saw what she'd been craving her entire life. He was right. Barry had always put her first, no matter what drama was going on. He'd always been there for her, in his quiet, sweet way. He'd always loved her unconditionally. Her heart swelled with love for this man she'd held at arm's length way too long.

Diane moved closer, and Barry set his laptop aside and wrapped his arms around her. "How have you been able to put up with me all this time? Most men would have left."

"Because I love you," he said. "I never thought of it as 'putting up with you.' I just wanted to be with you and share your life. And that's what we're doing, despite your fear of commitment. We're sharing our lives. I live here. My clothes are hanging next to yours in the closet, and my toothbrush is in your bathroom. We plan trips together and spend holidays together. We're a couple. And if that's all you're ever able to give me, it's all I need."

Tears filled Diane's eyes as she lay in Barry's arms. He was right. They'd been together all this time and nothing terrible had happened. How could she not trust Barry? She depended on him for so much. He was already in her heart. It was time for her to let him into her life completely.

* * *

Sunday afternoon, Diane showed up at Anna's apartment with a container of homemade chocolate-chip cookies. "Barry and I were busy in the kitchen yesterday," she said, setting the container down on the table. "It was cold and windy out, so we filled the house with the smell of fresh-baked cookies."

"Oh, I love cookies!" Anna said, delighted. "Especially homemade. Thank you for bringing them, dear."

Diane walked down to the dining room and poured two mugs of hot chocolate, then returned to Anna's room. The two sat sipping the sweet liquid and eating cookies like two little children sneaking a snack.

"Is that my wedding band," Anna asked, pointing to Diane's little finger.

Diane nodded. "I hope you don't mind. It was the only piece of jewelry I thought had been chosen from the heart. And it reminds me of you, which I like."

"I don't mind at all, sweetie. I gave it to you. And you're right. I think William did love me when he married me. At least, I'd like to believe that. So it is the only jewelry bought out of love."

Diane smiled. She was glad her grandmother felt that way too. "You'll never guess what my mother told me the other day. She's going on a cruise with her longtime friend. This is a huge breakthrough for her, and it's all because of you."

"Me?" Anna looked stunned. "How?"

"She's been re-evaluating her life since you've returned. She says it's time she stops waiting to die and enjoy life instead. For years, she drank heavily and harbored a lot of anger. But now, I think she's letting that anger go. At least, I hope so," Diane said.

Anna nodded, looking serious. "I hope so too. Do you think she'll be able to forgive me and come to see me?"

"I don't know," Diane said. "I'm sorry. But I'll keep trying. Stranger things have happened." Diane wished she could change her mother's mind about seeing Anna. She knew how much it meant to the older woman.

"I'll keep hoping for a miracle. It's funny that even after all these years, in my mind, she's still my little Joanie. I loved her so much and did everything in my power to protect her. But as she grew older, she was drawn to her father, even though he spent very little time with her. I suppose that's why. We always want the one thing we can't have."

CHAPTER TWENTY-SIX

Anna

Anna's days were filled with caring for Joan, and she loved every minute of it. The baby soon outgrew colic, and it wasn't long before she slept longer during the night, giving Anna a reprieve. After William's outburst that night, he kept his distance from the baby. It was as if he understood he'd gone too far, and he was careful and kind to the baby when he did interact with her—which wasn't often. William spent his days at work, loathing his job, and his nights out at the bars doing God knew what. Anna didn't ask, nor did she care. She had the child she'd always wanted, and that was enough for her.

On sunny days, Anna bundled up Joan, placed her in the stroller Edith had loaned her, and took Linda and Ronald to the park so they could run off some energy. As they played, Anna would walk around the park paths with Joan. Anna was finally losing the weight she'd gained during her pregnancy, but she realized she'd never be as thin as she'd been before. Edith let out a few of Anna's house dresses so she could wear them again, and made her a couple of new dresses for the winter months.

Anna was so thankful for Edith. She was a true friend.

Most nights, William came home for dinner and then went out again. Anna knew, from the perfume she smelled on him when he came home late at night, that he was cheating on her. But she didn't confront him about it. Anna knew she should, but she was fearful of his reaction. William gave her money each week for groceries and didn't complain when she needed a little extra to buy necessities for Joan, so Anna was thankful for that. If that was all their relationship was at the moment, she could live with it. Anna felt she had no other choice.

One evening in December after dinner, instead of rushing off to the bar, William stayed home. He turned on the radio, picked up little four-month-old Joanie, and began dancing around the living room with her. The baby smiled and cooed as he moved around the room, bringing a rare smile on William's face. Anna watched them, her heart swelling with love. This was the William she'd fallen in love with, the man she'd thought had loved her too.

William held out his free arm to Anna, and she joined them. He slipped his arm around her waist, and they danced in a tight circle, the three of them. The baby smiled and made happy gurgling noises as William sang softly to "Let Me Call You Sweetheart," and "As Time Goes By." Anna dropped her head on his shoulder, remembering when they'd gone out dancing over a year ago and how he'd held her and gazed into her eyes as if she were the only woman in the room. Back then, she was.

William kissed baby Joan on the head, and Anna put her down in her bassinette. After the dinner dishes were washed and put away, Anna went to sit on the sofa next to William as he smoked his last cigarette for the night.

"I miss the nights when you and I went out dining and dancing," he said, moving closer to her. "We were two professionals without a care in the world, enjoying life."

"That seems so long ago," Anna said dreamily. "But I love being a mother to Joanie. I wouldn't trade that for anything in the world."

William turned to her and smiled. "You're a good mother. And an even better wife. You put up with so much from me." He reached out and gently touched the side of her face. "I love you, Anna. I know it may not always seem that way, but I do."

A sweet chill ran through Anna as he pulled her close. Despite everything, she knew she still loved him. At least, she loved her memories of him and how they had been and still could be if he tried. He kissed her then, and that was all it took for her to remember how delightful it felt to be in his arms.

That night, Anna allowed him to make love to her without any expectations that he would change his ways. These were the type of nights that made her still love him. She might not always have him to herself, but she'd cherish the times like this when she did.

* * *

Auntie May rode the train to Buffalo the week before Christmas and spent three days visiting Anna and the baby. May stayed in a nearby hotel and came to the apartment every day after William had left for work. She was charmed by little Joan and held her nearly the entire time she was there. The trio borrowed a wagon from the building superintendent and, with Joan bundled up in her stroller, they went to the nearest tree lot and bought a beautiful Christmas tree, just as Anna and

May had done so many years ago. May had brought a few of her favorite decorations, and Anna had bought a few inexpensive ones, and they decorated the tree while singing Christmas carols. William didn't mind being left out of the festivities. In fact, he stayed away most of the time, avoiding May's watchful eyes.

May placed gifts she'd brought under the tree and told Anna to save them for Christmas morning. The day she left, she hugged Anna tightly, as if she might never see her again.

"Maybe I can visit this summer when Joanie is bigger," Anna said hopefully.

May only nodded, smiled, and kissed little Joan on the cheek goodbye before leaving. Anna missed her aunt the moment she'd gone. She wished they lived closer so she could seek her company and counsel whenever she needed it. But with the way her life was turning out, Anna thought it might be better if Auntie May didn't know everything.

Although William had been grumbling more than usual about his job, over the fact he'd yet to be moved up to an engineer position, they still had a delightful Christmas. It snowed that day, and Anna made a large breakfast and planned a turkey with all the trimmings for dinner. Mattie and Thomas didn't celebrate Christmas and went out with friends instead, which was fine with Anna.

William hadn't forgotten to buy his girls each a gift—a heart-shaped silver music box that played, "Let Me Call You Sweetheart" for Anna and a small doll with curly blond hair for Joanie. Anna loved her music box and hugged him close after she'd opened it. She'd bought William a new set of gold cufflinks, which he liked, and a couple of little baby toys for Joanie. They all sat down to a delicious meal and enjoyed listening to carols on the radio. It was a magical, rare night for the little family that Anna treasured.

Unfortunately, things didn't remain good for long. The next week, William got into a big fight with his supervisor and nearly lost his job. Thomas yelled at him later that night about his attitude at work, which only made matters worse. William left the apartment after dinner that night and didn't return until the early hours of the morning. Anna tried not to panic. She knew when things went wrong for William, he became angry at everyone around him. She made sure his clothes were always neatly pressed and ready, his breakfast was made on time, and if the baby cried at night, Anna was up in a flash, getting her a bottle now that she was no longer nursing. But Anna lived on pins and needles, waiting for William to explode.

One January morning, William got up as usual, dressed, and sat down to eat his breakfast. When he didn't rush out the door to drive to work, Anna sat down and waited but didn't ask what was happening. She knew better than to say anything.

"We're going to pack up our things and head to California," he announced after finishing his coffee. "I've had it with this place. There's a job waiting for me at an aircraft manufacturing company in Burbank."

Anna was stunned by his announcement but didn't argue. "When do you want to leave?"

"As soon as possible. I'm selling the car, and we'll take the train. You'll have to ship the furniture you absolutely need to keep and anything else you can't fit in a suitcase."

Anna tried to stay as calm as possible. "Do we have an address to ship it to?"

"Yes. My mother's house. We'll live there until we have enough money to rent our own place."

Four days later, and after several arguments between Thomas and William about his quitting his job, Anna hugged Mattie goodbye and said a tearful farewell to Edith. Anna had packed and shipped some of their things, but William had said they'd buy a crib for Joan when they got there. She was outgrowing the bassinette anyway. Once again, Anna was on the move, not knowing what to expect and how long they'd live in southern California.

* * *

Meeting William's mother, Mari, for the first time was a disaster. The short, round woman with the tightly pulled back graying hair and steely blue eyes charged Anna like an enraged bull.

"You!" she said, her Finnish accent as harsh as her grandmother's German had sounded. "You forced my son into marrying you because you were pregnant!"

Anna nearly fell over backward from the accusation. "I wasn't pregnant before we were married," she said defensively. "Why would you say such a thing?"

"My Bernice said you were. She could tell right away. Why else would William marry a woman older than him after only knowing her a few months?" Mari said.

"Because I love her," William interjected, coming inside carrying the suitcases. "Leave Anna alone and say hello to your granddaughter, Ma."

Mari's wrinkled face tightened, but she did reach out to hold Joan. Anna reluctantly handed the baby over to the older woman, afraid she'd scare Joanie. Surprisingly, Mari cuddled the baby and tickled her cheek, making Joanie laugh.

William whispered in Anna's ear as he walked past her.

"Mari means 'rebellious woman' in Finnish. You can see it suits her." He chuckled.

Anna sighed. She hoped she and Mari would eventually get along.

Mari had a small house in a nice neighborhood in Burbank, not far from Lockheed Aircraft, where William would be working. Bernice and William had both helped their mother buy the house five years before, which explained why William hadn't saved much money by the time Anna had met him. The older woman had worked hard her entire life raising the children on her own, working as a maid or a housekeeper. Anna had great respect for her for that. Being a single mother couldn't have been easy, especially during the Depression and then the war years. She supposed those hard times were what had made Mari a tough woman. Even now, at age fifty-two, Mari worked early mornings at a local bakery. Anna hoped that would give her a little time alone each morning since there wouldn't be much privacy sharing a home with her mother-in-law.

Anna discovered she loved southern California, especially the beautiful weather. Mari's three-bedroom bungalow sat on a large corner lot with a white picket fence around the front lawn and a fenced-in back yard that had a large lawn, fruit trees, and flowers. It was the perfect spot for Anna and Joan to enjoy the sunshine.

William, Anna, and Joan shared the tiny guest bedroom which was quite cramped by the time Anna bought a crib for the baby. But Anna didn't mind since she spent very little time in the room. Each morning around four a.m., Anna heard Mari moving around in the bathroom and kitchen before leaving for work. After the older woman left, Anna would rise, use the bathroom, and then start William's breakfast before Joanie woke up. It was a nice schedule, giving them time alone without Mari standing over them.

Anna bought a stroller in a second-hand shop so she could take Joan on walks through the neighborhood, meeting many of Mari's neighbors. She also helped Mari, who she called Mrs. Craine, by weeding the flower garden and mowing the grass with the push mower. Anna loved being outside and didn't mind doing those chores. Indoors, however, was where Mari ruled. Anna wasn't allowed to help with dinner except to do the most menial of jobs such as peeling potatoes or chopping carrots. In many ways, Mari treated Anna much as her grandmother had, as if she were useless and stupid. Anna did her best to get along with Mari, but it wasn't always easy.

One thing Mari didn't tolerate in the house was liquor. Considering what a heavy drinker her ex-husband Thomas was, it didn't surprise Anna that her mother-in-law had a hatred for alcohol. After the first couple of weeks of staying home after dinner, William began going out in the evenings to have a few drinks, which prompted many fights between him and his mother. Anna was disappointed that William was returning to his old ways but knew better than to say anything.

"A woman who cannot keep her man home is not a woman after all," Mari said harshly to Anna one evening after Joan had been put down to sleep.

Anna had been crocheting a new blanket for the baby's crib and looked up at Mari, startled. "I have no control over him," she said sadly. "He's his own man."

"Ach! He is a boy, not a man. A real man would be with his family, not out chasing other women in bars."

A lump formed in Anna's throat as she held back tears. She would not let this angry old woman have the satisfaction of making her cry. She sat silently as her fingers went through the motions of running the crochet hook in and out of the yarn.

Mari, who'd been reading the newspaper while rocking in her chair, set the paper down and stared at Anna. "William has always been impulsive and has never thought of the consequences of his actions. That is why I had so much trouble with him and had to send him east to his father's for a while. It didn't help, apparently, because his father wasn't a good influence either. Neither of them can keep a job for very long or stay in one place."

Anna remained silent. Mari was right about some of what she said. William didn't seem able to hold down a job for very long.

"It's that temper of his," Mari continued, shaking her head. "He won't suffer fools and keep his mouth closed. If I had talked back to every idiot I ever encountered, I'd never have been able to keep a roof over my children's heads. Sometimes, you just have to stay silent."

This time, Anna looked up at Mari and met the older woman's eyes. It was as if she understood what Anna had put up with so far with William. Maybe she too had put up with abuse from Thomas before throwing him out.

Mari went back to her paper then and didn't say another word.

As the months went by and they were still living with William's mother, Anna grew used to the tough woman. At least Mari enjoyed spending time with Joan, and sometimes Anna heard her talking softly to the baby while rocking in her favorite chair. William, however, became increasingly irritated at his mother always chastising him about his going out in the evenings.

"That woman drives me crazy," he'd mutter on nights he and Anna went to bed at the same time. "She thinks she can still tell me what to do."

"Maybe we could rent a place of our own soon," Anna said hopefully.

"I paid for this place. I should be allowed to use it," he shot back.

Anna only nodded. She missed having her own place and kitchen where she wasn't always being judged. But she didn't dare badger William, so she said nothing.

William had bought an older model car when they'd arrived to drive back and forth to work. Occasionally on the weekend, he'd ask Anna to bundle up Joan and make up a lunch basket, and they'd head to the coast. They'd go to the beach and sit on a blanket in the sand, a little umbrella over Joan to protect her skin. Anna loved the days they did this. It reminded her of the Fourth of July party she and William had attended at the Shipman's lake house. In those days, William wasn't as stressed as he always was now, and he'd been kind to her. Now, she wasn't sure from day to day how his mood would be. He was always careful around his mother, but sometimes, alone in their room, he'd berate her for some small infraction or slap her if she didn't say exactly what he wanted her to. Anna never knew when his temper would flare, and it kept her feeling like she was walking on pins and needles.

Once again, William hated his job. He ranted about how stupid his co-workers were and how much smarter he was and how he should be in charge. Anna only agreed with him, not wanting to give him a reason to take his frustration out on her. But when William was relaxed and happy, like the days they went to the beach, he was always kind and loving to Anna. His moods were a mystery to her, but she appreciated when times were good.

Late one night, after having been at the bar, William came home smelling of bourbon and another woman's perfume. Anna rolled over with her back to him, hoping he'd just pass out, but he had other ideas. When he pulled her to him, she cringed. She didn't want him to touch her after he'd been with another woman.

"Please, don't," she begged softly. "I'm so tired."

William froze a moment, and then he grabbed her and rolled her over, pulling himself on top of her. The slap across her face came so fast and hard, it made her head spin. "You're my wife," he growled in her ear. "And I'll do whatever I want to you."

Something primal rushed over Anna, and she began to fight him, but he held her down firm. They wrestled until the lamp on Anna's nightstand tipped over and hit the crib, waking Joan. The baby cried, startling William long enough for Anna to push him off her and get out of bed. She lifted Joan from the crib and held her tight. William glared at her in the darkened room, but soon the alcohol overtook him, and he rolled back on the bed, passing out.

Shaking and with tears in her eyes, Anna took Joan out to the living room and sat in Mari's rocker to soothe the baby. She was thankful Mari hadn't woken up from all the noise. Anna couldn't bear for Mari to see her shame.

Anna never returned to bed that night and instead slept on the sofa with Joan safe in her arms. Mari saw her there before going to work and only made the comment that it must have been a rough night with the baby. Anna nodded and waited until the older woman was gone before putting Joan in her crib and going into the bathroom. Looking in the mirror, Anna was horrified to see the large bruise on her cheek and near her eye. She quickly covered the tender bruise with makeup and was dressed as usual and making breakfast for William by the time he was up.

Anna's hand shook as she poured his coffee and handed him his plate of food, but he never even noticed. He only grumbled at her before eating and never said a word about the night before. She wasn't sure he even remembered what he'd done. When he finally left, she dropped onto a kitchen chair and wept. She was tired, her face was swollen, and her head ached. She wasn't sure how much more of his abuse she could endure.

Later that afternoon, when Mari returned home from work, she took one look at Anna and waved for her to follow her into the kitchen. Joan was safely tucked away in her crib, taking a nap, so Anna followed the older woman.

"Now I know what all the noise was about last night," Mari said, sliding the stepstool over in front of the built-in oven and climbing up to reach something in the cupboard above. She grabbed a stout bottle and stepped down, then brought it and two small glasses to the table.

Anna had her face turned away so the bruise wouldn't show, but Mari reached over and gently turned her face toward her. "Never be ashamed of something you didn't cause," Mari said. "It is he who should be ashamed." She opened the bottle and poured a little of its contents into each glass. "Drink up. You need this."

Anna took a sip and felt the sweet liquid burn its way down her throat. "What is this?" she asked.

"Apricot Schnapps," Mari said, then drank down her own glass in one swig. "Drink it down fast. It'll warm you from the inside out." Mari poured herself another shot.

"I thought you didn't allow alcoholic drinks in the house," Anna said, stunned.

"Ack! This isn't a drink. It's like a dessert." Mari laughed, which made Anna laugh too. Anna drank back the entire shot then and coughed from the burn.

Mari poured her another one. "Men think they own women, but they don't. You must not ever give in to your husband when it is important to you. Fight, Anna. With all your strength."

Anna's smile faded as she stared into the clear liquid. "I wasn't raised to fight back," she said softly. "It's not in my nature."

"You must be strong, girl, you hear? Because at some point, you must fight back. When it comes down to you or him, you must choose yourself."

A chill ran down Anna's spine. Mari had walked away from Thomas. Had it been when she'd had enough?

Mari lifted her glass. "To strength," she said.

"To strength," Anna said, lifting her own glass. Then she downed it in one swallow.

After that afternoon, Anna felt closer to Mari.

CHAPTER TWENTY-SEVEN

Anna

The months passed, and in August they celebrated Joan's first birthday. Mari brought home a cake from the bakery, and the three adults laughed as they watched her get icing all over her face. To Anna, it seemed as if Joanie was growing up quickly. She was already walking and loved following her father around when he was home. William would lift her in the air and twirl her around as the little girl shrieked with delight. It was clear that Joan adored her father despite his not being around very much.

The baby was also outgrowing her clothes and shoes quickly. Anna hated asking William for money, but she had no choice. He now gave grocery money to Mari instead of Anna, so if she needed anything for herself or the baby, she had to ask. For a woman who'd earned her own living at one time, it was hard for her to no longer have the freedom money gave her. Especially when William would grumble and groan about giving her even a few dollars for new clothes or shoes for Joan.

"What, do you think I'm a Rockefeller or something?" he'd

ask as he reluctantly handed Anna a few dollars. "Make it last."

Anna did try to stretch the money as best she could. Mari had a sewing machine, so Anna made most of Joan's clothes from fabric she found on sale at the dime store. As for herself, Anna continued to wear her old clothes from before they were married and had taken in the maternity dresses so they'd fit her better. She'd lost weight over the past year because of all the walking she now did, and her dresses just hung on her. But she didn't dare ask William to buy her clothes, so she made do.

By October, Anna could see that William's job and his nights out were taking a toll on his behavior. He'd started hiding bottles of bourbon in their bedroom nightstand and drank shots morning and night. He was irritable and self-absorbed, although he was careful how he treated the baby. He didn't even remember Anna's birthday on the twenty-sixth, but instead went out after dinner as usual. She'd hoped he'd have offered to take her out to dinner or at the very least, had bought her a small gift, but he did none of that. She was just another person in his life, and no longer special to him in any way.

Auntie May, however, sent her a card and a check for twenty dollars. Anna bought a new pair of much-needed shoes and stockings with the money and stashed the rest away in case she or Joanie needed something. When Mari saw the birthday card sitting on the dresser in Anna's room, she was instantly angry.

"Did that son of mine not buy you a gift? I had no idea it was your birthday," Mari said, her hands on her ample hips.

"It was a few days ago. I didn't want to make a big fuss of it," Anna said, sorry now that she hadn't hidden the card.

"I will bake you a cake," Mari said. "What is your favorite?"

"I like German Chocolate," she said. "But please don't go to all the trouble."

"No trouble at all. We will celebrate," Mari said, sounding determined.

That evening after dinner as William stood to leave, his mother said sternly, "Sit! We have cake for dessert in honor of Anna's birthday."

William stared at Anna in surprise as Mari went to the kitchen to get the cake. "So, you didn't bother to remind me of your birthday, but you told my mother? What are you trying to pull? You're trying to make me look bad." He stood and towered over a terrified Anna who sat next to Joanie's high-chair. She knew that tone, and it frightened her.

"I didn't say anything to your mother. She saw the card from Auntie May. I wasn't going to make a big deal about it," Anna said, her voice trembling.

Mari came in with the cake that had a single candle in the middle. She glared at William, making him sit down, then set the cake in front of Anna. Joanie clapped with glee when she saw it. "Make a wish," Mari said.

It was all Anna could do to blow out the candle, let alone make a wish. William's beet-red face and angry eyes made her tremble with fear. The baby clapped again after she blew out the candle, and Anna tried to relax and make this fun for Joan.

Mari cut pieces for everyone, and somehow, Anna ate hers despite the lump in her throat. Joanie got chocolate all over her face, which made Mari laugh, and Anna smiled at her daughter, but through it all, William just glared at her.

After they ate, Anna jumped out of her chair to help clear the table and was about to follow Mari into the kitchen when William grabbed her arm and swung her around.

"Never make me look bad in front of my mother again. Do you hear me?" he growled at her.

"I'm sorry," she said, her voice small.

He let go of her arm and stormed out, grabbing his coat on the way. That night, he came home later than usual, smelling of liquor and cheap perfume. Anna was curled up on the edge of the bed, hoping not to have a repeat of that last terrible night. She felt the bed move as he got in, then his hot breath was in her ear as he spoke in a slurred voice.

"I found someone to celebrate your birthday with. Someone who appreciates me for what I can do for her. Happy Birthday, honey."

Tears filled her eyes as he moved away from her and settled into bed. Why was William always trying to hurt her? She tried to do her best to take care of him and Joanie. She never complained or asked him to buy her expensive things. Still, if he wasn't hurting her physically, he was breaking her heart.

Mari's words rang in Anna's ears. *"At some point, you must fight back."* Anna wasn't sure she had the strength to fight William. She knew she couldn't win. She thought of her Auntie May and how strong and confident she'd always been. Anna had thought she'd grown up to be confident too, but she lost all that after marrying William. Or, maybe she gave it up. She didn't know which. All she knew was her that Auntie May would be very disappointed in her now, and that thought also tore at her heart.

Anna felt all alone in the world.

* * *

Winter in California was wonderful. It rained occasionally, but most days were warm, and the sun shone brightly. January came, marking the first year that Anna and William had been living in the small house with his mother. More and more, Mari trusted Anna to cook dinner in her kitchen and accepted her as a daughter.

"No more calling me Mrs. Craine," Mari said one afternoon as they worked together in the kitchen. Joan was sitting in her highchair eating cut-up grapes that Mari had brought home from the grocery store. "You must call me mom."

Anna's heart warmed. She was no longer afraid of Mari's brusque ways and had grown to love the older woman. "I'd love to call you mom," she said.

"Good. And this little one," Mari said, going over to Joanie to tickle her cheek. "She will be calling me grandma soon. I look forward to that day."

"Mama!" Joanie said, then giggled in her sweet little way. "Mama!"

Anna laughed. "That's right, baby. Mama. Now say Dada. Your dad would love to hear you say that."

"Mama," Joanie said.

"She knows the most important word," Mari said, winking at Anna.

Later, William came home grumbling as usual about his job. Anna listened quietly as she set the food on the table and moved Joan's highchair next to the table. As she set the little girl in the chair, Joan said, "Mama. Mama."

William smiled over at his daughter. "Good job, Joanie. Now say dada. Can you say dada?"

Mari came in with a platter of roast beef. "Maybe if you stay home more, she'll learn how to say your name."

Anna's whole body tensed at Mari's words.

"Hey. I'm home for dinner, aren't I?" William said defensively.

They sat down and passed the food around the table. Anna busied herself with filling Joan's plate with mashed potatoes, cooked carrots, and cut-up beef. "I've been trying to teach Joan to say dada," Anna said to try to placate William. "She'll pick it up soon, I'm sure."

"Of course she will," William said between bites. "She's smart like her old man."

Mari snorted but kept eating.

"Of course she is," Anna said quickly. "Just like her dad."

Later, after the dishes were washed and Anna had put Joan to bed, she was surprised to see William still at home. He was sitting on the front porch, smoking a cigarette. Anna took a sweater out of the closet by the door, pulled it on, and walked outside. William turned and looked at her.

"Join me?" he asked.

She sat on the chair next to his. A small, round table was between them, and his drink sat there. Anna knew it was his typical bourbon. "It's a nice night out," she said.

"It is. I do enjoy the California weather."

"I was surprised to see you still at home," Anna said tentatively. "It's nice." She smiled over at him.

"I know I should be here more often with you and Joanie," he said. "And not because my mother thinks so. I just can't stand being around her. Nothing is ever good enough for my mother, as you've found out."

"She and I had a rocky start, but we're getting along now," Anna said. "She loves Joanie, which is nice. Joanie needs family around her."

He nodded. "Neither of us has family, do we? My father doesn't count. There's my mom and your Aunt May. That's about it."

"And your sister Bernice and her husband," Anna reminded him.

"Yeah. She isn't much better than my mother. She always criticized me too."

Anna watched him as he took a long drag of his cigarette and then slowly blew the smoke out. She still didn't understand who William really was. She'd known the sweet, happy William when they'd dated, and then the angry version after they'd married. But Anna had also seen his vulnerable side, the little boy in him just wanting to be accepted. Maybe that was why she stayed with him. He did have a heart deep down inside. She knew it was there. He masked it often with anger, but if he were in the right place, the right job, somewhere he was happy and satisfied, she believed he could be a better person.

"I'm smart, you know," William said. "Really smart. I can teach myself something new just by watching someone else and then do it even better. I see what people do wrong, and I know how to improve upon it. But the older men at the places I work won't even listen to me. Just because I'm younger, they think I don't know anything. It's so frustrating."

"Yes, it would be frustrating," Anna said. "I know you're smart. But sometimes, a person has to wait in line for their turn. It's not fair, but it's the way things work."

William turned and stared at her, and suddenly Anna feared she'd said the wrong thing. But instead, he smiled. It was the same sweet smile he used to give her in the days when they were happy. "You're a smart lady. You have a degree, and you were a professional working woman. You could take care of yourself. So why did you marry me?"

His question took Anna by surprise. She searched her mind for the answer, but really, it was the simplest answer that counted. "Because I fell in love with you."

He smiled again and reached for her hand. "I'm sorry I forgot your birthday. I'm sorry for all the times I was angry at you. You don't deserve to be treated that way. You're a good person and a good mother to Joan. I'll try to be better."

Anna's heart melted when he kissed her hand, then held it as they sat there under the stars. Despite all that he'd done to her, she couldn't help but be moved by his words. She wished things would change, and they could be the happy family she'd always wanted. She'd have to wait and see.

But by May, he'd quit his job, and they were on the move again.

CHAPTER TWENTY-EIGHT

Diane

"Wasn't it difficult, constantly forgiving him?" Diane asked.

Anna smiled. "You have to remember, it was a different time. People didn't easily get divorced, and I was raised to do what I was told. It was always the woman's fault if her husband wasn't happy or if he strayed. Plus, I had Joan to consider. I couldn't bear to lose her if I did leave him, and things got ugly. I just did what I had to do to survive."

"But you were educated and could have supported yourself and your baby. You could have gone back to live with your Auntie May," Diane said.

"It sounds simple, doesn't it? But it wasn't that simple, believe me. Not then. But if I had it to do over again, that's exactly what I would have done. I don't think I'm going to be granted a second chance, though."

Diane nodded. Yes, it was always easy to see what should have been done after the fact. Hadn't she given her husband several chances before it had gotten so ugly she had to leave?

How could she judge Anna's choices when her own had been the same?

"I do understand why you stayed," Diane said. "I did it too. Until I couldn't any longer."

Anna reached over and placed her hand over Diane's. "We did the best we could at the time."

Diane smiled. "Yes. We did."

After putting her small recorder away, Diane offered to take Anna down to the dining room for dinner.

"Not tonight, dear. I've been feeling a bit tired lately. The nurse said she'd bring my dinner to my room."

"Oh. You should have said something earlier. I didn't mean to wear you out," Diane said, suddenly concerned.

"No, dear. Your being here always makes me feel better. I look forward to it. But tonight, I don't think I have the strength to be stared at while I eat. Max is a sweetie for sitting with me, but the others still think I'm an oddity." She chuckled. "Well, maybe I am."

"No, you're not. You're an amazing woman who's been through a lot. If the other residents took the time to get to know you, they'd see what I do," Diane said with certainty.

"I'm so happy I have you in my life." Anna smiled warmly. "After all those years being locked away, I'm grateful that you found me."

Diane hugged her grandmother. "I'm so happy I found you too," she said softly.

Diane arrived home to an empty house. Barry had left a note saying he was doing some work at his own house and would pick up a pizza on the way home. She smiled. He was always so thoughtful.

She went to the den and sat at her desk. Pulling the recorder out of her purse, she popped up the USB connector on it and plugged it into the computer. Then she downloaded the file from that night's conversation. Diane wondered if she should type out all the conversations so she'd have a hard copy in case she ever lost the files. It would be a lot of work but would be worth it to save the family history for future generations. She decided it would be a good project for the summer.

As she put in a load of laundry and folded some towels that Barry had left in the dryer, Diane's thoughts returned once more to her ex-husband. Anna hadn't yet come to the part of the story where she hit her breaking point, but Diane remembered her own perfectly. They had driven to a lake in the country about an hour away from home and found a quiet place to set up their small grill to make hamburgers. It was a beautiful Saturday in June, and the lake water was still cold despite the warm sun shining down on it. They'd brought their fishing poles so four-year-old Natalie could fish for the first time. It started out as a delightful family outing and ended as one of the worst days of Diane's life.

She remembered how excited Natalie was, running around in her yellow swimsuit and splashing ankle-deep in the lake water, then shrieking at how cold it was and running out. Natalie was laughing, and so was Jeffrey as he watched her and started the coals in the grill. Diane kept one eye on Natalie as she pulled the food from the cooler and placed it on the large blanket she'd laid on the grass.

Tired of running in the water, Natalie sat near her dad, watching as he tied a hook and sinker on his fishing line. She was transfixed, giving him her full attention. Diane draped a towel over the little girl's shoulders and went to the car for the rest of their supplies. When she turned, she noticed Natalie was too close to the flames of the small grill, and before Diane could call out to her, Natalie's towel caught on fire. Jeffrey had looked up at the very same moment and quickly dropped his fishing rod and grabbed the towel away from Natalie. Then he turned to his daughter, grabbed her arm, and began shaking her and screaming.

"What the hell is the matter with you? Are you stupid? You never, never go near a fire like that!" he yelled.

Natalie's eyes were wide and filling with tears. "I'm sorry. I didn't know I was so close," she said in her little voice.

"You didn't know you were so close? Are you an idiot? Couldn't you feel the heat of the fire?" Jeffrey's face was right in Natalie's, and the more he yelled, the more frightened the little girl looked.

A deep primal instinct ran through Diane at that moment. Picking up the crowbar from the back of the car, she ran over to them, frantic to stop him. "Stop it! Stop yelling at her! She understands, okay? You're scaring her."

Jeffrey backed away and turned blazing eyes on Diane. "She could have burned herself. She needs to learn not to go near a fire!"

"I think you've made that perfectly clear," Diane said, placing herself between him and Natalie. "She's crying and scared. Are you happy?"

"Screw you!" Jeffrey screamed in her face. That's when he eyed the crowbar. "What did you think you were going to do with that?" he asked, his tone menacing.

"I'll use it if I have to," she said, her words crystal clear and deadly calm. "You will never lay another finger on my daughter again."

Jeffrey glared at her for a long time, as if weighing his odds.

"Screw you!" he screamed again, then he turned, picked up one of the fishing rods, and broke it in two. "And screw this entire family day!"

Diane watched in disbelief as her husband stomped around, swearing and breaking things while Natalie cried behind her. Suddenly, it was crystal clear to Diane what she had to do. Jeffrey had called her terrible names and made her feel foolish and insecure many times, but this time he'd gone too far. He'd shook Natalie like a rag doll and called his own daughter stupid and an idiot. That was something Diane couldn't forgive.

Diane picked up her crying daughter and carried her to the car. Carefully, she buckled Natalie in her car seat. "It's okay, sweetie," Diane said soothingly. "Everything's okay." Diane pushed the hatchback closed and headed for the driver's side, the crowbar still in her hand.

"What the hell are you doing?" Jeffrey yelled at her. "Where do you think you're going?"

"Home," Diane said. "Find your own way back to the city, and don't bother coming to the house. The locks will be changed by then." She got behind the wheel and drove off, seeing Jeffrey's shocked face in the rearview mirror.

Once she was home, the finger-shaped bruises swelling up on Natalie's arms along with her tear-stained face told Diane she'd done the right thing. She wasn't going to let him ever hurt her daughter again.

Diane did have the locks changed immediately, and Jeffrey didn't return to the house that night. When he finally called her later that evening from his parents' house, he apologized for the way he'd acted and asked if it were okay if he came home.

"No," Diane said with more determination than she'd ever had throughout her marriage. "I allowed you to belittle me far too long. But calling our four-year-old daughter stupid was inexcusable. Shaking her and holding her arm so tightly that it bruised her is unforgivable. I will not let you treat her the way you've treated me all these years. I'm through, Jeffrey. I want a divorce."

When he began yelling and threatening her, Diane hung up. That night, for the first time in years, she finally felt able to breathe. After years of second-guessing herself and feeling incompetent because of his insults, she was finally going to be free of him.

And as Diane relived that memory now, she wondered what had made her grab the crowbar that day. Had she known all along that at some point, his verbal abuse would turn violent? Something deep inside of her must have known, or she never would have picked it up. And she knew for certain that if it had come down to it, she would have used it on him to protect her daughter and herself.

That thought sent chills up her spine.

"I could have been Anna," she whispered. "Had things happened differently, I could have lost my daughter and spent my life in prison, too."

That night, as Diane lay in bed curled up next to Barry, she felt better than she had in years. She knew she'd made the right decision leaving Jeffrey all those years ago, and she knew that Barry was not Jeffrey. He'd never once displayed anger toward her, and he'd always been kind and loving toward Natalie. It was time to let go of her fear of the past and start trusting again.

Diane smiled to herself. It was all because of Anna. Her bravery in sharing her story had given Diane the strength to face her own. It was the best gift anyone could have given her.

* * *

Wednesday afternoon, Diane showed up at Anna's eager to hear more of her story. But when she walked into her grandmother's apartment, she was surprised to see the older woman lying in her bed, the back adjusted so she was sitting up.

"Anna. Are you feeling okay?" Diane asked, a worried frown creasing her face.

"Hello, dear," Anna said, her voice sounding weaker than usual. "Don't fret about me. I was just feeling a little more tired than usual the past few days, and my doctor thought I should rest."

"I'm sorry. I had no idea. You should have called to tell me you weren't feeling well," Diane told her. "I don't want to tire you out."

"But I like it when you visit. It brightens my day."

Diane smiled. "I love visiting you. You've made my life so much fuller. And your story has helped me come to terms with my own past, which is big, believe me."

"Really? Well, you'll have to tell me about it," Anna said, looking pleased.

Diane pulled the chair next to the bed and sat down. "First, you said you saw your doctor. What did he say?"

"Oh," Anna swiped her hand through the air. "He basically told me I was suffering from old age." She chuckled.

Diane laughed. "I'm sure he said more than that."

"Well, I have a little issue with my heart. He adjusted my medication, thinking it was making me tired. But let's not talk about my health. Tell me about your big breakthrough."

Diane told her the story of the day she decided she'd had

enough of Jeffrey's abuse and finally had the strength to leave him. "There was no way he was ever going to treat our daughter the way he'd treated me. But I was surprised at the lengths I would have gone to protect Natalie from him. I would have hit him with that crowbar if I had to. I'm not a violent person, and the thought that I could become violent like that has scared me for years. But I'm not going to let my fear hold me back any longer. Barry isn't my ex; he's completely the opposite. I want to finally let go of the past and move forward with him."

Anna's face had grown serious while Diane related her story. After she was finished, Anna nodded her head. "Yes. It's surprising and scary the lengths we women will go to protect our children." She looked up into Diane's eyes. "I'm so glad you shared your story with me, dear. And I'm happy you didn't have to turn to violence to save your daughter. It's too high a price to pay, but one that is sometimes necessary."

Diane studied her grandmother's face. Her eyes looked far away as if she were thinking of that fateful day that had changed her own life. "I'm so sorry. I didn't mean to make you sad," Diane said.

"No, you didn't. I thought I knew William too, even though we were married after only a few months," Anna said. "I should've listened to my Auntie May and waited, but I was so eager to be a wife and mother, I just didn't. I paid for being impatient. I paid for it in many ways."

CHAPTER TWENTY-NINE

Anna - 1952

Anna once again packed up the family's meager belongings in May of 1952 and said a tearful goodbye to Mari, whom she'd grown close to over the past year-and-a-half. William had once again quit his job and was moving the family up to Ontario, Canada, to join Thomas and Mattie at their resort. Thomas had offered them room, board, and pay if they'd work from May to September.

"It's a good opportunity to save money," William told Anna as they made the long car drive from California to Ontario. "I've decided I want to work for myself, and this way, I can save money and hopefully buy a small business where I can be my own boss."

William had been talking about starting his own business for a while, and Anna thought it might be a good idea considering how much he hated working for someone else. But it scared her. He'd thought he'd like to run a bar, and that would mean his working nights and always being around liquor. But she kept her opinions to herself. Maybe he'd be a successful business owner and would finally settle down and not be on the move every year.

But first, she had to get through the next few months working for Thomas and Mattie. While Anna felt she'd be fine working for the pair, she was certain William and his father would eventually butt heads.

They drove for several days across country, and when they entered Minnesota, they drove up to the border. The resort was located on a lake about three hours north of the Minnesota-Canadian border, and about twenty miles from the nearest small town. After driving down a dirt road for miles, they came to a hill, and there below, with the lake all around, sat the lodge on a point plus several small cabins spread out nearly hidden among the trees. It was so beautiful, it nearly took Anna's breath away.

"Don't be fooled," William said. "It may be beautiful, but it's going to be a lot of work."

Anna realized that. But the sight of it was so amazing, she didn't let William's words ruin the moment.

Mattie seemed the most excited to see the trio when they arrived. She hugged Anna tightly and exclaimed at how big Joan had grown. "She's no longer a baby," she said, watching the toddler run around the lodge's grand living room. At twenty-one months old, Joanie was tall for her age and quite agile. She loved climbing on everything and was always busy. She was a handful for Anna, but she loved her dearly.

Thomas didn't give them as warm a welcome. "The place opens this weekend, so be ready to work," he grumbled. "And someone is going to have to keep an eye on that kid so she isn't always underfoot."

"That kid's name is Joan, and she'll be fine," William shot

back. "I'm ready to work. Always am."

"We'll see," Thomas said.

Mattie showed them their room which was upstairs in the lodge. It was basically a large storage room under the eaves, but there was a window and the room was large enough to put up a curtain to separate Joan's space from theirs. William carried up their suitcases. All the larger items they owned had been boxed up and stored in Mari's garage, waiting to be shipped to wherever they landed in October. At this point, Anna was learning not to accumulate items she loved because if it didn't fit in a suitcase or in the car, she couldn't keep it.

After they'd settled in, William went outside to work with Thomas and Mattie showed Anna what she'd be doing. She took her on a tour of the big kitchen where they'd be cooking three meals a day for the guests as well as baking bread and desserts daily. "The lodge has electricity powered by a generator, so we have running water and a bathroom, thank goodness. The gas oven is powered by propane. Thomas is cheap, though, so the generator is turned off by nine, and you'll have to walk around here with an oil lamp." A screened-in back porch was off the kitchen and faced the lake. Anna thought it would be a nice place to catch cool breezes in the evening.

Mattie showed her around the property. The docks were right outside the lodge, and Anna saw that Thomas hadn't wasted any time in getting William right to work. The two men were moving small wooden boats into the water and tying them to the long docks.

"We have six cabins of varying sizes, and it will be our job to clean them after the guests leave," Mattie said. "There's no power to any of the cabins, only oil lamps for light at night. There are also six outhouses, one for each cabin. The largest cabin has three bedrooms and its own kitchen, so there's a generator connected to it for groups who may want to cook their own meals."

Anna nodded. It seemed like this was going to be a tremendous amount of work. Not that she minded, but she was worried how she'd keep Joan occupied and safe while she worked all over the resort. Even now, trying to keep an eye on the little girl as Mattie showed her around was difficult.

"Don't worry about Joanie," Mattie said as if reading her mind. "We can take turns watching her depending upon who is in the safest spot. She can sit at the big table in the kitchen while we cook, and we'll give her things to do. It'll work out somehow."

"Thanks, Mattie," Anna said, grateful that she was kinder and more considerate to people's needs compared to Thomas. If he had his way, she was sure he'd put the little girl in a cage all day.

As Thomas had warned, the resort filled up that weekend. Anna tried hard to keep up with all the work while watching Joanie. It wasn't easy. Joanie was distracted easily and wanted to follow her mother around instead of sitting quietly. At mealtimes, Anna had to keep Joan in a highchair to stop the little girl from running in and out of the kitchen as Anna served the guests. But Joan hated being confined for a long time and would eventually start crying to be let down. Mattie would give her a cookie, or Anna would hand her a toy, but it wouldn't distract the girl for long.

"Make that kid shut up!" Thomas growled as he sat eating his dinner in the kitchen. William was a little more patient, but even he got annoyed with Joan's fussiness. It was frustrating to Anna, trying to care for Joanie and work at the lodge from sun-up to sun-down with no time off.

But one night after they'd been there working for a month, Anna lost her temper. Joanie was fussing again about being secured in her highchair. Anna had just come back into the kitchen after serving the guests dinner, carrying an empty platter. She watched in horror as Thomas stood over Joanie, ready to slap her face. Anna dropped the platter, which shattered on the floor, and grabbed Thomas's wrist before he could touch her child. "Don't you dare hit my baby," she growled, glaring up at him.

Red-faced, Thomas pulled his arm away from Anna. "I'll hit whoever I want in this house!" he yelled. "Make that brat shut up, or I'll smack *you* into tomorrow."

William had been watching the entire scene looking stunned, but his father's words moved him into action. He stood and stepped between Thomas and Anna. "You hit my wife and I'll make you wish you were dead," he told the older man.

Thomas snorted. "Look who's talking. Mr. Tough Guy. You only have enough nerve to hit someone in a skirt."

William was in Thomas's face in an instant, but Mattie pushed between them.

"Stop it! Both of you!" Mattie screamed, holding a frying pan in one hand. "Or I'll smack you both. And leave the baby alone," she said directly to Thomas. "She's too little to understand. You're the one who should know better."

Thomas stormed out of the kitchen, and William sat down to finish his dinner as if nothing had happened. Anna, still shaking from her stand-off with Thomas, started to pick up the fragments left from the platter.

"Leave it be, Anna," Mattie said gently. "Why don't you

bring dessert out to the guests while I clean this up?"

She nodded and went back to her work. Joanie, she noticed, was quiet after all that had transpired. Anna was sure that Thomas had scared her into silence.

That night as Anna got into bed beside William, she saw that he was staring at her with a silly grin on his face. "What's so funny?" she whispered, careful not to wake Joanie, who was asleep in a small bed on the other side of the curtain.

"You," he said. "I had no idea you had that kind of grit in you. Taking on Thomas is pretty gutsy." He chuckled.

Anna found no humor in what had transpired earlier in the evening. "I don't know what came over me tonight. I saw your father standing over Joan, and all I saw was red. I grabbed him before I even realized what I was doing. I won't let that man hit my child." She looked up at William. "No one will ever hit my child," she said with certainty.

William studied her a moment, letting what she'd said sink in. "Well, you made that perfectly clear to Thomas." He smiled. "And I think you even scared him."

Anna doubted that. Thomas wasn't a man who scared easily. "Thank you for defending me," she said in a gentle voice. "I have no doubt that your father is capable of hitting me."

William's face softened as he gently touched the side of her face. "I know I haven't been the best husband to you, and I'm sorry. But I'll never let him hurt you. Ever. If he lays a hand on you, tell me. I'll take care of him."

She nodded but remained silent. The last thing she wanted was to come between William and his father. Their relationship was rocky enough without her adding to it.

The weeks passed, and Anna made sure to keep Joan out of Thomas's way. July and August were the hottest months, and despite the fans that ran in the kitchen, it was sweltering in there. Mattie did all the baking early in the morning with the kitchen windows open to let in the cool lake breeze, but still, by lunchtime, it was blazing hot. Likewise, cleaning cabins was hot work too. There were no fans, and even if Anna opened all the windows, she was soaking wet by the time she'd changed the beds and swept the floors. Little Joan was always by her side, and Anna had even bought her a mini broom and dustpan set at the dime store in town so she could pretend to help her mama.

Working in dresses was difficult, so Anna had purchased two pairs of capri pants and a couple of sleeveless blouses in town with her leftover birthday money from Auntie May. She wore an old pair of Keds sneakers while she worked and tied a scarf around her hair to keep it out of her face. When Anna looked in the mirror, she laughed at herself. She looked like a much different woman than the one who'd worn fancy suits and heels to work only a couple of years before.

The biting flies and mosquitoes were thick in the woods and on the lake, so William always wore long pants and a long-sleeved cotton shirt. Anna wondered how he could stand the heat dressed that way, but he told her he'd rather be hot than chewed up by the bugs. Anna also noticed that William wore a pistol in a holster on his belt as he worked. Thomas wore one also. She asked him the first night she'd seen it why they each needed a gun.

"You never know what you're going to run into in the woods," he'd told her. "It's just safer to have one."

While the men did sometimes take people out on hikes in the surrounding woods, they spent most of their time in the boats, so the guns seemed unnecessary to her. But then, she remembered how her grandfather and uncles carried a gun around the farm too, so she supposed it wasn't so strange. She soon grew used to seeing the pistol on William's hip and forgot about it.

One thing Anna was grateful for was that the town was so far away. William was home every night, and usually so tired after working outside all day, he'd fall into bed early and go to sleep quickly. At least he wasn't drinking in a bar all night or coming home with another woman's perfume on him. And because he wasn't straying, their relationship was stronger. Even though they worked a lot, they also were able to take a little time to enjoy the beautiful area. William sometimes took Anna and Joan on boat rides in the evening, or they'd take walks in the woods before the sun went down, and the mosquitos ate them alive. They enjoyed spending the time together, and for the first time in a long time, Anna felt like they were a real family.

Many of the guests that came to the resort were old friends of Mattie and Thomas from their speakeasy and bootlegging days. Often, after the day was done, Mattie and Thomas would sit and drink with their friends, talking about the good old days. Anna was surprised and pleased that William rarely joined in. He'd go to bed instead, exhausted from his work day, content to hold her in his arms as he slept.

Near the end of August, a big family group rented the large cabin for a week. It was two young families with two kids each, and their unmarried younger brother. The men hired William to take them fishing at the best spots, while the women laid on the sandy shore and watched their children play in the water. Anna got to know the women quite well because they were always asking for snacks for the kids or towels or advice on

activities to do in town. Their children were all under the age
of five, so they watched them like hawks as the children played.
One of the women named Evelyn even invited Joan to join the
kids while Anna cleaned cabins.

"Oh, she'd love that. It's so boring for her here," Anna said.
"But are you sure?"

"What's one more?" Evelyn asked, then laughed. "I promise
we'll keep her safe. You've been so kind to us this week, it's the
least we can do."

Anna thought it would be good for Joan to play with other
children, and the women seemed very responsible, so she went
off to the two cabins that needed cleaning. The day was warm,
but there was a cool breeze coming off the lake. It had rained
the night before, pushing out the thick humidity from the
previous day. Anna carried her cleaning supplies in a bucket
and brought along a mop and broom.

She cleaned out the first cabin, then went to the other one
that was closest to the large cabin. As she changed the sheets in
the little bedroom, she heard a floorboard creak from the outer
area of the cabin. Startled, she turned and saw the man who
was staying in the bigger cabin with the two families.

"Did you need something?" she asked, her heart pounding
from his scaring her.

He smiled at her. "I saw the door was open and just thought
I'd come in and talk with you a moment." He was a handsome
young man, who looked to be in his twenties, with wavy brown
hair and deep brown eyes. He was slender, and very tan from
his time out on the boat this week.

"Oh, well, I was just cleaning out the cabin," Anna said.
"We have new guests coming tomorrow."

He nodded. "It's very busy here. They must keep you jumping."

"Yes, they do." She hesitated. It made her nervous being alone with this man she barely knew. "I thought all the men went out fishing this morning."

"Oh, they did. I didn't feel like sitting in a small boat all day, waiting to catch a fish." He grinned again. "I'm Adam, by the way." He lifted his hand to shake hers. "And you're Anna, right?"

Anna shook his hand quickly, then pulled away. "Yes. I am. My husband is one of the fishing guides out with the men today." She hoped the word 'husband' would make Adam leave.

"Oh, yes. And that cute little girl is yours too?"

"Yes. That's Joan. The women from your group are watching her right now."

"That's nice of them. Well, I thought I'd take a walk along the lake to the point. It's very rocky and a great place to sit and enjoy the scenery," Adam said. "Any chance you'd like to join me after you're done here?"

Anna was taken aback. Had he really invited her on a walk alone with him even after she'd said she had a husband? What on earth would William think? "I'm sorry. I have more work to do after I'm done here. I hope you have a nice walk."

"Oh. Okay. I'll see you around then," he said, then walked out the door.

Anna let out a sigh and went back to her work. The last thing she needed was for William to get jealous because another man noticed her. She stopped and thought about that a moment. Why would Adam give her the time of day? She glanced in the little mirror over the dresser. She looked like a charwoman in an old fairytale. Cinderella. She laughed. Yes, that's who she was, and Adam was most definitely not a prince coming to save her.

By the time Anna was finished serving dinner and washing dishes, she'd forgotten all about Adam. He hadn't come in for dinner with the rest of the group, so she didn't give him a second thought. She put Joan to bed, then came downstairs and went to sit a moment in the screened-in porch off the kitchen. The other guests had gone to their own cabins, Mattie was in her bedroom, and William and Thomas were still cleaning fish for the guests down at the little hut by the lake. The sun was low in the sky, painting the lake a beautiful orange color. In the distance, a loon cried. Anna closed her eyes as she sat back on the loveseat glider and listened to the loon's soulful call. These were the moments she didn't mind working at the lodge. She wouldn't want to do this for the rest of her life, but for now, it wasn't so bad. William was saving the money he and she were earning for the business he wanted to start, and hopefully, by this fall, they'd be somewhere else and begin again.

"Daydreaming, I see," a husky voice said.

Startled, Anna opened her eyes, and there stood Adam. She hadn't heard the outside door open. Quickly, she sat up. "I was just resting, enjoying the sounds of the lake and loons," she said.

"Well, maybe I'll join you," Adam said, choosing to sit right next to Anna.

She stood. "The men will be finished cleaning fish any minute now, and I'll have to wash and refrigerate the filets. It would be best if my husband didn't see you in here with me."

He grinned. "Who? Bill? Why? We're just talking."

Anna wrung her hands. "His name is William, not Bill. And he wouldn't see it that way. Please, just leave before they come."

Adam stood and walked closer to Anna. "It seems a shame

that someone as pretty as you has to fear your husband," he said in a soothing tone.

Anna backed away another step, and that's when she saw William walking up the path to the porch, his face set in a scowl. It was too late for Anna to flee into the kitchen. He'd already seen her.

The door flung open with a loud bang. "What's going on here?" William asked gruffly. He was holding the fish wrapped in newspaper.

"I just came to say goodnight to Anna, Bill," Adam said, a smirk on his face.

William's scowl deepened. "Come on, Anna. Let's get these in the kitchen." He stormed past her and through the door. Anna didn't look up at Adam. She followed William inside.

"What the hell was he doing out there with you?" William shot at her the moment they were alone in the kitchen. He dropped the fish into the stainless-steel sink with a heavy thunk.

"I didn't invite him," she said calmer than she felt. "I was sitting there alone when he came along." She went to the sink and began rinsing each of the fillets as if nothing was wrong.

"I don't like that guy sniffing around you," William told her. "You stay away from him."

Anna didn't reply. Anything she said right now would be wrong. After a moment's silence, William went outside again through the back porch. Anna sighed. They'd had a relatively calm few months here at the resort. She didn't want anything to change that. She hoped Adam understood the message from William's rude behavior that he wasn't welcome around her.

The next day was Sunday; usually the last day most guests stayed. Anna couldn't wait for the residents of the large cabin to check out the next day. Sunday was wash day for their own linens and sheets, and after the men left to take the guests fishing, Anna did several loads of laundry. Mattie was in the kitchen, preparing lunch for when the fishermen came back and was looking after Joan. They had managed to set up a little area in the corner of the kitchen for the little girl with toys that kept her occupied.

Anna carried the wet sheets outside and began hanging them on the line. There was a cool breeze, and the air was scented with cedar and pine from the trees that surrounded the resort. The clothesline faced the lake, and Anna enjoyed watching the many loons, geese, and ducks out on the water as she worked. It reminded her of the summers near Leach Lake when her father was at Aw-Gwah-Ching. Even after all these years, she missed her father and brother deeply. She'd barely known her mother, so it was more difficult to miss her. But her dear father remained in her heart.

"What's that sad look on your face for Anna?" a male voice asked from behind her.

Anna jumped at the sound. She turned and saw Adam there, only inches from her. "You have to stop startling me like that," she said brusquely. "I'm busy. I can't talk right now. Please, go."

Adam studied her a moment. "Don't worry. Bill is out in the boat, as usual."

"Don't call him Bill. He hates that. They'll be back for lunch any minute. Please. Leave me alone." She turned and lifted another sheet from the basket to hang, but Adam drew closer.

"Why is such a pretty woman like you with such a horrible man like Bill?" Adam whispered close to her ear. "You deserve so much better."

She stiffened at his nearness. This man didn't have real feelings for her, he just saw something he wanted and wouldn't take no for an answer. She'd been fooled by William's lines once; no man could fool her again. Anna turned. "Go away. Please."

A shadow came from out of nowhere behind Adam, grabbed him, and threw him to the ground. Anna was shocked to see William standing over the younger man. She'd been so intent on making Adam leave she hadn't heard the motors of the boats returning to the dock.

"Stay away from my wife!" William growled, his fists clenched at his sides.

Adam laughed as he lay on the grass. He stood, brushed himself off, and then stared William straight in the eye. "Your wife is too good for you, Bill. You don't deserve her."

Anna's eyes grew wide as she watched William's face redden with anger. William was a few years older than Adam and several pounds larger. He grabbed the younger man by the collar of his shirt with his left hand and punched him dead in the face with his right. Adam fell to the ground, and William was on him instantly, hitting his face over and over.

Anna rushed to the men and began screaming, "Stop it, William! Stop it! You're going to kill him!"

But William ignored her as he got his revenge on this man who'd been antagonizing him for days.

Thomas and the other men came running from the dock, and the other lodge guests who'd been heading in for lunch came running too. Everyone was yelling for William to stop, but it fell on deaf ears. William was so enraged, he was like an animal on prey.

Thomas tried to pull him off Adam, but it was useless. He resorted to kicking William in the side so hard that he fell off the other man. William was up in an instant, ready to punch whoever had kicked him, his eyes glazed and wild looking. Thomas stood his ground in front of his son.

"You're killing the man! Stop it!" Thomas yelled.

William stood still a moment, refocusing, his breath coming in short gasps. The other guests had run to Adam to help him.

Mattie came out of the kitchen, and when she saw the bloodied man, she ran back in and brought out wet towels and the first aid kit. Thomas grabbed William's arm and pulled him to the kitchen, waving for Anna to follow.

"What the hell were you thinking?" Thomas yelled at William, pushing him to sit down at the table. "You nearly killed that man!"

William looked dazed. His fists were cut up and bloody, and his breathing was still ragged. "He was bothering Anna," he said. "No man is going to take what I own."

Anna stared in disbelief. *No man is going to take what I own.* William thought he owned her. Like a piece of property. She shivered at the thought.

"Get some wet rags," Thomas barked at her, pointing to William's fists.

Anna moved to the sink and wet two washrags. She brought them over to her husband and carefully began cleaning the blood from his hands.

"I don't care what that man said to you or Anna. These are our guests. Do you know what a stunt like this could cost me?" Thomas said, his tone menacing. "You will single-handedly ruin our resort before we even get it off the ground. What if they get the sheriff? He could have you locked up for battery, or worse, attempted murder."

"I don't care," William said. "I was defending my wife. He provoked me."

"Ahh!" Thomas threw his hands in the air. "You'd better hope that guy is okay, that's all I can say." He stormed out the back door.

Anna was still gently wiping the blood from William's hands. He had several gashes from hitting Adam's face. William suddenly grabbed her wrist. "Look at me!" he insisted.

Her heart pounding, Anna raised her eyes to his. A storm still brewed there and could unleash its rage at any minute.

"Did you invite his advances? Did you tell him that you were too good for me? Is that what you think?" he asked, his anger rising.

"No! I told him to leave me alone. I never once invited him to talk to me." She was shaking. If William took his anger out on her, she'd never survive it.

A small cry came from the corner behind the table. In all the turmoil, everyone had forgotten Joanie was playing in that spot. Now, the little girl looked up at her parents with wide, fearful eyes. She'd seen and heard everything.

Anna looked from Joanie to William. He still had a tight grasp on her wrist. "I would never do anything to break up our family," Anna said softly. "You know that."

William stared at her another moment, then released her wrist. "Take care of our daughter," he said.

Anna hurried to pick up Joanie and could feel how frightened the little girl was. She stiffened at her mother's touch, not sure who to trust. Anna held her close and whispered in her ear that everything was fine until the little girl relaxed.

Mattie came back in, shaking her head, and finished making lunch. Anna placed Joan in her highchair and fed her, then helped Mattie. William only sat there, dazed.

When Thomas finally came back in, he was fuming and went directly to William. "They're taking him to the hospital in town. That means the doctors will ask how he got that way, and then the sheriff will be sent out here. You have less than an hour to pack up and leave before you're arrested."

Anna stopped stacking a platter with sandwiches and stared at Thomas in disbelief. "You mean we have to leave?"

He spun on Anna. "Of course you have to leave. Otherwise, this idiot will be in jail for God knows how long." He waved his hand at Anna to get going. "Go pack now! Take what you can and get out of here."

Anna turned to Mattie, and the older woman nodded. "Go on. It won't help anyone if William goes to jail."

William stood, his face no longer red, but his eyes staring daggers at his father. "I'll leave. But I'm not the one to blame. That jerk out there is. You make sure to tell the sheriff that."

"What does it matter now?" Thomas asked haughtily. "You've screwed up again. You always screw up. Now go and pack and get out of here."

Anna lifted Joanie out of the highchair and headed out to the main room. She had to pass the table of guests who were eating lunch to go upstairs. Everyone stopped talking and stared when they saw her as if she were the guilty one. She rushed upstairs and quickly packed their bags.

An hour later, they'd packed up their car and Anna hugged Mattie goodbye. "I wish we weren't leaving," she said tearfully. "I'm so sorry for what happened."

Mattie pulled back and looked her in the eye. "It's not your fault, so don't let William bully you into believing it is. He did it. You did nothing wrong."

Anna nodded, but she knew that somehow, she'd be blamed for what had happened.

Thomas was still so angry that he wouldn't even come to see them off. Not only had William brought trouble to their door, but they'd be left with no help for the next few weeks.

As William pulled down the dirt road, his hands still bloodied, he was deadly silent. Joan had been fussy for a few minutes, then had fallen asleep in the back seat, hugging her tired-looking dolly William had given her that first Christmas. After they'd gassed up the car in town, William headed south to the Minnesota border.

"Where are we going?" Anna asked timidly.

"Buffalo. But we need to get out of Canada fast, so we'll go by way of Minnesota."

"Why Buffalo?" Anna asked.

He turned to her. "I didn't make as much money as I'd planned, but I'm going to invest in a bar my uncle owns. He needs a partner. It'll be a start."

Anna nodded. She hadn't known William had been planning to go into business with one of Thomas's brothers. It sounded like a disaster waiting to happen.

William turned and stared hard at her. "You know, this move is on you this time."

She sat silent. She knew he would blame her. They had a lot of miles to go sitting in cramped quarters in the car, so the last thing she needed was to irritate William more than he already was.

Once they crossed the border, she noticed William relaxed. Like a con man playing a game on a mark, he'd beat the odds again.

CHAPTER THIRTY

Anna - 1953

A nna felt queasy as she rushed out of bed and into their tiny bathroom. It was seven in the morning, and although William didn't get out of bed until noon, she still woke up early to feed Joanie and start their day. But this morning, she was feeling green around the gills. Anna hoped she hadn't caught some bug that was going around.

Once she'd been sick, her stomach settled, and she padded out to the kitchen. It was January, and the small apartment was cold. They lived on the top floor of a four-story brownstone, and their radiator was the last to get any heat. Winter in Buffalo could be damp and bitter, and a poor heating system was the last thing anyone wanted.

She turned on the stove and opened the door half-way to heat up the kitchen. Anna was thankful that cockroaches hibernated in the winter so she didn't have to deal with the awful creatures scurrying about. William had found them the cheapest apartment possible, which meant it was even worse than the one they'd lived in the last time they were here. The tenants were questionable, and the bugs were disgusting. Since moving here six months ago, Anna had made friends with a few of the women who had children, but she kept her distance from the other tenants. Some shady-looking men lived on the second floor, and the first floor reminded her of a brothel— single women who had men coming in at all hours of the day or night. Anna had never been one to judge others, but she couldn't turn a blind eye to what she saw going on in the building.

William, however, ignored everyone and focused on working afternoons and nights at the bar he claimed to own half of. At first, he'd been excited, handing over his meager savings to his Uncle Lewis and working twelve-hour shifts at the bar. William made up business cards with the bar's name, The Last Drop Saloon, and his name with the title 'proprietor' under it. He'd learned from Lewis how to tend bar and already had the gift of gab—and lying—down pat, so he was a natural. But as the months passed and little money came in, William was becoming disillusioned at being an owner. When Anna asked meekly for grocery money or to buy necessities for Joan, who was growing like a weed, William grumbled and handed over a few dollars, much less than she needed. It seemed he brought home only tips, not a paycheck, and it was getting harder for Anna to squeeze as much value out of each dollar as she could.

Ever since William's violent behavior at the resort, Anna was growing desperate to find a way out of their marriage. *No man is going to take what I own.* She remembered the words he'd said to Thomas after the fight, and they gave her chills every time. William thought he owned her, and recently, he'd become even more possessive of her. Because he worked all day and into the night, he'd quiz her on what she and Joanie had done the day before, where she went and who she saw. She felt she was being interrogated. After she'd answer, he'd put his face close to hers and say menacingly, "I hope you're telling the truth." It chilled her to the bone. Anna wasn't sure how much longer she could take it. Plus, she'd found the pistol he'd carried in Canada in his nightstand drawer. It was loaded. She wondered why he'd kept it since it belonged to Thomas. It scared her to think of this weapon in the house with Joanie, especially being so close at hand when William was drunk or went into a rage.

Thomas and Mattie had moved back to Buffalo and were living in their old apartment building, but they rarely saw his father. Thomas was still angry with William for putting his business at risk, and he also thought his son was stupid for going into business with Lewis. At least that was what Mattie reported to Anna when she'd stop by with lunch after work for her and Joanie a couple of times a week.

"Lewis is a worst con-artist than Thomas," Mattie said seriously. "He'll wipe William out for sure."

"I could never tell him that," Anna said, disappointed to hear this was yet another dead-end job. "He wouldn't believe me anyway."

She was thankful for Mattie's visits and the food she brought for her and Joanie. Most days, Anna and Joanie ate bologna sandwiches or beef hot dogs and whatever vegetable Anna could afford to buy. Sometimes they had pancakes for dinner, each having one slice of bacon. There were always eggs in the house and bread for toast for William's breakfast. But other than that, she could afford little on the money he gave her.

The women in the building soon learned that Anna had a talent for embroidery, tatting, and crocheting. They'd seen the beautiful lace collars she'd made for Joanie's dresses and the tatted hems on the dresses she made from discarded scraps of fabric for her daughter's doll. Soon, women were asking her to make lacey items for them or to edge a blouse hem to make it look new again. The women told their mothers, sisters, and friends, and soon, Anna had enough work to keep her busy day and night. This, she thought, was precisely what she needed to earn extra money to stash away so she could someday disappear with Joan. Anna told the women not to come to her apartment door until after one in the afternoon so as not to disturb her husband. That way, he would never know she was earning money.

As the months went by, Anna used some of the money for necessities, but most of it was rolled up and hidden in an overturned teacup in the back of the cabinet. Since William would never drink his coffee out of a dainty teacup, she knew it was safe there.

Joanie was growing bigger and smarter every day. She was two-and-a-half years old and would sometimes play with the other children in the hall under Anna's watchful eye. Joan was a talker, learning new words daily. Anna taught her nursery rhymes like "Hey diddle diddle, the cat and the fiddle, the cow jumped over the moon," or "Twinkle, twinkle little star." Anna would recite them along with her mother, as well as sing songs they learned from the radio. Joanie was so quick at learning, Anna had to be careful what was said around her, so it wasn't repeated to William.

By March, Anna knew she was expecting another baby. She'd had morning sickness for weeks and had felt increasingly tired. The doctor confirmed she'd have the baby by October. Anna had mixed emotions over bringing another baby into the world. She loved the thought of Joan having a sibling. She remembered how much she'd loved her own brother, and how nice it would be for her children to have each other through the years. But another baby would make it harder for her to get away from William. She wasn't sure she could support both children alone.

It also scared her to share this news with William. He was becoming increasingly discontented with working at the bar. Lewis treated him like an employee, not a partial owner. They fought all the time. She feared the news that another baby was on the way would put William over the edge.

A few days later, William seemed like he was in a good mood when he woke up, so Anna sat at the table with him while he ate his breakfast. She'd made sure Joan was busy playing with her few toys across the room by the window. Tentatively, Anna said, "I have some news."

William was just about to take a bite of his eggs when he stopped and looked at her suspiciously. "What news?"

Anna swallowed the lump forming in her throat. "We're expecting another baby," she said softly.

He stared at her a moment, looking confused. Her words finally hit him. "Again?" he asked, setting his fork down. "How the hell did that happen?"

Anna took a breath. She had wondered the same thing since William rarely touched her anymore, and when he did, she used a diaphragm. But there had been that one night in late December when he'd come home late from the bar and basically forced himself on her. She hadn't been able to put in her diaphragm, even though she'd begged William to give her a moment.

"It had to be that one night in December," she said quietly.

She hated discussing this with Joan in the room.

"Christ! How am I supposed to support another child? We can barely pay for the one we have."

"William. Please don't yell. Joanie can hear you," Anna begged.

He stood and stormed into the bedroom, coming back with his suit jacket on. "I don't want to talk to you right now. You were supposed to take care of this. I told you I didn't want any more children." He grabbed his coat out of the closet and slammed the door on his way out.

Joanie was startled by the yelling and slamming of the door and began crying softly. Anna went to her and hugged her close, tears forming in her own eyes. "It's okay, sweetie. We're okay," she said.

William came home later than usual that night and was extremely drunk. This went on night after night. He ignored Anna each morning when she served his breakfast and ignored Joanie as well. He was having a tantrum like a child, and Anna was at a loss as to what to do.

"He'll get over it eventually," Mattie told her when she visited that week, bringing sandwiches for lunch. "The problem is, he never had a real father as a child, so he isn't comfortable being a father. He probably never even wanted children."

"That's what he said," Anna told her. "But he never told me he didn't want children. It just never came up. And it's not like I planned this. He didn't give me the option to be careful." Anna blushed when she said this. She wasn't comfortable talking about such intimate subjects.

Mattie studied her a moment. "I see," she finally said. "You're going to have to learn how to tell him no in no uncertain terms, or this could happen again."

Anna shook her head. "No one says no to William," she said softly.

Mattie nodded, a serious look on her face. She understood. She'd seen William's rage at the resort last summer, and she'd also witnessed the bruises he'd left on Anna in the past. "I'm sorry, Anna. The Craine men are a tough bunch. I wish there were something I could do to help."

But Anna knew there was nothing Mattie could do. Anna was the only one who could change her situation. But now that they had a second baby on the way, she felt she had no choices.

The months went by, and Anna grew larger. She took Joan to the park most days during the summer, even when the heat was unbearable. Anything was better than staying inside the apartment. Anna used the money she earned from the women for tatting and embroidery to buy items she'd need for the new baby. A small basket for him or her to sleep in, sleepers and rompers, a blanket to swaddle the baby in. She also had to buy new shoes for Joan to walk the hot streets in, and some summer clothes to wear. Joan was growing out of her clothes quickly, and it was getting harder to keep her in anything for very long. When William noticed the new items, he'd sneer and ask where Anna got the money.

"Auntie May sent a few dollars for baby items," she told him. Knowing how May was, he didn't question the lie. In truth, Anna hadn't written to May in a while. She'd sent news about the upcoming baby, but nothing more. As far as her aunt knew, they were doing fine and didn't need a handout.

On a warm morning in mid-July, as William was getting ready to leave for work, there was a knock on the door. Anna quickly answered it, terrified to find one of the women she'd made several lace collars for standing there.

"Hi, Anna," the woman said, smiling. "I came for the collars. Sorry to be early, but I have so many errands to run today."

Anna froze, not sure what to say. William was standing by the door, watching her, hearing every word. "Just a minute," Anna said, nearly closing the door.

"Who's that?" William wanted to know.

She thought quickly. "Oh, I made a few lace collars for a friend. She bought the thread for me to use." Anna retrieved the collars that she'd wrapped in tissue and bagged so they wouldn't get dirty. "Here you go. I hope you like them."

The woman held out the money she owed her, but Anna shook her head. "No need for that. That's what friends do for each other," she said quickly. Anna said goodbye to the stunned woman and shut the door quickly.

William stared at her with narrowed eyes. "Why was she going to pay you?"

"I have no idea," Anna said as casually as she could manage. "I made them as a favor. It keeps my hands busy while I sit at the park with Joan." She headed for the kitchen to clear away the dishes on the table, hoping that William would believe her. But he followed her into the small kitchen.

"Have you been selling your fancywork to women in the apartment building?" he asked.

Anna tried not to tremble. "No. Of course not. Sometimes the women give me thread to make them something, but then we trade for pieces of fabric and such. Never money."

"You're lying." He walked right up to her, backing her against the sink. "Are you making extra money behind my back and hiding it? Are you?" he yelled when she didn't answer.

"No. I'm just doing a little tatting for friends." Anna started to shake.

"What's the matter? Don't I give you enough money? Are you too good to live on what I make?" he screamed. "Where are you hiding the money? Where?"

When Anna didn't answer, he became enraged. William started opening drawers and cupboards in the kitchen and throwing stuff on the floor. He opened the dish cabinet and threw first one, then another dish. They fell to the floor and shattered.

"Stop! William, please stop! Don't break the dishes. I'll show you," she said. Anna walked over to the cabinet on wobbly legs and took down the teacup. She pulled the rolled-up bills out and handed them to him. "It isn't much—just a few dollars. I was trying to help, that's all. I needed a little money for baby things and new shoes for Joan." Her voice was small, and she backed away as he glared at the money she'd set in his hand.

"You were hiding money so you could leave me, weren't you?" he asked. "Weren't you?" he yelled.

"No. No. I wasn't going anywhere. You've been working so hard and putting so much into the bar. I just wanted to help."

The slap hit her so fast, she never saw it coming. She fell back against the sink and grabbed ahold of the counter so she wouldn't fall.

"Liar! Why do you lie to me? Do you think I'm stupid?" William took another step toward her, his hand raised. Anna turned away from him, crouching to protect the baby growing inside of her.

"Please. Don't," she begged pitifully. "Please don't hurt the baby."

He moved so close, she felt his hot breath on her neck. "You will never leave me, do you hear? Because if you even try, I will take the kids away from you so fast your head will spin. I'll tell everyone what a terrible mother you are. I'll make you so miserable, you'll wish you were dead."

Tears ran down Anna's cheeks as she let his threat sink in. She stood still as a statue, until she heard him walk away, then the front door shut. Only then did Anna allow herself to sink to the floor in relief.

"Mama?" Joan walked into the room in stocking feet, her little face looking frightened.

"Sweetie. Don't walk in here. You'll cut yourself. Mama is fine. I just dropped a few dishes." She pulled herself up and made her way to Joan, leading her out into the living room. Kneeling, she hugged her daughter tightly. "Mama's okay. Everything's okay," she said. Even though the words were a lie.

Inside her, Anna felt the baby move. She knew then that she could never leave William as long as she was alive. Fresh tears trailed down her face.

* * *

Anna never saw that money again. She supposed William spent it on drinking or another woman. He gave her very little money for groceries and necessities, and she did her best to stretch it. Anna no longer made pretty items to sell and told all the women no when they asked. If she hadn't been carrying a life inside of her, Anna would have felt like she had little to live for. Except for Joanie. She had to keep going for her daughter, and soon for her new baby.

Anna hadn't seen a doctor again after the pregnancy was confirmed. She couldn't afford it. She would have to take her chances on whoever was on call when she went into labor. Anna could only pray that the baby was doing fine, and all would go well.

As time went on, William was becoming angrier and more disagreeable. He constantly fought with Lewis, and several times his uncle threw him out of the bar because he was drunk while working. William always came home drunk now and thankfully passed out the moment he hit the bed.

Anna had moved Joan out into the living room to sleep on the sofa that opened into a bed. She wanted her to get used to sleeping out there, even though she was still young. Joan had turned three in August, and she and Anna had celebrated with a home-baked cake and funny hats they'd made from newspapers. Anna had bought her a little teddy bear at the dime store and had made the teddy a dress from an old flowered blouse of hers. William hadn't bothered to show up, even though Anna had told him they'd be celebrating, and he hadn't even bothered to buy Joanie a present. Anna hoped the little girl was young enough to not remember his forgetting her birthday.

One night in late September, with Anna's due date only a week and a half away, William came home at two in the morning after closing the bar. He shook Anna awake and told her to pack.

"Now?" she asked, dazed and exhausted from carrying so much extra weight around all day. "Why?"

"We're getting out of this hell-hole," he said, his suitcase already open. He was quickly shoving clothes into the bag. "Hurry up! We have to leave now."

She rose and did as she was told. Anna knew it wouldn't help to argue with him. She dressed quickly and then packed her clothes as well as Joan's and the few items she had for the baby. William took everything down to the car, even the bassinette Anna had purchased. Finally, she woke Joan, wrapped her in her blanket, and William carried her out to the back seat of the car. Thankfully, Joan quickly fell back to sleep.

As they drove away from the apartment building, Anna heard sirens screeching in the quiet night. A fire engine rushed past them, and then a police car.

"What's going on?" Anna asked. William didn't answer, he just kept driving. But instead of heading out of town, he drove in the direction the fire engine had gone. Anna saw the blaze long before they reached it, and when they slowly drove past the building on fire, her mouth dropped open. It was the bar William and Lewis owned.

William laughed. "I told him the electrical was shoddy, but he never listened to me. This will teach him." Then he drove on past the scene and out of town heading west.

Anna was stunned. His message was loud and clear. No one messes with William and gets away with it. Lewis had done something to make William furious, and this was how he retaliated. Anna knew that William had enough electrical knowledge to start a fire and make it look like an accident.

She didn't even ask where they were going. She slid down in the seat, wrapped her arms around the baby in her belly, and tried to sleep.

CHAPTER THIRTY-ONE

Diane

Diane's mouth had dropped open during the last part of the story, and she clamped it shut when she realized it. "He burned down the bar? Oh, my goodness! How did he always get away with such terrible stuff?"

Anna shook her head. "In those days, you could leave town and no one came looking for you. Plus, he was good at not leaving evidence. There was never any proof that he'd set the fire. Thomas told us that it was classified as an electrical fire, but we all knew it was William. On top of that, he owed two months back rent on our apartment. That's why we had to sneak out that night. He was always doing things like that. I felt terrible about it."

"It wasn't your fault. He earned the money, so it was his responsibility," Diane said.

"I suppose. But I still felt guilty. I wasn't raised to steal, but it didn't bother William at all."

Diane turned off her recorder and slipped it in her pocket. "I should let you rest. We've talked for a long time. I'm sure your dinner will be coming soon."

"I love talking with you, dear," Anna said, smiling warmly. "And we never know how much time we have, so the sooner I tell you everything, the better."

Diane frowned. "You'd tell me if you were really sick, wouldn't you?"

"I'm fine, dear. Just old. Who knows how long I have? I want you to know everything. Maybe someday, Joan will forgive me or at least try to understand why I did what I did. Knowing you have the whole story will give me closure before I go."

Diane stood and leaned over to hug Anna. "Don't leave me just yet, okay? I want to spend more time with you." She smiled at Anna and got her coat to leave. A nurse came in, bringing her dinner.

"Just on time," Diane said. "I'll see you Sunday, Anna. Take care."

"Goodnight, dear. I'll see you soon."

As Diane drove home, she thought about her grandmother and all she'd been through. Anna had to have been a strong woman to put up with all the terrible things William had done to her. And Diane didn't even know the entire story yet.

"I probably would have shot him long before she did," she mumbled to herself.

Later, as she and Barry ate baked chicken and rice for dinner, Barry asked, "Did you invite Anna for Thanksgiving Dinner next week? We still need to pick out a turkey."

She shook her head. "No, I didn't. I'm not sure my mother will come if Anna comes too. I know it won't give us much time to buy one, but I'll have to wait and ask mom on Friday."

He nodded. Diane appreciated how easy he made everything in their lives.

"I had an inquiry about my house today," Barry said, looking up at Diane. "My assistant knows I don't spend much time there, and she suggested to a new teacher that I might be willing to rent it to him. I guess I've never thought of doing that, but it's a good idea. What do you think?"

Diane stopped eating. "Oh. I don't know." Suddenly, the old panic rose inside her. If Barry rented out his house, that would mean he'd live with her permanently. She knew that was silly since he already lived with her. His clothes were in her closet, and his personal items were in the bathroom. But knowing it would be permanent scared her.

He smiled. "I see you're freaking out very quietly inside your head. Don't worry. We don't have to decide today. I just want you to consider it."

She sighed. "I'm that transparent?"

"It's okay." He reached over and placed his hand over hers. "It's hard for you. I understand. But it's expensive keeping a house when I actually live here most of the time. I promise I won't make you marry me if you let me live here." His eyes twinkled mischievously.

She laughed. "I thought I was over all this panic. And here it pops up at the thought of you giving up your house. It's stupid, really. You should rent it out—or sell it if you decide to. I agree it's silly for you to waste your time and money taking care of a house you don't live in."

His brows rose. "Are we having a breakthrough?"

"I already thought I'd had one, but now I have to make myself move forward. You should rent it if you can. It's a shame for the house to just sit there."

"You know," he took her hand in his. "If you decide you could stand me all the way through retirement, we could sell my house and use the money to buy a small place or a condo in a warmer climate and be snowbirds together."

She grinned. "That's a few years from now, but it's a nice thought."

"So, should I rent it?" he asked.

Diane took a stabilizing breath. "Yes. Rent it. It's only for the school year, so if I get tired of you, I could kick you out next summer."

"Then it's a plan," he said, grinning.

It's a plan, Diane thought as she finished her dinner. *Baby steps.* But she was proud of herself for being able to take this first step toward their relationship possibly becoming permanent.

* * *

Two days later, Barry was already moving the few personal possessions he had left in his house over to Diane's. He left everything else and rented it furnished.

"Don't you have any favorite furniture you want to keep?" she asked him.

"Everything I love is right here," he told her with a smile.

Barry always knew the right thing to say—not in a cheesy con-artist kind of way that William had used on Anna, but in a sweet way.

Friday afternoon, Diane showed up at her mother's place. She was going to invite her to come for Thanksgiving and ask her if she'd mind if Anna attended too. Diane had to steel herself to have enough nerve to bring up the subject.

She waited until they'd already eaten dinner and finished shopping. They were in Joan's apartment, putting items away when Diane broached the subject.

"Are you planning on coming to our house for Thanksgiving dinner this year?" Diane asked casually.

Her mother glanced her way. "Yes, if you want me there. Unless that woman is coming."

Diane sighed. Her mother already knew what she was up to. "I haven't asked Anna yet, because I wanted to ask you first if you'd mind her coming."

"I thought I've made it clear that I don't ever want to see her. It's not fair that you're making me the bad guy who has to say no to her coming to dinner."

"I'm not putting you on the spot, Mom," Diane said. "Obviously, you're always welcome to come for the holidays. I didn't want to invite Anna behind your back. If you don't want her there, that's fine. I won't invite her."

"But you'll be mad at me if I don't allow her to come," Joan said, crossing her arms.

"Mom." Diane sighed again. Her mother always made everything so difficult. "I'm trying to be considerate of your feelings. I won't be mad. I'll visit with her the night before instead. She'll understand."

"Oh, I'm so happy the murderess will understand," Joan said flippantly.

"Don't call her that," Diane shot back. "She's a nice person."

"Who happened to murder my father in cold blood."

Diane's own blood was boiling at this point, but she tried to speak calmly. Fighting with her mother never ended well. "You don't know exactly what happened, Mom. You said so yourself. You didn't *see* her kill your father."

"So, is that what she's saying now? That she didn't do it? What? Did the gun jump out of the nightstand all by itself and shoot him?"

Diane stopped a moment and looked at her mother curiously. "How much do you remember of that night? You said you were sent to the neighbor's apartment."

"I've already told you," Joan said louder than necessary. "That woman came out of the bedroom where my father had fallen asleep. She told me to take Matthew across the hall to the neighbor's place. I did what I was told."

"Did something happen before she told you to do that?" Diane asked. "Were they arguing? Did he hit her?"

"I don't want to talk about it," Joan yelled, turning away from her.

Diane walked around her mother and looked directly at her. "Mom. Why did you go to the parole hearing with Aunt Bernice twenty years after the murder? Did you hate your mother so much that you wanted her to serve more time?"

Joan's eyes widened, then narrowed. "She was supposed to serve a life sentence in prison. Aunt Bernice wanted to make sure she did."

"What about you, Mom? Why were you there? You were a child when it happened, and as you've said, you didn't see anything. Why would you go to speak against your own mother?"

"It wasn't my idea, okay?" Joan said tightly. "Aunt Bernice was determined to keep her in jail. She told me I had to go. She said my being there would have a higher emotional impact on the committee. You knew your Aunt Bernice. She could be very insistent when she wanted her way. I just went to please her."

"But did you want Anna to stay in jail?" Diane asked.

"I don't know what I wanted. I just did what Bernice told me to do."

"You were twenty-five, Mom. You were married. You had two kids already. Couldn't you have made up your own mind on whether or not you wanted to testify against your mother?" Diane asked, frustrated.

"Stop it! Stop bombarding me with questions! I told you I don't want to talk about it anymore. I don't want to even think about it anymore. Why can't you just let this go?" Joan turned her back on Diane again and walked a few steps away.

"I'm sorry, Mom," Diane said. "I'm just trying to understand what happened back then. I'm sorry I upset you."

Joan spun to face her. "Then don't ask me about it again. And if you want me to join you for Thanksgiving, don't invite her."

Diane nodded. "I won't invite her. I'm sure they'll have Thanksgiving dinner at the place where she lives. She isn't feeling well, anyway. So, I'm sure she didn't expect an invitation."

Her mother suddenly calmed down and studied her a moment. "What's wrong with her? Is she sick?"

Her question surprised Diane. "She said she was having a little problem with her heart medication. She was in bed the last time I saw her. Hopefully, she's feeling better now."

"Well, she's ninety-five. I suppose she has all sorts of issues," Joan said.

"Actually, she seems pretty healthy for her age. But she can't walk very well on her own anymore, and now there's this heart issue." Diane looked directly at her mother. "She won't live forever, though."

"Well, neither will any of us," Joan said, her tone bitter.

Diane left soon after that, disappointed that she hadn't been able to get any new information out of her mother about the day William was killed. She could tell her mother knew more but had either blocked it or refused to think about it. She'd just have to wait until Anna finished her story to learn more.

* * *

On Sunday afternoon, Diane went to see Anna. It was a cold, windy day, and she shivered as she walked down the hall to Anna's door. After decades of living in Minnesota, Diane was sick of the cold winters. The more she thought of Barry's idea of going somewhere warm every winter, the more she liked it.

"It's a blustery day out there," Anna said when Diane entered her apartment. Anna was sitting in her chair today, and that made Diane happy.

"But it feels good in here." She hung up her coat and went to sit near her. "You must be feeling better today."

"I am." Anna smiled, the soft creases in her face gathering together. "You're not going to get rid of me that easily."

Diane laughed. She liked it when Anna smiled. Her wrinkles didn't make her look sad or mean; she looked kind. It was difficult to think that this woman with the twinkle in her eyes and the smile on her face had spent so many years in prison.

"I had another breakthrough," Diane said. "Barry rented out his house and is living at mine permanently."

"Oh, that's wonderful, dear," Anna said, looking truly happy for her. "But wasn't he already living there?"

"Yes. But I always knew he had his own place to go back to if anything went wrong. Now, we're stuck with each other— kind of. At least until the end of the school year. At first, I thought I would freak out. But now, I don't mind. I'm doing my best to push away the fear that's keeping me from being happy."

"I'm so glad. Barry's such a nice man. You're lucky to have each other," Anna said.

"Well, I don't know if he's lucky to have little ole' paranoid me," Diane said, chuckling. "But I know I'm lucky to have Barry."

"Believe me, dear. He's lucky to have you, too."

Diane's heart warmed at Anna's words. She always said such sweet things. She wished she'd had someone like Anna in her life when she was young. Someone she could've run to after a terrible fight with her mother, or she could've stayed with when things were rough. At least she had Anna now, and that was what counted.

"A good man is a gift," Anna said. "I think about how I should have waited to marry, just as my Auntie May had told me I should. Maybe I would have become an old maid. Maybe I should have. Either way, I ended up alone."

"I'm sorry," Diane said. "I wish it had been better for you."

"I try not to regret my past. I really do," Anna said. "It took me a long time to learn that what William did to me was not my shame, it was his shame. If I had understood that back then, I would have had the nerve to leave him. Or at least ask for help. But times were different then. Women were looked down on by society. And if your husband abused you, well, people thought it was because you deserved it. It was a terrible time for women. It was a terrible time for me."

CHAPTER THIRTY-TWO

Anna — 1954

Anna pushed Matthew's stroller down the street toward the park with Joanie skipping beside her. It was a lovely June day, and she was enjoying the sunshine. After they'd driven away from Buffalo in the middle of the night last September, they'd ended up back in Minneapolis, much to Anna's relief. They were living in a run-down apartment building, a few blocks from her Auntie May's place, but at least it had two bedrooms. The second bedroom was little more than a closet, but it worked as a room for Joanie. The baby slept in the basket beside Anna's bed, but would soon need a crib. He'd grown so much since his birth in October. But Matthew was a happy baby and hadn't had colic as Joanie had, thank goodness. With William's constant dark moods since moving there, Anna was sure a crying baby would have put him over the edge.

They'd lived in a shabby hotel for a few days before William found the apartment, and then he pounded the pavement for work. Finally, he'd talked his way into a department manager's position at the Pillsbury Company, and although it sounded like a high position, the money wasn't very good, so they'd ended up in the low-end apartment building in the sketchy part of town. But Anna didn't care. She was happy to have a roof over her children's heads and food on the table, however meager it was.

William, however, pretended he was living the high life when he wasn't at home. He'd bought two new suits, tailored to fit, plus shiny new shoes while Anna still wore her old dresses and maternity clothes that she'd taken in to fit better after Matthew was born. William went out in the evenings after work with the other managers, or so he said, spending money on dining out and drinking while Anna squeezed every penny out of the little money he allowed her to put food on the table for her children. She never complained, though, because when she did, he'd slap her or shove her against a wall and tell her to shut up and be happy he gave her anything at all. She did what she could with what little she had and came up with ways to make something out of nothing.

Auntie May had been thrilled to have Anna and the children living so close again. She invited them to her apartment for dinner at least once a week and gave the children treats like homemade chocolate-chip cookies. She also gave Anna a key again, so she could come and go as she pleased. Anna took the opportunity to go there during the day with the children and use her aunt's sewing machine to make clothes for the children. She went through the old dresses that she'd left there and used the material to cut cute dresses for Joan and play clothes for Matthew.

The first time they were at the apartment while May was at work, Anna had been going through her closet when Joanie spied the old rag doll, Lily, on the chair in Anna's room. She went up to it quickly but refrained from touching it.

"Can I hold the dolly?" she asked her mother.

Anna smiled down at the sweet doll her brother had made for her all those years ago. She went to kneel next to her daughter, who was now almost four years old. "Of course you can play with her. But please be very gentle. She's almost as old as I am." Her heart melted when Joanie lifted the doll and hugged her. "Her name is Lily," Anna said.

Joanie's eyes lit up. "That's a pretty name," she said. And from that time forward, Joanie wouldn't go anywhere without her little doll, Lily.

As Anna looked over her dresses and suits from her past life before marriage, she felt like she was going down memory lane. The beautiful blue dress she'd worn with the crinoline underneath on that first date with William. The striped sundress she'd worn to the Fourth of July party. They would've all held wonderful memories for her if her life hadn't turned out the way it had. If William hadn't turned out to be a conman and a liar. Now, these dresses only reminded her of how naïve she'd been despite the tough childhood she'd endured. She'd believed in William then. Now, she believed in no one and only wanted to give her children the best she could out of a terrible situation.

Styles in dresses had changed over the past few years, so Anna altered a couple of her older dresses to look more modern and brought home a pair of shoes that still looked good. She'd made a sundress for Joan out of the blue and white seersucker dress she'd worn while dating William, and a pair of shorts and a top. The skirt had been so full, there was plenty of fabric.

Now, as they walked to the park, Joan was carrying Lily and wearing the striped top and shorts along with a pair of cheap sneakers Anna had purchased for her at the dime store.

Joanie skipped along as if she didn't have a care in the world, and that made Anna smile. She was happy that William's dark moods and angry outbursts hadn't turned Joanie into a scared, serious child—yet. But Anna knew from her own past that at some point, it could scar her. That was what worried Anna the most at night as she lay in bed, trying to sleep. How would William's behavior affect her children, and how could she stop it? She had no answer to either question.

They went home later that afternoon, and Matthew took a nap while Joanie played with Lily and her other doll and the little toy tea set that Anna had bought her for Christmas last year. Anna went to the kitchen to start cooking a small roast for dinner. She only bought meat when it was on sale and never paid full price for anything. That was the only way she could stretch her money. To her surprise, she heard the outer door open and shut, then William's voice calling for her.

Anna wiped her hands on her apron and walked out into the living room. She noticed Joanie making herself small in the corner where she was playing, trying to go unnoticed. This tore at Anna's heart.

"You're home early," Anna said, keeping her tone light. She always had to watch how she worded a sentence. That's why she didn't ask him why he was home early. He would have gone into a rage, telling her it was none of her business. Stating a fact was less risky.

William tossed his hat on the table by the door. "That damn place doesn't know what the hell it's doing. Screw them! I can find a better job than that."

Anna's heart sank. He'd lost another job. She prayed it wouldn't mean that they were moving again. "I'm sorry, dear," she said because there was no way she could ask him why he'd left.

"Well, I'm not sorry. I'll find something else. Something better." He glanced around and sneered. "Something that can pay for a better place than this dump."

Anna remained silent. She didn't dare agree with him. "I was just putting dinner in the oven," she said. "Will you be eating with us?"

"Where else would I eat?" he asked as if he ate with them every night. He turned and noticed Joan sitting in the corner with her doll. "Aren't you going to come see Daddy?" he asked. Usually, the kids were in bed when he came home, so Joan wasn't used to seeing her father at home so early. She hugged Lily close and walked over to William as Anna watched. Joan looked terrified.

"Is that a new outfit?" William asked his daughter, then turned and glared at Anna. "I didn't know we had so much money we could buy new clothes."

"Mama made it for me," Joan said softly.

William kneeled and looked at her. "I see. Well, you look adorable in it. And who is this?" He pointed to the dolly.

Joan relaxed a bit. "Lily. It was mama's doll."

"It was?" He turned to Anna. "Why haven't I ever seen it before?"

Suspicion filled his voice as it always did these days. "It's been at Auntie May's apartment all this time," Anna said. "When I was sewing clothes for the kids, Joan saw it and asked to play with it."

William turned back to Joan. "She sure is a nice little dolly." He hugged his daughter and smiled. Joan smiled back, looking very much like a miniature Anna. "You go ahead back to playing now, dear," William said. The little girl walked back to the corner and began playing with her doll again.

William studied Anna a moment. "Why does her outfit look so familiar?"

"I made it out of the sundress I wore to the Shipman's Fourth of July party," Anna said lightly. "The skirt was so full I was able to make her a dress and that little outfit."

William frowned, and Anna's heart skipped a beat as she wondered what she'd said wrong.

"I can buy my daughter new clothes," he said tightly. "You don't have to rip up old dresses to make her things."

Her heart pounded as she searched for the right words. "Oh, honey, I know you can," she said as calmly as possible. "But I'll never be able to wear that dress again after having two babies, so I didn't want the fabric to go to waste."

He looked her over, then nodded, satisfied with her answer. "Shipman. I remember that day. I wonder if he still works at 3M. I should give him a call." Taking off his suit jacket and tie, he headed into the bedroom.

Anna let out a sigh of relief. Talking to William was like walking a tightrope. At least this time, she didn't fall.

William did call Roger Shipman, but there were no positions available for him. Over the next couple of weeks, he called everyone he'd ever worked with, trying to round up a job. But everyone remembered what he was like to work with, and no one wanted to hire him. His mood grew even darker, and each night, he went off to the bar to drink and then came home in a stupor.

Finally, he took a job bartending in one of the bars he frequented. He'd been bragging about having owned his own bar in Buffalo when the owner asked if he'd like to work there. Anna was relieved that he had something to keep him busy. He worked three to midnight, but he didn't usually get home until after two. They were back on the same schedule as when they lived in Buffalo, which was fine with Anna. She liked having quiet evenings home with the kids.

William continued searching for a better job while he bartended, but with no success. His temper was growing worse the longer he couldn't find a decent job. He liked hanging out in the bars, but he didn't like working in them. He complained that customers treated him like trash, and many acted like he was below them.

"I'm smarter than all of those idiots," he complained to Anna. It was his usual complaint. He always thought he was smarter than everyone else. She couldn't help but wonder, though, if he were, why couldn't he get a better job? She remembered the night at the Shipman's party at their beautiful lake home how William had promised her that would be them someday. She'd believed him then. Now, she knew it had all been lies. Bragging and lies.

By fall, William was constantly frustrated and in a rage. They barely had enough money to pay rent, let alone buy food and clothes for the kids. Anna did without quite often, eating less so the children would have more. William worked longer hours at the bar in order to make more money, but it barely made a difference. Anna hesitantly suggested she could do sewing or babysitting for some of the women in the area, but he flat out refused.

"I make the money in this house!" he shouted at her. "Not you!"

She didn't mention it again.

Joan's birthday came, and the only presents she received were from Auntie May. Anna felt so guilty, but she didn't have a dime to spare to buy her daughter a gift. She'd sacrificed a little of the grocery money to buy ingredients to make her a cake, and that was all she could do. Auntie May gave Joan a cute mini cooking pan set and a set of Winnie-the-Pooh books. Joan was excited over the books because she loved it when her mother read to her before bed.

The only neighbor Anna had befriended was Mrs. Arnett across the hall. Her husband had retired from being a fire-fighter, and their grown children lived far away, so she often came out into the hall to visit with Anna as the children played. Although the Arnetts lived on a meager income, Mrs. Arnett always offered Joanie and William home-baked cookies or small candies when she saw them. Anna was thankful to have such a kind neighbor in the building.

In late September, William brought a girl home and announced to Anna that she'd be staying with them for a few months. Anna stared at him in disbelief. The girl was young, possibly in her teens, and she was thin with long, red hair pulled up in a ponytail. She was also obviously pregnant.

William didn't explain. "Take care of her. Her name is Liz, and that's all you need to know." Then he left again to go back to work.

Anna and Joan stared at the frightened-looking girl, both dumbfounded.

"I'm sorry," the young girl finally said, sounding pitiful.

Anna found her voice. "I'm Anna," she said. "And this is Joan and Matthew." She pointed to the highchair where the little boy sat, waiting for lunch. "We were just going to eat lunch. Are you hungry?"

The girl set down the small suitcase she'd brought and nodded. "Yes, please."

They didn't have much. Anna had heated up a can of

chicken noodle soup and had cut a ham and cheese sandwich in half for her and Joan to share. For Matthew, she'd cut up a hard-boiled egg and had put a little peanut butter on toast. She ended up giving the girl her half of the sandwich and some soup and made peanut butter toast for herself.

They didn't say much because Anna didn't want to talk in front of the children. Matthew was put down for a nap in the used crib Anna had managed to find in a second-hand shop, and then she asked Joan to play quietly while Liz helped her in the kitchen.

Liz quickly went to the sink to wash the dishes while Anna studied her. She was a little shorter than she was, but much thinner, which was why her belly was so pronounced. She wore a simple cotton dress with a full skirt, ankle socks, and light blue slip-on Keds. She looked like an all-American, apple-pie kind of girl—except she was pregnant. Anna wasn't sure she wanted to know who got her that way.

"I'll do that. You can dry," Anna told the girl, taking over the dishwashing while Liz dried them with an embroidered flour sack dishcloth. Mattie had sent her dozens of flour sacks from Buffalo that she got free at work. Anna always embroidered cute little animals on them to make them look cheery.

The two worked in silence until the dishes were finished. Afterword, Anna offered the girl a glass of iced tea she'd made earlier in the day, and she motioned for Liz to sit at the tiny table in the kitchen.

"Is your full name Elizabeth?" Anna asked.

The girl nodded, her ponytail swaying as she did. "But I like Liz. You know, like Elizabeth Taylor?"

Anna smiled. She remembered how she'd admired movie stars as a young girl. She hadn't been to a movie in ages, but everyone knew who Elizabeth Taylor was. "How do you know William?"

The girl's eyes brightened. "From the bar. I work there sometimes, serving tables for tips. I've been supporting myself since I was fourteen after my mother died. My father, well, he drinks a lot, and there was never any money. I quit school and started waitressing, but I make so much more in tips at the bar. The owner is a friend of my father's, and he lets me sleep in a little room off the kitchen." She dropped her eyes. "My father, well, he's not very nice. He used to hit my mother, and then me—a lot. But Augie, the bar owner, he's so kind. He'd never let anyone hurt me."

Anna's heart went out to this young girl with the heartbreaking story. How could she not feel compassion for her? Women had so few choices when the people in their lives let them down. "How old are you?"

"Seventeen."

"Seventeen? You're so young," Anna said, shocked.

"I didn't have anywhere to go. Augie said I couldn't work at the bar looking like this," her hands went to her belly, "and I couldn't go back to my father's place. I begged William to please let me live with him until the baby came. He didn't want me to, but then he finally said I could." She stopped and looked at Anna. "I hope you don't mind. I know you have your own children to look after, and I promise not to get in the way. I'll help as much as I can around here and with the kids. I just didn't want to go to one of those homes for unwed mothers. I couldn't bear to go to a place like that."

Anna frowned as she studied the girl. She didn't understand why this girl would ask to live with William or why he'd agree. There really could be only one explanation, and that's what confused Anna. Would William actually bring one of his women here for her to take care of?

"Liz, who do you think I am?" Anna asked.

The girl's brow furrowed. "Aren't you William's sister?"

Her words took a moment to sink in. Anna shook her head, trying to figure out what lie William had conjured up to trick this young girl. "No, dear," Anna said gently. "I'm his wife."

Liz's eyes widened. "Wife? He has a wife?" She turned so pale, Anna thought she might be sick.

"Are you okay?" Anna asked.

The girl looked to be in shock. "I didn't know. He never said he was married." She looked up at Anna with big blue eyes. "I'm so sorry. I didn't know. He said he lived with his widowed sister and her children." Liz clapped a hand over her mouth. "Oh, no. Those are his children, aren't they?"

Anna nodded. "Yes. Joan and Matthew are our children."

The girl rubbed her hands on each side of her head as if she were massaging a headache. "I'm so sorry. I'm so, so sorry," she said.

Her reaction told Anna everything. She knew for certain that William had fathered the girl's child. Bile rose in her throat, and Anna had to take a long drink of her iced tea to push it back down. She'd known all along that William was having flings with other women, but this was a girl. A seventeen-year-old girl. And he'd gotten her pregnant. Now, he expected her to take care of his mistake.

Anna patted the girl's arm, trying to soothe her. "I'm sorry, too."

That night, long after she'd given the young girl sheets to make up the sofa in the living room and everyone else was asleep, Anna lay in bed, waiting for William. When he finally came in, he stumbled around until his clothes were off, and he fell into bed. Anna had thought all night about what she'd say. She had to be careful not to anger him. But she was uncharacteristically angry, and she couldn't ignore what he'd done.

"William?" she said softly so as not to wake up Matthew. "That girl can't stay with us. You can't expect me to care for your pregnant girlfriend."

He turned toward her, and she could see his eyes. He didn't look angry, he looked worn out. "There's no other choice. She had nowhere to go. Do you really want to throw her out in the street?"

Anna took a steadying breath. "She isn't my problem, William. She's yours. You're asking too much of me this time. What will our children think?"

"They're little. They don't need to know anything. This isn't up for discussion. She's staying until the baby comes, and that's that."

"We can barely afford to feed our own children," Anna said. "How can we feed her too?"

"Just do it. I don't care how!" William said impatiently. "I can't deal with all this. She'll be gone in a few months." He rolled over to end the discussion.

Anna lay there under the covers, her heart hardening toward William and the young girl. "She's only seventeen," she said, not caring if he hit her to shut her up. "Seventeen. How could you?"

William stiffened next to her but didn't move. "She seemed much older. I didn't know."

Anna closed her eyes. How on earth was she going to live with this girl he'd slept with and gotten pregnant? She was only human. How much more was she supposed to put up with in this marriage?

Finally, she slept.

CHAPTER THIRTY-THREE

Anna — 1954

Anna didn't speak to William again about Liz and the baby growing inside her. At first, Anna ignored the girl's presence, giving Liz chores to do around the apartment but otherwise keeping her distance. Liz was trying so hard to help, that it was difficult for Anna to dislike her. The truth was, it was William she should hate, not Liz. Anna was sure William had used his sweet charm and silvery tongue to lure the girl in, just as he had with her. The only difference was he'd married Anna, although she wasn't entirely sure why anymore. As she looked back on their relationship, she believed he'd married her to get a promotion, plain and simple. He'd never planned on having a family or staying faithful to her. Now, he saw Anna and the children as a weight around his neck, but he was also a jealous man. There were many sides to him, some meaner than others, and Anna walked a thin line every day between those personalities.

At first, Anna saw the way Liz watched William's every move when he was home, her eyes bright with affection for him. Anna could tell that despite William being married and having lied to her, Liz was still in love with him. But as time wore on, and Liz heard the anger in his tone and saw the cruelty of his actions, the light in Liz's eyes faded, much as Anna's own light had dimmed over the years. Anna felt sorry for the young girl. To be used, impregnated, and then discarded by the man she thought had loved her hurt deeply. Anna understood that better than anyone.

But it was one afternoon when William was in a foul mood upon waking that Liz truly saw the type of man he was. It was a cold November day, and the children were playing inside the apartment because it was too frigid to take them to the park. William was sleeping until noon, as usual. Anna tried to keep the children quiet, and Liz did too, but Joan had snatched Lily away from Matthew, and the little boy began howling at the top of his lungs. No amount of soothing would calm him. Anna even offered him a cookie, but the little boy couldn't be placated.

William came out of the room, half-dressed, with his hair mused and his face red with anger. "Shut up! Shut up now!" he screamed, terrifying Matthew and causing him to cry even louder.

"Take him into the hall to play," Anna told Liz quickly. "Now!"

Liz picked up the heavy boy and took Joan's hand, pulling her along, but she wasn't fast enough. William charged at little Matthew, ready to hit him. Anna rushed between William and her children as Liz escaped out the door.

"Don't you dare hit my child!" she yelled, her eyes flashing at William.

He stopped, taken aback at the rage in Anna's voice. Then,

without warning, he backhanded her so hard, she fell to the floor. "This is my house!" he screamed. "No one tells me what to do in my house!" He turned and headed back to the bedroom.

The door was still open, and Liz gawked at Anna, having witnessed the entire scene. She ran into the apartment and kneeled beside her. "What can I do?" Liz whispered, obviously afraid that William might come out at any moment and hit her too.

Anna slowly sat up, blood trickling from the cut on her lip. The big ring that William wore on his left hand had hit her so hard, it loosened a tooth. "Watch the children," she said. "Don't worry about me." With Liz's help, Anna stood and then waved her away. By the time Liz had brought the children in from the hall, Anna was sitting at the dining table, holding a washcloth with ice in it to her lip.

Frightened from the yelling, the children had settled down, and Liz told them to play quietly so as not to upset their father again. Joan handed Matthew the doll, eager to keep him calm. The little boy hugged Lily tightly and rocked himself back and forth.

Liz sat down on the chair beside Anna. "I didn't know he was like this," she said quietly. "I grew up being beaten by my father. I thought William was different." She dropped her eyes, and tears began to fall.

Anna placed a hand on her arm. "I didn't know at first, either," she said. "He's not the man I dated and married. He's become a monster throughout the years, and it keeps getting worse. At least you know now."

Liz raised her eyes to Anna. "I'm so sorry. I'm sorry you got stuck taking care of me, and that you're being treated so terribly. You don't deserve it."

At that moment, Anna's heart opened up to this young girl. Liz hadn't known any better when she'd become involved with William. She hadn't done it to hurt Anna because she hadn't even known she existed. Right then and there, Anna promised herself that she'd keep this girl safe until the time she would leave them.

When Auntie May learned that a young pregnant girl was staying with them, Anna lied and said she was William's niece who'd gotten herself in trouble. Anna hated lying to her aunt, but she was also too embarrassed to tell her the truth. May only nodded, and then always included Liz in her invitation to dinner on Friday nights. For that, Anna was grateful. Because by now, Anna had begun looking at Liz as she would a little sister who she needed to take care of.

Liz's belly grew larger as the weeks passed. At Christmas, Auntie May gave Anna some money to put up a tree for the kids and buy a few gifts. Anna bundled up the children on Christmas Eve and borrowed a wagon from a neighbor, then she and Liz took them to buy a small tree at a sidewalk vendor. She wanted her children to have the same happy Christmas memories that she'd had with her Auntie May. Once home, they set up the tree, and May came over to help. William was working at the bar, as usual, so the little family celebrated without him. They sang Christmas Carols as they hung handmade decorations and cheap plastic balls Anna had bought at the dime store on the tree.

Liz was just as excited as the children were. "I've never had a Christmas tree before," she said as they plugged it in and the colorful lights brightened the room.

Auntie May had brought cookies she'd baked the week before with her theater friends. Chocolate chip, white sugar cookies, and ginger snaps. They made a full chicken that Anna had filled with chestnut stuffing, and May had brought homemade cranberry sauce. It was a nice Christmas, and the nicest one Liz had ever had. And when they opened their gifts after dinner, the children squealed with glee, and so did Liz. Anna had bought colorful building blocks for Matthew and a metal top that spun in circles when he pushed down the handle. Joanie's gift was large, and when she opened it, she shrieked gleefully. It was a metal Colonial dollhouse with plastic furniture. Anna had also bought her two small dolls that would fit in the house. Both children loved their gifts and sat playing with them immediately.

For Liz, Anna had bought her a warm wool coat and new gloves. The poor girl hadn't had a proper coat all winter and needed it desperately. Liz squealed like the kids and slipped it on immediately.

"It'll fit better after the baby is born," Anna said.

"I love it! It's so warm," Liz said and hugged her. The girl's excitement touched her and brought tears to Anna's eyes.

May had also brought gifts for the children, Liz, and Anna. She gave Anna two new casual dresses and two pairs of new stockings. Anna was thrilled and hugged her aunt. All her clothes were getting ragged, and the new dresses would make her feel pretty again.

Everyone was asleep when William came home that night. He nudged Anna awake when he got into bed.

"Where did that tree and all the gifts come from?" he asked.

Anna was groggy but immediately watched her tone as she answered. "Auntie May bought the tree for the kids and the gifts. She came over for dinner, too."

"Auntie May," he grumbled. "I've been working so much, I

forgot it was Christmas."

"I know," she said softly. "You've been working very hard. Auntie didn't mean anything by it. She gets lonely and wanted to spend Christmas Eve with us." Anna hoped her little lie would keep William from growing angry.

"Well, I guess it's okay then," he said. "But I could have done all that for the kids," he said.

"I know. Maybe next year," she said.

He agreed and finally fell asleep as Anna sighed with relief.

By mid-January, William's mood was growing darker. He'd applied for jobs at several places in town, but no one was hiring. He resented working as a bartender, but he had to make money somewhere. More and more, he picked fights with Anna over the cost of rent and food, and that they were now paying for Liz as well. Anna knew better than to remind him that the extra mouth to feed was his fault. She tried hard to appease William and did her best to stretch the little money he gave her as far as possible.

Liz was due in late February, and Anna still didn't know what the plan was for the baby. She'd grown to love Liz like family. One afternoon as the children played in the hallway with the other kids on the floor, Anna sat with Liz and drew up enough nerve to ask her a few personal questions.

"Do you know what you're going to do about the baby after it's born?" Anna asked.

Liz shook her head. "I don't know. William had said I should put it in an orphanage and let someone adopt the baby. I had thought that was a good idea, but the longer the baby is inside me, the more I'm falling in love with it." She raised her eyes to meet Anna's. "I know he won't support this baby, or even claim it. And I can't keep the baby and work to support it.

I just don't know what to do."

Anna nodded. She understood how Liz felt. Anna was also stuck in the same situation because she didn't know how she'd support her children alone. But through the months, she'd thought a lot about the baby Liz was carrying and how it was a half-brother or sister to her own children. How could William toss away his own child?

As January came to a close, Anna built up enough courage to approach William with an idea. She asked if he'd talk to her alone before going to work one afternoon. While Liz watched the kids, she and William went to the local coffee shop so he could order breakfast.

"So, what's this big discussion we need to have," William asked. They were sitting off alone in a corner booth away from the other patrons.

"I wanted to ask you a question," she said. "Please hear me out."

He sipped his coffee as he watched her. "Okay."

Anna took a deep breath. "Liz will be having her baby in less than a month. She has nowhere to go and no one to help her with the baby. Would you consider us adopting her baby and keeping it as our own?"

The shocked look on William's face nearly made Anna laugh. "Are you crazy?" he said in a hushed whisper. "You want to raise a bastard child?"

"Your bastard child," she said steadily. "And, yes. I want to keep the baby. Liz can't, and why would we give away a baby that is your own flesh and blood? Don't you care what happens to your son or daughter?"

He sat back in the booth and crossed his arms. "You are crazy. Is this to punish me? Do you figure every time I look at that child, I'll remember I cheated on you, and that you're so holy you're willing to raise it?"

Anna shook her head. "No. It's nothing like that. I've grown to care about Liz, and I want her child to have a family. Will you please at least think about it? Please? It's the right thing to do."

William shook his head. "No. I can't afford to pay for my own legitimate children. Why would I make my own children do without in order to pay for a bastard child? It's ridiculous." The waitress served his food, and he ate as if he didn't have a care in the world.

Anna watched him, sipping her tea. She was outraged by his cold words but didn't dare argue with him. She'd asked, and that was all she could do. But it tore at her heart to think that her children would have a sibling they might never know existed.

Before she and William parted ways so he could go to work, he asked, "You've really grown close to this girl, haven't you?"

Anna nodded. "She's a sweet girl."

"Hm," he said. "Well, then, I guess I do have a lot to think about."

Anna's heart lifted. "Are you serious?"

"Absolutely," he said. Then he turned and walked away.

Anna didn't say anything to Liz about the possibility of them adopting her baby. She didn't want to get the girl's hopes up. For the next two days, Anna's waited on pins and needles for William to tell her what he'd decided. She didn't press him because she knew how testy he could be.

On the third morning, Anna woke up to feed the children and saw that Liz wasn't on the sofa. She searched for Liz, but she wasn't in the kitchen or bathroom either. Panicked, Anna looked in the hall closet, and Liz's small bag and new coat were gone. Fear gripped her. Had Liz left, afraid of what would become of her baby? Or had William taken her somewhere?

When William awoke and came out for breakfast, he didn't say anything about Liz. Anna was a nervous wreck and finally asked, "Do you know where Liz went?"

A slow smile drew across William's face. "She's gone. I took her to a home for unwed mothers last night."

Anna's heart sank. "Where? I want to go see her," she said, desperately worried about the girl.

"No. It's none of your business. And I don't want you to search for her. She's gone, and that's all you need to know."

Anna dropped into the chair across from her husband, holding back tears that threatened to fall. She wouldn't give him the satisfaction of seeing her cry. "Why, William? Why would you take her away like that?"

He glared at her with contempt. "Because you two got too chummy, and there was no way I was going to let you keep that baby. It's absolutely ridiculous. You should have hated her, but you two became friends instead. I swear sometimes you haven't a brain in your head. The girl was carrying my child, and you wanted to keep it. Well, she's gone, and I'd better not hear of you going after her."

Anna nodded. What else could she do? She went into the kitchen and stared out the tiny window over the sink with a view of another brick building only a few feet away. Other than her children, her life was miserable. They lived in poverty, she lived in fear of her husband's outbursts, and every time there was a glimmer of something good in her life, he snatched it away. Instead of tears, Anna's heart hardened toward William. She'd find a way someday to take the children and leave. Because it was extremely clear to her now that leaving was her only way out.

CHAPTER THIRTY-FOUR

Diane

Anna's face was solemn as she said the last words. Diane watched her, her heart going out to this woman who'd been so badly treated and yet ended up in prison because of that awful man.

"Did you ever see Liz or her baby again?" Diane asked.

Anna shook her head. "No. I don't know if William did either. Despite his threats, I searched for her but couldn't find her. Some of those places required that the unwed mother stay for a year whether they kept the baby or gave it up. Maybe Liz did that, and afterward, it would have been too late to contact me. I would've been in prison by then."

"Oh." Diane hadn't thought about that. They were getting close to the end of her story. Diane had already heard enough to understand why Anna would shoot her husband, but there was still a piece missing. Something absolutely horrible must have happened that day to make her pull that trigger.

Anna changed the subject to how Diane was coping with the idea of Barry moving in permanently. "I'm getting used to it," Diane said. "It's not like much has changed because he was always at my house anyway. It's just knowing that if anything goes wrong, he has nowhere to go, and we have to work it out. Not that anything like that has happened over the past four years, but I'm always the pessimist." She laughed.

Anna smiled. "I think you're a very positive person. You're just nervous, and I understand why. But it's going to be fine. You both make a lovely couple."

Diane looked at Anna and thought about all she'd missed out on while in prison. She hadn't had the chance to raise her children or fall in love with a good man. In fact, Anna had never seen her son Matthew again. It was all so sad, and Diane felt guilty for whining about her own problems to Anna.

"You haven't mentioned your brother, Andrew. Did you ever reconnect with him in all those years?" Diane asked.

Anna gave her a small smile. "Can you hand me my keepsake box, dear?" she asked.

Diane stood and picked up the box from the end table, then handed it to Anna. Her grandmother dug in it as it perched on her lap. Finally, she pulled out an old envelope and gave it to Diane.

"Unfortunately, my husband's murder was in every newspaper in the nation, and Andrew saw it. They used my maiden name in the article, and Andrew recognized me right away. He sent that letter to me while I was in prison. It's the only one I ever received."

"Can I read it?" Diane asked.

"Of course."

Diane looked at the envelope first and saw it had been postmarked in Cody, Wyoming. Carefully, she pulled it out. The paper was stiff with age, and Diane was afraid of tearing it. She unfolded the letter carefully. It was only one page in length. The script was neat and easy to read.

> *My dearest Anna,*
>
> *When I read the newspaper article about you, I was in shock. I hardly believe my sweet little sister could have done what they said. I don't believe it. For you to do such a thing as they say, you would have had to been pushed pretty hard and treated badly. I'm so sorry, Anna. I wish I had been there to help you. After the way our grandparents treated you, you deserved so much better.*
>
> *I have been living in Wyoming since I wrote you that letter all those years ago. At first, I went from ranch to ranch, learning as much as I could about training horses. Finally, I settled in at a place where I have a little cabin all my own on the edge of the pasture where I can see nothing except horses and land for miles around. I love it here and plan on staying until the day I die.*
>
> *I love you, little sister, and hope that somehow, you are able to find a way out of that place. Please take care of yourself. I'm not a rich man and cannot help you financially, and for that, I'm sorry. But you will always be in my thoughts and prayers.*
>
> *Love,*
> *Your Andrew*

Chills ran up Diane's spine as she read the heartfelt letter. She turned the envelope over again, but there was no return address. She glanced up at Anna. "That's such a sweet letter. Why didn't he give you an address to write back?"

"He did. It was on another piece of paper in the letter. And I did write to him after I received this. But then, somehow, I lost the address. It was in care of the post office in a small town, but as the years went by, I've forgotten. Truthfully, at the time, I felt it was for the best. He didn't need to be reminded of his sister, who was in prison. He was living the life he'd always wanted and knowing that made me very happy. There was no sense in my bothering him with my problems."

"Did you ever hear from him again?" Diane asked.

Anna shook her head. "No. I don't know if he ever married or had children of his own, or if he's passed away. I'm sure, by now, he has. I hope wherever he was, he was happy."

Diane carefully folded the letter and slipped it back inside the envelope. She handed it to Anna, who set it on the pile of items in her keepsake box. Diane watched her, and a thought occurred to her. "How did the letter get in that box if Bernice had the box, and then my mother?"

"I put it in there recently. I'd kept a small box of items while I was in prison. After you gave this box back to me, I placed those items in there as well."

"Ah," Diane said. She took the wooden box from Anna and set it back on the table. "I was wondering what you're doing for Thanksgiving this week," she said, changing the subject. "I hope they have a nice dinner here."

"I'm told they do. Max has already asked me to eat with him." She chuckled. "As if anyone else was going to ask me."

"My mother always comes to our house for Thanksgiving. I tried to talk her into letting you come, too, but she put up a big fuss. I'm sorry. I really wanted you to spend the day with us," Diane said.

Anna smiled warmly. "I understand. Maybe by Christmas, my Joanie will come around."

Diane grimaced. "I'm not sure she will. But if she does, you'll be the first to know."

Diane left then to let Anna go down to dinner with Max. When she arrived home, Barry had dinner in the oven.

"Mm," Diane said, sniffing the air. "Mexican food?"

"Homemade Mexican food," Barry said, kissing her cheek. "Chicken enchiladas and rice."

"I'm so glad you like to cook," Diane said. "I hate cooking."

"We make a great pair," Barry said, smiling.

As they ate, Diane told Barry about William bringing home the pregnant girl and how he'd taken her away so Anna couldn't raise the baby.

"Wow. He was a piece of work," Barry said. "Can you imagine the nerve it takes to bring home a girl he'd gotten pregnant and tell his wife to take care of her? What a jerk."

"Right? I can't even imagine it. But he'd treated Anna so badly by that time that she didn't dare fight him on it. He was not a nice person by any stretch of the imagination."

Barry agreed.

"She showed me a letter she received from her brother Andrew. He'd seen a news article about her killing William and wrote to her. He was living in or around Cody, Wyoming back then."

"Really?" Barry's brows rose. "Did they write back and forth after that?"

Diane shook her head. "No. She wrote back, but never heard from him again. And she lost the address years ago." Diane sat there deep in thought. "I wonder if I could find his death certificate online if he's passed? He'd be ninety-eight if he were still alive. I doubt he is alive, though."

"I think you should try to find him," Barry said. "He could be alive. If not, you'll know what year he died. That might give Anna some closure."

That evening, Diane searched a variety of websites trying to find information about Andrew Bergman. It was hard to find any trace of him. Finally, after giving in and joining Ancestry and digging around, she found his birth certificate and several U.S. Census reports of him from when he lived around Dent. Trying different towns in the census records, Diane searched 1940, 1950, and 1960. She couldn't find him. Finally, she gave up for the night but was determined to search more this week to find a record of Andrew.

* * *

Diane had a short week at work and was busy getting everything tied up and ready for the following Monday. She planned on visiting Anna on Wednesday as she always did, then Thursday she'd have dinner with her mother and Barry. Just as she was finishing up work on Tuesday afternoon, Diane received a call from Pauline at Anna's care center.

"I'm sorry to have to tell you this," Pauline said, sounding upset. "Anna was taken to the hospital about an hour ago. She collapsed in her room, but she was still breathing when they came for her. I knew you'd want to know."

Diane's heart pounded as she wrote down the hospital information and thanked Pauline. She called Barry to tell him where she was headed, then drove directly to the hospital. Barry was already there, waiting for her at the emergency entrance.

They rushed inside, and Diane asked the woman at the desk if there was any news about Anna Craine.

"She's in ICU," the woman informed her. "Are you family?"

"Yes. I'm her granddaughter."

"You can go in and see her." The receptionist directed her to the fourth floor, and Diane and Barry went directly up.

"What if I lose her already?" Diane said, looking up at Barry. "I've just gotten to know her. I can't lose her now."

Barry placed his arm around her. "Anna has made it this far in her life. I'm sure she will fight to stay a little longer."

The nurse at the desk updated Diane on Anna's condition. "She had a mild heart attack. But she's still conscious and alert. That's encouraging for her age. We're going to keep her under observation overnight and then possibly for a while longer to make sure all is fine."

Diane let out a sigh of relief. "Can I see her?"

"Of course. Follow me." She led Diane and Barry down the hall and into a private room. All the rooms could be seen from the nurse's desk so they could be accessed easily.

Diane went inside the room, and there lay Anna with her eyes closed, tubes running all around her. A heart monitor beeped a steady rhythm. "Anna?" Diane asked softly.

The older woman's eyes fluttered open, and a smile appeared on her face. "Oh, sweetie. I'm so glad you came. She reached out her hand, and Diane immediately took it.

"Pauline called me. How do you feel?" Diane asked.

"Much better than I look," Anna said, chuckling. "I guess I had a mild heart attack, and they get very uptight around here when that happens."

Diane laughed. "I suppose they would."

Anna saw Barry standing by the door. "Come in, dear.

Come in. The more, the merrier."

"Well, you haven't lost your sense of humor," Barry said. "I'm glad you're feeling okay."

"Thank you, dear. Honestly, I don't even know what happened. I was standing up with my walker to get ready for lunch, and the next thing I knew, they were hauling me out to an ambulance. I don't remember any pain or falling down."

"I'm glad you didn't hurt yourself when you fell," Diane said. She and Barry sat in the chairs by the bed.

"Me, too. I could have broken one of my brittle bones. Unfortunately, now they want to keep me in the hospital for a few days." Anna shook her head. "I'm not a fan of hospitals."

"No one is," Diane said. "But they need to make sure you're well enough to go home."

Anna nodded. "Thank you so much for coming, dear. It's nice knowing that someone cares."

Diane smiled. "Of course I came. We're family."

"Family," Anna said softly. "I never get tired of hearing that word."

They visited for a time and then had to leave so Anna could rest. Diane went to see her again on Wednesday after school. They had already moved Anna out of ICU and into a regular room.

"One step closer to home," Anna said, sounding encouraged.

On Thursday, Diane picked up her mother and brought her to the house for Thanksgiving dinner. She didn't say a word about Anna being in the hospital, at least not until her mother asked where "that woman" was tonight.

"She's at the hospital," Diane said, keeping her voice calm. "Anna had a mild heart attack the other day, and she's resting there until she can go home."

Joan looked startled a moment, then regained her composure. "Well, I guess at her age, she's lucky to survive a heart attack."

"Yes. Very lucky. I hope to have a little more time with her before she leaves us," Diane said.

"I guess we always think we have all the time in the world," Joan said, talking to no one in particular.

"That's why it's good to say what you feel while you have the chance," Diane said gently, "instead of waiting until it's too late."

Diane knew she was pushing her mother, but she felt she had to. Much to her surprise, Joan didn't react the way she'd thought she would. She merely nodded, as if she were taking it all in.

Anna was released from the hospital on Sunday and was driven home in the care center's van. Diane was at Anna's apartment when she arrived and helped her into bed.

"Oh, my," Anna said, looking around. "What beautiful flowers." Diane had brought a bouquet of colorful flowers for her, and there was also a lovely bouquet from the staff of the care facility. What stood out the most, though, were the twelve red roses in the gorgeous cut crystal vase. "Are those from you, dear?" Anna asked, pointing at the roses.

"I'm afraid not," Diane said. She picked up the attached card and handed it to Anna. The older woman smiled. "Well, my, my. They're from Max."

"They're beautiful," Diane said. "He's a charmer, that one."

"Yes, he is." Anna grinned. "Where was he seventy years ago when I was looking for a good man?"

Diane laughed. They talked a little about her heart issue, and Anna assured her that she'd be fine with a bit more rest.

"It's just giving out after all these years," she said. "The people here will keep my meds on track for me, so don't worry. I just need to rest."

Diane left a little while later, not wanting to wear Anna out. She spent the rest of the day searching for information about Andrew online when suddenly she found his application for a social security number. She knew from her searching that they only share the numbers if someone has already passed. Using this information, she finally found the date and town of his death. Surprisingly, he'd died in Columbus, Montana, not in Wyoming. That was why she hadn't been able to find his death certificate earlier. She ordered a copy so she could share the information about Andrew with her grandmother.

Diane sat back and thought about Andrew and the life he must have led after running away from home at age fourteen. She couldn't even imagine it. Yet it seemed he'd led the life he'd dreamed of, and that was a good thing. She wished she'd met him. He died in 2012 at the age of ninety. If she'd known about him, she would have had plenty of time to meet him. But then, she didn't even know her grandmother was alive until just a few short weeks ago. She felt sad about all those lost years.

That next Wednesday, Diane visited Anna after school, but she didn't ask her to talk about the past. Diane knew what the next story would lead to, and she didn't want to upset Anna. So, they talked about safe things like Diane's daughter Natalie and what their plans were for Christmas.

"I hope I can have a small tree in here," Anna said. "Even if it's a fake one. I've missed celebrating Christmas."

"I'm sure we can put up something," Diane said. In fact, the whole place was starting to decorate for Christmas, but since Anna hadn't been out of her room yet, she hadn't seen any of it. Most of the doors had wreaths on them, and they had set up a large tree out in the entryway and another one in the dining room. Diane couldn't wait for Anna to see all the decorations when she was able to go eat in the dining room again.

Diane went shopping the next day after work and bought a small tree for Anna's room. She picked up a few sparkly decorations and a star to place on top. She also purchased a holiday wreath to hang on Anna's door.

At home, Barry was putting up the outdoor lights and had pulled out the Christmas decorations for inside as well.

"Isn't it a little cold to be out decorating the house?" Diane asked him when she came home. It had been in the thirties all day.

"I'm wearing four layers. I think I'll be fine," he said with a grin. "Besides. Natalie hasn't been home for months, and we want her to come home to a beautiful house, don't we?"

Diane smiled up at him. She couldn't wait for Natalie to come home for winter break. She had so much information she wanted to share with her, and she wanted Anna to meet her great-granddaughter.

On Friday, Diane went to her mother's and took her out to dinner. They ate at a little Italian place where her mother enjoyed their pasta dishes.

"Everywhere you go, there are Christmas decorations already up," Joan said, shaking her head. "When I was little, people waited until the week before to put decorations up. It drags the holidays out too long."

"People find joy in the holidays, Mom," Diane said. "That's why they put things up so early."

"It's ridiculous."

Diane wouldn't let her mother get her down. She and Barry

had put up their tree that week and the house looked festive. "Are you going to put up a small tree in your apartment this year?" she asked her mother.

"Nah. Why bother? I'll be coming to your house for Christmas anyway. When is Natalie coming?"

"She's flying in on the twenty-first and staying for two weeks," Diane said.

"Good. I can't wait to see her."

Diane smiled. One thing she could never fault her mother on was her love for her granddaughter.

After they did a little shopping, Diane dropped her mother back at her place. "I'll see you next week, Mom," she said as she got ready to leave.

"You never told me how Anna is doing," Joan blurted out.

Diane stopped, surprised. "I guess I didn't think you'd want to know. She's back at her place, and she's feeling better. She's on bed rest for a while, though."

"Oh. Okay." Joan hesitated as if searching for words. "Is she coming to your place for Christmas?"

Diane had already figured her mother wouldn't want her to invite Anna. "Would it be okay with you if she did?"

"It really isn't up to me, now, is it?" Joan didn't look her in the eye.

"Actually, it is, Mom. If you'd like her to come, I'll invite her. But if you don't want her there, I won't. I don't want to make anyone uncomfortable."

"Well, she's not going to live forever," Joan said, looking everywhere but at Diane. "And I guess it wouldn't be fair to Natalie to say her great-grandmother can't come to Christmas."

Diane waited, but her mother didn't continue. "So, are you saying I should invite Anna to Christmas dinner?"

Joan finally raised her eyes to Diane. "I'm saying I won't stop you if you want to invite her."

"Okay, Mom," Diane said, trying not to smile because she knew it would make her mom mad. "I'd like to invite her. If you change your mind, let me know."

Joan waved her away, and Diane took her cue and left.

"It's a Christmas miracle," Diane said to herself as she drove away. That thought made her smile all the way home.

CHAPTER THIRTY-FIVE
Anna - 1955

Throughout the spring and summer, William's moods and drinking were getting worse. Anna kept the children away from him as much as possible. She'd feed him his breakfast, and then take the children to the park, or on bad weather days, to Auntie May's apartment. May taught summer school half-days and enjoyed having Anna and the children around when they visited. Sometimes, though, after an especially bad night, Anna couldn't go to her aunt's place. Some bruises she could hide, but others, when William was sloppy drunk, couldn't be hidden with makeup.

Anna felt deeply ashamed. She'd allowed herself to stay in an abusive marriage when she should have left after the first time William hit her. How could she have known he'd get this terrible? She'd grown up watching adults hit children and each other as if it were an everyday occurrence. Her father had never hurt her, nor had her brother. But her grandmother could be especially mean both physically and verbally. But now, to be with a husband who treated her the same way was too much for Anna. In spite of her shame and her fear of William, she had to get out.

Throughout the summer, Anna spent as little as possible on groceries so she could save a little extra money and put it away for her escape. This time, however, she hid the money at her aunt's apartment in her old room. If William even suspected she was stashing money away, he'd never find it. Anna knew when she made her escape, she'd need a little money to get by. She was sure her Auntie May would let them stay there, but Anna knew she couldn't do that forever. She needed to eventually be able to stand on her own two feet.

One hot, humid Friday in August, Anna was clearing the table from dinner with the kids. Joan was putting her toys away because Anna had promised to take them for ice cream if they both behaved. Matthew sat in his highchair and was singing, "I scream, you scream, we all scream for ice cream," in his toddler's voice as Joanie giggled at him.

Anna wiped Matthew's mouth and picked up the last of the plates just as William stumbled in.

"What the hell is all the racket in here?" he said, slurring his words. The kids immediately quieted down upon seeing their father.

"William," Anna said, trying to sound upbeat. "What a surprise. You're home early." He glared at her, and she knew immediately that he was in a foul mood. Fear rose inside her.

"You're surprised, are you?" he asked, walking up to Anna and grabbing her wrist. He squeezed it so hard, she dropped the glass she'd been holding, and it shattered on the hardwood floor. "Why? Are you hiding something?"

"No. No. Not at all," she whimpered. "Please. You're hurting my arm."

He let go of her but not without giving her a shove. Anna reeled but was able to right herself before she fell.

"We're going to get ice cream, Daddy," Joan spoke up timidly. "Mama said if we were good, we could go after dinner."

"Oh, she did, did she?" William's narrowed eyes never left Anna. "So, we have so much money that you can take the kids out for ice cream?"

Anna knew he was baiting her. He was angry about something else, and he was looking for a reason to take his frustration out on her. She thought carefully before replying. "I just wanted to treat the kids, dear," she said softly. "Joanie's birthday is next week, and I thought it might be a nice early gift."

He looked down at Joan, who'd backed up against the sofa, and then back at Anna. "So, this is how it is? I work my tail off serving a bunch of drunken idiots all night long so you can waste my money on whatever you like."

Anna glanced over to Joan, and then to where Matthew sat in his highchair. William was standing between her and the kids. She knew that when he was this drunk, she had to lure him away from the children. "Sweetie," she said gently. "What's wrong? Did something happen at work?" She hoped if she gave him all the attention, it might diffuse his anger.

"Work," he said, sneering. "That bar isn't a workplace. It's a pit. I used to have a real job, you know? I lead engineer teams, and I designed important things—top-secret things. But look at me now. I'm stuck in this shit hole with you and these kids, working at a dead-end job."

He grabbed Anna again, this time on the upper arm, and she heard the broken glass crunch under his shoe. His grip was hard, his fingers biting into her skin. His eyes were bloodshot, and his pupils were large; so large his eyes looked black. Anna had seen him drunk before, but tonight he was out of his mind drunk.

"William, please. Please," she begged softly. "Not in front of the children. Please."

He cocked his head and stared at her with dead eyes, then suddenly he raised his other hand and backhanded her across the face, letting go of her arm at the same time. Anna fell hard onto the floor.

"Daddy, don't! Please don't hurt Mommy!" Joanie cried out, running toward her father.

Anna heard her daughter and tried to stand up. Her head was spinning, but she knew she had to get Joan away from William.

"I'll damn well do whatever I want!" he screamed at Joan. He shoved the little girl so hard that she flew across the room and fell into the pile of toys she'd been picking up. Anna was up in a flash, running toward her daughter, but William caught her and swung her around to face him, an evil grin on his face.

Anna began pounding on him with her loose hand, no longer able to control herself. "Don't you dare touch my daughter!" she yelled. "You leave my children alone!"

"I'll do whatever I want to *my* children," he yelled back. He grabbed her by the hair and pulled her face so close to his she could smell the alcohol on his breath. "I own you," he said, his voice sinister. "And I'll do whatever I want to you."

Joan was crying where she lay on the floor, and that made Matthew cry. William ignored them and dragged Anna by the arm toward the bedroom.

"It's okay," Anna said to the children, trying to soothe them as she was being pulled away. "Just stay here and wait for Mommy," she said. A lump grew in her throat as tears formed in her eyes at seeing her children so distressed.

William lifted her up and tossed her on the bed, and in a flash, he was on top of her. She lay very still, her body shaking. Anna knew better than to fight him. He was so much bigger than she was, and his anger seemed to make him stronger.

"I own you," he said again, staring at her with those dark, angry eyes. "I could kill you right now. I could kill all of you and walk away. I always get away."

Chills of fear rippled throughout Anna's body. She'd waited too long. He was right. He could kill them all and then disappear. Hadn't he done terrible things before? And he'd always walked away without paying for it. Her body shook, terrified.

William attacked her then in a way that couldn't be called anything else but rape. He hit her several times and forced himself on her. Anna tried not to cry out so as not to scare the children. She just let William have his way because she didn't have the strength to fight him.

Afterward, he rolled over and passed out. Anna lay motionless, feeling blood trickle down the side of her face. Anna felt as dead inside as William's eyes had looked. Slowly, she rolled off the bed and straightened her clothing as best as she could manage. Her body was still shaking with fear, but she didn't even notice. Anna walked out into the living room and tried to smile at the children. Looking up in the mirror by the door, she gasped. She looked ghastly. Her lip was swollen and bleeding, and her face was puffy with bruises starting to form. She hardly recognized herself.

Joanie stood beside Matthew's highchair, patting him gently, trying to calm him down. Both children stared at their mother with wide eyes.

Anna sat down heavily in a chair at the table. She had no

idea what to do next. She knew she should try to comfort the children. She wanted to. But she was afraid if she rose from the chair, she'd fall to pieces and never be able to help anyone, including herself. She'd done this to herself. She'd done this to her children. She was a terrible person, putting her children in harm's way. How could she ever live with herself if either of her children were hurt by that man she should have left years ago? Anna couldn't take it anymore. She couldn't let him hurt her or them again.

"Mama?"

Anna raised her eyes and focused on Joanie, who'd spoken. The little girl was hugging Lily tightly with one arm and had her other arm around her baby brother. At that moment, Anna knew what she had to do.

"Mama's okay," Anna said gently. Stiffly, she rose and lifted Matthew out of his chair, setting him on the floor. She bent over and kissed her little boy on the top of his head, then kissed Joanie on the cheek. "Joanie. Take your little brother across the hall to Mrs. Arnett's apartment and wait for me there. Okay, sweetie?"

Joan nodded her little head and took Matthew's hand. Clutching Lily, she walked out of the apartment just as Anna had asked.

Anna turned and walked stiffly back into the darkened bedroom. William was sound asleep, lying on his back, snoring. Quietly, she slid open the nightstand drawer. Anna reached inside and moved her hand around until she felt the cold metal of the gun. She lifted it out and stared at it a moment. Without any thought or hesitation, Anna placed the barrel to William's head and pulled the trigger.

* * *

A minute later, Anna walked out of the apartment and across the hall. Mrs. Arnett had already opened her door to see where the loud noise had come from.

"Anna? What happened?" the older woman asked, but then stopped and gasped as Anna walked right past her as if in a daze. Mrs. Arnett followed her into the apartment, where Anna sat down at the table and folded her hands in her lap. Mrs. Arnett, Joanie, and Matthew stared at her with wide eyes.

"Please call the police," Anna said to Mrs. Arnett. "I just killed William."

CHAPTER THIRTY-SIX

Diane

Anna looked up at Diane, still wringing her hands as she had throughout the story. It was a Sunday afternoon in mid-December, and Anna was once again sitting in her comfortable chair. They had decorated the apartment with the small tree the week before and hung garland around the edges of the ceiling. The lights twinkled, giving the room a festive look. But at this moment, neither woman felt festive. Despite Diane telling Anna she didn't have to recount what happened that fateful night, the older woman had insisted.

"Someone needs to know the truth," Anna had said.

And now, as Anna watched her, Diane was speechless. She was trying to grasp what had happened. But all she could picture in her mind was a broken Anna shooting William as he slept. Finally, she spoke.

"You shot William to protect your children. After the terror he put you though that night, no one could blame you for that."

"They did blame me, though," Anna said softly. "I was in

shock that first few days after I killed him. Whenever I was asked if I'd done it, I said yes. Because I had. It was the truth. The lawyer Auntie May had hired was so frustrated with me. He kept asking me questions about my life with William. Had he been hitting me? Had he threatened me? I was so ashamed, so I didn't answer. But my face told the whole story. My mug shot that night shows a woman with a bloody lip and a swollen and bruised face. One eye was nearly closed because it was so swollen. Still, they asked me if William had done it. Who else would have? I couldn't think straight. I just wanted to curl up and die. How could they have expected me to answer questions after all I'd been through?"

Diane winced. She hated seeing the pain on Anna's kind face. "What happened afterward?"

"Despite advice from the lawyer, I pleaded guilty of murder at my hearing. I was guilty. I'd shot a man in cold blood. No amount of explaining or excuses could change that. Later, after I was sentenced to life in prison, my lawyer told me that going to a jury trial probably wouldn't have saved me anyway. In those days, although women were allowed to serve on a jury, few did, especially for something as gruesome as a murder trial. No jury of twelve men was going to let me off with a defense of spousal abuse. Just the thought of it would have given them night-mares. Because if you let one woman off for murder because of abuse, you'd have to let all women off. And the men in those days couldn't have handled that."

"I'm sorry," Diane said softly, her heart breaking for Anna. "You had no way out, no matter what you did. It was either prison or die at William's hand."

Anna nodded. "I'm afraid it isn't much better today. The abused person still must prove it. Even if there are pictures.

Even if they've already contacted the police several times. In the end, if the abused kills the abuser, she has to prove it was self-defense."

Diane knew that was true. Now, more than ever before, she was thankful it had never come to that in her marriage.

"I wouldn't have had the strength to go through a jury trial," Anna continued. "The shame of abuse was always placed on the woman. People believed that women caused their husbands to abuse them. I couldn't have put my children through a trial either. I was afraid they'd drag poor Joanie in and make her tell them what she'd seen. I couldn't bear for that to happen to her. She'd been through enough."

Knowing now what her mother had seen that night, Diane agreed. She couldn't imagine making a young child testify against her own father. "How did your Auntie May react?" she asked.

Anna relaxed, and her face softened. It was as if telling her story had given her the relief she'd desperately needed. "Poor Auntie May. She hired the lawyer because she wanted me to fight, but there just wasn't any fight left in me. She knew all along what kind of man William was—a conman and a womanizer—but I didn't listen to her. I wish I had, but I can't change the past.

"At first, after I was sentenced, she would visit me twice a month. But I saw how much it hurt her to see me there. I finally took her off my list of visitors and wrote her a letter telling her why. I didn't want her to waste her time on me. She'd done so much for me already. She wrote to me once a month after that, telling me about things that happened at her work or with the theater group. She also deposited money each month in my account, so I could buy necessities." Anna shook her head. "She was such a dear. And I had been such a disappointment to her. She never said that, but I know I was."

Diane placed a hand over Anna's. "She wouldn't have kept writing to you if she thought you were a disappointment. I'm sure she loved you until the end."

Anna nodded, her eyes filling with tears. "After Bernice took the children, Auntie May was never allowed to visit them. That broke her heart. She lived a full life, traveled a little after she retired, and always kept her hand in the theater group until the day she died. She was ninety-two when she passed in 1983. I wasn't contacted until after her burial, so I wasn't able to request to attend her funeral. But she did leave me money in case I ever did get out of jail." Anna looked up at Diane and smiled. "That's how I'm able to stay in this nice place. The money she left me is paying for it. And I hope that I'll be able to give some to Joanie if any is left when I pass."

Diane smiled back at her. "That was so kind of your aunt. She had faith that you'd someday be free. What a wonderful gift."

"Yes. It was."

Picking up the digital recorder, Diane clicked it off. She now had the whole story, but it wasn't the end. Because her grandmother was still alive, and she hoped they'd have enough time to create a few memories of their own. "I haven't mentioned this because I was afraid my mom might back out, but she said she was fine with you coming to our house for Christmas dinner."

Anna's eyes lit up. "Really? Oh, my." She raised her hands to her face as fresh tears fell. This time, tears of joy. "That would be the perfect holiday gift."

Diane couldn't help but smile too. Bringing her mother

and grandmother together after all these years was practically a miracle. "Natalie will be there too. Four generations of Craine women. Won't that be amazing?"

"I never dreamt it would be possible. I'm so thankful," Anna said. She reached out her arms and Diane went to her and hugged her close.

"Me, too," Diane said.

* * *

All that week, Diane was busy at work finishing up before the winter break. There were tests to grade and final grades to figure and record. There was a teacher's Christmas party to attend and another one with Barry's co-workers. She was also running last-minute errands to buy gifts and other items before Natalie flew in the next Monday. Diane was unable to visit Anna that Wednesday, but she planned on seeing her on Sunday and also bringing Natalie over to meet her on Tuesday.

Friday night, Diane went to her mother's as usual. Joan was a creature of habit, and changing her shopping day was more trouble than it was worth. They did their typical dinner and shopping, and then once they were at Joan's apartment again, Diane helped her wrap the few gifts she'd purchased.

"Well, I'd better get going," Diane said after they'd finished. "Don't forget that I'll be picking you up Thursday afternoon for Christmas Eve."

Joan didn't answer, and when Diane looked up at her, she saw a frown on her mother's face. Immediately, Diane knew that her mother was going to back out of Christmas and seeing her mother.

"What's wrong, Mom?" she asked.

Joan nervously clasped her hands in front of her. "I've been thinking a lot about seeing your grandmother, and I just don't think I'm ready."

"Maybe it's just nerves," Diane said calmly. "Once you two get together, I'm sure you'll be fine."

Joan shook her head vehemently, like a child refusing to do what she was told. "No. I don't want to see her. I can't. Just thinking about her and what happened has been very upsetting—all those terrible memories. I don't want to think about them. I don't want to remember." Her mother sat in a chair and wrapped her arms around herself.

Diane had seen her mother behave in many different ways, but this was entirely out of character. She walked over and sat down beside her. "I'm sure it's difficult. I know what happened that day, and I'm sure you were traumatized by it. You were only five years old. How could you not be?"

Joan didn't answer. She just sat there, staring off in the distance.

"Mom. Maybe it's time to get it all out in the open. You've been holding those memories in for so long. Maybe it would be a relief to let your feelings out after all these years."

Her mother looked over at her, her expression turning hard. "I've spent my whole life trying to forget those memories."

"I know, Mom," Diane said.

"Do you?" Joan asked. "Do you know how much alcohol it takes to forget a traumatic experience?"

Diane sat back, surprised by her question. "No."

"Neither do I." Joan's face dropped. "I spent years drinking, trying to wipe that image out of my head, and it never went away. Never."

Suddenly, everything fell into place for Diane. Her mother's failed marriages. Her mother's drinking problem all those years. Joan had been running away from that tragic day her entire life. But nothing had made it go away. Even now, after years of being sober, her angry fits were just masking what was really wrong—her unresolved feelings about what happened that fateful night.

"I'm sorry, Mom," Diane said. "I'm so sorry. I wanted so much to get to know Anna that I hadn't realized how much this would affect you."

Joan shook her head slowly. "No. I'm the one who should be sorry. It was my fault. I was the reason my mother killed my father. She did it to save me." Tears filled her eyes, and she dropped her head in her hands, sobbing.

Diane sat there in shock. How had her mother known that Anna had killed him to save her and Matthew? Joan had only been five years old. How had she figured out that Anna's actions had anything to do with her?

"It wasn't your fault, Mom," Diane said, placing her arms around her mother's shoulders. She'd never seen her mother fall to pieces like this. Anger, yes. The only emotion allowed in their house had been anger. But tears? They weren't the type of family that touched each other, let alone hugged. Diane wasn't sure now how to react to her mother's emotions.

"It was my fault," Joan insisted. "I ran at my father that night when he hit my mother. I'd seen him shove her and push her around, but that night he slapped her so hard, she fell to the floor. I can see it as clearly as if it were yesterday." She grabbed a handful of tissues from the box that Diane had given her and swiped at her eyes. "I ran to him and asked him not to hurt her. When he turned toward me, his eyes were scary—like some kind of evil monster. He shoved me so hard, I flew across the room and fell on a pile of toys. I didn't move. I was afraid if I moved, he'd hit me just like he'd hit mom."

Diane's heart clenched at hearing her mother's version of the story. Diane's childhood hadn't been perfect, but her mother had never allowed anyone to hit her. How horrible it must have been for Joan to see that, and to be hurt that way by her own father.

"My mom ran to him, telling him not to hurt me," Joan continued. "I remember him yelling, saying something like he owned me, and he owned her, and he could do whatever he liked. I was so frightened, I couldn't move. My dad had scared me before with his yelling, but now he was hitting me. I didn't want him to hit me like he hit my mother." Fresh tears filled her eyes.

"I'm so sorry, Mom," Diane said, knowing how useless her words sounded. "But you have to know that your mom was just protecting you. You weren't to blame for anything that happened."

Joan shook her head. "He pulled her into their bedroom, and after a few minutes, I finally got up, grabbed Lily, my doll, and ran to Matthew because he was crying. I kept telling him he was okay and not to cry, or he'd make daddy angry again. I remember Mom coming out of the room then, blood dripping from her lip, and her eye was swollen. I knew then that my dad must have hit her more, and in that moment, I hated him. I hated him for being so mean to my mom and to me."

Diane was shocked at the detail her mother remembered. She hadn't forgotten any of it after sixty-five years.

Joan took a breath, then continued. "She asked me to take Matthew to the neighbor's apartment, and I did what she asked. I was actually relieved to leave our apartment in case daddy came back out. The neighbor, I don't remember her name, was about to get us some cookies and milk when we all heard a loud bang. Then my mother came in, looking like she was stunned or something. Bruises were starting to swell up on her face, aside from the cut lip and swollen eye. But there was something else. She had blood splattered on her face, dress, and arms. At the time, I thought it was her blood. But as time went on, I realized it must have been my father's blood."

"Oh, my God!" Diane was horrified. "I had no idea that's what you saw. I'm so sorry." Diane hadn't realized how Anna must have looked to her children and Mrs. Arnett when she walked in after killing William.

"I'll never get that image out of my head," Joan said. She was no longer crying. Instead, she looked dazed. "I don't think my mother would have killed my father if he hadn't hit me that night. I've had to live all my life with the fact that I was the reason my father died."

"But Mom," Diane said. "You weren't the reason. It was so much more than that. Your mother had lived through years of abuse from William. It happened because she couldn't take it anymore, and she certainly wasn't going to let him hurt her children."

"After the police came and took her away," Joan continued, "I thought for sure they'd let her come back for us. But then Bernice and Jim came to pick us up, and we weren't allowed to ask where our mother was. Aunt Bernice would just say, 'She'll rot in prison for the rest of her life.' I hated hearing that, so I learned quickly never to ask about my mother or father again."

"That's terrible." Diane was appalled at how her Aunt Bernice had acted. "She had no right to turn you against your own mother."

Joan looked up at Diane. "That's why I can't see Anna. How can I face her after I went to the parole hearing and told them she was guilty and that she'd killed my father in cold blood? I alluded to the fact that she had planned on killing him all along. I never believed it, I just said what Bernice told me to. I remember the dull look in my mother's eyes that night. She wasn't angry or vengeful when she told us to go across the hall. She was drained of life. But I told the parole board that she'd planned it because Bernice wanted me to say it. It was because of me that Anna didn't get out of jail then. I've regretted it my whole life."

Diane's heart went out to her mother. She had no idea her mother had been carrying this guilt all these years. "That wasn't your fault, Mom. It was Bernice's fault. It was her hatred of Anna that made her want to keep her in jail all those years."

"I still did it. I was an adult with children, but I let Bernice talk me into going and saying those things."

Diane sat back, also feeling drained by all her mother had told her. When Anna had told her what had happened, Diane hadn't thought about it from her mother's perspective. Now, she understood why her mother might not be able to reconnect with Anna. Her pain and guilt had tormented her all her life.

"I'm so sorry you've had to carry this with you all your life, Mom," Diane said gently. "But I can assure you that Anna doesn't blame you for any of it. She just wants to see you again. She calls you Joanie, and she's sorry she missed all these years of being your mother."

Joan wiped her eyes again and looked at her daughter. "I just don't think I have the strength to face her."

"Okay, Mom," Diane said soothingly, understanding how hard it might be for her. "I'll leave it up to you. If you don't want to see her Christmas Eve, maybe you could spend Christmas Day with us instead, and I won't invite Anna."

Her mother nodded.

"But, please think about seeing her. Maybe it will finally put this whole terrible memory to rest once and for all," Diane told her. "She loves you, Mom. Still. She's always loved her children. You can see it in her eyes."

Fresh tears trickled down Joan's face. "I'll think about it," she said. "But I can't promise anything."

Diane was content that her mother would think about it. She hoped Joan would come to the realization that seeing her mother might heal her pain. But now, after hearing what her mother had felt all these years, Diane wouldn't press her to see Anna if she chose not to.

Diane stayed a while longer with Joan to make sure she was okay. By the time Diane left, her mother was almost back to her old self, practically kicking her out because it was late. When Diane walked into her house a while later, she dropped onto the sofa where Barry was sitting, watching the news.

"Must have been a long night," he said. "You're home late."

Diane curled up next to him, taking his arm to wrap around her. "It's been a hell of a night. Wait until I tell you what my mother told me."

"I'm listening," he said, turning down the television.

Diane looked up at him, thankful she had someone in her life who was always there for her.

CHAPTER THIRTY-SEVEN

Diane

Monday afternoon, Diane picked up Natalie at the airport, and they both talked non-stop the entire way home. Diane was thrilled to have her daughter home, even if it was only for two weeks. Despite having grown up in Minnesota, Natalie looked like a California girl with her light blond hair pulled up in a ponytail and her blue eyes sparkling.

"How do you stay so tan in northern California?" Diane asked.

Natalie grinned. "A couple of friends and I drove down to Laguna Beach for a three-day break a couple of weeks ago. This is what's left of my tan."

"Lucky you. I wish I could drive a few hours and be in the sun."

Barry was waiting for them with the grill going and steaks ready to cook. After hugging her hello, Barry said, "I hope you haven't turned vegetarian on us. I'd hate to waste these steaks."

Natalie laughed. "I'm born and raised as a Minnesotan. I doubt I'll ever turn vegetarian."

As they ate, Natalie told them all about school and her life in California. She'd been there for almost four years and had made so many new friends that Diane had never even met.

"I want to come out and meet all your friends," Diane said. "I feel like I don't know anything about your life anymore."

"You should come. And Barry, too. You can play tourist and see all the sites."

"In the winter," Barry said. "That way we can get out of the snow."

"Have you thought of where you're going to apply for med school?" Diane asked her daughter. She wished she'd come back to Minnesota, but she knew better than to press her on it.

"Well," Natalie hesitated.

"You are going to med school still, aren't you?" Diane asked.

"Yes. I plan to. It's just that I applied to continue at Stanford," Natalie said. "I know you'd like me to come home for school, but I really love it out there." She bit her lip. "Are you disappointed?"

Her mother shook her head. "Never. I mean, I'd love for you to come back for school, but it sounds like you have a full life there. I hope you're accepted if that's what you really want."

Natalie smiled. "It is what I want. I feel so comfortable there. And it's such a great school."

"I know it is." Diane was extremely disappointed, but she wanted what was best for Natalie.

Diane updated Natalie on everything Anna had told her about the night she shot William and then what her mother had recounted about that night.

"Wow! Imagine carrying that with you your entire life," Natalie said about Joan. "I know grandma had her issues when you were growing up, but it now makes sense, doesn't it?"

Diane nodded. "Yes. It does. It's still hard for me to excuse my mother's behavior when she had children to raise, but I can at least understand it."

"Maybe I can talk grandma into coming over Christmas Eve," Natalie said. "She has trouble saying no to me." She gave a mischievous grin.

"That's actually a good idea," Diane said. "She's putty in your hands. But first, I'd like to take you to meet your great-grandmother tomorrow. You're going to love her. She's the sweetest person I've ever met."

When Diane and Natalie visited Anna the next day, Natalie did fall in love with her. Anna teared up when she saw Natalie and asked if she could hug her.

"I never thought I'd see any of my family again, let alone my great-granddaughter," Anna said. "You're so beautiful. And I hear you're smart, too. You're studying to be a doctor."

The three women visited for a while, and Diane sat back and enjoyed watching her daughter with Anna. It was so amazing to think that only a few weeks ago, Diane thought she had no grandparents. Now, Anna was an integral part of her life, and it was so gratifying that Natalie could meet her too.

After they'd all chatted a while, Diane pulled an envelope out of her purse and handed it to Anna. "I have something for you, and I hope it doesn't upset you," she said.

Anna carefully opened the envelope and pulled out the official-looking document. She slipped on the reading glasses that hung around her neck on a chain. "Oh, my." Anna looked up at Diane, surprised. "How did you find this?"

"I did a little research online. I thought it might give you closure," Diane said.

Anna read off the date. "Two thousand twelve. Andrew

lived a long life." She smiled over to Diane. "Thank you. This is good news. Even though Andrew has passed, I know where and when. I'm so happy he had a good long life."

"Can I see?" Natalie asked. Anna handed her Andrew's death certificate, and the young woman looked it over. "Wow, Mom. It's great you found this."

"I wish I had met him," Diane said. "He sounded like a wonderful person. I hope that someday if I get a chance to travel around, I can stop at his grave and leave flowers."

"That would be very sweet," Anna said. Tears filled her eyes. "I'm happy he hasn't been forgotten."

"Me too," Diane said, patting the older woman's hand.

They made plans to pick Anna up on Thursday afternoon and then left. Diane noticed that Anna tired easily, and that worried her.

"I'm worried it might be too taxing for Anna to spend the day with us on Christmas Eve," Diane told Natalie. "How did she seem to you?"

"She did seem tired," Natalie said. "We'll see how it goes that day, and if she starts to look tired, we'll take her back early in the evening."

The next day Diane stayed home with Barry to bake cookies and other treats for Christmas while Natalie went to work her magic on her grandmother. Later that afternoon, Natalie came back with a grin on her face.

"She's coming," Natalie announced. "I told Grandma how sad I'd be if she didn't spend Christmas Eve with us like she always has."

"Good job," Diane told her. "I knew you could do it."

"Oh. And Grandma told me to tell you that you play dirty." She laughed.

Diane and Barry laughed along.

"Hey, whatever it takes," Diane said.

Thursday morning, Diane was nervous. What if her mother broke down when she met Anna after all these years? What if the two quarreled? The day could end up a disaster.

"Hey," Barry told her before they headed downstairs to make breakfast. "It's going to be okay. There will probably be a lot of tears, but they'll be happy tears."

Diane stared at him, stunned. "Are you a mind reader now? How did you know what I was thinking?"

"Because I know you," he said, pulling her into a hug. "And you look worried. This is a day to be happy. You're bringing together a family that has been broken for decades. That's amazing."

"It is," she agreed. "But it's scary, too."

"It'll be fine," Barry told her.

Looking into Barry's serene face, Diane couldn't help but believe him.

Later, Diane and Barry went to pick up Anna first, and Natalie took Barry's car to pick up Joan. They wanted to time it so Anna was settled at the house before Joan arrived.

"My what a lovely home," Anna said as she walked inside, using a walker. "I've always dreamed of owning my own home, but it just wasn't to be."

Diane showed her to the living room where they'd set up the tree. The fireplace was lit, and there was a comfortable chair for Anna to sit in.

"This is so cozy, dear," Anna said. "And your tree is beautiful!" Her eyes lit up as she gazed at the Christmas tree. "It reminds me of all the Christmases with Auntie May."

Diane was pleased she could give Anna a nice Christmas

after all the years she was in prison. Every year Diane took the holidays for granted, some years resenting all the work involved with decorating, shopping, and baking. But now, after meeting Anna, she was thankful for all the lovely Christmases she'd been able to enjoy.

Anna was settled in the living room with a cup of hot cocoa and a plate of cookies when Diane heard Natalie and Joan arrive. She rushed out into the foyer and saw her mother and Natalie carrying several shopping bags filled with Christmas gifts.

"Hi, Mom," Diane said. "Merry Christmas. Why don't you let me take those for you?"

"Merry Christmas," Joan said, but not at all festively. Diane looked over her head at Natalie, who shrugged. It was always difficult to gauge Joan's moods.

"And stop making faces over my head. It's not like I can't see you," Joan barked.

Diane grit her teeth. It seemed her fear that the day might end badly was correct.

"Well, is she here?" Joan asked, her voice quieter now.

"Yes," Diane said. "Anna's in the living room. She's very excited to see you, Mom. So please try to be nice."

Joan frowned at her. "Of course I'll be nice. I'm not that terrible of a person." She handed over the last of the packages, all except for one bag. "I'll keep this," she said, pulling it close.

The three walked into the living room. Barry was sitting on the sofa, talking to Anna when they appeared. Diane took a breath and held it as Anna turned her head and saw her daughter for the first time in decades.

"Joanie," she whispered, her eyes filling with tears.

Joan stood there, frozen, staring at her mother. Her lip

quivered, and tears filled her eyes. She walked into the room, set the package down, and bent to hug Anna. "Mom."

The two women began to cry, and Diane let out her breath. Tears filled her eyes also as she watched the women reunite. It was a sweet, heartfelt moment.

Natalie ran to get tissues and passed them around, and everyone wiped their eyes. Joan and Anna were talking softly to each other, but as Diane placed the packages under the tree, she could hear them.

"I'm so sorry, Mom," Joan said sorrowfully. Natalie had brought her a chair to sit on next to Anna.

"But dear. You shouldn't be sorry. I was the one who did wrong," Anna told her, holding her hand tightly.

"But you did it to save me," Joan said. "I knew it was my fault the moment it happened. If dad hadn't shoved me across the room, you never would have killed him."

Anna shook her head. "No, dear. I was upset that he'd done that to you, but it was so many other things that made me finally lose my mind and do it. He'd been like that toward me for years. I couldn't let him hurt my children. I couldn't go on like that. It wasn't your fault, dear. Please, never think that."

Joan hugged her again, and it was as if all the decades had melted away, and she was a little girl happy to have her mother again.

"I brought something for you," Joan said, lifting an item wrapped in tissue paper out of the bag. "You have to be careful, though. It's very old and very fragile."

Anna's face lit up as she accepted the item. Carefully she unwrapped the tissue paper, and then a smile filled her face. "Lily. Oh, my goodness. You still have Lily after all these years."

Diane and Natalie moved in for a closer look. The little rag doll was old and nearly threadbare, her fabric darkened from many hugs, and her dress faded. "That's the doll your brother made for you?" Diane asked, amazed. "Mom. You had it all along?"

Joan nodded. "I was hugging it the day mom sent us to the apartment across the hall. I had it when Bernice came to collect us, and I wouldn't let go of her. I was careful with Lily, just as my mother had said I should be. As I grew older, Bernice threatened to toss Lily into the garbage because she was so old and faded, so I wrapped her up and hid her. I've kept her with me all these years."

Once again, Anna's eyes filled with tears. "Thank you for taking care of my doll," she said to Joan. "And for loving her enough to keep her."

Joan reached for her mother's hand. "I think I kept her because I still loved you all these years," she said, tears filling her eyes. "Somewhere deep down inside of me, I never wanted to believe you were the terrible person Bernice said you were. I remember how kind and loving you were to Matthew and me, and I remember how much you loved us. Lily reminded me of that, every time I grew angry at you for not being there for me."

"I'm so sorry," Anna said. "I wish I'd handled things differently. I wish I'd had the strength to walk away."

"You did what you had to do to survive," Joan said. "I know that now."

Diane watched in wonder as her mother turned into an entirely different person around Anna. She wondered if this might change Joan's outlook completely. Diane knew that her mother's drinking had been sparked by losing her mother and father so suddenly and violently. Maybe this was what her mother had needed all along to heal.

They sat down to a delicious meal and then opened gifts beside the tree, everyone in a happy, festive mood. Joan sat by her mother the entire night as if trying to reclaim a little of what she'd lost all those years ago. They talked about their last Christmas together with Auntie May and Liz and how much fun it had been. Joan was shocked to learn that Liz had been carrying her father's child. She'd never known that and told Anna that she had been a saint to not only let the woman live with them, but also include her in family gatherings.

"That's just one small story among many your mother has told me," Diane said to Joan. "You two need to spend time together so she can tell you everything."

Joan sobered. "I'm not sure if I'm ready to hear everything. But spending time together will be a must from now on."

"I'm so happy to hear that, sweetie," Anna said. "You have no idea how happy you've made me."

Joan smiled at her mother. "I think I do."

When it was time to take Anna and Joan home, Joan asked if she could ride along to Anna's place first to spend more time together.

Diane drove with Natalie in the passenger seat and the two older women in the back. There was giggling and whispering between them, making Diane glance at Natalie with raised brows.

"There those two go again," Joan said loudly. "Thinking I don't notice them making faces."

Diane laughed. She couldn't believe that all four generations of Craine women were sitting together in the car. It really was a Christmas miracle.

* * *

When Diane arrived home, the fire was going out, and the tree lights were unplugged. Natalie said goodnight and headed to her room. All the dirty dishes in the kitchen were stacked in the dishwasher, and it was running. With a happy sigh, she headed upstairs, where she assumed Barry was already in bed.

Barry was still fully dressed, sitting on the bed, reading a book. "So. How did the night end?"

"Wonderfully." Diane sat on the bed beside him. "And the best part is the dish fairies loaded the dishwasher." She laughed.

"They are very efficient," Barry said.

Diane smiled over at him. Barry looked relaxed and happy. She wanted to curl up beside him and fall asleep in his arms. "It turned out to be a wonderful holiday, didn't it?" She sighed.

Barry smiled. "Yes, it did. All your worrying was for nothing."

"That's why I have you. To calm me down when I start to freak out," she said, grinning.

"And to do the dishes after a family gathering," he said.

She laughed. "And to curl up with at the end of a hectic day. You always make those days so much easier to endure."

He pulled her closer. "So, are you saying that you couldn't live without me?"

"Pretty much," she said, teasing.

Barry's expression turned serious. "I have one more gift for you, but I wanted to give it to you in private. No pressure that way."

Diane's brows raised. "No pressure?"

He pulled a small box out of his nightstand drawer and handed it to her. She knew immediately what was in that box.

"Open it," he said softly.

Taking a breath, Diane opened the lid. Inside sat a beautiful